DATE DUE

GAYLORD			PRINTED IN U.S.A.

The Future of Public Employee Retirement Systems

The Future of Public Employee Retirement Systems

EDITED BY

Olivia S. Mitchell and Gary Anderson

OXFORD
UNIVERSITY PRESS

OXFORD
UNIVERSITY PRESS

Great Clarendon Street, Oxford ox2 6DP

Oxford University Press is a department of the University of Oxford.
It furthers the University's objective of excellence in research, scholarship,
and education by publishing worldwide in

Oxford New York

Auckland Cape Town Dar es Salaam Hong Kong Karachi
Kuala Lumpur Madrid Melbourne Mexico City Nairobi
New Delhi Shanghai Taipei Toronto

With offices in

Argentina Austria Brazil Chile Czech Republic France Greece
Guatemala Hungary Italy Japan Poland Portugal Singapore
South Korea Switzerland Thailand Turkey Ukraine Vietnam

Oxford is a registered trade mark of Oxford University Press
in the UK and in certain other countries

Published in the United States
by Oxford University Press Inc., New York

© Pension Research Council, The Wharton School, University of Pennsylvania, 2009

British Library Cataloguing in Publication Data

Data available

Library of Congress Cataloging in Publication Data

Data available

Typeset by SPI Publisher Services, Pondicherry, India
Printed in Great Britain
on acid-free paper by
CPI Antony Rowe, Chippenham, Wiltshire

ISBN 978–0–19–957334–9

1 3 5 7 9 10 8 6 4 2

Contents

List of Figures

List of Tables

Preface

Many millions of pension plan participants all over the world have recently awakened to the sad fact that financial market collapse can—virtually overnight—erode a lifetime of saving for old age. The shock is made worse by the fact the global age wave is also cresting, with rising numbers of elderly and declining working-age populations to support them. This volume focuses on the retirement systems provided to public sector employees, paying careful attention to their costs, their benefits, and their future in light of these current financial and demographic challenges.

There is no question but that those covered by public pensions are often the subject of 'pension envy': that is, their benefits might seem more generous and their contributions lower than those offered by the private sector. Yet this volume points out that such judgments are often inaccurate, since civil servants hold jobs for with few counterparts in private industry, such as firefighters, police, judges, and teachers. Often these are riskier, dirtier, and demand more loyalty and discretion than would be required of a more mobile labor force in the private sector. In any event, there remains ample room for comparative and analytic judgment. Accordingly, one focus of this book is on financial aspects of these schemes, addressing the cost and valuation debate. Another is the political economy of how public pension asset pools are perceived and managed, an increasingly important topic in times of global financial turmoil. And finally we undertake an international comparison of public retirement system reform, exploring ways that public pensions can be strengthened in the United States, Japan, Canada, and Germany. We are thus happy to represent the vigorous debate currently underway by academics, financial experts, regulators, and plan sponsors, all seeking to define a new future for public retirement systems.

Previous research studies directed at the Pension Research Council and the Boettner Center of the Wharton School of the University of Pennsylvania have focused on public and private pensions as well as retirement adequacy in the United States and around the world. As with all of our research volumes, we owe much to our fine contributors, coeditors, and conference participants. In this instance, Gary Anderson served as a wonderful co-organizer and we owe him many thanks. The Senior Partners and Institutional Members of the Pension Research Council are also very much appreciated for their intellectual and financial support. The Wharton School provided conference facilities and funding, permitting the initial research findings to be reported. Additional financial sustenance was received from the Pension Research Council, the Boettner Center for Pensions and Retirement Research, and the Ralph H. Blanchard Memorial Endowment at the Wharton School of the University of Pennsylvania. The manuscript was expertly prepared and carefully edited by Andrew Gallagher and Matt Rosen, with assistance from Hilary Farrell.

On behalf of these institutions and individuals, we thank all of our fine collaborators and supporters for their help and intellectual guidance in these times of financial turmoil.

Olivia S. Mitchell

Pension Research Council
Boettner Center for Pensions and Retirement Research
The Wharton School

The Pension Research Council

The Pension Research Council of the Wharton School at the University of Pennsylvania is an organization committed to generating debate on key policy issues affecting pensions and other employee benefits. The Council sponsors interdisciplinary research on the entire range of private and social retirement security and related benefit plans in the United States and around the world. It seeks to broaden understanding of these complex arrangements through basic research into their economic, social, legal, actuarial, and financial foundations. Members of the Advisory Board of the Council, appointed by the Dean of the Wharton School, are leaders in the employee benefits field, and they recognize the essential role of social security and other public sector income maintenance programs while sharing a desire to strengthen private sector approaches to economic security. More information about the Pension Research Council is available on the Internet at http://www.pensionresearchcouncil.org or send email to prc@wharton.upenn.edu.

Notes on Contributors

Neveen Ahmed is a doctoral candidate in Economics at North Carolina State University studying US financial markets and public pensions. She received her MA in economics from North Carolina State University and her BSc in Economics from Cairo University.

Beth Almeida is the Executive Director of the National Institute on Retirement Security, a not-for-profit organization that conducts research and education programs on US pensions. She has worked previously with the International Association of Machinists and Aerospace Workers and led research initiatives at the University of Bonn's Center for European Integration Studies; the European Institute for Business Administration; and the Center for Industrial Competitiveness at the University of Massachusetts-Lowell. She received her bachelor's degree in International Business from Lehigh University and her master's degree in economics from the University of Massachusetts-Amherst.

Gary Anderson is a consultant on public pension issues; previously he served as Executive Director of the Texas Municipal Retirement system which covers municipal employees and retirees for many Texas cities. He is also an Advisory Board member of Wharton's Pension Research Council, and has served with the National Association of State Retirement Administrators and the Government Finance Officers Association. He received his BA in Political Science from Texas A&M University, and his MA in Public Management from the University of Houston-Clear Lake City.

Brad M. Barber is a Professor of Finance at the Graduate School of Management, UC Davis. His recent research focuses on pension fund activism, analyst recommendations, and investor psychology. At UC Davis, he teaches courses in investment analysis and corporate financial policy. He received his Ph.D. in Finance and his MBA from the University of Chicago, and his BS in Economics from the University of Illinois.

Keith Brainard is the research director for the National Association of State Retirement Administrators. His work focuses on governmental pension plans and defined benefit pensions; he also maintains the Public Fund Survey, an online compendium of public pension data. Mr. Brainard previously served as manager of budget and planning for the Arizona State Retirement System, and he provided fiscal research and analysis for the

Texas and Arizona legislatures. He received his MA from the LBJ School of Public Affairs at the University of Texas-Austin.

Robert L. Clark is Professor of Economics and Professor of Management, Innovation, and Entrepreneurship at North Carolina State University. His research examines retirement decisions, the choice between defined benefit and defined contribution plans, the impact of pension conversions to defined contribution and cash balance plans, the role of information and communications on 401(k) contributions, government regulation of pensions, the development of public sector retirement plans, and Social Security. He also studies economic responses to population aging in developed countries and international retirement plans, especially Japan. He serves on Wharton's Pension Research Council Advisory Board and is a Governor of the Foundation for International Studies on Social Security. Professor Clark earned his BA from Millsaps College and his MA and Ph.D. from Duke University.

Lee A. Craig is Alumni Distinguished Professor of Economics at North Carolina State University. His research focuses on long-run changes in US agricultural productivity growth, the evolution and integration of agricultural commodity markets, the gold standard and the history of business cycles, and the history of public sector pensions and pension finance. He has been affiliated with the National Bureau of Economic Research; a trustee of the Economic History Association and the Cliometric Society; a fellow of the Center for Demographic Studies at Duke University; a fellow of the Seminar für Wirtschaftsgeschichte, Universität München, Germany; and a member of the North Carolina Academy of Outstanding Teachers. Professor Craig received his BS and MA from Ball State University and his MA and Ph.D. from Indiana University.

Roderick B. Crane is the Director of Institutional Client Services at TIAA-CREF, where he develops and executes strategies for the state and local government 401(a), 457, 401(k), and 403(b) markets. He was previously a senior consultant with The Segal Company and Mercer Human Resources Consulting where he worked with large state and local governments on the design and administration of their defined benefit and defined contribution retirement programs as well as their deferred compensation and retiree health savings plans. He has also served as staff legal counsel for the North Dakota Legislative Assembly and its public employee retirement oversight committee. He earned his BA in economics from the University of North Dakota and the Juris Doctor from the University of North Dakota School of Law.

Jeremy Gold provides pension finance consulting to sponsors of defined benefit pension plans on investment analysis from an asset/liability point of view, and strategic benefit advice from a corporate finance perspective. He previously headed Morgan Stanley Pensions, served as Consulting Actuary/Account Executive at Buck Consultants, and worked with pension consulting firms and insurance companies. He is a Fellow of the Society of Actuaries; an Elected Board Member of the Society of Actuaries; a member of the Pension Practice Council of the American Academy of Actuaries; and a member of the Financial Economics Task force of the International Actuarial Association. He received his Ph.D. from the Wharton School of the University of Pennsylvania.

Michael Heller is Vice President or Actuarial Consulting Services at TIAA-CREF, where he manages a number of actuarial functions primarily focused on providing advice and assistance in the design and funding of both defined benefit and defined contribution retirement plans. He earned his BS in mathematics from the from the City College of New York; he also is a Fellow of the Society of Actuaries, a Member of the American Academy of Actuaries, and an Enrolled Actuary.

Edwin C. Hustead is former Senior Vice President in charge of the Arlington, Virginia Hay Group actuarial practice and all Hay governmental actuarial and benefits consulting. He is responsible for analyzing the financial condition of governmental employee retirement plans such as the Pennsylvania State Employee's Retirement System. He has consulted with Congress in the design and implementation of the Federal Employees Retirement System and has worked with the Society of Actuaries committees generating the UP94, GAR94, and RP2000 mortality tables. He was previously Chief Actuary of the Office of Personnel Management of the US Government. He received his BA in Mathematics from Franklin and Marshall College. He is also a Fellow of the Society of Actuaries, a member of the American Academy of Actuaries, and an Enrolled Actuary.

Toni Hustead was Chief of the Veterans Affairs and Defense Health Branch at the US Office of Management and Budget (OMB) in the Executive Office of the President where she was in charge of assisting the President in creating and implementing policies and budgets associated with veterans' benefits and defense health issues, overseeing the management of these programs, and ensuring that they aligned with other Presidential priorities. As OMB's only actuary, she was involved with accrual budgeting of Federal entitlement programs. She was previously an international benefits consultant for the Hay Group where she served as European Director of Benefits Consulting. She also was Chief Actuary for the Department of Defense and assisted the House Legislative Counsel's Office in its drafting of the legislation that actuarially funded the Military Retirement System. She is a member of the American Academy of Actuaries and an Associate of the Society of Actuaries.

Kelly Kenneally is a communications advisor to the National Institute on Retirement Security, a not-for-profit organization conducting research and education programs on US pensions. Her expertise is in the areas of finance, corporate affairs, technology, energy and environment, and retirement security. She has previously served as White House deputy director of the President's Commission on Fellowships, and as communications director with Micron Electronics; she held prior positions at MCI WorldCom, Edelman Public Relations, and the American Nuclear Energy Council, and the Maryland General Assembly. Kelly earned her BA in Government and Politics from the University of Maryland and she has undertaken graduate coursework in Political Management at George Washington University.

Gordon Latter is head of Pension and Endowment Strategy in the Merrill Lynch Global Securities Research and Economics Group where he provides expertise on retirement programs and provides risk management and strategic asset allocation advice. He has previously served as a primary consultant for pension clients at an actuarial consulting firm, Leong & Associates, Actuaries & Consultants Inc. where he performed sophisticated forecasts and asset/liability modeling. He earned a Bachelor of Commerce degree in Mathematics at the University of Manitoba. Mr. Latter is also a fellow of the Society of Actuaries, a fellow of the Canadian Institute of Actuaries, and a member of the Society of Actuaries Task Force on Financial Economics.

David Madland is the Director of the Work/Life Program at the Center for American Progress. His research interests include retirement, economic insecurity, health care, campaign finance, taxes, and public opinion. He received his BS from the University of California at Berkeley and his Ph.D. in Government from Georgetown University.

Raimond Maurer holds the endowed Chair of Investment, Portfolio Management, and Pension Finance in the Finance Department at the Goethe University of Frankfurt. His research focuses on asset management, lifetime portfolio choice, and pension finance. He serves in professional capacities for the Society of Actuaries, the Association of Certified International Investment Analysts, and the Advisory Board of the Wharton School's Pension Research Council. He received his habilitation, his Ph.D., and his Diploma in business from Mannheim University.

Ken McDonnell is Program Director of the American Savings Education Council in Washington, DC, a nonprofit national coalition of public and private sector organizations seeking to raise public awareness about long-term personal financial independence. His research interests include pension investments and employee benefits. He received his BA and his MA from Northern Illinois University.

Stephen T. McElhaney is Mercer's senior public sector actuary where he serves as a lead public sector retirement consultant for US retirement plans providing actuarial, design, compliance and strategic consulting services. He has assisted the Governmental Accounting Standards Board during its development of several key accounting standards and he also serves on the Board of Directors of the Conference of Consulting Actuaries. Steve received his BA in mathematics from Washington and Lee University, and he is a fellow of the Society of Actuaries, a member of the American Academy of Actuaries, a fellow of the Conference of Consulting Actuaries, and an Enrolled Actuary.

Olivia S. Mitchell is the International Foundation of Employee Benefit Plans Professor and the Chair of the Department of Insurance and Risk Management; Executive Director of the Pension Research Council; and Director of the Boettner Center on Pensions and Retirement Research at the Wharton School. Concurrently, Dr. Mitchell is Research Associate at the National Bureau of Economic Research and a Co-Investigator for the AHEAD/ Health and Retirement Studies at the University of Michigan. Her areas of research and teaching are private and public insurance, risk management, public finance and labor markets, and compensation and pensions, with a US and an international focus. She received her BA in Economics from Harvard University and her MA and Ph.D. in Economics from the University of Wisconsin-Madison.

Silvana Pozzebon is Associate Professor in the Department of Human Resources Management at HEC Montréal (École des Hautes Études Commerciales de Montréal). Her research and publication interests include pensions as well as occupational health and safety management. She earned her bachelor's degree in economics from Concordia University, and her MS and Ph.D. from Cornell University's School of Industrial and Labor Relations.

Ralph Rogalla is a Research Associate in the Department of Finance at the Goethe University of Frankfurt. His research focuses on the management of assets and liabilities of pension funds. He received his Diploma in Economics from Technical University Berlin and he worked as a research intern at the European Central Bank. He earned his Ph.D. from the University of Frankfurt.

Junichi Sakamoto is the Chief Adviser to the Pension Management Research Group of the Nomura Research Institute. He was previously the

Director of the Actuarial Affairs Division, Pension Bureau of the Ministry of Health, Labour and Welfare, in the Japanese Government. In that capacity, he was responsible for the actuarial affairs of the 2004 reform of social security pension schemes in Japan. He is also a part-time lecturer at the University of Tokyo, the Nihon University and the Sophia University. He received his BS and MS in Mathematics from the University of Tokyo, Japan.

M. Barton Waring is the Chief Investment Officer for Investment Strategy and Policy at Barclays Global Investors, Emeritus, having expertise in pension investment policy. He earned his JD in law from Lewis and Clark College, and his MPPM in Finance from Yale University.

Paul J. Yakoboski is Principal Research Fellow at the TIAA-CREF Institute, where he conducts research on retirement income security, saving and planning for retirement, and retiree health insurance. He was previously Director of Research for the American Council of Life Insurers, Senior Research Associate with the Employee Benefit Research Institute, Senior Economist with the US General Accounting Office, and Director of Research for the American Savings Education Council. He received his BS in economics from Virginia Tech, and his MA and Ph.D. in economics from the University of Rochester.

Parry Young is an independent consultant on pension and other postemployment benefit issues related to US state and local governments. He previously worked as a credit analyst in Standard & Poor's Public Finance Department in New York, specializing in municipal bond ratings in the Western states as well as the credit implications of retirement issues. He served in a variety of rating areas including short-term debt, structured, housing, and corporate. He is an associate member of the Government Finance Officers Association and the Governmental Accounting Standards Board Pension Accounting Research Project Advisory Committee. He earned his BA in English Literature from New York University and his MBA in Finance and Investments from Baruch College.

Abbreviations

AAL	Actuarial Accrued Liability
AARP	American Association of Retired People
ABO	Accumulated Benefit Obligation
AGA	Association of Government Accountants
AICPA	American Institute of Certified Public Accountants
ALEC	American Legislative Exchange Council
ARC	Annual Required Contribution
ASB	Actuarial Standards Board
ASOPs	Actuarial Standards of Practice
ASRS	Arizona State Retirement System
ATR	Americans for Tax Reform
bcIMC	British Columbia Investment Management Corporation
BLS	US Department of Labor Bureau of Labor Statistics
bps	basis points
CAFRs	Comprehensive Annual Financial Reports
CalPERS	California Public Employees Retirement System
CalSTRS	California State Teachers' Retirement System
CDC	Collective Defined Contribution
COLA	Cost-of-Living Adjustment
CPP	Canada Pension Plan
CRSP	Center for Research in Security Prices
CSRS	Federal Civil Service Retirement System
CVaR	Conditional Value at Risk
DB	Defined Benefit
DC	Defined Contribution
DoD	Department of Defense
DOL	US Department of Labor
EAN	Entry Age Normal
ELSAs	Earnings Limitation Savings Accounts
EPI	Employees' Pension Insurance
ERISA	Employee Retirement Income Security Act
FAS	Financial Accounting Standard
FAS	Final Average Salary
FERS	Federal Employees Retirement System
FMAA	Federation of National Public Service Personnel Mutual Aid Associations
GAO	US General Accounting Office

GASB	Government Accounting Standards Board
IAP	Individual Account Plan
IASB	International Accounting Standards Board
IT	Information Technology
JFMIP	Joint Financial Management Improvement Program
JNR	Japan National Railway Company
JR	Japan Railway Company
JT	Salt and Tobacco Monopoly Enterprise
MAA	Mutual Aid Association
MVA	Market Value of Assets
MVABO	Market Value of the Accumulated Benefit Obligation
MVL	Market Valuation for Liabilities
NASRA	National Association of State Retirement Administrators
NP	National Pension
NPERS	Nebraska Public Employee Retirement System
NRA	Normal Retirement Ages
NTT	Nippon Telegraph and Telecommunications Enterprise
NYCERS	New York City Employees' Retirement System
OMB	Office of Management and Budget
OPEB	Other Post-employment Benefits
OPTrust	Ontario Public Service Employees Union Pension Trust
PAYGO	pay-as-you-go
PBI	Permanent Benefit Increase
PBO	Projected Benefit Obligation
PERA	Public Employee Retirement Association
PERF	Indiana Public Employees' Retirement Fund
PERS	Public Employees' Retirement System
PPCC	Public Pension Coordinating Council
PVFB	Present Value of Future Benefits
PVFEC	Present Value of Future Employee Contributions
PVFNC	Present Value of Future Employer Normal Costs
QPP	Quebec Pension Plan
REITs	Real Estate Investment Trusts
RPPs	Registered pension plans
RRSPs	Registered Retirement Savings Plans
SERA	State Employees' Retirement Association
SERS	Nebraska School Employees Retirement System
SSA	Social Security Administration
TCRS	Tennessee Consolidated Retirement System
TIPS	Treasury Inflation-Protected Securities
TPC	Total Pension Costs
TRA	Teachers' Retirement Association
TRF	Teachers' Retirement Fund

TRP	Thrift Savings Plan
TRS	Alaska Teachers Employee Retirement System
UFCW	United Food and Commercial Workers
URS	Utah Retirement Systems
USBLS	US Bureau of Labor Statistics
VA	Veterans Affairs
VaR	Value at Risk
VAR	Vector Autoregressive
VBO	Vested Benefit Obligation

Chapter 1

The Future of Public Employee Retirement Systems

Olivia S. Mitchell

Pension systems are a central component of the compensation package for workers in virtually every developed nation, and nowhere is this more important than for public sector employees. In the United States, for instance, state and local pension systems cover over 27 million active and retired workers (GAO 2008) and federal pensions cover 10 million active and retired workers. In other countries, as we detail in the following text, public sector pensions are also taking center stage, wielding impressive financial and political clout, while at the same time portending huge costs.

The growth of these public pension systems has spurred hot debate of late, for several reasons. First, some private-sector employees envy their public sector counterparts due to the relatively generous benefits negotiated by strong unions that traditionally represent civil servants. Second, some politicians argue that pension and healthcare benefits paid to police and firefighters, schoolteachers, and other civil servants, have become too expensive for the public purse. In the private sector benefits costs have been cut by replacing defined benefit (DB) pensions by defined contribution (DC) plans; this has not yet occurred to any large extent in the public arena. And finally, the costs of maintaining public sector pension plans have come under the microscope of late, as municipalities, states, and other governmental units facing difficult financial times and volatile capital markets realize they must cut corners. These stresses are challenging many aspects of the public employee labor contract and raise questions about how such employees are attracted to the public sector, retained and motivated on the job, and retired, via the entire compensation package of wages and benefits.

This volume takes up these and other themes pertinent to the future of public employee retirement systems. In the first section, we build on our prior work (Mitchell and Hustead 2000) to focus on financial aspects of these schemes, addressing the cost and valuation debate in the public arena. Next, we offer an examination of public retirement system reform, exploring actual and proposed efforts to bring public pensions into better financial status in countries from the United States to Japan, and Canada to

Germany. Several chapters provide case studies illustrating specific aspects of risk management and the process of reform. Last, we take up the political economy of how these asset pools are perceived and managed, an increasingly important topic in times of global financial turmoil.

This volume will be of substantial importance to a wide range of readers. Public sector employees and their representatives will find the comparisons and arguments over pension asset and liability valuation of keen interest. Public administrators and policymakers seeking an explanation of what makes these plans so costly will gain a new understanding of how the arguments stack up. In addition, private sector employers and plan sponsors can learn much from efforts to reform these retirement systems in states and countries around the world. Finally, investors and the taxpaying public more generally may be at risk to cover these long-term promises, so it behooves them to pay close attention to the financing and investment practices of these plans, along with their valuation. In what follows we offer an overview and summary of key findings.

Costs and benefits of public retirement systems

Policymakers and scholars have recently become embroiled in a debate over what valuation and accounting methodology should be used for pension plan assets and liabilities. In the case of *corporate* pensions, there is relatively widespread agreement regarding how to do this valuation. In the United States, for instance, the Financial Accounting Standards Board (FASB) requires mark-to-market reporting of corporate pension assets and liabilities, and the UK Financial Reporting Council and the European International Accounting Standards Board (IASB) have similar views. Though the implementation of the approach regarding timing and details may differ slightly across countries, the general movement over the last decade has been to adopt a market-based approach to valuing private sector pension assets and liabilities.[1]

In the case of public employee pensions, however, there is far more controversy about whether an *actuarial* or *market-based* approach should be preferred and by whom (the latter is often termed the Market Valuation for Liabilities or MVL for short). As an example, Andrew Wozniak and Peter Austin (2008: 3) argue that '[g]iven the long-term nature and security of public pensions, plan management is generally focused on long-term cost, not short-term market related solvency. Many practitioners take the view that long-term cost is minimized if investment earnings are maximized thus reducing contributions while covering future benefit payments and plan expense.' A similar view is offered by a former member of the Government Accounting Standards Board (GASB), Girard Miller who states (2008: 2): 'By retaining the traditional practice of using reasonably probable investment returns as the basis for discounting future obligations . . . actuaries and accountants faithfully support the primary purpose of a public pension plan—which is to establish a funding plan that has the best possible chance of equitably balancing the interests of today's taxpayers and tomorrow's retirees. Many . . . would agree with me that using risk-free rates of return to value public plans (which enjoy a long-term horizon and capacity to prudently assume equity risks) will almost assuredly overburden today's taxpayers.

Such an MVL regime would perversely shift the entire normal market risk premium to the benefit of future generations at the expense of their forebears.' But other experts disagree, including David Wilcox (2008: 1) who notes:

Some have argued that because state and local governments do not exist to generate a profit, or because public plan sponsors cannot go out of business or be acquired by a competitor, market-based estimates are irrelevant for them. Others have argued that policymakers need other information aside from market-based estimates in order to make sound decisions on behalf of their constituents . . . in order to be useful, an estimate of plan liabilities must provide an analytically sound answer to a coherent, well-specified question. Market-based estimates of plan liabilities meet that test.

The first section of this volume provides several perspectives and insights into this vexed question. In his chapter, Stephen McElhaney notes that US public sector entities are permitted wide choice over cost methods and assumptions. This, in effect, allows them not to mark to market either their pension promises or their retiree health benefit obligations. One result is that it is not possible to compare public pension scheme liabilities, assets, and therefore funding rates across the broad array of states, cities, and municipalities with each other, nor with their private sector counterparts. For instance, on average, public pension plans use an 8 percent discount rate, while private sector firms must use lower long-term bond rates to determine the market value of liabilities. Given current practice, the author calculates that promised state and local government pension and health-care liabilities total about $2.4 trillion, versus dedicated pension assets of less than $2 trillion. Underfunding would be far greater in public sector plans if discount rates comparable to those used in the private pension arena were adopted.[2]

These and other differences between public and private pension accounting practice are permitted by the Governmental Accounting Standards Board on the argument that private businesses can go bankrupt, whereas governments financed via the involuntary payment of taxes are much less likely to default. Nevertheless, the governmental accounting group has announced its intention to review its public pension financing rules in the next several years, to determine whether changes in practice are required. McElhaney does not believe that GASB will, however, move to a fully mark-to-market framework. Instead he suggests that public plans should at a minimum be asked to certify that the assumptions they use in valuating theses plans reflect their actuary's best judgment. Currently, the plan actuary must certify that his assumptions are reasonable and in compliance with accepted standards, but he need not confirm that the results are congruent with his best estimate.

Another contrarian view to traditional public sector pension valuation practice is offered by Jeremy Gold and Gordon Latter. In their chapter, these authors contend that actuaries are skilled at developing long-term projections and budgets, but they worry that the projections tend not to be tightly linked to economic realities and market conditions. Their gravest concern arises when pension asset and liability figures differ which produces a misallocation of resources. To illustrate their case, the authors select four defined benefit plans from different regions of the United States and report both actuarial and market value measures of plan liabilities and funding ratios. The chapter shows that the four plans have funding ratios ranging from 66 to 106 percent using the conventional actuarial accrued liability approach. By contrast, using the authors' preferred measure of market value of liabilities, the plans are only 50–80 percent funded. What this means is that the costs of offering a pension promise when interest rates are 4 percent is massively more expensive than when rates are 12 percent.

A defense of the traditional public employee DB plan is central to M. Barton Waring's chapter where he alludes to the mythical Greek sea monsters Scylla and Charybdis, who inspired the expression 'between a rock and a hard place.' He argues that DB plans are important to retain despite the perception that they may be risky and expensive, since in his view, the DC model does not work particularly well either. The author finds that the average balance in a DC plan today is only about $150,000, so that DC participants cannot expect to live well in retirement with such a small accrual. While DC plans could, in theory, provide as much income security as DB plans, they would need to have much higher mandatory contributions than usually found and annuitization features that are not often automatic. In terms of the mark-to-market debate, he contends that the MVL approach must prevail inasmuch as public and private plans borrow in the same capital markets and face the same interest rates.

In his view, a 'tough love' plan of action is needed to control risk in underfunded plans and change reporting, contribution, and benefit policy. Most crucially, in his view, public plans would do well to simply agree to adopt a regular reduction in the discount rate used until they reach the long-term government bond rate. When it comes to benefits, he suggests that labor and management must review existing levels using current market data to fend off possible legislation that might be tougher on the overall package. Waring further argues that the real reason public pension systems adopt a traditional actuarial viewpoint is not that they do not understand the economic discount rate. Rather, he suspects that plan sponsors are 'worried about what the legislature is going to do if they walk in and say the pension liability is 40 percent more than what they said it was.' Since the majority of state pensions make explicit in the state constitutions a commitment to pay public sector employee benefits (GAO 2008), marking the liabilities to market would impose a rude shock to managers seeking to smooth contribution flows.

Pension funding volatility is the subject of Parry Young's chapter, which notes that state and local governments have experienced substantially higher volatility in pension funding ratios, and hence contributions, of late than ever before. In many jurisdictions, he finds that this volatility has been a substantial burden for the planning and budgeting process. Young points out that annual required contributions to public plans can vary due to many factors such as benefit and demographic changes, larger than anticipated investment gains or losses, and changes in the actuarial assumptions. He cites data showing that state and local government employers' plan contributions rose from 10.5 percent of payroll in fiscal 1997, to 6.8 percent in 2002, to 14.7 percent in 2003, and 29.5 percent in 2004. Yet, state revenue patterns are such that money has not always been available to boost government contributions over the last decade. Young also notes that recent declines in capital market values have created serious funding shortfalls for many public pension funds. He argues that rate volatility is the natural result of holding riskier assets, implying that by addressing market values and volatility with wise choice of assets, plan sponsors can immunize themselves substantially against such shocks.

In a chapter devoted to a comparison of the relative costs of hiring public versus private sector employees, Ken McDonnell shows that the average state and local worker costs employers substantially more in wages and benefits than in the private sector. For instance, total compensation costs were 51 percent higher for state and local employers compared to private firms, which results from 43 percent higher wages and salaries, and 73 percent higher employee benefits including pensions. The author outlines possible explanations for these differences and concludes that they are in part due to higher unionization rates raising wages and benefits in the public sector. In addition, there are differences with regard to both occupation and industry mix: for example, public sector workers in the 'service sector' category include skilled and risky jobs such as police and firefighter, whereas private sector service workers tend to be less skilled waiters/waitresses, and work in cleaning and building services functions with traditionally lower wages. The compensation differences are even larger for health insurance benefits, where state and local government employer costs are 235 percent higher per hour than for private employees, and 330 percent higher for state and local government employers.

Turning to administrative costs of public sector plans, Edwin Hustead reviews a set of DB and DC plans offered in different states in America to explore the range and diversity of pure, hybrid, and individual account schemes. He notes that in the public sector, most US pensions were originally established as DB programs. Hence the systems that today have DC elements have usually added these features alongside a traditional DB plan. In his analysis, he finds that DB annual plan expenses are rather low, totaling only about 0.1 percent of assets. One reason they are so low is that these plans are large and have been in place for decades. By contrast, the public DC plans are typically much newer and hence smaller. Here he finds that annual administrative costs amount to about 0.2 to 0.3 percent of assets. Hustead's research also captures costs in the federal government retirement systems, which differ from the states in having a separate administrative organizational structure for DC and DB plans. Here administrative costs are small and similar across plan types. For the Federal DB case, he reports annual costs of 0.3 percent of contributions or 0.02 percent of assets, while DC expenses are 0.4 percent of contributions or 0.04 percent of assets. His overview suggests that large public sector retirement systems which are either exclusively defined benefit or exclusively defined contribution would have similar administrative costs, holding constant plan size.

In the final chapter in this section, Toni Hustead takes up the question of how policymakers, participants, and taxpayers might think more clearly about how to report and finance Federal employee pensions. In the United States, there are more than 30 Federal pension plans that cover over 10 million active and retired participants; the two largest of these are for Federal civilian employees, namely the Federal Civil Service Retirement System (CSRS) which covers civilian employees who entered service before 1984, and the Federal Employees Retirement System (FERS) which covers all new hires after 1983 (plus employees who elected to transfer from CSRS to FERS). A third large plan covers military participants and their families, the Department of Defense (DoD) Military Retirement System. The author notes that recent changes in federal government pension accounting now require each employing US Federal agency to budget for the accruing liability of retirement for its current personnel. And the US Congress has set up Federal trust funds which are supposed to receive annual payments sufficient to cover benefits earned that year and amortization amounts to pay off past unfunded liabilities. Nevertheless, as these trust funds are invested in Federal securities, the Treasury is permitted to spend the receipts similar to

Social Security Trust Fund bonds. Ultimately then, these Federal schemes can be described as at least partially funded, though in fact they still depend on policymakers' willingness to raise money to pay the bills when retirees need to be paid.

Implementing public retirement system reform

Public pension reforms are also underway in other developed nations. Raimond Maurer, Olivia Mitchell, and Ralph Rogalla review civil servant pension systems in Germany, where most state schemes are tax-sponsored, non-contributory unfunded DB plans. State governments finance the programs by raising taxes and sometimes by investing in government bonds that they typically issue themselves. Their chapter goes on to explore an alternative approach using a model that lays out some of the risks and rewards of moving from a pay-as-you-go (PAYGO) system to a partially funded pension plan. The analysis begins with an actuarial valuation of pension promises due to current and retired workers. Next the authors project 50 years out, to estimate the payroll-related contribution rate necessary to fund the pension obligation. Then, using a Monte Carlo framework and a stochastic present value approach, combined with a conditional value at risk measure, the authors can determine what asset allocation minimizes the worst-case pension costs. The authors report that pre-funding the plan at 20 percent of payroll and investing 30 percent of the assets in equities and 70 percent in bonds sharply curtails the worst-case pension costs. Finally, they outline contribution rates and asset allocation when a plan sponsor is required to stick to a set level of risk. They point out that debate on whether to pre-fund public pension obligations will require being explicit about the level of risk that the plan fiduciary is willing to take on. This, in turn, requires a hard look at risk bearing for future and present generations.

In her study on Canadian public plans, Silvana Pozzebon notes that Canadian public employees are relatively free of pension envy. That is, there has been no backlash against public sector employees due to their generous pensions; instead, these plans continue to be seen as a way to attract workers to the fields of education and health care. These plans do, however, face challenges, as provincial governments seek to protect budgets against sharp increases in unfunded pension liabilities and demographic pressure due to workforce aging. The Canadian public sector exploded between the 1960s and 1970s, and now a large group of workers is nearing retirement age. As one example, the Ontario Teachers' Pension Plan began investing in equities in 1990 and has been seen as one of the best-performing retirement programs in Canada. Yet it now faces deficits and they cannot expect the government to pick up the tab.

How Japan copes with the demographic shift is the subject of much interest due to that nation's status as the most rapidly aging country on earth. Junichi Sakamoto describes the foundation and development of Japan's civil service pension systems, which from 1985 have been gradually merged with systems covering private sector workers. The author traces the development of Japan's pension system back to the new government after Meiji Restoration in the nineteenth century, which initiated Japan's transformation to an industrial economy. The government established a superannuation system for civil servants and members of the armed forces on the theory that they had given their lives to the nation. In the early twentieth century, other public employees began to form mutual aid associations around their workplaces. After World War II, the two types of public pension plans merged, and local government workers gained coverage in 1962. Meanwhile, private sector employees had no pension coverage until 1942 when Japan created the Employees' Pension Insurance (EPI) scheme, modeled after the German pension insurance system. As the nation went through industrial change in the 1960s, the system was stressed. As employees were made redundant by changing technology in some schemes, fewer workers remained to support older beneficiaries. The mutual aid association for Japan Railway employees nearly collapsed and eventually was absorbed by the EPI scheme. Responding to growing imbalances, the government called for consolidation of private and government sector plans in 1985; only in 2007 was a bill introduced calling for all four remaining schemes to merge. One continued sticking point is whether to require the self-employed and farmers to join the scheme.

Just as public pension schemes around the world have experienced change, so too have US public pension plans continued to evolve. Keith Brainard's chapter contends that the prevailing retirement plan model in public sector jobs is still a DB pension, but his further examination shows that many public systems also offer a DC plan alongside the DB plan. His work provides examples from states introducing hybrid plans and other innovations, including Nebraska which in 2003 introduced a cash balance plan for state and county workers. Existing DC participants received a one-time opportunity to switch, and 30 percent chose to take advantage of the offer. In 2007, the plan offered a second chance to participate and an additional 4 percent opted in. The Minnesota Teachers' Retirement Association offers so-called 'Earnings Limitation Savings Accounts' that comply with Internal Revenue Service rules and encourage teachers to return to work after retiring. These plans are designed to provide added income security for the teachers and improve the pool of educators for the state. Brainard notes that permitting employees to return to work is sometimes criticized as encouraging 'double dipping,' but the Minnesota plan overcomes this argument by depositing pension benefits into an individual account that becomes accessible as a lump sum at age 65. The Arizona State Retirement System has an investment earnings-based Cost of Living Allowance (COLA) paid for through earnings that are greater than actuarial assumptions. About two-thirds of state and local plans have automatic COLAs and others rely on ad hoc COLAs granted by legislation, but the author argues that dropping a new COLA into a defined benefit plan where it has not been pre-funded over the years proves quite expensive. Another innovative approach is seen in Oregon, where the legislature established a new hybrid plan that mandates individual contributions. The DC contributions are professionally managed by the DB fund managers, giving participants the chance to hold a portfolio that they otherwise would not have access to, and it avoids having participants navigate the investment market on their own.

A discussion of best practices in the public DC pension arena is taken up in the chapter by Roderick Crane, Michael Heller, and Paul Yakoboski. The authors review key features of state plans for general employees as well as several public higher education plans, and they highlight several practices they deem innovative. These include defaulting participants into target date life cycle funds and providing a limited (15–20) set of participant-directed investment choices. They argue that this menu, linked with investment advice and investment education, is likely to enhance retiree well-being. They also contend that it is useful to ensure that pension contributions total at least 12 percent of pay if the workers are covered by Social Security, or 18–20 percent of pay if not. In terms of the payout process, they laud the fact that all but three of the state plans and all of the higher education plans offer an annuity option at retirement, and most offered some exposure to equities after retirement.[3]

The political economy of public pension reform

An understanding of the political economy of public pension reform is facilitated with an historic overview of how these systems have evolved over time. The chapter by Robert Clark, Lee Craig, and Neveen Ahmed describes how US public pensions date back to the Colonial Era, when Britain's North American colonies established disability pensions for members of the militia. The chapter traces how municipalities began to offer pensions to teachers, firefighters, and police officers during the mid-nineteenth century, and these plans grew with civil service reforms that curbed patronage. States then offered pensions to employees beginning in the early twentieth century and were spurred by the 1935 Social Security Act, which specifically excluded public employees. In the 1950s, the Social Security Act was amended to include public sector employees, allowing government units to enter or withdraw from the system voluntarily.

By 1961, all but five states had public pension plans; as of 1991, Social Security became mandatory for public employees with no pension plan.

Turning to an analysis of today's public employee pensions, the authors report that public sector employee DB pensions offer benefit replacement rates of around 56 percent of the worker's income at the time of retirement. The majority of public sector workers are also covered by Social Security. Meanwhile, and by sharp contrast, private sector DB plans have been on the wane, and many corporate employers have now terminated or frozen them, with a switch to DC plans. Clark and colleagues examine trends in replacement rates over time, where they find that state plans tend to be more generous relative to private-sector plans. The key question is whether states can continue to afford the relatively generous benefits in view of rapid population aging and fiscal stress.

A different view of the political nature of public pensions is offered by Brad Barber (2009), who explains that management adds one level of costs for shareholders seeking the maximum value for their investment in a corporation. Good governance typically limits those costs as shareholders in scandal-ridden companies, such as Tyco and Enron, learned firsthand in recent years. For pension funds, an extra layer of costs is associated with the portfolio manager that accumulates investments and then acts as a shareholder for the beneficiaries. Another cost can occur if fund managers have a political, moral, or personal agenda that does not align directly with shareholder value. In public funds, he adds, the portfolio manager is actually a triumvirate of the investment manager, the pension board, and the legislative body overseeing public-sector retirement plans. When it comes to activism, fund managers can have varying effects. Some may be self-serving autocrats forcing their own political agendas, while others can be a benevolent enforcer reducing agency costs, which benefits not only for investors but the market as a whole.

Barber offers as an example the California Public Employees' Retirement System (CalPERS) with its history of activism since 1984, when the system gained authority to invest 25 percent of its assets in equities. Three years later, CalPERS launched its governance program aimed at improving corporate performance by using its weight as a shareholder to block corporate poison pills. In 1992, it became more aggressive, publishing an annual focus list of companies it would attempt to influence. In addition to public crusades, CalPERS does extensive behind-the-scenes negations at companies to influence governance. Barber has tracked the performance of the CalPERS focus list over the past 15 years and finds a slight advantage, but not enough to be scientifically determinative. Nonetheless, he says, interventions in corporate governance such as fighting a poison pill or eliminating classes of stock have sound theoretical underpinnings to suggest they do create shareholder value. Beyond corporate governance issues, pension fund managers have become involved in other forms of activism. Barber notes that CalPERS has been ordered by legislation to use its influence to demand corporations divest from businesses in South Africa, Sudan, and Iran. In addition to legislative demands, the CalPERS board has also taken stands against corporations on social grounds. In 2000, overriding the recommendation of its staff, the board ordered the fund to divest from tobacco companies, stating that tobacco stocks were risky because of litigation. The CalPERS board has become involved in labor strife with a grocery chain, which in his view, imposed reputational consequences on the pension fund.

Barber does believe that activism originating from a fund's investment committee aimed at governance, which he calls *shareholder activism*, can be rational. And when funds take on broader social causes, what he terms *social activism*, beneficiaries and taxpayers may pay a price. Divestment policies, he notes, automatically put funds at a disadvantage in terms of investment performance. In his view, there is no question that constraints on investment opportunity hurt the fund; rather the only question is how much and whether it is material. He believes that public pension funds can endanger their returns with such action, meaning that they may lose their original objective of protecting retirees.

An alternative different perspective is offered by Beth Almeida, Kelly Kenneally, and David Madland (2009) who note that public plan retirement assets per participant are twice those in the private sector. They also indicate that existing public employee pension obligations could be met with an increase in contributions of less than 1 percent of payroll. At the same time, they acknowledge that opposition to traditional DB pensions is moving into the public arena. Public sector plans are influenced by public opinion because voters and taxpayers have a say in the design of the plans, either through ballot issues or the representatives they elect. Almeida adds, however, that most voters know very little about the issue. For instance, many workers cannot say whether their own retirement scheme is a DB or a DC plan. The authors analyze survey data and find that among the voting public, public sector employees, women, and those who have DB plans themselves tend to be most supportive of public sector pensions, while those with an individualistic ideology are less supportive. Republican-party affiliation has no effect, after controlling for other factors including ideological perspective. Other research indicates that states with Republican-controlled legislatures have been more aggressive than other states in attempting to change public plans from defined benefit to defined contribution. The authors find the results interesting because it would appear that individual voters are not clamoring for change, so they attribute the debate at least in part to partisan politics.

The authors then provide four case studies, for Alaska, Colorado, California, and Utah, where there have been recent debates about switching from DB to DC plans. In those states, they argue that anti-tax, libertarian groups have taken an ideological stand against public defined benefit plans. Yet these efforts had only mixed success in drawing the public and elected representatives to their cause. The authors conclude that the challenges to public defined benefit plans do not appear to stem from well-articulated critiques or well-established economic consideration, nor from widespread public dissatisfaction. Rather, interest groups seek to dismantle defined benefit plans as part of their agenda.

Conclusion

At present, most US public employee plans appear to have sufficient assets to continue paying retirement benefits for some time. In fact, as the GAO (2008: 19) notes, some analysts suggest that a public plan funding level of 80 percent could be a sensible target, since '... it is unlikely that public entities will go out of business or cease operations as can happen with private sector employers, and state and local governments can spread the costs of unfunded liabilities over a period of up to 30 years under current GASB standards. In addition ... it can be politically unwise for a plan to be overfunded; that is, to have a funded ratio over 100 percent. The contributions made to funds with "excess" assets can become a target for lawmakers with other priorities or for those wishing to increase retiree benefits.'

Nevertheless, the doomsayers also have a point. The current economic environment has produced a 'perfect storm' for public pensions, where low interest rates are spiking liabilities, depressed equity markets are whittling away assets, and economic recession is drying up state and local tax revenue. In fact, the GAO (2008) has noted that almost two-thirds of the plans it reviewed contributed less than necessary to meet annual required levels, with the shortfalls being most pronounced among the worst-funded plans. Such behavior implies that taxpayers and public employees will have to pay more in the future, and it may also lead to curtailed retiree benefits (Barrett and Green 2008). Inasmuch as public employee pensions are not guaranteed by the federal government, it is even possible that public sector plans might default. Whereas this has not happened to date in the United States, it is true that a few cities and towns (including Cleveland, OH, and Bridgeport, CT, as well as Vallejo, CA) have declared bankruptcy.

Accordingly, the task ahead is to ensure that public sector retirement systems do have a future, one that is both affordable and resilient to economic and demographic pressures. It is incumbent not only on plan fiduciaries and the politicians to whom they report, but also the taxpaying public and those in the investment arena, to ensure that these commitments are transparently valued and financed in the most cost-effective and generationally fair manner.

Notes

[1] Nevertheless, recent research (Coronado et al. 2008) on US corporate pensions suggests that corporate pension liabilities and assets are not yet fully reflected in company share prices.

[2] For instance, a recent study by Novy-Marx and Rauh (2008) contends that accrued benefits under the 50 US state retirement systems are underfunded by \$2 trillion, on the assumption that the benefit promises can be valued at a risk-free discount rate. They suggest that this is reasonable if the pension payouts cannot be abrogated, consistent with the fact that many public pension payments are backed by the full faith and credit of the sponsoring state governments.

[3] An alternative model called the Collective Defined Contribution (CDC) scheme advanced by the Dutch is also of some relevance, though not taken up in this volume in detail. See Bovenberg (2008).

References

Almeida, Beth, Kelly Kenneally, and David Madland (2009). 'The New Intersection on the Road to Retirement: Public Pensions, Economics, Perceptions, Politics, and Interest Groups,' in O.S. Mitchell and G. Anderson, eds., *The Future of Public Employee Retirement Systems*. Oxford: Oxford University Press.

Barber, Brad M. (2009). 'Pension Fund Activism: The Double-Edged Sword,' in O.S. Mitchell and G. Anderson, eds., *The Future of Public Employee Retirement Systems*. Oxford: Oxford University Press.

Barrett, Katherine and Richard Green (2008). *Promises with a Price*. Pew Charitable Trusts' Center on the States. Philadelphia, PA.: Pew Charitable Trusts.

Bovenberg, Lans (2008). 'Frontiers in Pension Finance and Reform: Institutional Innovation in the Netherlands,' in D. Broeders, S. Eijffinger and A. Houben, eds., *Frontiers in Pension Finance*, Edward Elgar.

Brainard, Keith (2009). 'Redefining Traditional Plans: Variations and Developments in Public Employee Retirement Plan Design,' in O.S. Mitchell and G. Anderson, eds., *The Future of Public Employee Retirement Systems*. Oxford: Oxford University Press.

Clark, Robert L., Lee A. Craig, and Neveen Ahmed (2009). 'The Evolution of Public Sector Pension Plans in the United States,' in O.S. Mitchell and G. Anderson, eds., *The Future of Public Employee Retirement Systems*. Oxford: Oxford University Press.

Crane, Roderick B., Michael Heller, and Paul J. Yakoboski (2009). 'Defined Contribution Pension Plans in the Public Sector: A Benchmark Analysis,' in O.S. Mitchell and G. Anderson, eds., *The Future of Public Employee Retirement Systems*. Oxford: Oxford University Press.

Coronado, Julia, Steven Sharpe, Olivia S. Mitchell, and S. Blake Nesbitt (2008). 'Footnotes Aren't Enough: The Impact of Pension Accounting on Stock Values.' *Journal of Pension Economics and Finance*, 7(3): 257–276.

Gold, Jeremy and Gordon Latter (2009). 'The Case for Marking Public Plan Liabilities to Market,' in O.S. Mitchell and G. Anderson, eds., *The Future of Public Employee Retirement Systems*. Oxford: Oxford University Press.

Government Accounting Office (GAO) (2008). *State and Local Government Pension Plans: Current Structure and Funded Status*. Statement of Barbara D. Bovbjerg, Director of Education, Workforce, and Income Security, before the Joint Economic Committee of the US Congress. July 10.

Hustead, Edwin (2009). 'Administrative Costs of State Defined Benefit and Defined Contribution Systems,' in O.S. Mitchell and G. Anderson, eds., *The Future of Public Employee Retirement Systems*. Oxford: Oxford University Press.

Hustead, Toni (2009). 'Thinking About Funding Federal Retirement Plans,' in O.S. Mitchell and G. Anderson, eds., *The Future of Public Employee Retirement Systems*. Oxford: Oxford University Press.

Maurer, Raimond, Olivia S. Mitchell, and Ralph Rogalla (2009). 'Reforming the German Civil Servant Pension Plan,' in O.S. Mitchell and G. Anderson, eds., *The Future of Public Employee Retirement Systems*. Oxford: Oxford University Press.

McDonnell, Ken (2009). 'Benefit Cost Comparisons Between State and Local Governments and Private Industry Employers,' in O.S. Mitchell and G. Anderson, eds., *The Future of Public Employee Retirement Systems*. Oxford: Oxford University Press.

McElhaney, Stephen T. (2009). 'Estimating State and Local Government Pension and Retiree Health Care Liabilities,' in O.S. Mitchell and G. Anderson, eds., *The Future of Public Employee Retirement Systems*. Oxford: Oxford University Press.

Miller, Girard (2008). 'Presentation by Girard Miller: Comments before the Public Interest Committee of the American Academy of Actuaries.' Washington, DC: September 4. http://www.actuary.org/events/2008/forum_statements_sept08/oral/miller.pdf

Mitchell, Olivia S. and Edwin Hustead (2000). *Pensions for the Public Sector*. Pension Research Council. Philadelphia, PA: University of Pennsylvania Press.

Novy-Marx, Robert and Joshua Rauh (2008). '*The Intergenerational Transfer of Public Pension Promises*.' University of Chicago GSB Working Paper No. 08–13. Chicago, IL: University of Chicago Graduate School of Business.

Pozzebon, Silvana (2009). 'The Outlook for Canada's Public Sector Employee Pensions,' in O.S. Mitchell and G. Anderson, eds., *The Future of Public Employee Retirement Systems*. Oxford: Oxford University Press.

Sakamoto, Junichi (2009). 'Unifying Pension Schemes in Japan: Toward a Single Scheme for Both Civil Servants and Private Employees,' in O.S. Mitchell and G. Anderson, eds., *The Future of Public Employee Retirement Systems*. Oxford: Oxford University Press.

Waring, M. Barton (2009). 'Between Scylla and Charybdis: Improving the Cost Effectiveness of Public Pension Retirement Plans,' in O.S. Mitchell and

G. Anderson, eds., *The Future of Public Employee Retirement Systems*. Oxford: Oxford University Press.

Wilcox, David (2008). '*The Disclosure of Market Value of Assets and Liabilities by Public-Sector Defined-Benefit Pension Plans*: Comments before the Public Interest Committee of the American Academy of Actuaries.' Washington, DC: September 4. http://www.actuary.org/events/2008/forum_statements_sept08/oral/wilcox.pdf

Wozniak, Andrew and Peter S. Austin (2008). *US Public Pensions at a Crossroad: Which Way Forward?*, May. New York, NY: BNY Mellon Asset Management. http://www.melloninstitutional.com/public/library/documents/knowledge/pdfs/US_Public_Pensions_final.pdf

Young, Parry (2009). 'Public Pensions and State and Local Budgets: Can Contribution Rate Cyclicality Be Better Managed?' in O.S. Mitchell and G. Anderson, eds., *The Future of Public Employee Retirement Systems*. Oxford: Oxford University Press.

Part I

Costs and Benefits of Public Employee Retirement Systems

Chapter 2

Estimating State and Local Government Pension and Retiree Health Care Liabilities

Stephen T. McElhaney

Recently concern has been raised about public sector unfunded retiree liabilities. Some observers declare a looming crisis in public pension and retiree health-care funding (Pew 2007). Others charge that this crisis is even worse than it might appear, because public sector retirement system liabilities are not computed using appropriate assumptions and methods (Ennis 2007; Gold and Latter 2009). Here we do not resolve the question of whether such a crisis exists. But because public debate relies, at least in part, on the numbers being published in public financial reports, it is important to review the basis of these calculations as a measure of their credibility. This chapter examines the principles under which the calculations of unfunded liability are derived. Our attention focuses on general actuarial principles as set forth in Actuarial Standards of Practice; accounting principles for retiree benefit plans in the private sector; accounting principles for retiree benefit plans in the public sector; comments regarding the differences between private- and public-sector financial reporting; and estimates of the overall magnitude of public sector retiree liabilities.

Measurement issues

The primary guidance given to actuaries with respect to measuring retirement-related liabilities, both in the public and private sectors, is provided by the Actuarial Standards Board (ASB) in its Actuarial Standard of Practice (ASOP) No. 4, entitled *Measuring Pension Obligations and Determining Pension Plan Costs or Contributions* (ASB 2007). Within the scope of ASOP No. 4, paragraph 1.2.a is the measurement of pension obligations, including 'determinations of funded status, assessments of solvency upon plan termination, and measurements for use in cost or contribution determinations' (ASB 2007). Section 2.1 of that circular defines the term 'Actuarial Accrued Liability,' which is used almost universally for communicating funded status of public sector retirement programs. A plan's Actuarial Accrued Liability (AAL) is dependent upon the particular actuarial cost method and is defined as the 'portion of the actuarial present value of projected benefits...not provided for by future normal costs' (ASB 2007).

Section 3.11 of ASOP No. 4 gives guidance with respect to selection of an actuarial cost method. Actuarial cost methods are generally chosen to be consistent with the funding objectives of the pension fund and/or the sponsoring organization. Specific actuarial cost methods include the Entry Age Normal Method, the Projected Unit Credit Method, the Traditional Unit Credit Method, Frozen Initial Liability Method, the Attained Age Normal Method, and the Aggregate Method as well as variations of these methods. Of these methods, only the Entry Age Normal Method, the Projected Unit Credit Method, and the Traditional Unit Credit Method directly calculate an Actuarial Accrued Liability at each actuarial valuation date. For the Frozen Initial Liability Method and the Attained Age Normal Method, an Actuarial Accrued Liability is calculated at one particular actuarial valuation date and not updated at future dates except as to amortize such liability to the extent funded by contributions to the plan. The Aggregate Method does not determine any Accrued Liability, and plans that use the Aggregate Method therefore can give the illusion of being 100 percent funded at all times. The methods that determine Actuarial Accrued Liability at each valuation date are sometimes called 'immediate gain methods,' while the methods that do not directly determine Actuarial Accrued Liability at each valuation date are sometimes called 'spread gain methods.'

ASOP No. 4 provides very broad guidance with respect to selection of a specific actuarial cost method. Each of the specific methods listed in the earlier paragraph would probably meet the very broad guidelines of ASOP No. 4 for almost any public sector retirement program. The circular does not provide guidance with respect to actuarial assumptions except to refer to ASOP No. 27—*Selection of Economic Assumptions for Measuring Pension Obligations* (ASB 2005*a*), and ASOP No. 35—*Selection of Demographic and Other Noneconomic Assumptions for Measuring Pension Obligations* (ASB 2005*b*).

The first of these, ASOP No. 27, is especially important in assessing governmental retiree liabilities, since it provides guidance with respect to selection of the discount rate used for valuing liabilities. In most instances, the selection of discount rate has more influence on the magnitude of the calculated liability than any other single assumption. Under this document, the discount rate should be selected based upon the expected long-term investment return, unless the specific purpose of the measurement should be based upon a different assumption. ASOP No. 27 suggests that the actuary's determination of the investment return assumption should consider factors which include the plan's investment policy, investment volatility, manager performance, and cash flow timing. In addition, ASOP No. 27 states that the determination of economic assumptions includes development of a best-estimate range, rather than a single result, and that the actuary should select the assumptions from within this range. For an investment return assumption where the investment policy includes potentially volatile assets such as equities, such a best-estimate range may span 200 basis points or more. Two actuaries analyzing the same data could reach substantially different conclusions with respect to choice of an investment return assumption, resulting in substantially different measurements of plan funded status.

ASOP No. 35 provides guidance with respect to demographic assumptions such as turnover, retirement, disability, and mortality. While selection of unreasonable demographic assumptions can have a material effect on the magnitude of actuarial liabilities, for purposes of this chapter, it has been assumed that such assumptions have been selected reasonably with appropriate reference to the experience of the plan. (This comment also applies to other economic actuarial assumptions covered by ASOP No. 27 such as future salary growth and inflation.)

A different document, ASOP No. 6—*Measuring Retiree Group Obligations* (ASB 2001), provides guidance with respect to selection of assumptions which are unique to non-pension benefits such as retiree health care and retiree life insurance. For retiree heath care, these assumptions include assumed rate of health-care claims and future trend rates. As with ASOP No. 35, it is assumed that such assumptions are selected reasonably.

To summarize, Actuarial Standards Board practices on measurement issues with respect to unfunded retirement liabilities are quite broad. Different funds and different actuaries can and do reach different conclusions regarding the magnitude of unfunded liabilities for retirement programs that are essentially very similar.

Private sector measurement

For private sector organizations in the United States, measurement of retirement liabilities is covered primarily by three accounting standards issued by the Financial Accounting Standards Board (FASB):

- Financial Accounting Standard (FAS) No. 87: *Employers' Accounting for Pensions* (FASB 1985)
- Financial Accounting Standard (FAS) No. 106: *Employers' Accounting for Postretirement Benefits Other Than Pensions* (FASB 2004)
- Financial Accounting Standard (FAS) No. 158: *Employers' Accounting for Defined Benefit Pension and Other Postretirement Plans—an amendment of FASB Statements No. 87, 88, 106, and 132(R)* (FASB 2006)

The standards to measure liabilities are described in FAS No. 87 and FAS No. 106, while FAS No. 158 covers how such liabilities should be disclosed in financial statements. Among other requirements, FAS No. 87 and FAS No. 106 set the specific requirements with respect to selection of the actuarial cost method and the discount rate. The actuarial cost method used is the Projected Unit Credit Method for all plans. Further, the discount rate should reflect the rates at which the obligations could be effectively settled. FAS No. 87, paragraph 44 suggests that this rate could be based upon current market rates of 'high-quality fixed-income investments currently available' (FASB 1985).

The suggestion to use current market rates for fixed-income investments anticipates a liability determination which is independent of the plan's expected return on investments. Implicit in this requirement is that such assumption would be modified to current rates at each measurement of the liability. As a rule, this type of measurement is known as a market value liability. Discount rates using this approach will almost always be lower than discount rates based upon the plan's long-term investment return, and therefore the actuarial liability calculated using a current market fixed-income rate will generally be higher than an actuarial liability using an investment return assumption.

Public sector measurement

For state and local public-sector organizations in the United States, measurement of retiree liabilities is covered by two accounting standards issued by the Governmental Accounting Standards Board (GASB):

- Governmental Accounting Standards Board Statement No. 27: *Accounting for Pensions by State and Local Governmental Employers* (GASB 1994)
- Governmental Accounting Standards Board Statement No. 45: *Accounting and Financial Reporting by Employers for Postemployment Benefits Other Than Pensions* (GASB 2004)

In contrast to the FASB requirements described earlier, these two statements provide guidance with respect to selection of actuarial cost method and discount rate. Any of the actuarial cost methods described for general measurement purposes under ASOP No. 4 may be selected.

This flexibility may be desirable from the standpoint of long-term planning since the best fit of any cost method depends upon both the plan structure and the financial requirements of the sponsoring organization. However, this flexibility also makes it difficult to compare the funded status of different organizations. Also, as has been noted previously, some actuarial cost methods do not recalculate the actuarial accrued liability at each actuarial valuation date, so that the reported funded status of various retirement programs may not be fully comparative to the extent such comparability would be desirable. And finally the discount rate is based upon each entity's estimated long-term yield on investments.

For pension benefits under GASB No. 27, the discount rate is to be the estimated long-term investment yield for the plan. For other post-employment benefits (OPEB) under GASB No. 45 paragraph 13c, the discount rate is to be the 'estimated long-term investment yield on the investments that are expected to be used to finance the payment of benefits.' The different language used in GASB No. 45 reflects the fact that most pension benefits are funded within pension trust funds, whereas most other post-employment benefits, including retiree health care, have historically been paid for directly from current budgets on a pay-as-you-go basis. For a plan operating in a pay-as-you-go environment, the long-term investment return would be based upon returns on an employer's general assets, which are usually invested in very short-term fixed-income instruments. This rate might actually be lower than the market bond rate derived for purposes of FAS No. 87 or FAS No. 106. For OPEB that are fully funded through a trust, the discount rate would be selected using the same principles as for funded pension trust. For OPEB that are partially funded by a trust and partially funded by employer assets, the discount rate is selected by blending the appropriate fully funded and pay-as-you-go discount rates.

A result of the GASB discount rate requirements is that disclosed liabilities for a particular OPEB plan will vary substantially, depending upon whether the plan is funded or unfunded. Such a difference is expected to cause many public sector plan sponsors to consider pre-funding of OPEB obligations. It should be noted that pre-funding of OPEB obligations is not common in the private sector due to two primary differences with respect to funding between public and private sector employers:

- For private sector employers, the choice of discount rate under FAS No. 106 is the same whether the plan is funded or unfunded.
- Most pre-funding instruments for private sector employers are not very tax effective. Tax issues are not an issue for public sector employers who are not subject to federal income tax.

The choice of discount rate is usually left to the plan sponsor. For public retirement systems, the final decision is typically made by the retirement board with input from the actuary. As with the flexibility in choosing the actuarial cost method, this practice in adopting a discount rate causes issues in having comparability of results among different retirement systems. Two systems with very similar asset allocation and investment polices may choose different discount rates for reasons that may be unique to the system or board. Also, there has been a tendency not to update the discount rate due to the effect such a change would have on the reported amount of unfunded Actuarial Accrued Liability. In some instances, systems have changed to more aggressive investment polices in order to justify the current discount rate, which means that the assumptions drive the asset allocation policy instead of the other way around.

Comments regarding measurement differences

GASB's approach to the discount rate for public plans has been criticized on two fronts. First, the flexibility in selecting the discount rate based on expected investment returns results in a wide range of such discount rates, making it difficult to compare funding levels across various public organizations. Second, there is a growing movement advocating that any determination of retiree liabilities should be market-related, perhaps following FAS No. 87 and FAS No. 106. This position was taken by Ennis (2007) who stated that allowing a plan sponsor to contribute less because the fund has increased its risk causes public pension plans to appear cheaper than would be dictated by proper economics. The author argues for using a settlement rate similar to that used by private sector organizations that disclose under FAS Nos. 87 and 106.

In addition, some members of the actuarial profession have advocated that public-sector organizations should disclose retiree liabilities using a market value approach independent of expected returns on plan assets (Ruloff 2007; Gold and Latter 2009). The argument is that the market value of liabilities is the only way to capture the intrinsic value of promised benefits, so that reporting under any other methodology would mislead as to benefits promised.

In 2006, GASB issued a white paper entitled *Why Governmental Accounting and Financial Reporting Is—And Should Be—Different* (GASB 2006). Here the organization stated that governments are accountable for resource use in ways that differ from business enterprises. This is due in part to business revenues being a 'voluntary exchange between any willing buyer and seller' whereas the revenue for government entities results from an 'involuntary payment of taxes.' Therefore, the article contends, governmental accounting should address the need for 'public accountability information by helping stakeholders assess how public resources are acquired and used, whether current resources were sufficient to meet current service costs or whether some costs were shifted to future taxpayers and whether the government's ability to provide services deteriorated from the previous year' (GASB 2006: 1–2).

With respect to pension and other post-employment liabilities, GASB (2006:13) argued that the accounting approach adopted for GASB Nos. 27 and 45 'explicitly harmonizes accounting with the actuarial funding characteristics of public pension plans' (apparently meaning compliance with the ASOPs described earlier in this chapter) and that the approach 'was based on research studies conducted with financial statement users at the time the pension standards were being developed.' Also, GASB noted that the approach makes it possible to charge 'each period a level percentage of normal costs' which in turn 'equitably spreads the burden of an ongoing benefit program among different generations of taxpayers.'

At present, there remain substantial differences in how retiree liabilities are reported for public and private organizations. In practice, the wide range of acceptable practices and assumptions leads to problems of comparability from one public organization to another.

Magnitude of public sector liabilities

A number of recent studies have sought to document the value of pension and retiree health care liabilities in the public sector. In 2007, the Pew Center on the States issued a report covering public sector retirement benefits promised by state governments (Pew 2007). This report estimated total state pension liabilities of $2.35 trillion, of which $1.99 trillion was funded, leaving a total unfunded liability of $361 billion. For OPEB, the total liability was estimated at $381 billion, of which $11 billion was funded, leaving an unfunded liability of $370 billion. Therefore, the states' unfunded liability for both pensions and OPEB was estimated as $731 billion.

This liability excludes promises made by local governmental entities and most public school teachers. Local governmental liabilities are somewhat difficult to estimate since there is no central filing and compilation of financial disclosures. Spiotto (2006) estimated that pension liabilities of state and local governments could approach $700 billion to $1 trillion over the next 10 years. Obviously this figure is a very rough estimate, and it probably places the states' share of the total unfunded liability at between one-third to one-half of the total for all state and local governmental organizations.

The OPEB liability has not yet been disclosed in annual financial statements of most government units, and the first such disclosures occurred in 2008. One estimate quoted in *The New York Times* valued the total OPEB liability at $1 trillion (Freudenheim and Walsh 2005) This estimate will likely turn out to be on the low side. More recently, Credit Suisse issued a report entitled *You Dropped a Bomb on Me, GASB*. In this report, OPEB liabilities for all US state and local governments were estimated at $1.5 trillion (Zion and Varshney 2007). These figures are based upon the current requirements reported under GASB Nos. 27 and 45. Accordingly, the lack of uniformity in how individual liabilities are derived is substantial.

Further, while most governmental plans use either Entry Age Normal or Projected Unit Credit, there are many systems that use a method that does not re-determine actuarial accrued liability at each valuation date. For some of these, it may have been years since a determination has been made. It also is not yet known which methods will be used for disclosure of OPEB liabilities, although it is presumed that the great majority of the calculations will use either Entry Age Normal or Projected Unit Credit. Another consideration is that the discount rate is based upon a reasonable range for the projected rate of investment return. Thus plans with similar asset allocation and investment policies may have selected substantially different investment return assumptions. For many public sector retirement systems the choice of discount rate is made by the system board of trustees, so the actuary is required merely to state that the rate is reasonable, rather than representing his best estimate. Even a difference of 0.5 percent in the discount rate can lead to large differences in the Actuarial Accrued Liability. Finally, for OPEB, it is not known how many of the plans will fully fund benefits through trust funds. The number could substantially change the overall actuarial liability since selection of discount rate depends on the funding approach. Adding the liabilities for funded pension plans to unfunded OPEB plans means adding liabilities determined with an average discount rate of 8 percent to liabilities determined using discount rates in the 4 percent to 5 percent range, creating an 'apples and oranges' situation.

Potential changes for public sector measurements

If the public sector were to adopt a market-value approach to measuring retiree liabilities similar to the private sector, liabilities would surely change substantially (see Gold and Latter [2009]). Pension liabilities would certainly increase, but OPEB liabilities might decrease. The overall financial effect is difficult to measure, but for pension benefits, the reported unfunded liabilities for some organizations could potentially double or triple. GASB apparently has believed up to this point in time that the current methodology provides the most relevant information to users of public sector financial statements. But efforts can be made to make the current disclosures more meaningful, particularly by making changes in the selection of actuarial cost method and selection of the investment return assumption.

For actuarial cost methods, the choices could be limited to those methods that directly determine an actuarial accrued liability at each valuation date. This would restrict choice of actuarial cost method to Entry Age Normal, Projected Unit Credit, or Traditional Unit Credit. Some of the unfunded liabilities currently being reported under spread gain methods may be misleading users as to the actual funded status of the plans.

The choice of the investment return assumption is too important to be manipulated in order to obtain a desired result. For private sector calculations under the Employee Retirement Income Security Act (ERISA) prior to 2008, the choice of the investment return assumption (as well as other actuarial assumptions) had to be certified annually by the plan's actuary as being his or her best estimate. (Note that starting in 2008, funding rules under ERISA have been changed to calculate liabilities in a manner similar to the FASB market value approach.) It is logical that calculations for financial disclosure of public sector retirement benefits should likewise be based upon the actuary's best estimate. In many instances the assumptions adopted by a retirement system board will be identical to the actuary's best estimate, but in those instances where the actuary's recommendation is not adopted by the board, the public and users of financial statement information should understand the effects of such a decision. This requirement would also place more discipline on retirement system boards if they elect to disregard the actuary's recommendation.

Conclusion

The magnitude of unfunded liabilities by state and local governments in the United States has great importance to taxpayers, bond holders, and public employees. Consequently, the measurements of these liabilities should be performed in a manner which provides the most useful information possible to these groups. Determining the parameters for these measurements will present challenges in the years ahead to those who create the standards.

References

Actuarial Standards Board (ASB) (2001). *Measuring Retiree Group Obligations*— Revised Edition, No. 6. Actuarial Standard of Practice. Washington, DC: Actuarial Standards Board.

—— (2005*a*). *Selection of Economic Assumptions for Measuring Pension Obligations*— Exposure Draft, No. 27, Sections 3.4 and 3.6.3. Actuarial Standard of Practice. Washington, DC: Actuarial Standards Board.

—— (2005*b*). *Selection of Demographic and Other Noneconomic Assumptions for Measuring Pension Obligations*—Exposure Draft No. 35. Actuarial Standard of Practice. Washington, DC: Actuarial Standards Board.

—— (2007). *Measuring Pension Obligations and Determining Pension Plan Costs or Contributions*—No. 4. Actuarial Standard of Practice. Washington, DC: Actuarial Standards Board.

Ennis, Richard (2007). '*Moral Hazard in Public Pensions.*' Working Paper. Chicago, IL: Ennis, Knupp, and Associates.

Financial Accounting Standards Board (FASB) (1985). *Employers' Accounting for Pensions*, No. 87. Statement of Financial Accounting Standards. Norwalk, CT: Financial Accounting Standards Board of the Financial Accounting Foundation.

—— (2004). *Employers' Accounting for Postretirement Benefits Other Than Pensions*, No. 106. Statement of Financial Accounting Standards. Norwalk, CT: Financial Accounting Standards Board of the Financial Accounting Foundation.

—— (2006). *Employers' Accounting for Defined Benefit Pension and Other Postretirement Plans—An Amendment of FASB Statements No. 87, 88, 106, and 132(R)*, No. 158. Statement of Financial Accounting Standards. Norwalk, CT: Financial Accounting Standards Board of the Financial Accounting Foundation.

Freudenheim, Milt and Mary Williams Walsh (2005). 'The Next Retirement Time Bomb,' *The New York Times*, December 11.

Gold, Jeremy and Gordon Latter (2009). 'The Case for Marking Public Plan Liabilities to Market,' in O.S. Mitchell and G. Anderson, eds., *The Future of Public Employee Retirement Systems*. Oxford: Oxford University Press.

Governmental Accounting Standards Board (GASB) (1994). *Accounting for Pensions by State and Local Governmental Employers*, Statement No. 27, paragraph 10c Norwalk, CT: Governmental Accounting Standards Board.

—— (2004). *Accounting and Financial Reporting by Employers for Postemployment Benefits Other Than Pensions*, Statement No. 45, paragraph 13.c. Norwalk, CT: Governmental Accounting Standards Board.

—— (2006). *Why Governmental Accounting and Financial Reporting Is—And Should Be—Different*, White Paper. Norwalk, CT: Governmental Accounting Standards Board, pp. 1–2, 13.

Pew Center on the States (2007). *Promises with a Price*. Philadelphia, PA: The Pew Charitable Trusts, p. 4.

Ruloff, Mark (2007). *Financial Economics and Public Funds*. Washington, DC: Society of Actuaries Annual Meeting, October 17.

Spiotto, James E. (2006). 'If the Pension Bomb Stops Ticking, What Happens Next?' Presentation at *A Forum on Public Pension Funding*, Chicago, IL, February 28.

Zion, David and Amit Varshney (2007). '*You Dropped a Bomb on Me, GASB.*' Americas/United States, Equity Research, Accounting & Tax. March 22. New York, NY: Credit Suisse Securities (USA) LLC.

Chapter 3

The Case for Marking Public Plan Liabilities to Market

Jeremy Gold and Gordon Latter

Career employees of US state and local governments such as teachers, civil servants, police, firefighters, and sanitation workers are usually covered by defined benefit (DB) public pension plans. The financial positions of such pensions are typically reported in documents called Comprehensive Annual Financial Reports (CAFRs). Public pension plan CAFRs usually include extensive data about plan assets, cash flows, expenses, investment policy, and performance. This information is helpful to watchdogs and other parties interested in monitoring the financial integrity of pools of assets that can run into hundreds of billions of dollars.

Information about public plan liabilities, however, is far more difficult to obtain. A typical CAFR will disclose the actuarial methods and assumptions used in the liability calculations, including plan provisions, data on participant ages, projections on salaries and service, and actuarial methods. The measure of the actuarial liabilities is highly dependent upon the methods and assumptions chosen by the plan actuary, or contained in local statutes and regulations. Actuarial assumptions are typically consistent with Actuarial Standards of Practice (ASOPs), especially ASOP No. 4 and ASOP No. 27 (for economic assumptions), and ASOP No. 35 (for demographic assumptions). The economic assumptions (expected returns on invested assets, future inflation, and salary increases) are designed to facilitate a long-range budgeting process and are not intended to reflect current market conditions. The actuarial liabilities developed in accordance with these long range projections are not well-linked to economic values and leave several important pension financial questions unanswered.

This chapter focuses on three such questions of particular importance to public pension plan valuation:

1) Will future taxpayers be paying for services provided to current and previous generations of taxpayers, or might the opposite be true?
2) How can we compare the funding level and benefit security of one public pension plan with plans in other US jurisdictions?

3) What is the market value of benefits earned by public employees in any given year, and what does this tell us about their total compensation?

As a preview of our arguments below, we propose that a useful approach can be modeled after the CAFR for the New York City Employees' Retirement System (NYCERS) for the 2007 fiscal year (New York City Employees' Retirement System & New York City Public Employee's Group Life Insurance Plan 2007: 149). Developed by Robert C. North, Jr., Chief Actuary of the New York City Office of the Actuary, the report includes supplementary information not generally available. For instance, the analysis provides several measures of plan assets and liabilities. For reasons discussed below, we identify the Market Value of the Accumulated Benefit Obligation (MVABO) shown in the rightmost column as the Market Value of Liabilities (MVL) for the plan. The same report shows several measures of the plan's funded ratio, defined as assets divided by liabilities. We suggest that the 'North Ratio' or the market value of assets (MVA) divided by the MVABO, is the most useful measure of the plan's financial status. This ratio helps us to answer the three questions shown above.

The remainder of the chapter discusses the importance and relevance of the Market Value of Liabilities. Next we examine the ordinary disclosures of several public pension plans and make rough estimates of their MVLs. We then consider the implications of MVL disclosure and conclude with some thoughts for policymakers.

Market value of pension liabilities

In 2006, the Society of Actuaries and the American Academy of Actuaries identified three defined benefit pension liability measures (Enderle et al. 2006):

1. Market liability is determined by reference to a portfolio of traded securities that matches the benefit stream in amount, timing, and probability of payment.
2. Solvency liability is determined by reference to a portfolio of default-free securities that matches the benefit stream in amount and timing.
3. Budget liability is the traditional actuarial accrued liability used to develop a schedule of contributions to be made to the plan over time.

The budget liability depends on choices made by the plan with respect to the actuarial funding method to be used and upon assumptions made in accordance with ASOP. Budget liabilities are not marked to market and do not address our three pension finance questions.

Focusing on the other two measures, the market liability equals the solvency liability if payment is certain. In many jurisdictions, pension payments are highly protected by the taxing power of the government sponsor and collateralized by the plan assets. Although the main purpose of pension funding in the private sector is to provide collateral, Peskin (2001) observes that the primary rationale for public sector funding is to assure intergenerational equity—that is, that each generation of taxpayers pays for the public services it consumes contemporaneously. In practice, while there are jurisdictions in which benefits may not be perfectly secure, in what follows we deem the MVL to be well-measured assuming that the probability of payment is nearly certain. Robert North's use of Treasury securities to measure New York City's public pension MVL is consistent with this approach.[1]

The Employment Relationship and the Role of the Pension Plan. Economists distinguish principals from agents. Principals are those with 'skin in the game'; it is their pocketbooks that will be more or less full as a result of the economic activity in question. Agents are those whose decisions affect the welfare of the principals. In the public plan arena, the principals include taxpayers, plan participants (employees, retirees, and beneficiaries), and lenders. Many agents are involved, including elected officials, plan trustees, plan administrators and their staffs, investment officers, asset managers, rating agencies, consultants, and actuaries.

Governments hire employees to provide services to taxpayers and other residents. These employees are compensated by taxpayers in (at least) two ways: current cash compensation (salaries), and promises of future cash (pensions). To avoid either burdening or subsidizing future taxpayers, current taxpayers should generally expect to finance the cost of today's services today, even if a deferred component of public employee total compensation may not be paid out for decades.

A public pension plan is like a reservoir: it allows taxpayers to pay today for benefits that will support retirees tomorrow. Unlike water held in reserve, however, pension assets may be expected to earn investment returns over time. Because of these returns and the risks associated with them, a generationally neutral taxpayer/employee compensation system requires sophisticated financial analysis. How much is tomorrow's promise worth today? Who bears what risks along the way? The balance of this section answers these questions using the tools of financial economics.

Financial Economics and Traditional Actuarial Pension Practice. Financial economists and actuaries use quantitative methods to estimate the value today of money to be paid in the future. Although the root process, discounted cash flow, is common to both disciplines, the analysis of risk and who bears it can be quite different. The differences between actuarial and financial techniques have been discussed in the actuarial literature at least since Bühlmann (1987).[2]

The actuarial process is designed to develop a budget for the inflow of cash into the pension plan such that money will be available to meet benefit promises as they come due. The process depends on regular budget updates which smoothly adjust incoming cash flows to take account of emerging demographic and financial experience. By contrast, financial economists emphasize market values and are interested in measuring the pension contracts that link employees and taxpayers over time. The three questions we pose typify the concerns of financial economists.

Value When Employment Ends. Employees acquire pension wealth in accordance with the formulas embedded in their DB pension plans. When employment ends, the vested plan participant owns an annuity whose value reflects the probability that the recipient will be alive at each payment date, including ancillary benefits that may entitle his beneficiary to receive payments after the former employee's death. In the public sector, in contrast to the private, it is common for future benefits to include post-employment cost-of-living increases.

In practice, survival probabilities may be difficult to estimate and the annuity might be hard to value for any given individual, but the law of large numbers allows accurate estimates to be made for annuitant cohorts. The asset pricing models favored by financial economists (e.g., the Capital Asset Pricing Model) imply that the expected cohort cash flows may be valued using rates of return on fixed income securities (the yield curve). Assuming that pension default is unlikely, we can determine the value of benefits that are not inflation protected using the Treasury yield curve, and the value of inflation-indexed benefits using the Treasury Inflation-Protected Securities (TIPS) curve. Practical concerns may refine these measures when default is possible or when, as is frequently the case, inflation protection is limited.

Nominal market rates are currently almost certainly no greater than 5 percent annually and real rates are below 2 percent. This is importantly different from nominal rates used by public pension plan actuaries which are, and have been for many years, in the neighborhood of 8 percent.

Value During the Employment Career. The pension wealth of an employee still working clearly cannot be lower than the value of the benefit promise assuming that the employee quits today. This 'walk-away' or exit value is identified as the Vested Benefit Obligation (VBO) by private-sector actuaries and accountants. A somewhat larger number is the Accumulated Benefit Obligation (ABO) which augments the VBO by taking into account the probability that an employee will become eligible for early retirement subsidies or other ancillary rights that will increase the value of the benefits already earned. Neither the VBO nor the ABO attaches any value to benefits based on future service and future pay increases. A measure that does take into account future salary (but not future service) is called the Projected Benefit Obligation (PBO). All three measures take into account plan-specified post-retirement cost-of-living increases when these are con-tractually 'owned' by the employee.

Consider a public sector employee who is eligible to retire immediately. He/she is advised that if he/she retires today, he/she will receive an annuity of $20,000 annually for life based on his/her current service and work history. If he/she works another year, the benefit will be recomputed as, say $22,000, giving him/her credit for an additional year of service and for his/her then-higher salary. Note that he/she has no economic interest in the benefit that might be calculated based upon today's service and tomorrow's salary. That benefit would reflect a PBO value for pension wealth today. The employee compares, instead, his/her accrued benefit today (a $20,000 annuity beginning now) versus his/her accrued benefit next year (a $22,000 annuity beginning then).

Because the ABO and the VBO are often close in value, we do not declare one the preferred measure of pension wealth. We do, however, reject the PBO as a pension wealth measure (Gold 2005).

What is the Value of the Benefit Earned Each Year? The present value of accrued benefits at market rates may be followed from time $t-1$ to time t, assuming that new benefits (ΔAB_t, with market value $MV\Delta AB_t$) are earned at year end and benefits (P_t) are paid during the year:

$$MVL_{t-1}(1+\tilde{r}) + MV\Delta AB_t - P_t(1+\tilde{r}/2) = MVL_t$$

where $\tilde{r}$ is the total liability rate of return.[3] The $MV\Delta AB_t$ may be computed by the plan's actuary who identifies the changes from $t-1$ to t in the accrued benefits of active employees and discounts the associated cash flows, applying the same yield curve used to develop MVL_t from AB_t. When an actuary reports the MVL, we can estimate the $MV\Delta AB_t$ as follows:[4]

$$MV\Delta AB_t = MVL_t - MVL_{t-1}(1+\tilde{r}) + P_t(1+\tilde{r}/2)$$

The $MV\Delta AB_t$ is an important economic datum, whether computed for the retirement system or for individual employees. It is the pension wealth newly acquired by today's employees and it is properly viewed as the cost incurred by today's taxpayers.[5]

What is the Value of the Pension Promise to Taxpayers? Because the plan owes what the participant holds as pension wealth, we can tentatively conclude that the MVL is equal to the MVABO.[6] But this measure has not been widely accepted, with many actuaries arguing that the Actuarial Accrued Liability (AAL, measured using expected rates of return on plan assets) computed as part of the plan's budgeting process is the best measure of plan liabilities. The Governmental Accounting Standards Board (GASB 1994*a*, 1994*b*) which governs reporting in this area agrees. In the private sector, the Financial Accounting Standards Board (FASB 1985) tells businesses to report the PBO as a balance sheet liability.

We defend the MVABO as the most economically relevant measure of taxpayer obligations and compare it to the MVA to assess the financial state of public DB plans. Let us consider arguments that the MVABO is too high or too low a number. Some say MVABO is too high because it uses a nearly risk-free discount rate, while the plan invests in risky assets expected to exceed the risk-free rate over time. Those who make this argument often accompany it with the assertion that the plan will be around for a long time and is virtually certain to meet all of its obligations when due (Almeida, Kenneally, and Madland 2009). In effect, this argument says that riskless benefit promises funded by risky assets can be measured at the expected rate of return on those risky assets. This arbitrage-defying argument implicitly says that $100 worth of risky assets is more valuable today than $100 worth of risk-free assets (Bader and Gold 2005). It fails to account for the risk borne by future taxpayers who must make good on the benefit promises even if the risky assets fail to perform (Gold 2003).

The MVL cannot be less than the MVABO, since public pensions are subject to the ordinary rules of the financial markets and cannot magically promise benefits below the value that the capital markets assign to similar, default-free securities. Some contend that the MVABO is too low because it fails to recognize future pay increases, strong (often state constitutionally guaranteed) prohibitions of benefit reductions including benefits not yet earned, and valuable options held by employees. As it is typically calculated, the MVABO may underestimate the value of some options, but it also values some options that are not yet vested such as the right to retire early and receive a particularly valuable early retirement benefit. While these issues can cut both ways, in concept the MVABO should include and properly measure all options. With the caveat that the MVABO is imperfect, we accept it as the best practical measure of the MVL for public pension plans.

In the private sector, arguments are often made against recognizing future pay increases in today's benefit liabilities (Bodie 1990; Gold 2005; Sohn 2006). The proposition is that benefits based on future pay increases are not included, just as future pay increases are not. There is no current obligation to pay more in the future than the economic value that the employee will render in the future. In the public sector, this argument can be challenged because benefits and pay are negotiated between agents of the employees (union representatives) and of the taxpayers (elected officials). In the private sector, a company that overpays its workers will not be able to compete for customers and capital. Forces that might make this true in the public sector (where taxpayers consume services and provide capital) are not obvious and may not exist.

Disclosure of the market value of benefit promises and the incremental value associated with each year of employment (the MVΔAB) is a necessary component in the development of negotiating discipline.

Summary: How Market Values Help Policymakers. To sum up, we have argued future taxpayers will have to pay for future benefit promises as these are earned, plus the MVL, less the MVA (i.e., Question 1 from above). If the MVs are equal (i.e., the North Ratio is 100%), future taxpayers will pay for future benefit accruals as these are earned; none of the services they consume will be subsidized by earlier taxpayers nor will they be called upon to pay for benefits already earned. Equality of MVL and MVA defines a system that is fair to future taxpayers. If the plan is in deficit (MVA less than MVL, North Ratio below 100%), taxpayers to date have underpaid; if the plan is in surplus, the opposite is true.

We also have addressed how public plan funding levels and benefit security can be compared across jurisdictions (i.e., Question 2 from above). Specifically, a comparison of North Ratios will indicate which jurisdiction has been better funded by current and prior taxpayers. A system with a higher North Ratio has paid for more of its earned benefits than a system with a lower ratio. Any system with a North Ratio greater than 100 percent may be said to be protecting its participants and treating its future taxpayers well. Although it is unlikely that taxpayers will choose their residences on the basis of public plan financial status, areas with very low funding ratios are likely to face higher taxes in the future. Information about future taxes may affect home prices today.

And finally, the MVΔAB$_t$ is the market value of benefits being earned by public employees in year t (i.e., Question 3 from above). In recent years, the combination of an aging workforce and low market discount rates (and still high actuarial rates) implies that the MVΔAB$_t$ is generally much higher than the actuarially required contribution reported in actuarial reports and CAFRs.

Estimating the market value of liabilities for public pension plans

Despite the importance and usefulness of the MVL and MVΔAB measures, these values are rarely calculated and almost never disclosed by public plans in the United States. Decisionmakers with responsibility for plan activities, including plan trustees, administrators, and elected officials, do not usually ask their actuaries to calculate market values, and financial analysts working for rating agencies and bond investors do not have the necessary tools and information to make independent assessments even if they were inclined to do so. Part of the problem is that precise measurement of the MVL and the MVΔAB can only be done by actuaries working with reliable plan data, appropriate computer software, and detailed descriptions of the benefits being earned.

In this section, we seek to estimate the MVLs for four arbitrarily selected public pensions located in the Southeast (SE), Northwest (NW), Northeast (NE) and Midwest (MW), using publicly-available information contained in the CAFRs. Table 3-1 summarizes the relevant data extracted from the four CAFRs.

We rely on the MVL information provided in the NYCERS CAFR to derive a crude estimate of the value of benefits newly earned by its members, namely, the MVΔAB. CAFRs commonly disclose the AAL. We make two adjustments to convert the reported AAL into an estimated MVL. The first adjustment from AAL to ABO (based on actuarial assumptions) requires a change in accrual pattern. The second adjustment converts the ABO to MVL; this requires a change to market observed discount and inflation rates.

The first adjustment requires converting the AAL to an ABO. Because the ABO and AAL are identical for former employees, we need to adjust the accrual pattern for active employees only. The majority of public pension plans calculate the active AAL using the Entry Age Normal (EAN) actuarial method.[7] The EAN AAL equals the present value of future benefits (PVFB) less the present value of future employer normal costs (PVFNC) less the future employee contributions (PVFEC):[8] AAL = PVFB − PVFNC where present value is computed using the actuarial discount rate (expected rate of return on plan assets).

Consider a 50-year-old employee who has worked for 20 years and is expected to work an additional 10 years. Assuming a simple plan design where the annual accrual is $1,000 (payable at retirement), this employee would have accrued an annual benefit of $20,000 payable at age 60; the projected annual pension at retirement will be $30,000. Typical actuarial assumptions would value this annuity at $300,000[9] at age 60. Discounting this figure at 8 percent for 10 years, and assuming no pre-retirement decrements (mortality, early retirement, etc), the PVFB is $138,958.

Under the EAN method, normal cost is the level annual contribution at entry (e.g., age 30) that will accumulate to the present value of $300,000 at retirement. Level annual contributions of $2,648 accumulate with 8 percent interest to $300,000 over 30 years. The present value of future normal costs from now (age 50) until retirement (age 60) is $17,770.[10] Plugging these figures into the above formula yields: AAL = $138,958 − $17,770 = $121,188. Our 50-year old has accrued an annual benefit of $20,000

TABLE 3-1 Summary of data from four public pension plans' Comprehensive Annual Financial Reports (CAFRs: $mm for aggregate financial values)

Location of plan[a]	SE	NW	NE	MW
Actuarial accrued liability (AAL)				
Active member contributions	$58	$1,104	$1,794	$2,616
Retirees and beneficiaries	55,534	8,667	5,676	12,217
Active (employer portion)	55,386	3,073	4,160	5,492
Total AAL	$110,978	$12,844	$11,630	$20,325
Actuarial asset value (AAV)	$117,160	$8,443	$8,888	$14,858
Funded ratio (AAV/AAL)	106%	66%	76%	73%
Market value of assets (MVA)	$116,340	$8,591	$9,972	$13,784
Active demographic data				
Annual payroll	$25,148	$1,513	$1,821	$2,859
Number of actives (000)	665	34	52	74
Average annual salary (000)	$38	$45	$35	$39
Average age	44	45	n/a	n/a
Average service	10	9	n/a	n/a
Key plan provisions				
Retirement age[b]	59	60	60	60
Post-retirement COLA[c]	3.00%	CPI	CPI	1.5%
Key assumptions:				
Investment return	7.75%	8.25%	7.50%	7.50%
Salary increase[d]	5.50%	4.50%	5.50%	4.50%
Inflation assumption	n/a	3.50%	4.00%	4.00%

[a] Locations refer to Southeast (SE), Northwest (NW), Northeast (NE) and Midwest (MW). Some retirement systems comprise several plans, making data collection and judgment difficult.

[b] The approximate age at which the full accrued benefit is payable as a life annuity has a large impact on the factors used to convert the EAN AAL to an estimated ABO. The retirement age drives the 'years to retirement' employed in Adjustment 1. The retirement age differs markedly between different types of employees (e.g., uniformed, clerical, teachers, administrators, etc.).

[c] Cost of living adjustments after retirement. The consumer price index (CPI) may be used as an automatic annual benefit increase factor. In the southeast, the plan specifies an annual 3 percent increase independent of the CPI; in the mid west, the benefit is increased by the lesser of 1.5 percent or the CPI; for all practical purposes this may be treated as a straight 1.5 percent annual increase.

[d] Our conversion factors are highly dependent on the assumed rate of salary increase. Most plans assume greater salary increases at younger ages (when employee growth contributes to individual productivity) and report a single compound growth rate which, over an entire career, produces the same expected final salary. But our conversion looks at mid to late career active employees whose future expected increases are smaller. In the southeast, for example, we reduced the compound 6.25 percent to 5.5 percent based on additional information contained in the CAFR.

Source: Authors' computations, see text.

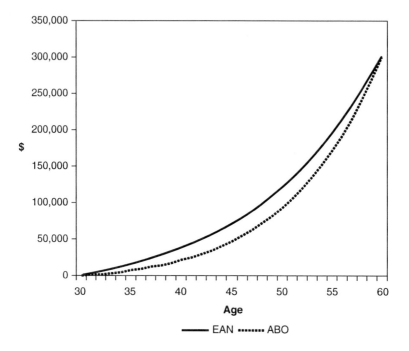

Figure 3-1 Comparison of Entry Age Normal (EAN) liabilities to Accrued Benefit Obligation (ABO) liabilities. Assumed salary scale: 0 percent. *Note:* Formula: 1 percent * final salary * years of service. *Source:* Authors' computations; see text.

payable at age 60. Multiplying by our age 60 annuity factor and discounting for 10 years at 8 percent, we calculate the actuarially valued ABO as $92,639.

Figure 3-1 displays the EAN AAL and the ABO year by year from entry age 30 until retirement at age 60. For our 50-year-old with 10 years left to retirement, the ABO is estimated to be 76 percent (92,639/121,188) of the EAN AAL. Table 3-2 provides sample conversion factors at various ages for our (flat dollar) plan.[11]

Most public plans, however, compute pensions as a percentage of final average pay. For such plans, the entry age normal cost is expressed as a percentage of each year's pay. Table 3-3 calculates sample conversion factors where the actuary has assumed a 5 percent salary increase at every age.[12] For our 50-year-old, with 10 years left to retirement, the ABO is estimated to be 54 percent (56,872/104,917) of the EAN AAL. We see (Table 3-4) that conversion factors decrease as the salary assumption increases. Figure 3-2 displays the EAN AAL and the ABO year by year from entry age 30 until retirement at age 60 with an assumed 5 percent salary increase.

TABLE 3-2 Factors used to convert Entry Age Normal (EAN) Accrued Actuarial Liabilities (AAL) to Accumulated Benefit Obligation (ABO). Assumed salary scale: 0 percent

Age	PVFB	Salary	Normal Cost	PVFNC	EAN Accrued Actuarial Liability	Accrued Benefit Payable at age 60	ABO	Conversion Factor (%)
30	29.813	100.000	2.648	29.813	0	0	0	
35	43.805	100.000	2.648	28.269	15.536	5.000	7.301	47
40	64.364	100.000	2.648	26.001	38.364	10.000	21.455	56
41	69.514	100.000	2.648	25.433	44.081	11.000	25.488	58
42	75.075	100.000	2.648	24.819	50.256	12.000	30.030	60
43	81.081	100.000	2.648	24.156	56.924	13.000	35.135	62
44	87.567	100.000	2.648	23.440	64.127	14.000	40.865	64
45	94.573	100.000	2.648	22.667	71.905	15.000	47.286	66
46	102.138	100.000	2.648	21.833	80.306	16.000	54.474	68
47	110.309	100.000	2.648	20.931	89.378	17.000	62.509	70
48	119.134	100.000	2.648	19.957	99.177	18.000	71.480	72
49	128.665	100.000	2.648	18.906	109.759	19.000	81.488	74
50	138.958	100.000	2.648	17.770	121.188	20.000	92.639	76
51	150.075	100.000	2.648	16.543	133.531	21.000	105.052	79
52	162.081	100.000	2.648	15.218	146.862	22.000	118.859	81
53	175.047	100.000	2.648	13.788	161.259	23.000	134.203	83
54	189.051	100.000	2.648	12.242	176.808	24.000	151.241	86
55	204.175	100.000	2.648	10.574	193.601	25.000	170.146	88
56	220.509	100.000	2.648	8.771	211.738	26.000	191.108	90
57	238.150	100.000	2.648	6.825	231.325	27.000	214.335	93
58	257.202	100.000	2.648	4.722	252.479	28.000	240.055	95
59	277.778	100.000	2.648	2.452	275.326	29.000	268.519	98
60	300.000	100.000	2.648	0	300.000	30.000	300.000	100

Notes: Formula: 1 percent * final salary * years of service. This table develops for one employee, hired at age 30, retired at age 65, benefits begin at age 65, with salary increasing 5 percent annually throughout his career, the entry age normal liability accrual (EAN AAL) and the ABO. The ratio (conversion factor) may be applied to a published EAN AAL to derive an ABO. To do so, however, for all the active employees in a plan, one must judge how the range (30 to 60) should be modified and which row (age) is representative of the active employee population. If, for example, the full range were deemed appropriate and the liability-weighted average employee were deemed to be age 53, the conversion factor would be 65 percent.

Source: Authors' computations, see text.

TABLE 3-3 Factors used to convert Entry Age Normal (EAN) liabilities to Accumulated Benefit Obligation (ABO) liabilities. Assumed salary scale: 5 percent

Age	PVFB	Salary	Normal Cost	PVFNC	EAN Accrued Actuarial Liability	Accrued Benefit Payable at age 60	ABO	Conversion Factor (%)
30	29,813	23,138	1,493	29,813	0	0	0	
35	43,805	29,530	1,906	33,717	10,088	1,477	2,156	21
40	64,364	37,689	2,432	36,666	27,698	3,769	8,086	29
41	69,514	39,573	2,554	37,046	32,468	4,353	10,087	31
42	75,075	41,552	2,681	37,328	37,747	4,986	12,478	33
43	81,081	43,630	2,815	37,499	43,582	5,672	15,329	35
44	87,567	45,811	2,956	37,542	50,025	6,414	18,721	37
45	94,573	48,102	3,104	37,442	57,131	7,215	22,745	40
46	102,138	50,507	3,259	37,178	64,961	8,081	27,513	42
47	110,309	53,032	3,422	36,730	73,580	9,015	33,150	45
48	119,134	55,684	3,593	36,075	83,059	10,023	39,803	48
49	128,665	58,468	3,773	35,188	93,477	11,109	47,644	51
50	138,958	61,391	3,962	34,041	104,917	12,278	56,872	54
51	150,075	64,461	4,160	32,605	117,470	13,537	67,718	58
52	162,081	67,684	4,368	30,845	131,235	14,890	80,449	61
53	175,047	71,068	4,586	28,727	146,320	16,346	95,375	65

54	189,051	74,622	4,815	26,210	162,841	17,909	112,858	69
55	204,175	78,353	5,056	23,250	180,925	19,588	133,314	74
56	220,509	82,270	5,309	19,802	200,707	21,390	157,225	78
57	238,150	86,384	5,574	15,811	222,338	23,324	185,150	83
58	257,202	90,703	5,853	11,223	245,979	25,397	217,737	89
59	277,778	95,238	6,146	5,975	271,803	27,619	255,732	94
60	300,000	100,000	6,453	0	300,000	30,000	300,000	100

Notes: Formula: 1 percent * final salary * years of service.

This table develops for one employee, hired at age 30, retired at age 60, benefits begin at age 65, with salary increasing 5 percent annually throughout his career, the entry age normal liability accrual (EAN AAL) and the ABO. The ratio (conversion factor) may be applied to a published EAN AAL to derive an ABO. To do so, however, for all the active employees in a plan, one must judge how the range (30 to 60) should be modified and which row (age) is representative of the active employee population. If, for example, the full range were deemed appropriate and the liability-weighted average employee were deemed to be age 53, the conversion factor would be 65 percent.

Source: Authors' computations, see text.

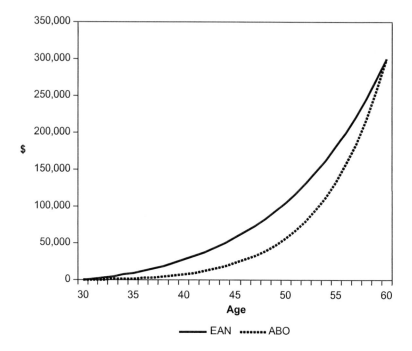

Figure 3-2 Comparison of Entry Age Normal (EAN) liabilities to Accrued Benefit Obligation (ABO) liabilities. Assumed salary scale: 5 percent. *Note*: Formula: 1 percent * final salary * years of service. *Source*: Authors' computations; see text.

Based on the data in Table 3-1 and the factors in Table 3-4, the analyst uses judgment and experience to choose a conversion factor. Although many considerations could influence the choice of a conversion factor, the most important is the number of years left until retirement. We estimate the liability-weighted average number of years to retirement after reviewing each of our four plan provisions, actuarial assumptions, and summary member data disclosed in the respective CAFRs. Applying this approach to our four public plans we develop the relationship of the AAL to the ABO shown in Table 3-5. Although the NE plan's CAFR did not provide an average age (an important element in our estimate of years to retirement), it did disclose an ABO-like value in accordance with FAS No. 35 (FASB 1980). For the other three plans, we assume a 65 percent conversion factor. If the plan provisions and demographics in combination with the actuarial assumptions differ significantly from the four samples provided here, the conversion factor will be different.[13]

The second adjustment converts the ABO to the MVL. Latter (2007) reports that the average actuarial discount rate for the two largest plans

TABLE 3-4 Converting Entry Age Normal (EAN) liabilities to
Accumulated Benefit Obligation (ABO) liabilities:
various salary assumptions

Years to Ret Age		Salary Scale Assumption (%)		
	0	4.50	**5.00**	5.50
25	47	23	**21**	20
20	56	31	**29**	28
15	66	42	**40**	38
10	76	56	**54**	53
5	88	75	**74**	73
0	100	100	**100**	100

Notes: Formula: 1 percent * final salary * years of service. Conversion
factors are shown based on years to retirement and various assumed salary
increases. Factors based on 5 percent (bold) come from Table 3-3.

Source: Authors' computations, see text.

in each of the 50 United States is 8 percent. Figure 3-3 shows that this
assumed return is significantly higher than the Treasury spot curve at
March 31, 2008.

Actuaries who perform valuations for public plans can readily develop
the cash flows that underlie the ABO. Because these underlying cash flows
are not presented in CAFRs, we rely on a hypothetical set of cash flows
that approximate the ABO term structure for large public plans—ignoring
post-retirement increases for cost of living. We adjust these cash flows for
cost-of-living provisions and then value them twice: using the plan actuary's
assumptions, and market assumptions. The ratio of these values for the
hypothetical population is then applied to the ABOs developed in the first
adjustment. For technical reasons, we make these calculations separately
for retired and active populations.

TABLE 3-5 First adjustment: converting the Actuarial Accrued Liability (AAL) to
Accumulated Benefit Obligation (ABO)

Location of plan	SE	NW	NE	MW
1. Active AAL	$55,444	$4,177	$5,954	$8,108
2. Conversion factor	65%	65%	n/a	65%
3. Active ABO [(1)*(2)]	$36,039	$2,715	$3,873	$5,270
4. Retired and beneficiaries	55,534	8,667	5,676	12,217
Total ABO [(3)+(4)]	$91,574	$11,383	$9,549	$17,488

Notes: See Table 3-1. Factor of 65 percent based on Table 3-4 with about seven liability-
weighted years to retirement.

Source: Authors' computations, see text.

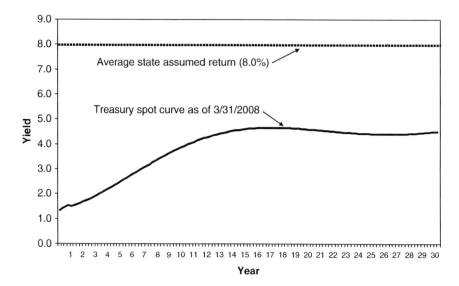

Figure 3-3 Nominal interest rates: actuarial versus market. *Source*: Authors' computations; see text.

The SE plan specifies that benefits will increase 3 percent annually after retirement regardless of the actual inflation rate. The actuarial valuation already embeds these increases and we need only adjust for the difference between the nominal actuarial discount rate (7.75%) and the Treasury spot curve. As shown in Table 3-6, our hypothetical population liabilities increase by factors of 1.3366 (retirees) and 1.9506 (actives). We apply these to the retiree and active ABOs brought forward from Table 3-5 to estimate an MVL of $144,528 million.

The MW plan provides post-retirement benefit increases equal to the lesser of CPI and 1.5 percent. In theory, a capped CPI formula requires an option model. This would be especially true if the cap were, say, 4 percent and would be likely to apply in some years and not in others. As a practical matter, the 1.5 percent cap is likely to apply in every year and thus we proceed as if the MW plan, like the SE plan, specified a fixed benefit increase rate. We use our hypothetical population to derive factors of 1.3142 (retirees) and 1.8613 (actives). Our MVL is estimated to be $25,864 million.

Because many public plans provide a cost-of-living adjustment (COLA), we need to adjust for the difference between actuarial and market real returns. Latter (2007) reports that the average inflation assumption for the two largest plans in each of the 50 United States is 3.5 percent. Figure 3-4 shows that this average assumed real return of 4.35 percent

TABLE 3-6 Second adjustment: converting the Accumulated Benefit Obligation (ABO) to a Market Value Liability (MVL)

Location of plan	SE	NW	NE	MW
Plan economic assumptions				
Nominal discount rate	7.75%	8.25%	7.50%	7.50%
Inflation (COLA)				
assumption	n/a	3.50%	4.00%	n/a
Real discount rate	n/a	4.59%	3.37%	n/a
PV of hypothetical plan Retirees:				
1. Plan nominal discount rate	$72,200	$69,834	$73,435	$73,435
2. Treasury yield curve	96,505	96,505	96,505	96,505
3. Plan real discount rate	#N/A	90,936	100,444	#N/A
4. TIPS yield curve	119,568	119,568	119,568	119,568
5. Adjustment factor				
(2/1 or 4/3)	1.3366	1.3149	1.1904	1.3142
PV of hypothetical plan Actives:				
1. Plan nominal discount rate	$86,008	$78,417	$90,135	$90,135
2. Treasury yield curve	167,770	167,770	167,770	167,770
3. Plan real discount rate	#N/A	127,657	162,672	#N/A
4. TIPS yield curve	266,675	266,675	266,675	266,675
5. Adjustment factor				
(2/1 or 4/3)	1.9506	2.0890	1.6393	1.8613
Conversion of ABO to MVL				
1. Retiree ABO	$55,534	$8,667	$5,676	$12,217
2. Adjustment factor	1.3366	1.3149	1.1904	1.3142
3. Retiree MVL [(1)*(2)]	74,229	11,396	6,757	16,055
4. Active ABO	36,039	2,715	3,873	5,270
5. Adjustment factor	1.9506	2.0890	1.6393	1.8613
6. Active MVL [(4)*(5)]	70,299	5,672	6,349	9,809
7. Total MVL [(3)+(6)]	$144,528	$17,067	$13,106	$25,864

Note: See Table 3-1.

Source: Authors' computations, see text.

(1.08/1.035 − 1) is significantly higher than the TIPS spot curve at March 31, 2008. Figure 3-5 compares the Treasury Spot curve (from Figure 3-3) to the TIPS curve (from Figure 3-4) as of March 31, 2008. The inflation curve represents the difference between these two curves.

The NW and NE plans provide for full CPI indexing after retirement. Table 3-6 shows assumed nominal discount rates of 8.25 percent and 7.5 percent and inflation rates of 3.5 percent and 4 percent for these plans. We use our hypothetical populations to estimate the impact of replacing these actuarial assumptions with market rates of discount and inflation. Benefits that will grow at the full CPI may be estimated by discounting non-inflated cash flows using real rates of return. We compute the values of the retiree cash flows by discounting at the actuarially assumed real rates

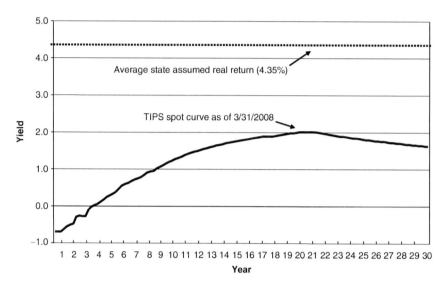

Figure 3-4 Real interest rates: actuarial versus market. *Source*: Authors' computations; see text.

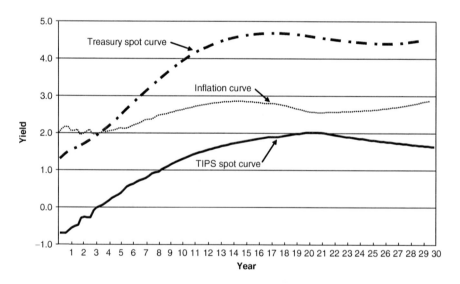

Figure 3-5 Treasury interest rates, real and break-even inflation rates (as of 3/31/2008). *Source*: Authors' computations; see text.

TABLE 3-7 Comparison of funded status: Actuarial vs. Market

Location of plan	SE	NW	NE	MW
Actuarial Accrued Liability (AAL)	110,978	12,844	11,630	20,325
Actuarial Asset Value (AAV)	117,160	8,443	8,888	14,858
Funded status	106%	66%	76%	73%
Market Value of Liability (MVL)	144,528	17,067	13,106	25,864
Market Value of Assets (MVA)	116,340	8,591	9,972	13,784
Funded status	80%	50%	76%	53%

Note: See Table 3-1.

Source: Authors' computations, see text.

(4.59% for the NW and 3.37% for the NE) and then repeat the calculation using the market's real rates found in the TIPs curve. We take the ratio of the market value to the actuarial values (119,568/90,936 = 1.3149 and 119,568/100,444 = 1.1904 respectively) and, in the last panel of Table 3-6, we apply these to the retiree ABOs determined in the first adjustment.

For active lives, the ABO benefits are indexed only after the employee retires. During the period between now and benefit commencement, we need to discount benefits at nominal rates. Real rates are used thereafter. This calculation leads to multipliers for the active members of the NW and NE plans of 2.0890 and 1.6393, respectively. The multipliers are higher for actives than for retirees primarily because the benefits will be paid for longer periods, thereby growing more with inflation. For both actives and retirees, the NW plan multipliers are higher than those for the NE because the NE actuary has been much more conservative (and thus closer to the market).

In the final panel of Table 3-6, we apply all of our respective multipliers to the active and retired lives ABOs determined by the first adjustment producing our final estimate of MVL on line 7. Table 3-7 compares the actuarial funded status to our crude mark to market funded status. In this market environment (Figures 3-3 and 3-4), one would anticipate lower market funded ratios after applying the adjustments. Indeed, in three cases (SE, NW, and MW) the market funded status is lower than the actuarial funded status. The funded status for the NE plan is unchanged since the actuarial economic assumptions are relatively conservative and the MVA is higher than the AAV.

$$MV \Delta AB_t = MVL_t - MVL_{t-1}(1 + \tilde{r}) + P_t(1 + \tilde{r}/2)$$

and applying it to the detailed MVL information provided in the NYCERS CAFR, we can now obtain a rough estimate of the benefits newly earned by its members, or the MVΔAB. At time *t*-1, the market value, duration, and implied market interest rate are $55.4 billion, 12.7 years, and 4.2 percent, respectively. At time t, the market value, duration and implied market interest rate are $49.8 billion, 11.7 years and 5.4 percent, respectively. From the CAFR we see the annual pension payments are $3.0 billion. From this information we estimate a liability return ($\tilde{r}$) of −9.5 percent. Plugging these figures into our formula results in ($bn):

$$MV\Delta AB = 49.8–55.4 * (1 − .095) + 3.0 * (1 − .095/2) = 2.5$$

Discussion

Many in the public plan community argue that differences between the private (corporate) sector and the public sector are sufficient to exempt public plans from the market discipline that constrains corporate plans. This view has been also espoused by the Governmental Accounting Standards Board (GASB 2006) which contrasts the valuation (and investor) focus of private sector accounting with the accountability (for the use of resources) focus applicable to public financial reporting. This and other distinctions justify financial reporting in the public sector different from that in private enterprise. When it comes to pensions, GASB (2006: 8) says:

The longer term view of operations of government is consistent with focusing on trends in operations, rather than on short-term fluctuations, such as in fair values of certain assets and liabilities. Immediate recognition of changes in fair values of assets set aside in employee benefit plans is appropriate accountability reporting in the employee benefit plans that hold those assets. However, it is not appropriate for government employers to immediately recognize those fair value changes or changes in accrued actuarial liabilities resulting from a change in benefit plan terms. These short-term fluctuations could produce a measurement of the period's employee benefit costs, which are included in cost of services, that may be less decision-useful for governmental financial report users.

We respect the distinction between valuation and accountability between the private and public sectors, but we disagree with how this difference is applied to public pension plans. The conclusion—that recognition of the value of changes in benefit terms is less decision-useful—is not supported by distinctions between private and public accounting objectives. The decision to modify plan terms cannot be well made in the absence of market values for the very benefit changes being considered. Some in the public plan community use the GASB's lack of recognition requirement to justify non-disclosure of MVL, annual MVΔAB, and MVΔAB attributable to plan amendments. While we agree that governments are not the same as corporations, we nonetheless view a public DB plan as a financial institution. In this sense, it has more in common with insurance companies and private sector pension plans than with either a government or a corporation.

Insurance companies and DB plans make long-term promises in exchange for current cash. The long-term 'reservoir' aspect of these institutions implies that they have high ratios of assets on hand to benefits currently being paid. Many opponents of market disclosure for public plans use the long-term nature of the commitments to justify discounting future promises using the expected return on plan assets. Their long-term nature is also used to justify the amortization of liabilities created instantly (upon plan amendment) over long periods (usually as a constant percentage of payrolls assumed to rise perpetually). We believe that ignorance of the market values of current liabilities and reporting that defers recognition of significant increases in current liabilities attributable to plan amendments is no more justified for a government-sponsored DB plan, than it is for a corporate DB plan, than it is for an insurance company. The different nature of the sponsor does not port down to the plan nor does it reduce the decision-usefulness of market values (Gold 2003).

In recent years, many public plan actuaries have argued that the long-term nature of public pension plans allows risk-sharing across generations with benefits for all. This argument does not survive serious scrutiny. Especially suspect is the argument that returns from risky investing can be front-loaded for the benefit of today's taxpayers and public employees, without injury to future generations of taxpayers. If future taxpayers bear all the risks, why are they not entitled to all the rewards? If the current generation gets rewards without risks, should future taxpayers settle for rewards that are below those available to other market participants exposed to the same risks? Indeed, unfunded benefits conferred on today's employees come at the expense of tomorrow's taxpayers (Bader and Gold 2003).

We note that Cui, de Jong, and Ponds (2007) argue that risk-sharing across generations, although it cannot add value, can enhance generational welfare (utility). That analysis postulates fairly valued trades (intergenerational commitment contracts) between generations implemented by adjustment technologies that can be modeled as the trading of contingent claims across generations. Gains and losses on risky investments incurred by one generation can then be passed on to future generations in accordance with these commitments. History, however, suggests that each current generation tends to be more willing to pass on losses than gains, raising serious governance questions that remain to be addressed.

Actuarial opponents of the application of market economics to public plans argue that the MVL reflects a 'termination' concept, while the ongoing nature of public plans renders the MVL irrelevant. A distinction between corporate and public plans, they say, is that corporate plans terminate so the MVL measures an improbable event in the public sector.

We counter that the MVL measures accrued pension wealth (independent of plan termination), a standard concept in labor economics. Similarly, the MVΔAB measures changes in pension wealth, an important component of total employee compensation.

It is frequently argued that the MVL cannot be measured as well for public plans as for private sector plans, because the employment contracts are different. We acknowledge these contractual differences but note that failing to measure the MVL makes it difficult to make good decisions about public sector employment contracts and total compensation. The lack of information about market values leads to many of the very contract provisions that are then cited as the reason why market value cannot be reliably measured. Unfortunately, societal interests are not well served by such circular reasoning and argument.

Threats to the Existence of Public Pension Plans. Agents in the public pension arena argue that the disclosure of market-based information about plan liabilities might be used by opponents of DB plans to terminate these arrangements. As evidenced by proposals in California[14] and elsewhere, some in the political arena do oppose public DB plans, and they are likely to use information that reveals the financial cost and volatility of riskily invested DB plans in their efforts. Such opponents generally advocate defined contribution (DC) plans because such plans have a more certain, and usually lower, cost than current DB pensions. They also point to the private sector, saying that elements of FAS No. 87 reporting have led the corporate sector astray. Thus, the argument goes, reporting MVL will threaten the existence of public DB plans.

We agree that DC plans are less able than DB plans to provide lifetime income to retired civil service employees. Nonetheless, we argue that DB plans will be strengthened by pertinent market value information. In the financial security arena, market values are key to rational decisionmaking. Particularly under today's economic conditions, traditional actuarial methods and assumptions tend to understate the cost of DB plans. Under all economic conditions they understate the volatility. In the period from 1975–85, however, these same methods and assumptions substantially overstated benefit values and cost. Decisions should not be driven by the position that overstating costs for a decade or more may be balanced by understatement for some other period.

The lesson that should be taken from the MVL and MVΔAB is that it costs more to provide a given level of retirement income in times of low interest rates (real and nominal, as appropriate) than it does in times of high rates. A system supported by honest reporting of market values would recognize that more of today's total compensation needs to be set aside in low interest rate periods. While the converse, that less needs to be set aside when rates are high, may seem to be a welcome message when applicable, the bottom line is that more of today's total compensation needs to be deferred if DB pension promises are to be paid for by those consuming the services today.

Those who favor DC plans seek to set aside smaller amounts in a fashion that is less risky to government employers (and thus future taxpayers), even if those plans eventually prove to be inadequate to protect retirees. It is critical to acknowledge that good pensions are more costly today than they were in the early 1980s. That is, pension funding must rise; risky investments do not produce free lunches (future taxpayers bear the risk); and benefits may have to be less generous than they have been to date. The pressure on DB plans is not a by-product of additional measurement and reporting. No economic sector can escape the hard rules of the capital markets. Trends around the world make this more true today than ever before. Alternatives to wasteful deployment of resources arise everywhere. The public plan sector with an estimated $3 trillion in assets and perhaps as much as $4 trillion in MVL is no exception. The economics that rules the other roughly $120 trillion of capital assets and financial institutions will prevail in the public pension arena.[15] Ignoring the market realities and hoping for the best might, in the short run, prolong the life of plans that may (in today's interest rate environment) be more generous than affordable. But those who wish to perpetuate and enjoy the benefits of DB pension plans should welcome the disclosure of these important numbers as part of a sustainable long term strategy.

Full identification and recognition of MVΔABs (combined with MVAs and MVLs that reveal existing funding shortfalls) might come as a shock to the system if released in today's interest rate environment. The consequences will not occur at one moment in time, however, and some adjustment period will be necessary (perhaps more than a decade). But the first response should be that pressure is increased on state and local governments to get their fiscal houses in order. This additional information should make it easier for elected officials to negotiate future total compensation that is more affordable and sustainable. Employees will be able to compare funding levels and benefit security between their plan and those in other jurisdictions. Employees with better funded plans can anticipate less pressure on their future benefits and wages than employees with poorly funded plans.

Pushback by Privately-Employed Taxpayers. Since 1950, public employment in the United States has grown relative to the private sector, and public sector workers' importance as voters has grown as well. This voting power is used skillfully by those who negotiate wages and benefits on their behalf, and it has become easy and routine for elected officials to grant benefit improvements especially when the costs are systematically understated. As a result, public employees today enjoy generally better pension benefits than their private sector counterparts, and the disparity is increasing even as, in many areas, public employees' wages are catching or have caught up to private wages of those in similar positions (Brainard 2009; Clark, Craig, and Ahmed 2009). Many private-sector employees now have jobs comparable to those held by public employees (e.g., office workers, private carters, private school teachers).

Disclosure of the annual equivalent compensation cost (MVΔAB) will facilitate comparison of total compensation between sectors, and it may exert some countervailing pressure on public officials and strengthen the hand of those who represent taxpayers. Accordingly, the additional information we recommend may lead to better decisionmaking and a new balance of interests between taxpayers and public employees.

Quality of Estimates. The estimation process described above adjusted first, for the pattern of accrual (AAL → ABO), and second, for the difference between actuarial assumptions and market observations of discount and inflation rates (ABO → MVL). Each of these adjustments depends on many moving parts, and the standard CAFR actuarial disclosures are not designed to facilitate such re-estimation. It is possible that our MVL estimates might be off as much as 20 percent, which is not a trivial matter. The most uncertain part of our process is the estimation of the AAL/ABO relationships illustrated in Figures 3-1 and 3-2 and the selection of the number of years to retirement which we use to choose our conversion factor (Table 3-4). We are more confident about the second adjustment where we are less dependent on the behind-the-curtain actuarial machinery. Despite our concerns over the reliability of our estimates, we believe that our analysis is likely to be more accurate than financial analyses that rely on, rather than penetrate, the dynamics of traditional actuarial methods.

Interest Rate Sensitivity. Economists often look at partial derivatives of decision measures to assess the impact of small changes in the inputs used to compute those measures. Actuaries often do a similar analysis that they call sensitivity testing. Interest rates are frequently the subject of such analyses. The funding ratios measured using common actuarial methods and assumptions look very stable. In the extreme case—aggregate funding—the funding ratio is always 100 percent. Funding ratios measured at market can be quite volatile, primarily because of asset/liability mismatches. Despite some caveats about the accuracy of our estimates, we are confident that our measures will be relatively robust. If, for example, TIPS rates change and we estimate retiree liabilities for a fully indexed plan, the re-estimated retiree MVL will be consistent and sensitivity will be reflected properly.

Market Value of Benefits Earned. For the year ended June 30, 2006, employers participating in NYCERS and its employees contributed less than $1.4 billion to that plan. Because the plan's AAL is virtually identical to its AAV, no contributions are made with respect to unfunded past service costs and the entire $1.4 billion represents normal cost. In the same fiscal year, we have estimated the MVΔAB to be $2.5 billion. This is the value of future benefits newly acquired by active employees and it represents the normal cost using the traditional unit credit actuarial cost method combined with market rates of discount. In fiscal 2006, therefore, New York City contributed substantially less to the plan than the new pension wealth acquired by its employees. Accordingly, our approach implies that approximately $1 billion in value received by today's employees will be paid by future taxpayers. As of June 30, 2006, the NYCERS plan MVA and MVL were $37.3 billion and $49.8 billion respectively, representing a market deficit of $12.5 billion. None of this deficit is recognized in cost calculations under the traditional actuarial methods, and all of it, plus interest, will have to be paid for by future taxpayers. Future taxpayers are on the hook for both the existing $12.5 billion shortfall and the newly added $1 billion, and must pay either in cash or by taking uncompensated market risk (Gold 2003).

Conclusion

The market value of DB public pension plan liabilities, in conjunction with the available market value of plan assets, are measures that have the potential to shine light in an arena where employees, taxpayers, and lenders have not had access to the information needed to make independent assessments. To our knowledge, only the New York City plan actuary makes these computations and discloses the results to date. We propose that all public pension actuaries make these additional disclosures using reliable plan data, appropriate computer software, and detailed descriptions of the benefits being earned.

   To illustrate this point, we arbitrarily selected four public plans to make the adjustments necessary to convert the disclosed budget liability or AAL into an estimated MVL. Our adjustments are rough, but they produce a much lower market funded status (versus actuarial) for three plans. Nonetheless, most public sector DB plans today report in accordance with GASB Nos. 25 and 27 (GASB 1994*a*, 1994*b*). A GASB white paper (GASB 2006) discusses the distinction between accounting for private enterprises (where the emphasis is on financial valuation) and accounting for public sector activities (where the emphasis is accountability and the husbandry of scarce resources). Although this distinction is important and appropriate, we believe that the actuarial values disclosed in accordance with GASB Nos. 25 and 27 do not serve accountability as well as they would if they were to include the MVL and the MVΔAB.

Advocates of the status quo argue that the MVL is a concept that appears in private sector accounting (the ABO defined by FAS No. 87) because private plans can terminate, whereas they assert that public plans have an 'infinite horizon.'[16] This misses the more general economic importance of the MVL as a measure of wealth held by employees and owed by taxpayers. It is this property of the MVL that makes it appropriate to all DB plans, to decision making about these plans, and to answering the three questions raised herein. Other status quo advocates contend that market-based calculations inject spurious volatility into funding ratios and plan costs. The volatility, however, is real. The cost of providing benefits when market interest rates are 4 percent is significantly greater than when rates are 12 percent.

This chapter advocates the calculation and disclosure of the market value of liabilities (MVL) and the annual equivalent compensation cost (MVΔAB) for public sector pension plans. Market-based information is critically important input for those who wish to make fiscally responsible decisions.

Notes

[1] Some have suggested that using a relevant swap curve instead of Treasury rates provides a better market measure of the liability. We take an agnostic view with respect to the technical advantages of one or the other measure and accept either as a useful way to estimate MVL.

[2] The theme has been carried forward by D'Arcy (1989) and Hardy (2005) and, into the pension arena, by Exley, Mehta, and Smith (1997), Bader and Gold (2003), and Enderle et al. (2006).

[3] Liability returns are computed analogously to asset returns (Leibowitz 1987) reflecting both the passage of time and changes in the beginning and ending discount rate curves.

[4] This is the Traditional Unit Credit (TUC) Normal Cost computed at market rates.

[5] Actuaries, elected officials, and other agents usually assert that the 'cost' of the plan is equal to the actuarially required contributions. Economists, and the markets they defer to, disagree.

[6] Earlier we used the term ABO to define the recognized accrual pattern (i.e., a liability that does not anticipate future service or pay increases). Henceforth, we use the term ABO to mean the value of such accrued benefits when discounted using the plan's actuarial assumptions. We use MVABO to mean the value discounted using market rates.

[7] Some states and localities (e.g., New York State) use the aggregate actuarial funding method to determine an annual contribution. Under this method the AAL is set equal to the actuarial value of plan assets (leading to the meaningless tautology that the plan is always fully funded). Attempting to estimate an EAN

AAL from the aggregate figures would require more in-depth analysis. Fortunately, GASB (2007) requires disclosure of the EAN AAL for all plans using the aggregate funding method.

[8] Although most public pension plans require employee contributions, we set the PVFEC to zero to simplify the exposition. This affects the sharing of cost between the employer and the employees but does not change the AAL.

[9] Using the RP2000 Combined Healthy Male mortality table and an assumed interest rate of 8 percent the non-indexed single life annuity value at age 60 equals 9.9238. We round to 10.0 to simplify the exercise: $300,000 = $30,000*10.0.

[10] This equals $2,648 * 10-year annuity at 8 percent.

[11] The benefit payable at 60 under this plan is the same as under a plan specifying 1 percent of final salary for each year of service where the final pay is $100,000 (i.e., 1%*100,000*30 = $30,000).

[12] The model was built to produce the same $30,000 pension, irrespective of salary increase assumption.

[13] In most jurisdictions separate plans are established for uniformed (or safety) employees. Such plans provide for much lower retirement ages. A common provision allows retirement at any age after 20 or 25 years of service. Many police and firefighters retire in their mid 40s.

[14] This refers to a 2005 California proposal reported by Delsey and Hill (2005), later dropped by Gov. Schwarzenegger (Gledhill 2005).

[15] The latest US only figure from the Federal Flow of Funds was $61.984 trillion (Federal Reserve Board 2007). Non-US figures are assumed to be at least as great as the US figure.

[16] See Findlay (2008). But Revell (2008) reports an instance of a governmental plan sponsor declaring bankruptcy, citing unaffordable pension and health care costs for its employees. The seeming permanence of public plans is often cited as a reason to discount liabilities at rates reflecting expected returns on risky assets, but Kohn (2008) proposes that low-risk liabilities must be discounted with low-risk discount rates.

References

Almeida, Beth, Kelly Kenneally, and David Madland (2009). 'The New Intersection on the Road to Retirement: Public Pensions, Economics, Perceptions, Politics, and Interest Groups,' in O.S. Mitchell and G. Anderson, eds., *The Future of Public Employee Retirement Systems*. Oxford: Oxford University Press.

Bader, Lawrence N. and Jeremy Gold (2003). 'Reinventing Pension Actuarial Science,' *The Pension Forum*, 14(2): 1–13.

—— —— (2005). 'What's Wrong with ASOP 27? Bad Measures, Bad Decisions,' *The Pension Forum*, 16(1): 40–46.

Bodie, Zvi (1990). 'The ABO, the PBO and Pension Investment Policy,' *Financial Analysts Journal*, 46(5): 27–34.

Brainard, Keith. (2009). 'Redefining Traditional Plans: Variations and Developments in Public Employee Retirement Plan Design,' in O.S. Mitchell and G. Anderson, eds., *The Future of Public Employee Retirement Systems*. Oxford: Oxford University Press.

Bühlmann, Hans (1987). 'Actuaries of the Third Kind,' *ASTIN Bulletin*, 17(2): 137–38.

Clark, Robert L., Lee A. Craig, and Neveen Ahmed (2009). 'The Evolution of Public Sector Pension Plans in the United States,' in O.S. Mitchell and G. Anderson, eds., *The Future of Public Employee Retirement Systems.* Oxford: Oxford University Press.

Cui, Jiajia, Frank de Jong, and Eduard Ponds (2007). 'Intergenerational Risk Sharing within Funded Collective Pension Schemes.' SSRN Working Paper. Rochester, NY: Social Science Electronic Publishing.

D'Arcy, Stephen P. (1989). 'On Becoming an Actuary of the Third Kind,' *Proceedings of the Casualty Actuarial Society*, 76: 45–76.

Delsey, Gary and John Hill (2005). 'State pension revamp sought,' *Sacramento Bee Online*, January 5. http://dwb.sacbee.com/content/politics/story/11935889p-12823013c.html.

Enderle, Gordon, Jeremy Gold, Gordon Latter, and Michael Peskin (2006). *Pension Actuary's Guide to Financial Economics.* Joint AAA/SOA Task Force on Financial Economics and the Actuarial Model. Washington, DC: Society of Actuaries and American Academy of Actuaries. http://www.actuary.org/pdf/pension/finguide.pdf.

Exley, C. Jon, Shayam J. B. Mehta, and Andrew D. Smith (1997). 'The Financial Theory of Defined Benefit Pension Schemes,' *British Actuarial Journal*, 3(4): 835–966.

Federal Reserve Board (2007). *Flow of Funds Accounts of the United States.* http://www.federalreserve.gov/releases/z1/Current/data.htm.

Financial Accounting Standards Board (FASB) (1980). 'Statement of Financial Accounting Standards No. 35, Accounting and Reporting by Defined Benefit Pension Plans,' March. Norwalk, CT: Financial Accounting Standards Board.

—— (1985). 'Statement of Financial Accounting Standards No. 87, Employers' Accounting for Pensions,' December. Norwalk, CT: Financial Accounting Standards Board.

Findlay, Gary W. (2008). 'Market valuation non sequiturs: Pressure to change how public plans measure liabilities,' *Pensions & Investments*, June 23: 12.

Gledhill, Lynda (2005). 'Governor gives up on overhaul of public pensions,' *San Francisco Chronicle*, April 8: A1.

Gold, Jeremy (2003). 'Risk Transfer in Public Pension Plans,' in O.S. Mitchell and K. Smetters, eds., *The Pension Challenge: Risk Transfers and Retirement Income Security.* Oxford: Oxford University Press, pp. 102–15.

—— (2005). 'Retirement Benefits, Economics and Accounting: Moral Hazard and Frail Benefit Design,' *North American Actuarial Journal*, 9(1): 88–111.

Governmental Accounting Standards Board (GASB) (1994a). 'Statement No. 25, Financial Reporting for Defined Benefit Pension Plans and Note Disclosures for Defined Contribution Plans,' November. Norwalk, CT: Governmental Accounting Standards Board.

—— (1994b). 'Statement No. 27, Accounting for Pensions by State and Local Governmental Employers,' November. Norwalk, CT: Governmental Accounting Standards Board.

—— (2006). 'Why Governmental Accounting and Financial Reporting is—and Should Be—Different,' March. Norwalk, CT: Governmental Accounting Standards Board.

—— (2007). 'Statement No. 50, Pension Disclosures,' May. Norwalk, CT: Governmental Accounting Standards Board.

Hardy, Mary R. (2005). 'We Are All "Actuaries of the Third Kind" Now,' *North American Actuarial Journal*, 9(2): 3–5.

Kohn, Donald L. (2008). 'The Economic Outlook.' Speech at the National Conference on Public Employee Retirement Systems (NCPERS) Annual Conference, New Orleans, Louisiana, May 20.

Latter, Gordon J. (2007). 'Public Plans Take Center Stage,' *Merrill Lynch Pensions & Endowments*, April 18.

Leibowitz, Martin L. (1987). 'Liability Returns: A New Look at Asset Allocation,' *Journal of Portfolio Management*, 13(2): 11–18.

New York City Employees' Retirement System & New York City Public Employee's Group Life Insurance Plan (2007). *Comprehensive Annual Financial Report for the Fiscal year Ended June 30, 2007*. Finance Division of the New York City Employee's Retirement System. New York: New York.

Peskin, Michael W. (2001). 'Asset/Liability Management in the Public Sector,' in O.S. Mitchell and E.C. Hustead, eds., *Pensions in the Public Sector*. Philadelphia, PA: University of Pennsylvania Press, pp. 195–217.

Revell, Janice (2008). 'Fat pensions spell doom for many cities,' *CNNMoney.com*, June 3. http://money.cnn.com/2008/06/02/pf/retirement/vallejo.moneymag/

Sohn, William J. (2006). Letter to the Financial Accounting Standards Board re: Proposed Statement of Financial Accounting Standards—Employers' Accounting for Defined Benefit Pension and Other Postretirement Plans, an Amendment of FASB Statements No. 87, 88, 106, and 132(R). May 31.

Chapter 4

Between Scylla and Charybdis: Improving the Cost Effectiveness of Public Pension Retirement Plans

M. Barton Waring

Defined benefit (DB) pension plans are under a great deal of pressure today, and there is much pressure to replace them with defined contribution (DC) plans. Particularly in the public sector, pressure is on because DB plans are not viewed by many as cost-effective or financially sound. Unfortunately there is a kernel of truth in these concerns, but this chapter argues that the worst problems may be avoided with careful effort. Yet public plans cannot simply become more cost-effective by reducing staff, adopting index funds, or clamping down on travel expenses. There are more fundamental issues to address, issues at the very center of how benefits levels are set and financed. They are significant enough to make the difference between a plan that is long-term healthy, providing benefits for generations, and one that will sooner or later fall over of its own weight. Deferring discussion of the issue until later will simply make the problem worse and insure failure.

In what follows, we first discuss the consequences of the shift from DB to DC plans so as to demonstrate the need for reforms required to save DB plans. Next we review the major policy decisions faced by DB plan fiduciaries, showing what can be done to better manage these plans and improve their cost effectiveness and financial soundness. While much of the discussion applies to all types of DB plans, we devote special emphasis to public employee plans. Further, while we speak mainly of pensions in the United States, many of the same issues are crucial for plans from other countries.

Why not defined contribution?

The pros and cons of DB versus DC are well known (Waring and Siegel 2007*a*, 2007*b*) and may be summarized with two key observations. First, because DC plans usually lack any method for purchasing an annuity (and where they do, they are exorbitantly priced), it takes roughly 50 percent more money at retirement for a DC plan to provide the same lifetime income security as would a DB plan. This is because DC participants each have to plan for their *maximum possible life spans*, while in a DB plan, they only have to fund to their *average life expectancy*. This makes a dramatic difference. Second, for most participants, the rate of savings in DC plans is far too low to provide any serious lifetime benefit at all. Median balances for those age 65 (or otherwise measured at about the time of retirement) are less than $70,000 across a variety of surveys. Clearly this does not provide for a meaningful retirement income. Accordingly, the bottom line is that a DC plan requires a great deal *more* money to be set aside than a DB plan for a comparable lifetime retirement income, yet in practice, it collects much *less* money in contributions and earnings. There are also other problems with DC plans including high fees, too many withdrawals and loans, poorly chosen active management, and poorly designed personal investment policies.

While every effort should be made to make DC plans work more effectively, it is often difficult to boost contribution rates to reasonable levels, perhaps by making them mandatory or limiting early withdrawals. These and other needed reforms all present significant difficulties, although there are improvements that can be made at the margin. For these reasons, we propose that 'the worst DB plan is better than the best DC plan.' There may be a bit of hyperbole in this assertion, but the sad fact is that it is not much. Our view is that we must preserve and protect DB retirement plans wherever they still exist.

Key pension policies

There are four key pension policies which must be managed explicitly or implicitly by every DB pension plan fiduciary, oversight committee, or board. Between them, they completely shape the plan's cost effectiveness and financial soundness. These include accounting and reporting policy, benefit policy, contribution policy, and investment policy. We discuss each of these in turn to show their relative importance and their interconnections.

When seeking to manage the costs and risks of a plan, most attention is devoted to investment policy, with contribution policy perhaps also having its quick annual 'day in court.' Virtually no attention is paid to accounting and reporting policy, and very little to benefit policy. Nevertheless, these priorities are completely backwards. Furthermore, they have often been treated as if they were stand-alone policies, but they are heavily intertwined and not at all independent.

Accounting and reporting policy: the ugly stepchild

Today's pension accounting and reporting policies are based on actuarial approaches that have little to do with financial and funding reality. This is especially true for US public employee DB plans, which have not had the benefit of some of the small reforms that have taken place on the corporate DB plan side. One explanation is that the actuarial methods underlying these policies were invented long ago, well before the development of modern portfolio theory and of the financial engineering knowledge that we have today. Though these policies are misguided in some key ways, they are strongly defended by a significant (although decreasing) portion of the actuarial community. And because they make the pension financing problem look rosier for the plan sponsor than it really is, trustees and other fiduciaries show a natural bias toward continuing with the old methods. As mentioned earlier, the four key policies are all interrelated, and today's archaic accounting and reporting policies permeate every other policy decision and make it impossible to properly manage the cost effectiveness of today's DB retirement plans. What follows discusses what would change if market-based accounting and reporting methods were adopted that would dramatically improve fiduciaries' ability to manage their plans.

The Discount Rate. The most important accounting and reporting problem for DB pensions is the discount rate and how it is set. It has been hotly debated in the US corporate DB plan environment and has now been brought closer to an adequate rate. But on the public employee plan side this topic is still ripe for discussion.

The discount rate is the most crucial accounting and reporting policy issue because it immediately and directly affects the stated size of a pension plan's liabilities, and thus the required level of annual contributions (and pension expense levels for private pension plans). The question is whether this discount rate should be based on expected returns on the asset portfolio, as actuaries have recommended in the past, or on some other market-based rate. Most financial economists contend that the discount rate should be the rate appropriate to a liability-matching portfolio of government bonds—that is, of a portfolio having the same market risks as the liability.

To explain why it is wrong to use the expected return on assets as the discount rate, we turn to a thought experiment. Let us assume the pension plan can be simplified to a single person and a single benefit payment, so that key ideas are not obscured by the apparent complexity introduced when looking at a plan covering thousands of people and responsible for years of monthly payments. Let us further assume that you are the sole trustee for a plan with this single employee, and further posit that this employee is retiring today. The retirement benefit is $100,000, in a single payment to be made 10 years from today. Your tasks are to decide the right discount rate to use in evaluating the cost of this retirement plan, and to arrange a contribution that will provide security for the benefit.

We consider two approaches to setting the discount rate: the conventional asset return approach, and the risk-free government bond rate approach. The first, also termed the 'expected asset return' approach, traditionally used by actuaries, concludes that the present value of the liability and the cash contribution needed to fund it is $46,320, assuming that the plan invests the money in a conventional pension plan asset mix (about 70% equity-like assets and the other 30% bonds) having an expected return of 8 percent per year. If this fund were to grow on average (arithmetic) at this rate of return, it would indeed provide the required $100,000 at the end of 10 years.[1]

But such a portfolio has risk in it, so it cannot perfectly hedge the liability. The actual average return might very well be less than 8 percent per year. Accordingly, one cannot know with certainty whether the obligation will be fully funded or not at the end of the 10-year period. This investment policy has a risk level, expressed as a standard deviation of returns, of about 12 percent per year (this is a typical value for such a policy). But a risk level of 12 percent for one year is a whopping 38 percent over 10 years, lending huge uncertainty to the final portfolio value.[2] It means that the fund may earn far too much—or, more importantly, *far too little*. No one would be happy if instead of $100,000, the fund contained only $62,000 (that is, 38% too little) at the planned payout date, and this is only a one standard deviation downside event.

There is an important semantic issue involved in this discussion. The 'expected' return of 8 percent is not an expectation of the same sort as when one says, 'Son, I *expect* you to be home at 11 o'clock tonight.' In finance, the probability of the desired expectation happening doesn't go up just because one wants it to, as is implied in our use of the word in ordinary conversation. Rather, it is a *statistical* expectation, the center point in a wide range of possible outcomes, more formally known as 'realizations' once they have occurred.

It is fair to quip that, at least with respect to ordinary use of our language, 'the expected return is not to be expected!' (Kritzman 2000: 65). One might do better than the expectation, but one might also do worse—but it is very unlikely that anyone will achieve exactly the level that was 'expected.' In summary, what risk means for investments is that the actual realized return will be different from the expected return, and the value we put on risk (the 12% and 38% numbers in this example) tell us by how much the realizations might ordinarily differ from the expectation.

A second approach to setting the discount rate is to imagine that one will invest $64,390 in a hypothetical 10-year zero-coupon government bond at 4.5 percent, which would pay the required $100,000 in 10 years with *certainty*. This approach to setting the discount rate does set a higher present value than the first example, and thus a higher immediate required contribution. But the obligation would be completely hedged and fully secure at all times during the 10-year period. Thus, 4.5 percent is the discount rate, rather than 8 percent as in the previous example, and it really does require a greater initial investment in order to assure the security of the benefit.

This second approach is the so-called 'defeasing' alternative, one which provides a perfect hedge for the required payment obligation. There is no market event that can happen, no interest rate change that can occur, that will alter the complete security of this benefit under this investment plan. Accordingly, financial economists and market players say that the right discount rate for a future cash flow is the expected return found in the financial markets for an asset, or portfolio of assets, with similar market-related risk characteristics as has the cash flow under analysis. By definition, if a perfect hedge is found in the market, it has the same market-related risks as the obligation being hedged. So we know that the expected return of the hedging asset is also the economically correct discount rate (and equivalently the expected return) of our liability. This makes intuitive sense even for non-economists, since the hypothetical matching portfolio would make the obligation completely safe, as demonstrated in our two examples. For this reason it is natural to think that the discount rate that gives us today's present value for that future obligation in such a safe manner is the 'right' discount rate. And so it is.

Now, as a fiduciary, one could bow to pressure to reduce today's apparent cost of funding this pension obligation and choose the first alternative. This constitutes an assertion that the present value of the liability is much smaller today and that a much smaller contribution is required to securely fund it. But where is the money going to come from if investment results are bad and the fund comes up short? If results are just one standard deviation below the expectation, the plan will be short by more than a third of the required $100,000 at the end of 10 years. This shortfall probability should be taken into account, the probability (not the certainty) that an additional substantial future contribution will be required. Otherwise, the trustee must explain to the retiree that his or her obligation may depend on the future creditworthiness—or lack thereof—of the plan sponsor who is obligated to make up the difference. If this was more widely understood, employees would no doubt object—even public bodies can face taxpayer revolts or otherwise be unable to pay significant shortfalls.

Ultimately the plan might earn the full expected return, but it might not, and one could question whether hoping to 'get lucky' is the proper role of the fiduciary. Further, the expected return of the assets is not the right way to set a discount rate. In fact, economists say that the expected asset return has nothing whatsoever to do with the discount rate needed to establish benefit security for a liability of this type. The investment illustration, being hypothetical, illustrates a complete hedge which in turn demonstrates that the market-related risks are matched, which is the test for sourcing a discount rate. This would still be the discount rate for the example liability even if the fund's assets were actually invested in lottery tickets. Billions of dollars trade every day on the world's exchanges in full reliance on this latter method of setting discount rates for all types of assets and liabilities.

Despite the logic suggested by the financial approach, its strong theoretical underpinnings, and its nearly universal use in real-life Wall Street investment banking practice for valuing other streams of future cash flows, the traditional actuarial approach of relying on the expected return of the assets to establish the discount rate is still in common use in public plans. This is despite the fact that the 'Law of One Price' is one of the most fundamental ideas in economics, stating that any asset or any liability can have only one price.[3] Discount rates are simply ways to state future obligations in terms of today's prices. There cannot be multiple present values for pension liabilities. Instead, there is only one, based on the price of the hedging asset, which is—in the case of a liability that must be completely secured and that has no other market related characteristics—government bonds. Thus the discount rate is the expected return of those bonds.

The Benefit of Changing to a Market Value Based Discount Rate Method. Present values for pension liabilities based on the expected return of the asset portfolio are actually not 'present values' of a secured liability at all. They are something else entirely, and while they may be written with a dollar sign in front of them, they are not actually stated in dollars. In the past I have called these units something else, something significantly less valuable, in order to keep them separate mentally from dollars; let us term them 'Sasquatches.'[4] The question is, would you want your retirement fund to be funded in full by fungible dollars or by the same number of Sasquatches?

In our view, if we were to make this important accounting and reporting policy change, from Sasquatches to properly discounted 'dollars of present value,' it will beneficially inject itself into each of the other policies. The key issue is that the fiduciaries must expect that their statements of funded status, their statements of required contributions, and all other financial statements show the liabilities in properly measured dollars, not in Sasquatches, that is, using economically appropriate discount rates for calculating present values. It is often the case that the switch to a lower discount rate and the recognition of the true, but higher liability will be expensive and may cause some angst. But it is the only path to managing healthy pension plans at reasonable cost, since the liability is already as large as it is. Switching from a faulty measuring stick to a good one does not change the true size of the liability; instead, it only changes the portion of the liability to which we are admitting, and sound practice requires admitting the truth. Moving from recognizing only part of the liability (by using Sasquatches) to recognizing all of it (in true dollars of present value) can only help make the benefit more secure and the sponsoring organization more financially sound.

Smoothing and Amortization. Another aspect of pension accounting and reporting policy that tends to distort reality and one that interferes with the ability of pension fiduciaries to properly understand their plan's true financial status is the practice of smoothing. Because conventional practice does not always mark the discount rate to market on a regular basis, the pension liability as reported appears to be more stable than it actually is. Like any other bond-like stream of payouts, the liability fluctuates in value with every change of rates, going up in size with rate decreases and down in size with rate increases. It must be so, but some insist that the liability is stable, when of course it is not.[5]

Why is the failure to mark-to-market a problem? If the accounting and reporting procedures allowed pension fiduciaries responsible for a plan to see this natural fluctuation, their natural reaction might be to *hedge* those fluctuations, adopting investment policies that dampened the pension plan's surplus or deficit volatility. By contrast, if the volatility is not reported, then this important task will not get done. This is why nearly all US DB pension plans with liabilities that could be entirely hedged with a long duration bond hold only 25 or 30 percent of their assets in bonds (this small portion is in short duration Lehman Aggregate Index-benchmarked bonds). As a result, US pension plans could not be much more unhedged and exposed to interest rate risk if they tried intentionally. In the following text we show just how large this unhedged and mismatched surplus volatility is, but in round numbers, it is close to the same as the volatility of the 10-year bond.

The practice of amortizing newly awarded pension benefits also distorts the fiduciaries' perception of plans' true funding status. Perhaps there should be a mechanism for allowing a period of time to fully fund newly awarded benefits, but there should be no time lapse for recognizing a newly awarded benefit as part of the overall liability. Fiduciaries must see the full size of the liability if they are to have sufficient information to adopt responsible benefit, contribution, and investment policies. In the past, reported values for pension liability and for required contributions have been subject to a great deal of manipulation through management of the discount rate and amortization assumptions. Accordingly, few fiduciaries take the numbers generated by today's archaic methods perfectly seriously. But with market value-based economically-sound approaches to valuation, this can be remedied, so fiduciaries will have the information necessary to make hard-headed and clear-eyed decisions to protect and preserve their plans.

Benefit policy

How big should benefits be? When a sponsor, through a retirement plan, promises a dollar of benefits to be paid at some point in the future, it will require a contribution by the sponsor at some point in time, either at its lower present value now or at its full future value later.[6] So the only way to control the cost effectiveness of a DB plan is to control benefit levels. Yet when the present value of those future benefits is stated in terms of Sasquatches rather than real dollars, and it is allowed to be interpreted by all interested parties as if it really were dollars, strange things can happen. Benefits tend to look less expensive than they actually are. In the example earlier, they appeared to be only about 72 percent as expensive in the first alternative as in the second, but this is an artificial example and is most likely an understatement. In actuality, the apparent cost can easily be only 50 percent of the true cost.

As a result, benefits are awarded more quickly and easily than they would be if the units of measure were in true dollars. This means that DB pension plans have grown more generous over time, and in many cases may out-weigh the sponsor's ability to comfortably pay the true cost as it comes due, absent exceptionally strong investment returns. This may seem to be quite positive from the employee's perspective, at least at first blush. But it is not good for the employer, and if the error is sufficient, it can even endanger the plan sponsor as well as the health of the plan. It could even result in the DB plan's replacement by a DC plan. Both employers and employees will be better off over the long haul if they negotiate benefit levels and contri-bution rates based on economically-accurate benefit valuations and costs.

Cost-Of-Living Adjustments (COLAs) are another area where today's accounting and reporting practices permit manipulating the true size of the liability, as it is seldom clear to fiduciaries how significant granting a COLA actually is. By not formally adopting COLAs as a policy but going through the process of 'considering' a COLA grant each year, only the present values of COLAs already awarded must be counted in present value computations for the reported liability. Yet if there is a reasonable expectation that in future years COLAs will be awarded sufficient to cover (say) 50 percent of inflation for retirees, shouldn't that expectation be valued right now, so that the true financial impact of the desire to provide that level of COLA protection is apparent, even if stated separately? A policy of regularly giving out full COLA coverage might cost an additional 30 to

50 percent of the no-COLA liability. These are expensive benefits, and they will require expensive contributions. All will be better-off if the true economic cost of the long-term plan for awarding COLAs were computed and reported along with the other liability valuation figures.

Another common threat to sound benefit policy and cost control arises when a plan's financials at the end of a year show it to be 'fully funded' according to the actuaries, and as a result, there is pressure to increase benefits. But since the liability is usually stated in Sasquatches and not in dollars, the plan isn't fully funded at all, so an increase in benefits will in actuality take a plan that is truthfully and economically in deficit and makes it even more so. New benefits cannot be justified on the grounds that the plan has excess assets when the excess is measured using traditional measures.

Controlling pension plan cost effectiveness is all about making sure that the benefit level is 'right'—no more, and no less than it should be, as a part of the total compensation package required to attract, retain, and motivate the kind of employees that the employer wants to have. Too small, and the quality of the work force may suffer; too large, and the finances of the sponsoring organization will suffer.

Under today's accounting and reporting practices, fiduciaries managing public employee pension plans do not have the right information for controlling the level of benefits. Managing what are in reality Sasquatches rather than dollars will not result in optimal benefit levels or optimal contribution calculations. It should be clear that all interested parties—labor, management, taxpayers, regulators, rating agencies—have the same interest in having good information. No one can properly evaluate the level of benefits, the appropriateness of that level, the adequacy of the planned funding, or the organization's ability to provide the required funding, if the liability is not measured in terms of proper, Law of One Price, dollars.

Contribution policy

The true cost of a DB pension plan is best understood in terms of the present value of the benefits, that is, the liability. In practice, however, the cost is 'felt' year-by-year as a stream of cash contributions made by the employer to the fund. So for many advisors operating under the belief that the traditional approaches to valuing plans and calculating contributions are valid, controlling costs has meant to minimize the present value of the future contribution stream. We challenge this by noting that the present value of all future contributions (plus assets on hand) has to equal the present value of future benefits promised, the liability, or benefits will not be paid. It then follows that the present value of the future contribution stream cannot be minimized, or managed in any other way, once the benefit level is fixed.

This view contradicts widely held beliefs, but its accuracy is evident as soon as one starts using the tools of financial economics. In fact, the only thing that can be decided under the heading of contribution policy is the rate at which benefits are funded with cash contributions. This question is simply a matter of deciding how fast the contribution 'payments' are made and how soon the liability 'mortgage' is paid off. Contribution policy cannot make the pension more or less expensive. It is analogous to amortizing the mortgage on one's home: larger payments amortize it faster, and smaller payments amortize it more slowly (or if too small, the balance grows instead of shrinking). Pension contributions set with methods that provide too slow an amortization or accrual of benefits reduce benefit security, which is the primary concern of contribution policy and of market-based accounting.

The breakdown of the required contribution into its component or elemental parts is often not made fully clear to the pension board. There are usually several components to it. Among which the most common are the 'normal cost' or 'service cost,' an amount to be accrued, and contributed, for benefits deemed to have been earned this year. There are several 'methods' of determining the amount 'earned' through another year of service, so this number is often manipulated to reduce contributions. This is the 'base' contribution, the amount that would be paid in each year at a plan where all benefits were fully funded (under the terms of the method used, not necessarily by an economically sound method).

An amount representing a 'catch-up' contribution to pay for recently awarded benefits that are being amortized into the liability over time. These benefits should already have been acknowledged and stated with the valuation of the rest of the liability, since they have been granted, but this is not required and often it is not done. When they are not shown, constituencies will not know that the plan is in a hole and that it will require discipline and contributions to get out of it. If these values were reported, the fiduciaries and other constituents might be watching more closely to make sure that the amortization period is no longer than sensible. Another 'catch-up' payment to 'amortize' the plan's deficit, with the stated intention of getting the plan back to fully funded status over a multi-year period. This also is heavily manipulated in that sometimes the amortization period is set for as far out as 30 years. Given that it is based on a Sasquatch version of the liability, obviously this method will never bring a plan to true full funding status. Reasonable fiduciaries that understand this might well want to see a much shorter period of time for catching up.[7]

In practice, contribution policy tends to get a great deal of attention during that moment when it comes up for discussion each year, because no one likes to make (or ask for) large payments. So a good deal of effort often goes into finding creative methods of avoiding or minimizing this year's contribution, in a manner that wouldn't be contemplated under market-based accounting. The beneficiary, worrying about benefit security, ideally wants the contributions to be made relatively earlier rather than later, but from the sponsor's perspective, the temptation is to defer them as late as possible. Many fiduciaries have probably been led to believe that a contribution not made is a contribution avoided forever. But it is not; it is only deferred, and it will have to be made later, with interest! Sponsor cash might be preserved for the moment, to meet other demands, but the plan will still need it and benefit security will suffer for lack of it.

Again, market-value-based accounting and reporting policies would facilitate a much better understanding of contribution policy and its effect on benefit security and the funding status of the plan.

Investment policy

Many pension plan trustees and officers seem to think that the way to improve the cost effectiveness of the DB plan is to make the investments perform better. Of course if that were feasible merely by forming the intention, it could be a great solution. But inevitably the attempt to generate better performance involves taking on more risks, and investment risks are real. Thus investing with a higher expected return target, in order 'to help pay for the plan,' may very likely end up making the plan cost a good deal more.

It is not rare for a pension board, pension trustees, labor representatives, and the public attendees, to turn in unison to the Chief Investment Officer (CIO) after hearing the disappointing funding level report from the actuary or administrator. In a grave voice, the board chairperson asks the question all of them are thinking, but in one more gracious form or another, the gist of the question is always: 'What are you going to do to get us out of this mess?' As if by some alchemy the CIO could skillfully make a single large (and correct!) bet that would bail out the plan, and as if the shortfall was the CIO's responsibility. In fact, the responsibility is much more that of the board than of the CIO. But to the extent that it accepts responsibility, the board may be thinking that the DB plan is not cost effective, is risky, that it cannot be controlled, and perhaps the organization should switch to a DC plan. None of those conclusions are in fact true, but they are understandable given that they are trying to run the plan with bad information. And there has been until recently little way for them to know that their information sources were less than fully accurate.

Informed by good information, it would be clear that there are three ways, and only three ways, to get an underfunded plan back in balance. The first way is to make a large contribution or series of contributions sufficient to make up the balance. This is a contribution policy response, and it is completely effective. Yet the suggestion would be unwelcome, as cash contributions are always hard to find and painful to raise. The second way is to revisit benefit levels to ensure that more benefits are not being promised than are required to make an appropriate total compensation package of salary and benefits sufficient to attract, retain, and motivate the work force. This is a benefit policy response, and it can also be immediately effective in bringing a plan back into balance. This suggestion will likely also be unwelcome, and understandably so, particularly by the work force.

All this explains why all involved want the CIO to solve the problem with a few death-defying feats of investment transmutation: the other choices seem unpalatable. But the investment policy choice is the weakest possible means of bringing a plan back into balance, and brave efforts through a more aggressive and thus more risky policy may make the plan worse, not better-off. Nevertheless, many plans today are putting all their energy into just such investment policy solutions, using hedge funds, infrastructure funds, higher equity allocations, and other increases of risk. These may all be good things to do, helpful on the margin if carefully considered in terms of their added risk. Yet they are not going to solve any significant funding problems—not, at least, without the sponsor also just 'getting lucky'! And there is increased risk of being very unlucky. It is not unfair to ask whether the focus on investment policy is not evidence that many plans are in denial of the true nature of the funding problem.

Liability-relative Investing. There is an 'elephant in the room' with respect to investment policy, ignored while sponsors work diligently to improve their strategy in every way except the one that will really do some good. Few if any sponsors have yet to adopt liability-relative investing— investing the assets and the liability together as a single portfolio, with the liability treated as an asset held short—as their primary mode of developing investment policy and strategy. The problem is being slowly addressed on the corporate DB plan side, but is woefully under-attended to by public employee DB plans. Yet the failure to do so (coupled with the continued use of traditional actuarial information) is the major reason, why the fiduciaries might perceive that the plan is too risky and out of control.

Surplus optimization, optimizing on the surplus, or on the portfolio consisting of assets minus the liabilities, is how liability-relative investing should be undertaken.[8] Waring (2008*b*) shows that it provides without doubt the single biggest opportunity to improve investment policy for virtually all DB plans: The 'normal' level of surplus volatility seen by today's pension plans is around a 13 or 14 percent standard deviation. Experience in surplus risk analysis shows that about half of the surplus variance (the square of standard deviation) will be from interest rate volatility that could be avoided if the plan used surplus asset allocation to develop its strategic asset allocation policy. If it did, it would be holding a portfolio that is fully duration-matched to the liability, cancelling out the funding ratio volatility that comes from interest rate movements (the sponsor would also be holding the portfolio of risky assets [equity etc.] that it wants).

To use a numerical example, let us assume that the fully hedged, liability-matched 'standard deviation of the surplus' would be 10 percent, for a given plan with a given exposure to equities and other risky assets. This gives a surplus variance (standard deviation squared) of 100. If that same plan were like most plans today and were not liability-hedged, experience says that there would be an additional contribution of about 100 in variance. This gives a total variance of 200. So the standard deviation of surplus for the unhedged plan is then the square root of 200, or 14 percent—again, consistent with experience for today's typical, asset-oriented investment policies in DB plans. Note that half of this plan's variance risk is avoidable if it just held a liability-matching asset portfolio. Avoiding this risk through surplus optimization is the most important single action a sponsor can take to improve its investment policy, and to reduce the appearance that the plan is out of control or unreasonably risky.

This can be readily done, by holding first the 'liability-matching asset portfolio' mentioned earlier, normally using swaps and other derivatives to hedge out the liability risks (Waring 2004a). (The liability risks consist mostly of real interest rate risk and inflation risk.) Then it is time to decide how much of a 'risky asset portfolio' the plan wants to hold in the hope of good returns that will help pay for the plan (Waring 2004b, 2008a, and 2008b). Today's typical risky asset exposures are quite aggressive, with 70 + percent of the portfolio dedicated to equities and other risky assets. This seems quite high, particularly once the problem is properly reframed in surplus context. It is perhaps acceptable for financially strong and growing organizations with relatively small plans. But the risk represented by this level of aggressiveness is real, and could seriously damage the funded status of the plan. Since bad markets tend to go with financial stress in all organizations, it is likely that when 'risk happens' the organization will be too strapped to be able to make up the loss with a large contribution, and at that point the plan is going to remain underfunded and will face a risk of failure.

Sadly, few public plan sponsors have adopted surplus approaches to date. Falling interest rates and falling equity markets are the two worst things for pension plan financial health, and both are happening simultaneously at present. They both happened earlier in the decade as well. This is causing a dramatic increase in plan deficits, worse for plans that entered this period of market turmoil already underfunded. Had these plans adopted a liability-matching asset portfolio a couple of years ago, the falling interest rates would not have hurt them. Had they reduced the level of their equity exposures, the market's losses would not have hit them so hard. (We note that hedge funds have not solved this problem!)

To sum up, the truly effective means for controlling funding levels are by making big special contributions or by rationalizing the benefit program. Understandably, neither one of these is very attractive, but ultimately they may be necessary at many plans. Any such efforts must be informed by good, economically sound valuation information in order for both sides to give credibility to the need. Much lower in the hierarchy of effectiveness, some carefully chosen amount of asset risk can be used to try to help pay for the plan as an appropriate investment policy decision, but fiduciaries should be careful lest they expose the plan to even larger risks than they would truly be comfortable experiencing. Ultimately there is absolutely no good reason not to move toward holding a full liability-matching asset portfolio, which will halve the risk (measured as variance) faced by typical plans. Regardless, investment policy will seldom have the power required to make an underfunded plan become fully funded.

Between Scylla and Charybdis

According to our view, the vast majority of public plans are underfunded. Yet fiduciaries and other stakeholders have not insisted on reforming accounting and reporting policy, even though it would dramatically improve their ability to truly understand their plan's financial posture. The main explanation is that they fear negative legislative reaction. It is possible that lawmakers will simply terminate the plan if told that the true value of the benefits that have been promised is much higher than had been previously acknowledged. On the other hand, if boards do nothing, the underfunding problem will progressively get worse until plans fall over of their own weight. This is just as serious and is also a real concern, even if it is not as immediate. DB boards must wend their way between these competing dangers. They cannot avoid future risk by avoiding the immediate risk while denying the fact that the traditional actuarial approach is badly failing them.

There is no easy way out of this dilemma for public DB plans. The strong levers for fixing the fact that a plan is underfunded are to put more money into it and/or to re-evaluate benefit levels, both very effective but unattractive alternatives. A strategy designed and followed to accomplish just these tasks, facing up to these difficulties, has several elements. First is a move to improved accounting and reporting policy. A fiduciary could announce a move to reduce the discount rate by 0.5 percent every year for six years or until he gets to a market discount rate, whichever comes first. The book liability valuation will then come up to fair market value in annual doses, rather than all at once. The actuary can be asked to begin reporting to the board immediately, on a non-book basis, the true value of the liability today, so that constituents know what they are dealing with. The board must acknowledge that good decisions cannot be made without good information, and so market-based information is needed about the value of the liabilities and about the market value impact of every decision, including contribution policy and investment policy. And the actuaries must be required to buy into these goals and sign on to serve them without reservation.

A second advance would focus on contribution policy. Here the actuary would be asked to provide information on the contribution level required to bring the plan to fully funded status on a market value basis within 10 years, with all current benefit levels considered (i.e., without amortization of recent new benefits). This information will be invaluable to the fiduciaries in understanding both the actual contribution policy decision in this year and in subsequent years. It is needed to define how much the legislature must be asked to contribute, and to evaluate whether these amounts are within the realm of the possible.

A third advance pertains to benefit policy. If the contributions required to be on a path to full funding on a market basis within a 10-year time frame are too onerous to be legislatively feasible, it would probably be wise for labor and management to undertake a joint effort to revise the benefits to a level that can be afforded over the long term. While this is difficult, especially for labor, it is worth remembering that 'the worst DB plan is better than the best DC plan.' It is important to preemptively take on this task and put a meaningful and hard-nosed plan in place, before the legislature takes stronger action.

A fourth element would be to adopt sensible investment policy. One could immediately move to adopt a surplus asset allocation approach to developing investment policy, including holding a liability-matching asset portfolio which will consist mostly of interest rate derivatives with long durations. This will dramatically reduce the risk to the plan's market valued or true surplus, starting immediately. In addition, the board will have to give some careful thought to how much risky asset exposure, with the attendant risk of loss, the fund can bear. Bad years are becoming more 'normal,' so while the investments will help pay for the benefits, the more aggressive the investment policy, the more likely that it will make the plan more expensive.

Ultimately the questions that all must grapple with are how large benefit levels can be and still be affordable over the long term, and who will pay for these benefits (assuming some combination of employer and employee contributions, as is relatively common among public employee DB plans)? These questions can only be addressed accurately with good, economically sensible, market-value-based information.

Conclusion

Our aging populations need support during their retirement years, and they are growing too large to be supported on a pay-as-you-go basis by the shrinking working-age population. This means that retirement plans must be financially sound without requiring generation-shifting contributions where today's workers have to make up for yesterday's workers' failure to save. To be financially sound, these plans have to be pre-funded and cost effective. Their periodic cost needs to make sense in the context of the total compensation—salary, medical care, pensions, and other benefits—required to attract, retain, and motivate employees.

All this suggests that plan sponsors must learn what the plan costs and liabilities are, with real and valid numbers. Today we lack such numbers, so the first order of business is to grapple with accounting and reporting policies, putting them on a market basis so that we do have real numbers to manage. With that done, boards will make better benefit policy decisions and contribution policy decisions. In turn, this better information will motivate better investment policies and strategies, in a liability-relative framework. Saving DB plans means making them financially sound. This is an urgent matter, but is in the best interests of all constituents.

Notes

[1] Given the expected variability or standard deviation of 12 percent, the fund will have to grow at a somewhat higher arithmetic average rate of about 8.7 percent, in order to achieve the geometric average (or compound rate) of 8 percent over the time horizon.

[2] The 38 percent figure is just the standard approximation, assuming a normal distribution, of the 10-year standard deviation, i.e. 12 percent times the square root of 10 years. More correctly we would use the lognormal approximation, but we would lose in intuition what we gained in accuracy. Note further that 38 percent is just one standard deviation (over a 10-year holding period): It is quite possible—there is about a one in six likelihood—for results to be more than one standard deviation below the expectation, even much more.

[3] More precisely, the Law of One Price (or the no-arbitrage condition) requires a market that is efficient. In practice, if a market approaches efficiency, there should be little difference in prices for identical goods in the identical place.

[4] Actuarial 'expected rate of return'-based discount rates have been lower than the Treasury bond rate for 20-odd years, but during the inflationary period of the 1970s and early 1980s, there were periods when the reverse was true. In that unusual situation, Sasquatches were actually more valuable than dollars. Before this period, fewer equities were held in pension portfolios, and the difference between the expected return on the assets and the proper discount rate was not typically very large, so it did not create a problem. The problem started when the portfolio diverged aggressively from its liability benchmark.

[5] People who insist that the liability is stable may be relying on the observation that the future values (benefit promises) are quite stable. The present value, however, is not and cannot be stable because present values fluctuate with interest rate (discount rate) changes.

[6] To eliminate credit risk, regulations in the United States and other places require certain plans to be fully funded, a status that is assumed to be intended in this discussion even where there is no explicit regulation (as for US public employee DB plans).

[7] For a comparison, under the Pension Protection Act, US corporate plans now must plan on getting to full funding within seven years on a valuation basis that is much closer to market value than that used by public DB plans.

[8] If the plan is in deficit, the surplus thus defined is a negative number. It is easier to talk about the (positive or negative) surplus than to switch back and forth between surplus and deficit, depending on the sign of the number.

References

Kritzman, Mark P. (2000). *Puzzles of Finance*. Hoboken, NJ: John Wiley & Sons.

Waring, M. Barton (2004*a*). 'Liability-Relative Investing: Be Dual Duration Matched *and* on the Surplus Efficient Frontier,' *Journal of Portfolio Management*, 30(4): 8–20.

—— (2004*b*). 'Liability-Relative Investing: Surplus Optimization with Beta, Alpha, and an Economic View of the Liability,' *Journal of Portfolio Management*, 31(1): 40–53.

—— (2008*a*). 'Managing Pension Funding Risk,' in H. G. Fong, ed., *Innovations in Investment Management*. New York: Bloomberg Press, pp. 29–83.

—— (2008*b*). 'Surplus Asset Allocation and the *Three* Fund Theorem: Practical Policy Suggestions for Investors with Liabilities,' Unpublished manuscript.

—— and Laurence B. Siegel (2007*a*). 'Don't Kill the Golden Goose: Saving Pension Plans,' *Financial Analysts Journal*, 63(1): 31–45.

—— —— (2007*b*). 'Wake Up and Smell the Coffee! DC Plans Aren't Working: Here's How to Fix Them,' *The Journal of Investing*, 16(4): 81–99.

Chapter 5

Public Pensions and State and Local Budgets: Can Contribution Rate Cyclicality Be Better Managed?

Parry Young

The payment of annual pension contributions is an ongoing concern for government sponsors of pension plans worldwide (Brainard 2008). During every budget cycle, the financial officers of US state and local governments must deal with this issue, as most are sponsors of defined benefit (DB) plans. Unlike more stable, slow-growing costs such as building maintenance or even payroll, employer pension contributions are unpredictable even over the medium term. In an industry like government, which tends to be service-oriented and thus quite labor intensive (almost three-quarters of school district expenses, e.g., may be related to people), benefit costs are a major cost factor.

To make matters even more interesting from a planning perspective, employer pension costs may be volatile in either direction, up or down. The actuarial methods used to determine rates generally aim for rate stability, but they have been unable to contain volatility in recent times due to a confluence of factors. This chapter reviews some of the major strategies used by employers to try to tame such rate fluctuations. Next we look at historical practices and also actions and adjustments made in response to recent pressures. New approaches may provide ideas for employers currently grappling with this issue.

Pension contributions

DB pension plans receive revenues from two principal sources: contributions and investment income earned on those contributions. The contributions come from employees, generally at a fixed rate, and employers, at a rate reset annually. In some cases the employer may pick up the employees' share. The employer contribution rate reflects the Annual Required Contribution (ARC) calculated by the system's actuary. It includes the cost allocated to the current fiscal year plus an amount to amortize unfunded actuarial accrued liabilities. In most years the majority of employers contribute 100 percent of the ARC but some employers may pay only 60 or 70 percent (or 0%) of the ARC. A contribution of less than 100 percent of the ARC may reflect a weakness in the employer's current financial position, or specific funding policies or restrictions. In rare instances, a payment may be more than 100 percent of the ARC. Reasons for this 'over-payment' would include a catch-up for underpayments in prior years, for example.

Not paying the full required amount in any one year or over a period of time tends to add to contribution volatility, in that these shortfalls will most likely have to be made up with correspondingly higher payments at some future point. Barrett and Greene (2007) reported that only 50 percent of the state pension funds received the full ARC from their sponsors in 2006. Pension funding statutes, procedures, and policies vary greatly from state to state and even between local systems within a state. For example, in California, the code mandates that the full pension contribution be paid annually by certain counties, including Los Angeles, San Diego, and Sacramento counties. If the county board of supervisors fails to make the appropriation to the retirement system, the county auditor is required to take any available monies from county funds and deposit them with the retirement system (California Government Code Section 31581).

The Recent Record of Contribution Volatility. The experience of US public pension funds over the past decade presents ample evidence of employer contribution rate volatility. Data for state and local government employers shows pension contribution rates declining from a high of 10.5 percent of payroll in fiscal 1997 to a low of 6.8 percent in fiscal 2002, before rising again (see Figure 5-1 and Table 5-1). The compilation covers the 12 fiscal years from 1995 to 2006 (NASRA 2008). For the five fiscal years ended in 2002, rates declined in each year by a mean of 8.3 percent. Even though the average rate never fell below 6.8 percent of payroll, many fund sponsors actually experienced contribution 'holidays' (no employer contribution) during this period. This declining rate trend reflected the strong improvement in funded ratios (the actuarial value of assets divided by the actuarial accrued liabilities) during the 1990s. Driving this improvement were an increased emphasis on equity investments by public funds and very strong investment returns for these public plan assets. Public funds increased their allocation to domestic equities to 45 percent in 2000 from 39 percent in 1992, and international equities to 16 percent from 4 percent during the same period (PPCC 1993, 2001). The average annual increase for the S&P 500 index of domestic equities for fiscal years 1995–2000 was an extremely robust 22.2 percent, more than double historical averages.

While the idea of a pension contribution holiday may sound attractive to an employer, especially if it is experiencing fiscal stress from other quarters,

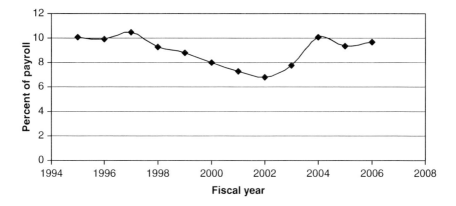

Figure 5-1 Employer contributions as percent of state and local government payroll. *Source*: NASRA (2008).

such a reprieve actually has at least one negative side effect. This danger is that the sponsor falls out of the (good) habit of appropriating for and making pension contributions. When the contribution holiday is over and the time to make contributions comes again, which is inevitable, it seems as if the current pension cost is now a new expense. This new cost will likely cause the sponsor's budget to increase at a faster pace than the normalized one and it tends to be difficult for revenues to keep pace in offsetting the increase.

Employer contribution rates to public plans continued to decline in 2001 and 2002, in spite of reversals in investment returns because it generally

TABLE 5-1 Employer contributions as a percent of state and local government payroll

Fiscal Year	Percent of Payroll	Percent Change
1997	10.5	—
1998	9.3	−11.4
1999	8.8	−5.4
2000	8.0	−9.1
2001	7.3	−8.8
2002	6.8	−6.8
2003	7.8	+14.7
2004	10.1	+29.5
2005	9.4	−6.9
2006	9.7	+3.2

Source: NASRA (2008).

takes at least a year or two for these changes to be reflected in the actuarial rates. This delay is due to slow reporting and the active methods in place to moderate such swings. In fiscal 2000, the S&P 500 index rose 5 percent, and then it fell dramatically in fiscals 2001 (16%) and 2002 (19%). Such performance contributed to a rapid decline in public plan funding ratios and, subsequently, to the concomitant increases in employer contribution rates. The mean employer rate increases for fiscals 2003 and 2004 were a sizable 14.7 percent and 29.5 percent, respectively (NASRA 2008). For most governmental units such increases represented painful budget hits, underscoring the desire for rate stability.

It may be argued that recent contribution rate volatility is the unintended side effect of the pursuit of higher return-higher risk asset allocation strategies that have evolved over the last two decades. When public pension portfolios were more conservative and consisted largely of fixed income instruments, rate volatility was not a major issue. The more recent, equity-oriented portfolios have increased asset and rate volatility, but they have also added tens of billions of dollars of investment income which would not have been earned under the more conservative strategies. Without that income, funding shortfalls would have required higher contributions, the other revenue source. On a net basis, public pension systems are ahead of the game financially but in exchange they have had to manage wider rate swings. It is unlikely that a switch to a significantly lower investment return policy in return for reduced rate volatility would be widely popular. The resultant loss of income and the negative effect such a change would have on the calculation of plan liabilities and average contributions would be a very high price to pay.

Strategies to modulate rate volatility

Large changes in public pension asset values from investment income variability and their effect on funded ratios must be held responsible for a large part of contribution rate swings over the last 10 years. Asset changes are much more volatile today compared to liability increases which have a history of more predictable growth. Asset peaks and valleys translated into advances and declines in funding ratios ahead of corresponding changes to contribution rates. Most US public funds use some kind of an actuarial smoothing process whereby gains or losses are spread over various periods, generally three to five years, without which methods the recent rate change experience would have been even more volatile. However, existing controls proved to be largely inadequate to the task of reining in contribution rate increases, in most cases.

Asset Valuation. In response to significant changes in employer contribution rates, the actuarial staff of the California Public Employees Retirement System (CalPERS), the largest US public pension fund with assets of almost $250 billion, instituted a study of this issue earlier in the decade (Seeling 2008). The objectives of the asset smoothing study included finding the best method which, at the same time, would: minimize the negative impact on the plans' funded status, minimize volatility in employers' contributions, and minimize average future employer contributions. Based on this study, the CalPERS board adopted a new set of policies to address the problem which reduced employer rate volatility by at least 50 percent. These new policies included the spreading of asset gains or losses over 15 years compared to the prior policy of three years. The system also changed the corridor for the actuarial value of assets to a minimum of 80 percent of market value and a maximum of 120 percent compared to the previous corridor of 90 to 110 percent, respectively. Employers who have a funded status of more than 100 percent would now have to make a minimum contribution of the plan's normal cost less a 30-year amortization, whereas under the earlier policies there was no minimum contribution.

The effect that these recommended changes would have on the employer rates for one class of CalPERS employees, school employees, can be seen in Figure 5-2 (see CalPERS 2005). Actual employer rates (round data points) declined sharply after fiscal 1998 and were at 0 percent for four straight fiscal years—1999–2002—and then began a rapid rise. Normal cost (dotted line) increased in fiscal 2002 reflecting the effectiveness of benefit increases. Giving effect to the recommended smoothing methods (triangular data points)—assuming the recommended changes were implemented 10 years earlier—would yield employer rate changes with the same general trends but not as sharp. Note that there would be at least some annual contributions in each year under the proposed new methods.

The 2008 issue paper on smoothing policies by CalPERS' Chief Actuary Ron Seeling provided an update on the topic. He stated that '... about 75 percent of all public agency plans experienced an employer rate change of less than 1 percent of pay between 2005–2006 and 2006–2007. The remaining 25 percent of plans included those that improved benefits and had a planned change in employer rate' (Seeling 2008: 9).

Liability Increases and Employer Rates. While asset changes have been the major factor in contribution volatility of late, increasing liabilities cannot be overlooked as another significant component. In 2008, CalPERS stated that about 80 percent of the decline in its funded status earlier in the decade was the result of the decline in asset values and 20 percent from benefit increases. Any increase in liabilities above assumed amounts (actuarial losses) would put upward pressure on rates. Benefit increases

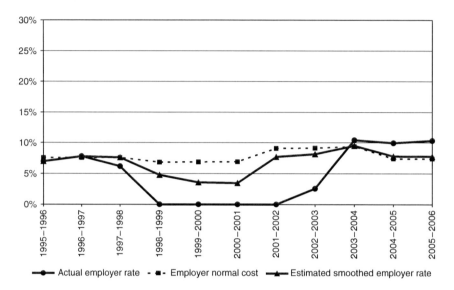

Figure 5-2 Estimated impact of recommended method as if implemented 10 years ago. *Note:* Actual employer contribution rates versus estimated rates under recommended rate stabilization method: schools. *Source:* GALPERS (2005).

have historically been a factor driving this disparity, but certain uncontrollable factors have also been pushing up liabilities in recent years. These factors include plan experience which differs from the expected, including demographic changes such as members living longer. Demographic factors can result in sizable additions to liabilities and may be ongoing (not just one-time). Furthermore, changes to actuarial assumptions can boost liabilities. Any decrease in the investment return assumption would increase liabilities, for example, and recent trends have seen public funds lowering their investment return assumption more than raising it.

Employer contribution rates go up when pension benefits rise (all other things equal), adding to asset change-related rate pressures. Too often benefits have been enhanced without fully vetting the long-term consequences of such a move. Part of the problem of benefit increases is that there is frequently a time period disconnect between the current administration granting the increase, and the future administrations and taxpayers to be charged with the fulfillment of these promises. This may be viewed as the shifting responsibility for benefit enhancements from one group to another. Further, not having a long-term plan for identifying the new revenue source to cover the increased costs in later years places this strategy in the same category as unfunded mandates: requiring funds to be used for a specific purpose in the future but with no solid plan to pay for it. New sources for financing new pension benefits are rarely identified, in practice.

Another problem is that pension benefit enhancements have often been made when other alternatives were not then economically feasible. For example, benefits may be increased when management believes its labor's compensation is below where it should be but the budget cannot absorb salary increases at that time. The thought (or hope) is that, by the time that higher contribution rates are required, the government's financial position will have improved to accommodate these increased costs. Misconceptions related to pension funding levels have also led to benefit increases and added to employer rate pressures. This situation can occur when a pension system has a funded ratio of more than 100 percent and is perceived to be 'over-funded' or to have 'excess assets,' two unfortunate terms. In the late-1990s some public pension plans with funding ratios exceeding 100 percent came under pressure to increase benefits based on the fallacy that the assets exceeding accrued liabilities were no longer required by the system and could be allocated to plan members. The investment losses in 2001 and 2002 brought home the fact that the so-called excess funds were actually needed to maintain sound funding levels. Increasing benefits based solely on a point-in-time overfunded position should be strongly discouraged.

Checks on Benefit/Liability Increases. Granting new benefits without fully vetting the ramifications is a potential problem that some governments have sought to correct. For example, the state of Georgia has a constitutional requirement which requires 'actuarial soundness' in pension systems, as follows: 'It shall be the duty of the General Assembly to enact legislation to define funding standards which will assure the actuarial soundness of any retirement or pension system supported wholly or partially from public funds and to control legislative procedures so that no bill or resolution creating or amending any such retirement or pension system shall be passed by the General Assembly without concurrent provisions for funding in accordance with the defined funding standards' (Georgia State Constitution Article III Section X Paragraph V). Georgia state statutes require a minimum period of one year between the introduction of any retirement bill which would have a fiscal impact and its effectiveness. This provision allows for a reasonable amount of time to examine the ramifications of a proposal, preventing changes from being rushed through a busy session. Further, an actuarial investigation must be performed to fully highlight the economics of each proposal. Too often benefits in other jurisdictions are enhanced without adequate study of the full, long-term effects on costs. Before a benefit change bill in Georgia can become effective, it must be concurrently funded.

Another method used to contain benefit (and rate) increases has been adopted by San Francisco. This city requires that any proposed benefit changes must be approved by voters. This feature carries the implicit understanding that voters, as taxpayers, hold the ultimate responsibility for paying any increased pension costs in employer rates resulting from benefit improvements. Therefore, at least some portion of the citizens on the hook for paying increased contributions must agree to do so. San Francisco's historically strong funded ratio may, at least in part, be attributed to this protective mechanism.

Decreasing Volatility Through Rate Floors. As we have seen, strict implementation of actuarial recommendations can still result in employer rate volatility. For instance, many employers were pleased in the 1990s when their annual actuarial valuations reported that their Annual Required Contribution was in fact zero, due largely to the above average investment return climate. In response, some systems have decided to override the actuarially determined rate when it produces a low or zero contribution result, so as to ease potential contribution shock in the future (the experience of fiscals 2003 and 2004). New York State offers an example. In May 2003, Governor George E. Pataki signed into law a bill requiring the state and local sponsors to make a minimum contribution of 4.5 percent of payroll into the state pension system. At the time of the law's passage, the State Comptroller estimated that, had the bill been implemented in 1998, an additional $4.8 billion in employer contributions would have been collected which would have resulted in a reduction in fiscal 2004 rates by 2 percentage points.

Automatic Stability: Fixed Rates. Strategies that mitigate rate volatility must include those that outright restrict rate changes. An illustration of this would be establishing a set contribution rate which may not be changed without legislative action. A by-product of such an approach, however, is that if rates cannot be raised to offset actuarial losses, then funding status may suffer. For example, California State Teachers' Retirement System (CalSTRS) Defined Benefit Program has statutory contribution rates for members (6% of earnings) and employers (8.25%). In addition, the state as a non-employer contributor makes a payment (3.3% in 2006), resulting in a total contribution rate of about 17.6 percent. A presentation to the CalSTRS board in 2006 found that the unfunded actuarial obligation for the DB program as of 2005, was $20.3 billion and did not amortize over any time period (CalSTRS 2006). To achieve full funding, the program would have to attain the equivalent of an increase of 3.753 percent of salaries over 30 years. Earlier, in December 2005, CalSTRS' staff had presented the board with 13 options to address the funding shortfall, including certain changes to benefits, increases in contributions, the sale of pension obligation bonds, and the extension of the amortization period for the unfunded obligation. Clearly, the fixing of the contribution rate does not assure funding stability.

Conclusion

Contribution rate volatility is a major concern for public sector DB plans. Rates have increased rapidly in recent years due to a number of factors including significant investment losses, benefit increases, and demographic changes, leaving managers with little time to adapt. As traditional smooth-ing techniques have not held rates in check, planners have explored, and some have adopted, new strategies to help ease rate swings. These include the extension of period over which asset gains and losses are spread (changed from 3 to 15 years in CalPERS's case) and the implementation of minimum rates (4.5% of payroll in New York State). Others have con-trolled liability growth by keeping close checks on benefit changes (Georgia requires an actuarial valuation to fully vet costs and San Francisco requires voter approval). No one strategy is a perfect fit for all plans, but financial officers looking for rate volatility solutions can benefit from the experience of those that have made changes in the past.

In spite of the efforts to reduce DB plan contribution rate volatility, some volatility will remain as long as US public pension fund asset allo-cation strategies continue to emphasize the higher-risk, equity asset classes, which include greater volatility by definition. It is unclear as to how far the principal stakeholders in these systems, including members, employ-ers, taxpayers, and the pension funds themselves, will move down the scale toward a less risky investment profile in exchange for a more stable rate environment. The costs of reduced rate volatility under this scenario include lower investment returns and higher average rates.

References

Barrett, Katherine and Richard Greene (2007). *Promises with a Price, Public Sector Retirement Benefits.* Pew Center on the States. Washington, DC: Pew Charitable Trusts.

Brainard, Keith (2008). *Employer Contributions Compilation, 2008.* Georgetown, TX: National Association of State Retirement Administrators.

California Government Code, § 31581.

California Public Employees' Retirement System (CalPERS) (2005). 'CalPERS Rate Stabilization Study.' April. Sacramento, CA: California Public Employees' Retirement System.

California State Teachers' Retirement System (CalSTRS) (2006). '*Strategic Packages for Addressing Unfunded Actuarial Obligation,*' September 8. Sacramento, CA: California State Teachers' Retirement System.

Georgia State Constitution, Article III § X, ¶V.

National Association of State Retirement Administrators (NASRA) (2008). 'Employer Contributions Compilation, 2008.' Washington, DC: NASRA.

Public Pension Coordinating Council (PPCC) (1993). *1993 Survey of State and Local Government Employee Retirement Systems.* Washington, DC: NASRA.

Public Pension Coordinating Council (PPCC) (2001). *2001 Survey of State and Local Government Employee Retirement Systems.* Washington, DC: NASRA.

Seeling, Ron (2008). *Issue Paper: Governmental Employer Funding of Defined Benefit Plans and CalPERS Employer Rate Smoothing Policies.* California Public Employees' Retirement System Chief Actuary. Sacramento, CA: California Public Employees' Retirement System Post-Employment Benefits Commission, February 20.

Chapter 6

Benefit Cost Comparisons Between State and Local Governments and Private Industry Employers

Ken McDonnell

It is often argued that compensation patterns for public sector employees are higher than in the private sector. This chapter examines some of the reasons for the observed differences in total compensation costs between US state and local government employers and private industry employers. We examine compensation costs by industry, occupation, union status, and employee benefit participation.

The evidence seems to be broadly supportive of the general point. For instance, overall total compensation costs were 51.4 percent higher among state and local government employers ($39.50 per hour worked in 2007) than among private industry employers ($26.09 per hour worked in 2007); see Tables 6-1 and 6-2. Total compensation costs consist of two major categories: wages and salaries, and employee benefits. For both of these categories, state and local government employer costs were higher than those of private industry employers: 42.6 percent higher for wages and salaries, and 72.8 percent higher for employee benefits.

Changes over time

Participation Rates. From 1998 to 2007 there was very little change in participation rates among full-time employees in state and local governments. In 1998, 86 percent of full-time employees participated in health insurance. By 2007, this percentage had declined but only slightly to 82 percent; see Table 6-2. For other insurance benefits such as life and disability, participation rates increased in a range of 2 to 5 percentage points. Participation among full-time employees in retirement/savings plans showed little change from 98 percent in 1998 to 95 percent in 2007. Participation increased for full-time employees in defined contribution (DC) plans from 14 percent in 1998 to 21 percent in 2007 while it declined but only slightly in defined benefit (DB) plans, from 90 percent in 1998 to 88 percent in

TABLE 6-1 Employer costs for employee compensation[a] and percentage of full-time employees participating[b] in employee benefit programs: state and local governments: 1998 and 2007

Employee Benefit Program[b]	1998			2007		
	Total Compensation Costs ($/hour)	% of Total Compensation Costs	% Participation	Total Compensation Costs ($/hour)	% of Total Compensation Costs	% Participation
Total compensation costs	27.28	100.0	c	39.50	100.0	c
Wages and salaries	19.19	70.3	c	26.26	66.5	c
Total benefits	8.10	29.7	c	13.24	33.5	c
Paid leave	2.11	7.7	c	3.07	7.8	c
Vacations	0.72	2.6	67	1.08	2.7	69
Holidays	0.69	2.5	73	0.99	2.5	76
Sick	0.53	1.9	96	0.76	1.9	95
Other	0.16	0.6	c	0.24	0.6	c
Supplemental pay	0.23	0.8	c	0.35	0.9	c
Overtime and premium[d]	0.11	0.4	c	0.18	0.4	c
Shift differentials	0.05	0.2	c	0.07	0.2	c
Nonproduction bonuses	0.07	0.3	33	0.10	0.3	33
Insurance	2.15	7.9	c	4.50	11.4	c
Life	0.05	0.2	86	0.07	0.2	88
Health	2.05	7.5	86	4.35	11.0	82
Short-term disability	0.02	0.1	20	0.03	0.1	25
Long-term disability	0.03	0.1	34	0.04	0.1	38

Retirement and savings	1.94	7.1	98	3.04	7.7	95
Defined benefit	1.80	6.6	90	2.73	6.9	88
Defined contribution	0.14	0.5	14	0.31	0.8	21
Legally required benefits	1.63	6.0	c	2.29	5.8	c
Social Security and Medicare	1.28	4.7	c	1.75	4.4	c
OASDI[e]	1.00	3.7	c	1.34	3.4	c
Medicare	0.28	1.0	c	0.41	1.0	c
Federal unemployment insurance	f	g	c	f	g	c
State unemployment insurance	0.04	0.1	c	0.05	0.1	c
Workers' compensation	0.30	1.1	c	0.49	1.2	c

Notes: Because of rounding, sums of individual items may not equal totals.

[a] Data are representative of all employees and includes all employers whether the employer offers a type of benefit or not.

[b] Includes workers covered but not yet participating due to minimum service requirements. Does not include workers offered but not electing contributory benefits.

[c] Data not available.

[d] Includes premium pay for work in addition to the regular work schedule (such as overtime, weekends, and holidays).

[e] Stands for Old-Age, Survivors, and Disability Insurance.

[f] Cost per hour worked is $0.01 or less.

[g] Less than 0.05 percent.

Source: US Department of Labor (1998, 2007a, 2000, 2008).

TABLE 6-2 Employer costs for employee compensation[a] and percentage of full-time employees participating[b] in employee benefit programs: private industry

Employee Benefit Program[b]	Total Compensation Costs ($/hour) (1997)	% of Total Compensation Costs (1997)	% Participation (1996/97)	Total Compensation Costs ($/hour) (2007)	% of Total Compensation Costs (2007)	% Participation (2007)
Total compensation costs	17.97	100.0	c	26.09	100.0	c
Wages and salaries	13.04	72.5	c	18.42	70.6	c
Total benefits	4.94	27.5	c	7.66	29.4	c
Paid leave	1.14	6.3	c	1.76	6.8	c
Vacations	0.57	3.2	90	0.90	3.5	90
Holidays	0.39	2.2	84	0.58	2.2	88
Sick	0.13	0.7	53	0.22	0.8	68
Other	0.05	0.3	c	0.06	0.2	c
Supplemental pay	0.51	2.9	c	0.78	3.0	c
Overtime and premium[d]	0.21	1.1	c	0.27	1.0	c
Shift differentials	0.05	0.3	c	0.07	0.3	c
Nonproduction bonuses	0.26	1.4	43	0.44	1.7	52
Insurance	1.09	6.1	c	1.99	7.6	c
Life	0.05	0.3	74	0.04	0.2	69
Health	0.99	5.5	70	1.85	7.1	64
Short-term disability	0.03	0.2	42	0.05	0.2	45
Long-term disability	0.02	0.1	32	0.04	0.1	37
Retirement and savings	0.55	3.0	62	0.92	3.5	60
Defined benefit	0.26	1.4	32	0.43	1.7	23
Defined contribution	0.29	1.6	47	0.49	1.9	50

Legally required benefits	1.62	9.0	c	c	2.21	8.5	c	c
Social Security and Medicare	1.08	6.0	c	c	1.55	5.9	c	c
OASDI[e]	0.87	4.8	c	c	1.24	4.8	c	c
Medicare	0.21	1.2	c	c	0.31	1.2	c	c
Federal unemployment insurance	0.03	0.2	c	c	0.03	0.1	c	c
State unemployment insurance	0.12	0.6	c	c	0.16	0.6	c	c
Workers' compensation	0.39	2.2	c	c	0.48	1.8	c	c

Notes: Because of rounding, sums of individual items may not equal totals.

[a] Data representative of all employees and includes all employers whether the employer offers a type of benefit or not.

[b] Includes workers covered but not yet participating due to minimum service requirements. Does not include workers offered but not electing contributory benefits.

[c] Data not available.

[d] Includes premium pay for work in addition to the regular work schedule (such as overtime, weekends, and holidays).

[e] Stands for Old-Age, Survivors, and Disability Insurance.

[f] Cost per hour worked is $0.01 or less.

[g] Less than 0.05 percent.

Source: US Department of Labor (1997, 2007a, 1999a, 1999b, 2007c).

2007. For leave benefits, there was a modest increase in participation rates in the range of 1 to 3 percent.

Participation rates among full-time employees in private industry showed an increase in leave benefits, particularly in paid sick leave plans which increased from 53 percent of full-time employees in 1996/97 to 68 percent by 2007; see Table 6-2.[1] Participation in health insurance declined from 70 percent in 1996/97 to 64 percent in 2007 and in life insurance from 74 percent to 69 percent. For disability insurance, both short-term and long-term, participation rates increased in a range of 3 to 5 percent. Among retirement/savings plan participation the overall percentage change was slight, from 62 percent in 1996/97 to 60 percent in 2007, yet the participation rate change by plan type was significant, particularly in DB plans which experienced a decline of 9 percentage points from 32 percent in 1996/97 to 23 percent in 2007.

Benefit Costs. For both state and local governments and private industry, benefit costs increased as a percentage of total compensation with the percentage increase for state and local governments greater. From March 1998 through September 2007 benefit costs, as a percentage of total compensation among state and local governments, increased from 29.7 percent to 33.5 percent while in private industry benefit costs increased from 27.5 percent to 29.4 percent (from March 1997 through September 2007; see Tables 6-1 and 6-2). For both employer types, the main driver in benefit cost increases was health benefits. For state and local governments, health benefits increased from 7.5 percent of total compensation to 11.0 percent, from March 1998 through September 2007 while for private industry health benefits increased from 5.5 percent of total compensation to 7.1 percent from March 1997 through September 2007.

Work force comparisons

A primary explanation for differences in total compensation costs between state and local government employers and private industry employers is that of their respective work forces differences in compensation. This is evident from a comparison of data arrayed by industry and occupation group.[2]

Industry Groups. State and local government workers are highly concentrated in the education sector. This grouping includes teachers and university professors, two categories of employees with high unionization rates and high compensation costs. Table 6-3 shows that 52.7 percent of all state and local government employees were employed in this sector, in 2007, and total compensation costs for the education sector were $42.48 per hour worked. By contrast, the private industry group with the largest

TABLE 6-3 Employment and total compensation costs, by industry group and union membership, state and local governments and private sector: 2007

	State and Local Government			Private Sector	
	Employment	Total Compensation Costs ($/hours)		Employment	Total Compensation Costs ($/hours)
Total	19.39 million	39.50	Total	116.35 million	26.09
Education	52.7%	42.48	Construction	6.7%	29.39
Hospitals	5.4	33.62	Manufacturing	12.1	30.82
General administration	31.1	36.53	Trade, transportation, and utilities	22.7	22.41
Local government utilities	1.2	a	Information	2.6	39.11
Local government transportation	1.3	a	Financial activities	7.2	34.95
Other	8.2	a	Services	47.9	24.91
			Professional and business services	15.6	30.44
			Education and health services	15.8	27.55
			Leisure and hospitality services	11.9	11.59
			Other services	4.7	21.87
Members of a Union[b]	36.2%	45.00	Members of a Union[b]	7.4%	35.92
Non-Union Workers[b]	63.8	34.50	Non-Union Workers[b]	92.6	24.94

a Data not available.
b Data for 2006.

Source: Department of Labor (2007a, 2007b), U.S. Department of Commerce (2008), and unpublished data from the U.S. Department of Labor.

number of workers was services, accounting for 47.9 percent of all private-sector workers. Here total compensation costs for services were $24.91 per hour worked.

Another factor affecting total compensation costs is union membership. Union presence in an industry tends to be positively correlated with total compensation costs and benefit participation. Table 6-3 shows that 7.4 percent of private industry workers were members of a union in 2006, compared with 36.2 percent of workers in state and local governments. Among private industry employers total compensation costs for unionized workers were $35.92 per hour worked compared with $24.94 per hour worked for non-unionized workers in 2007.

Occupation Groups. The concentration of occupations among state and local government employers is also quite different from private industry employers. Table 6-4 shows that a large percentage of state and local government employees in 2007 were concentrated in teachers (27.0%) and in service occupations (31.8%). Teachers had the highest total compensation costs among state and local government employers, $53.39 per hour in 2007. By comparison, the largest percentage of private industry workers was among sales and office occupations (27.3%) and service occupations (25.7%) where compensation costs were low, $20.86 per hour worked for sales and office and $13.00 per hour worked for service workers.

The largest gap in compensation costs between state and local government and private industry workers was among service occupations. The total compensation costs for these workers in state and local governments were $30.74 per hour in 2007 compared with $13.00 per hour in the private sector. This difference is due primarily to the type of occupations in the services category. Among state and local governments, the US Department of Labor Bureau of Labor Statistics (BLS) categorizes police and firefighters among the service occupations. Police and firefighters have a high participation rate in a DB plan. Among private industry employers, occupations such as waiters/waitresses and cleaning and building services functions are categorized as service occupations, and these jobs traditionally have low wages.

Public–Private differences in employee benefit costs

As noted earlier, benefit costs of state and local government employers were 72.8 percent higher than those of private industry employers in 2007. Next we review factors contributing to this difference.

Benefit Costs. The two most important voluntary benefit programs provided by employers are health insurance and a retirement/savings plan. Important cost disparities exist for these two benefits comparing state and

TABLE 6-4 Employment and total compensation costs in state and local governments and private sector by occupation group, ages 16 and older

	State and Local Governments		Private Sector	
	Employment (2006)	Total Compensation Costs ($/hour) (2007)	Employment (2006)	Total Compensation Costs ($/hour) (2007)
Total	18.48 million	39.50	118.35 million	26.09
Management, professional and related	13.4%	48.35	18.0%	46.22
Professional and related	7.2	47.95	9.3	43.21
Teachers[a]	27.0	53.39	2.2	39.28
Sales and office	14.1	27.00	27.3	20.86
Service	31.8	30.74	25.7	13.00
Natural resources, construction, and maintenance	5.3	34.34	18.8	29.57
Production, transportation, and material moving	3.1	30.86	6.9	22.64

[a] Includes postsecondary teachers; primary, secondary, and special education teachers, and other teachers and instructors.

Sources: Author's tabulations from the Current Population Survey March 2007 Supplement, EBRI (2007) and unpublished data from the U.S. Department of Labor.

local government employers, and private industry employers. Tables 6-1 and 6-2 indicate the average cost for health insurance benefits for state and local government employers was $4.35 per hour, compared with $1.85 per hour for private industry employers, a difference of 235 percent.

The difference is even larger for retirement/savings plans, which benefits cost state and local government employers $3.04 per hour worked versus $0.92 per hour worked for private-sector employers, a difference of 330 percent. One reason for this divergence is that DB retirement plans are more prevalent among state and local governments than they are in private industry.

Participation. Another reason for the observed difference in benefit costs is that state and local government employees are more likely to participate in employee benefit programs than are their private industry counterparts. Health insurance participation rates among full-time employees in state and local governments were significantly higher than rates among full-time employees in private industry as is depicted in Tables 6-1 and 6-2.

The disparity is larger for retirement and savings plans. Virtually all full-time employees in state and local governments participated in some type of retirement/savings plan, versus about 60 percent of full-time employees in private industry. Further, the majority of public sector workers have a DB plan and these DB plans tend to be more expensive to provide than DC plans. The administrative burdens and costs of operating DB plans is often cited by corporate plan sponsors as a major disincentive to operating this type of retirement plan (VanDerhei and Copeland 2001).

Conclusion

Observed differences in compensation costs between public and private-sector employers are summarized. One explanation for these differences distinctions has to do with the different concentrations of workers by industry and occupation. Another relates to the composition of the benefit package and benefit participation rates. State and local government retirement and health insurance costs are two to three times those of private employers.

Data Appendix

The datasets used in this study include the following:

For compensation costs: US Department of Labor (DOL) (1997). *Employer Costs for Employee Compensation-March 1997*. Washington, DC: Bureau of Labor Statistics; US Department of Labor (DOL) (1998). *Employer Costs for Employee Compensation-March 1998*. Washington, DC: Bureau of Labor Statistics; and US Department of Labor (DOL) (2007a). *Employer Costs for Employee Compensation-September 2007*. Washington, DC: Bureau of Labor Statistics.

For benefit participation private industry: US Department of Labor (DOL) (1999a). *Employee Benefits in Medium and Large Private Establishments, 1997*. Washington, DC: Bureau of Labor Statistics; US Department of Labor (DOL) (1999b). *Employee Benefits in Small Private Establishments, 1996*. Washington, DC: Bureau of Labor Statistics; and US Department of Labor (DOL) (2007c). *National Compensation Survey: Employee Benefits in Private*

Industry in the United States, March 2007. Washington, DC: Bureau of Labor Statistics.

For benefit participation state and local governments: US Department of Labor (DOL) (2000). *Employee Benefits in State and Local Governments, 1998.* Washington, DC: Bureau of Labor Statistics; and US Department of Labor (DOL) (2008). *National Compensation Survey: Employee Benefits in State and Local Governments in the United States, September 2007.* Washington, DC: Bureau of Labor Statistics.

For employment by industry: US Department of Labor (DOL) (2007*b*). *Employment and Earnings, December 2007,* 54(12). Washington, DC: Bureau of Labor Statistics.

For employment by occupation: Employee Benefit Research Institute (EBRI) (2007). *EBRI Estimates from the Current Population Survey, March 2007 Supplement.* Washington, DC: Employee Benefit Research Institute.

Notes

[1] To obtain an accurate comparison of benefit participation among full-time employees in private industry, the author combined data from the BLS Survey on Small Private Establishments with the BLS Survey on Medium and Large Private Establishments. This made the comparison with the 2007 data more accurate because the 2007 is representative of small, medium, and large private establishments. Data in the 2007 Bulletin are reported for full-time employees but not for full-time employees by firm size.

[2] Readers should be aware that the term 'service' is not used in the same way for the industry groupings and occupation groupings: that is, not all service workers are employed in the service industries.

References

Employee Benefit Research Institute (EBRI) (2007). *EBRI Estimates from the Current Population Survey, March 2007 Supplement.* Washington, DC: Employee Benefit Research Institute.

US Department of Commerce (2008). *Statistical Abstract of the United States, 2008.* Bureau of the Census. Washington, DC: US Government Printing Office.

US Department of Labor (DOL) (1997). *Employer Costs for Employee Compensation-March 1997.* Washington, DC: Bureau of Labor Statistics.

—— (1998). *Employer Costs for Employee Compensation-March 1998.* Washington, DC: Bureau of Labor Statistics.

—— (1999*a*). *Employee Benefits in Medium and Large Private Establishments, 1997.* Washington, DC: Bureau of Labor Statistics.

—— (1999*b*). *Employee Benefits in Small Private Establishments, 1996.* Washington, DC: Bureau of Labor Statistics.

US Department of Labor (DOL) (2000). *Employee Benefits in State and Local Governments, 1998.* Washington, DC: Bureau of Labor Statistics.

—— (2007*a*). *Employer Costs for Employee Compensation-September 2007.* Washington, DC: Bureau of Labor Statistics.

—— (2007*b*). *Employment and Earnings, December 2007*, 54(12). Washington, DC: Bureau of Labor Statistics.

—— (2007*c*). *National Compensation Survey: Employee Benefits in Private Industry in the United States, March 2007.* Washington, DC: Bureau of Labor Statistics.

—— (2008). *National Compensation Survey: Employee Benefits in State and Local Governments in the United States, September 2007.* Washington, DC: Bureau of Labor Statistics.

VanDerhei, Jack and Craig Copeland (2001). 'The Changing Face of Private Retirement Plans.' *EBRI Issue Brief* no. 232. Washington, DC: Employee Benefit Research Institute.

Chapter 7

Administrative Costs of State Defined
Benefit and Defined Contribution Systems

Edwin C. Hustead

In the private sector, the relative administrative costs of defined benefit (DB) and defined contribution (DC) systems can have a major impact on the decision to select one plan over the other. This chapter examines the administrative costs of the two types of plans in the public sector and their potential impact on the type of plan selected by a public sector employer. We begin with a comparison of DB and DC administrative expenses for the Federal government and for seven state-wide plans. We then discuss the impact that administrative expenses might have on the choice of a plan and other reasons that might impact on a choice between the two types of plans.

Prior studies

My previous paper (Hustead 1998) on administrative expenses in private sector pensions showed that annual administrative expenses for DB plans (3.1% of payroll) were twice those of DC plans (1.4% of payroll) for employers with only 15 employees. This was one of several reasons that might lead small employers to adopt a DC plan instead of a DB plan. The DC advantage in administrative expenses also held for large private sector employers but the difference was smaller. For instance, for employers with 10,000 employees, the administrative expenses for DB plans were 0.23 percent of payroll compared to 0.16 percent for the same size DC plans. Such a relatively small difference as a percentage of payroll would not have been a major factor in deciding between a DB and a DC plan. For comparison with measures used in this chapter, it is reasonable to consider the administrative expenses of large private sector plans to be around 2 percent of plan contributions for employers of 10,000 employees because private sector plan contributions are usually less than 10 percent of payroll.

Most state-wide public plans include many more than 10,000 employees and almost all public employers already have a DB plan, so the impact of administrative expenses in the public sector is much different. Public employers tend to confront one of two questions when considering adoption of a DC plan. First, and by far the most common, is whether to supplement the pre-existing DB plan with a DC plan. Second, some employers consider whether to replace the DB plan with a DC plan. As a practical matter, this second consideration tends to be limited to future employees and current employees who elect the DC plan.

Administrative costs of state and Federal retirement plans

This chapter uses two measures of administrative expenses. One is as a percentage of average plan assets, and the other is as a percentage of employee and employer contributions. Table 7-1 shows the amount of administrative expenses and the two measures for seven states that have both a DC and a DB plan. Two measures are used because one or the other can be problematic in some situations. Most importantly, the employer contribution to a DB plan can fluctuate widely in response to economic conditions. These seven states, and most other states, have a separate agency that administers the pension plans. The data were derived from the most recent audited financial statements posted on the Web sites of the administering agency. Table 7-1 is followed by a brief summary of the plans available in each state. This includes information on the name of the report, fiscal year, and administrating agency.

We summarize the state plan structures as follows:

- The Florida Retirement System administers two DB plans for most employees. Employees have been offered a DC plan as an alternative to the DB plans since 2002. There are also DC plans for specific groups. As of 2007, there were 680,000 employees in the primary DB plan and 82,000 members in the DC plans. Financial results are for the fiscal year ending June 30, 2007.
- The Ohio Public Employees Retirement Systems has offered two alternatives to the traditional DB plan since 2003; one of these is a DC plan and the other is a combined DB/DC plan. As of 2006, 369,000 employees were in the traditional DB plan, 5,600 in the DC plan, and 6,100 in the combined DB/DC plan. Data are for the year ending December 31, 2006. Public employees in Oregon are in a DB plan administered by the Oregon Public Employees Retirement System. Since 2004, the employee contributions have been deposited in a DC plan so all members are in both a DB and a DC plan. Data are for the year ending June 30, 2007.
- Colorado employees are covered by a DB plan and can make voluntary contributions to a DC plan. The plan is administered by the Colorado

TABLE 7-1 Annual administrative expenses for state retirement plans as a percentage of contributions and assets

State and type of plan	Administrative Expenses (millions of dollars)	Administrative Expenses as a Percentage of	
		Employee/employer contributions in year	Average Assets
Florida DB	16.1	0.53	0.01
Florida DC	0.15	0.07	N/A
Ohio DB	44.9	2.07	0.07
Ohio DB/DC	4.5	12.86	4.84
Ohio DC	3.9	11.94	5.51
Oregon DB	35.6	5.83	0.06
Oregon DC	7.3	1.66	0.16
Colorado DB	20.7	2.02	0.06
Colorado DC	4.3	2.33	0.34
Montana DB	2.9	0.64	0.09
Montana DC	0.4	1.87	0.16
North Dakota DB	1.0	2.42	0.10
North Dakota DC	0.01	0.78	0.26
West Virginia DB	3.0	0.19	0.10
West Virginia DC	2.2	2.55	0.26

Sources: Author's computations from data provided to the author by the Florida Retirement System, Ohio Public Employees Retirement Systems, Oregon Public Employees Retirement System, Colorado Public Employees' Retirement Association, Montana Public Employees' Retirement Board, North Dakota Public Employees Retirement System, and the West Virginia Consolidated Public Retirement Board.

Public Employees' Retirement Association and the data are for the year ending December 31, 2005.

- Montana has a traditional DB plan and an optional DC plan. Employees hired after 2002 have had the option of joining either plan. The plan is administered by the Public Employees' Retirement Board. Data are for the year ending June 30, 2006.
- The North Dakota Public Employees Retirement System began as a DC plan in 1966 and was changed to a DB plan in 1977. An optional DC plan was established in 2000 for some employees. Data are for the year ending June 30, 2006.
- Teachers in West Virginia hired before July 1, 1991 are covered by a DB plan and those hired after that date are covered by a DC plan. As of June 30, 2004, there were 19,000 teachers in the DB plan and 21,300 in the DC plan. The plans are administered by the West Virginia Consolidated Public Retirement Board and financial data are for the year ending June 30, 2007.

By most of the measures, the DC plan administrative expense percentages are larger than those of the DB plans in Table 7-1. This is partly explained by the fact that the DB plans have been established for a much longer time and are much larger than the DC plans. Some of the differences may also be related to the accounting methods used to allocate administrative costs. In some cases, costs may be based on a detailed functional study of costs. In other cases, rough allocations of line items may be used. For example, it is very unlikely that the functional costs of a free-standing DC plan for North Dakota would be less than $10,000. The cost of DC plans that are added to the responsibilities of an existing agency are undoubtedly much lower than they would be if there was no agency already administering a DB plan.

Table 7-1 also shows that administrative expenses for a large state-wide plan are relatively small. The state-wide DB plans administrative costs are all 0.1 percent or less of assets. DC plan expenses are higher but all of these plans are much smaller than the DB plans in the same state.

Table 7-1 focuses exclusively on state-wide plans. In many states municipal and county plans also participate in the state-wide plans. Large independent city and county plans would be expected to have similar results to the state plans. Smaller independent city and county plans probably have expenses that are much greater as a percentage of assets for both DB and DC plans because of their size.

The Federal Employees Retirement System (FERS), established in 1986, includes both a DB plan and a DC plan. The Federal government set up a separate administrating agency when it established the Thrift Savings Plan (TSP) as part of the new Federal Employees Retirement System to administer the DB plan. The TSP has grown very large over the years and now holds almost $200 billion in assets. Table 7-2 compares the administrative costs of the Federal DB and DC plans.[1] As would be expected, the costs are quite small as percentages of contributions or assets. Administrative costs are somewhat higher for the TSP but the administrative expenses of both plans are less than 0.05 percent of the assets. One reason that the DB plan costs are so low is that the DB funds have to be invested in special issues, so there is no need for the types of investment decisions and costs that are borne by state plans.

Other expenses

Two types of administrative expenses are not included in the tables because they are not readily available. One of these is the administrative expense incurred by the employing agencies in collecting the contributions by the employees, which are then forwarded to the pension plan administrative

Table 7-2 Administrative expenses of Federal plans

	Defined Benefit Plans CSRS/FERS for the year ended September 30, 2006	Defined Contribution Plan Federal Thrift Savings Plan for the year ended December 31, 2006
Administrative expenses in year ($)	142	81
Employer/employee contributions in year ($)	50,300	19,601
Average assets ($)	680,500	189,942
Administrative expenses as a percent of contributions (%)	0.28	0.41
Administrative expenses as percent of average assets (%)	0.02	0.04

Note: CSRS is the Civil Service Retirement System and FERS is the Federal Employees Retirement System. Amounts in millions of US dollars.

Sources: Author's compilation of data from Federal Office of Personnel Management (2007) and Federal Thrift Savings Plan (2008).

agency. Since all of the DB plans in the two tables are contributory, this administrative cost is probably about the same for both types of plans. The other type of expense not included is the charge made by the organizations that invest the DB and DC funds. These charges are usually deducted from the investment earnings. Bauer and Frehen (2008) and French (2008) provide some analysis of the relative administrative expense of public DB and DC expenses.

Organizational structure

Tables 7-1 and 7-2 show that public plan administrative expenses are generally a small percentage of the assets of each of the retirement systems. In general, this is true of both DB and DC plans. This consistently low level can be explained by the administrative organizations of the state retirement funds. Most state retirement plans tend to have several functional areas, including collection of employee contributions, determination of benefits, payment of retiree benefits, investment management, and information technology. Some of the functions are more extensive for DB plans and others for DC plans but the overall size and cost of the agency would be about the same for either a DB or a DC plan.

Since most public plans, including all of those in Tables 7-1 and 7-2, are contributory, there must be a process to collect and track contributions from employees and their agencies. This function is larger for DC plans because of the need to direct the contributions to the appropriate funds and to track and report on those funds. The determination of benefits for separating employees is similar in scope for both DB and DC plans. The individual calculations for retirees are very complex for a DB plan. However, the individual determinations and communication of options is much greater for the DC plans for those who have not reached retirement eligibility. The retiree benefit payment and communication is much greater for the DB plans since the function is not necessary for those employees who remove their funds from the state plans at termination.

The investment operation is greater for DB plans since the office must carefully determine and track investment policy for the funds. However, this is also a major function for DC plans since the office has to select the options and monitor the investment options for employees. The information technology function would be similar in scope and detail for both the DB and DC plans.

Trends in DB/DC plans in the public sector

A report by the National Conference of State Legislators (NCSL 2005) summarized the number and type of state DC plans, and it found that were only three systems that had DC plans as the primary plan for new employees, while none had the DC plan as primary for employees working at the time the DC plan was adopted. The first such plan was for the District of Columbia employees in 1987. This was followed by a change to a DC plan for newly hired West Virginia teachers in 1991 and Michigan state employees in 1997. Six state systems offered a choice of a DB or a DC plan. Four other states direct employee contributions to a DC plan and employer contributions to a DB plan.

There are approximately 100 state-wide plans in the United States. The typical state has a plan for teachers and another for employees. Only three of these plans are primary DC plans and even those continue to maintain a DB plan for employees hired before the adoption of the DC plan. This is in sharp contrast to the private sector where the large majority of plans is DC plans.

Conclusion

If a large private sector employer were to consider putting all employees in either a DC plan or a DB plan, then the employer could anticipate that administrative expenses would be very low relative to plan assets or contributions. Based on the information provided in Tables 7-1 and 7-2, a large state plan of either type would probably have administrative costs of around 0.1 percent of assets per year.

In practice, however, almost all states have existing DB plans, so large public plans are not faced with a choice between the two types of plans. Rather, states are often faced with the choice of whether or not to add a supplemental DC plan to the DB plan or move to a DC plan. The choice is made easier because the administrative costs of the new plan will be small when the function is assigned to the agency that administers the DB plan.

In many states, there have been proposals to completely replace the existing DB plan with a DC plan, at least for new employees. If that were done, there would be a short-term increase in administrative costs to introduce the DC plan, but ultimately the administrative costs would drop to levels near those for a DB-only plan. Since administrative costs are a small percentage of assets or contributions the long-term administrative costs do not affect the decision of whether or not to adopt a DC plan to replace the DB plan. The short-term costs of introducing the plan do have to be considered but even these are only a small part of the total long-term cost of the DC plan.

Perhaps the greatest deterrent to adoption of a DC plan is that it may not be feasible, or sometimes even legal, for a public employer to replace a DB plan by a DC plan for existing employees' future service. Many states including Pennsylvania have a legal prohibition against reducing benefits for existing employees' future service. DC plans distribute benefits differently from DB plans, so even though some employees would receive greater benefits with a DC plan, there would be a class of employees who would receive lower benefits in a DC plan.

In states with a legal prohibition against changing benefits for current employees, it would be expected that the class of employees with lower benefits would succeed in overturning a DC plan for their future service through the courts. In states without such a legal prohibition, there is strong, and usually successful, opposition to changing future benefits for existing employees. This opposition includes employee unions as well as legislators who are often covered by the existing retirement plan.

Private sector employers who have moved from DB to DC plans have often done so because they would achieve immediate and substantial savings. Without the ability to change plans for current employees, that opportunity is generally not open for public sector employees. In fact, moving from a DB plan to a DC plan for public sector employers under these conditions might result in a substantial increase in contributions in the short run.

Notes

[1] Administrative expenses for the Civil Service Retirement System/Federal Employee Retirement System (CSRS/FERS) plan were obtained from the Office of the Actuaries of the Federal Office of Personnel Management. The remaining data in Table 7-2 are derived from annual reports of the CSRS/FERS and the Federal Thrift Savings Plan (TSP) administrators.

References

Bauer, Rob and Rik Frehen (2008). 'The Performance of US Pension Funds.' SSRN Working Paper. Rochester, NY: Social Science Electronic Publishing.

Federal Office of Personnel Management (2007). *Civil Service Retirement and Disability Fund Report for the Fiscal Year ended September 30, 2007*. Washington, DC: Office of Actuaries of the US Office of Personnel Management.

Federal Thrift Savings Plan (2008). 'Statement of Net Assets and Changes in Assets for 2005 and 2006.' Birmingham, AL: The Federal Retirement Thrift Investment Board. www.tsp.gov.

French, Kenneth R. (2008). 'The Cost of Active Investing.' SSRN Working Paper. Rochester, NY: Social Science Electronic Publishing.

Hustead, Edwin C. (1998). 'Trends in Retirement Income Plan Administrative Expenses' in O.S. Mitchell and S. J. Schieber, eds., *Living with Defined Contribution Plans*. Philadelphia, PA: University of Pennsylvania Press, pp. 166–78.

National Conference of State Legislatures (NCSL) (2005). 'Defined Benefit and Defined Contribution Retirement Plans.' Denver, CO: National Conference of State Legislatures. www.ncsl.org/programs/fiscal/defineretire.htm.

Chapter 8
Thinking about Funding Federal Retirement Plans

Toni Hustead

This chapter takes up the question of how to think about retirement plans for Federal employees. In the United States, a Federal retirement plan is one established or maintained by a Federal agency for any of its officers or employees. There are currently almost 34 Federal pension plans covering more than 10 million individual participants including employees, retirees, and survivors. In practice, since more than 97 percent of these members are concentrated in three plans, these are the focus of this chapter (GAO 1996). Two of the three plans which cover over 5 million participants are for Federal civilian employees. The Civil Service Retirement System (CSRS) covers civilian employees who entered service before 1984. The Federal Employees Retirement System (FERS) covers all new hires after 1983, plus employees who elected to transfer from CSRS to FERS during one of the two open seasons. The third plan, covering more than 4 million participants, is the Department of Defense (DoD) Military Retirement System.

A brief history of Federal retirement plan funding

The Employee Retirement Income Security Act (ERISA) of 1974 set minimum funding and reporting standards for corporate or private-sector pension systems. This law requires private firms to fully fund these pension plans by holding investments other than their own securities, to protect employees against the loss of earned benefits if the companies were to go out of business. Public Law 95–595, enacted in 1978, extended most of the reporting requirements of ERISA to Federal retirement plans. That law did not extend the funding and investment requirements of ERISA to Federal plans, because the presumption was and continues to be that the Federal government will not go out of business. In addition, reneging on promised pension benefits to Federal civilian employees (including members of Congress) or military members is not considered a viable possibility. Currently, annual payments to Federal retirees are a small proportion of the overall Federal budget each year. For example, in FY 2007, Federal retirement benefits were $ 0.1 trillion (3.7%) of the $2.7 trillion net Federal outlays (OMB 2007).

Prior to this adoption of the ERISA-like reporting standard, most Federal retirement plans were either not funded, which means they pay benefits when due without any fund accumulations (referred to as 'pay-as-you-go'), or partially funded. For standard reporting purposes under the new law, each plan was required to determine and report to the public its unfunded liability and the annual cost of the benefit accrued by current employees. To determine these costs, most plans used the most common actuarial funding method used by large private employers at that time, the entry-age normal cost method. The reports were ultimately incorporated into the financial statements of the agencies.

These reports became instrumental in educating the public and policymakers on the true cost of Federal civilian and military employees, and they are likely the reason that pay-as-you-go financing was replaced with fully funded mechanisms in the 1980s for some of the larger systems. To fully fund each system, Congress passed legislation that set up unique Federal Trust Funds that annually receive payments to cover the benefits earned during the year as well as annual amortization payments to pay off the unfunded liabilities. The assets of the Trust Funds are invested in Federal securities, so the funds also receive annual investment income. Benefits payments are made out of the fund to plan participants. Hence, these Federal capital assets back the promises made to plan participants. In 1984, the existing Military Retirement System was fully funded. By contrast, the financing of the Civil Service Retirement System has not been changed. Since 1984, nearly all *new* major entitlements for civilian and military employees enacted have included legislative language that fully funds the new benefits. These include the new civilian Federal Employees Retirement System in 1984, new military education benefits for reservists in 1985, a new military retirement plan for those entering service after mid-1986, and a new plan to cover health benefits for military retirees over age 64 in 2001. Under these 'accrual budgeting' arrangements, Federal agencies transfer funds from their own budgets to the relevant Trust Funds equaling the benefits earned in that year, and Treasury is responsible for making unfunded liability payments to the funds as well and interest income payments. Agency budget appropriations include the accrual funds needed to make such transfers, and hence, they reflect a more 'transparent' view of the true cost of each Department's manpower and decisions.

Federal retirement fund assets

Federal retirement assets must be held by law in plan-specific Trust Funds that are invested in special issue US Treasury securities that yield interest comparable to marketable US obligations with similar maturities. Fund managers ensure that there is enough cash in the funds each year to cover benefits, and they invest all excess income over this amount. When securities are redeemed by fund managers to pay benefits, the Treasury either borrows from the public or uses then current tax receipts to cover its security obligation. When funds are moved from one account in the Federal government to another account there are equal and opposite accounting transactions that cancel each other out in the overall Federal financial statement. For example, when an agency transfers cash from its account to the Trust Fund, it is a debit to the agency and a credit to the Trust Fund for an equal amount, and the transactions cancel each other out inside the overall Federal budget. Likewise, when a Trust Fund invests excess cash in Federal securities, it is a debit to the Trust Fund and a credit to the Treasury, and these two transactions cancel each other out inside the overall Federal budget. When the Trust Fund pays benefits to plan participants, there is a debit but no associated credit in the Federal budget. Hence, while Trust Fund balances grow to large levels, the fact that they are 'self-invested' means that the overall Federal budget does not need to have the cash on hand until benefits fall due. This makes the process appear to be only a bookkeeping mechanism, since the end result is that Federal funding does not allow for the transfer of liabilities from future generations of taxpayers to today's taxpayers.

If the US government were to change the Federal Trust Fund investment policy from US Treasury special issue securities to private sector securities, this would result in significant new Federal budget outlays that would directly impact the Federal deficit. For example, at the end of FY 2007, all Federal Trust Fund balances equaled $3.7 trillion, and they are expected to increase by an average of $0.3 trillion a year over the next six years. These numbers are large because they include Social Security and Medicare Trust Funds. Focusing only on civilian and military retirement plans, the Federal Trust Fund balances equaled $0.9 trillion, and are expected to increase by an average of $0.1 trillion annually. Converting these current and/or future fund assets into private assets in the current deficit situation, would mean that the government would have to immediately borrow the money from the public (increasing the deficit), find an uncontroversial portfolio in which to invest these large sums, and then run the risk that the planned return on investment would be insufficient to cover obligations as they fall due. Investing trillions of dollars of Federal funds in the private market would also raise fears of political interference in private corporations or place unwanted mandates on investments.

There are two groups of funds in the unified budget of the Federal government: Trust Funds and Federal Funds. Total Trust Fund outlays resulted in a $248.7 billion surplus in FY 2007, but federal fund outlays had a deficit of $410.7 billion for a combined total unified budget deficit of $162 billion.

The FY 2009 President's Budget stated that the Federal government would only be able to fund benefits in the true sense of the word by increasing saving and investment in the economy as a whole. It went on to state that this could only be accomplished if annual Trust Fund surpluses were not used to reduce the unified budget deficit, and if Federal fund deficits were unchanged. This would reduce Federal borrowing and increase future incomes and economic sources to support benefits, as long as this savings is not accompanied by a reduction in private savings. The FY 2009 budget did not envision this happening anytime soon, as the deficit for that budget year was projected to increase to $407.4 billion despite nearly a $300 billion Trust Fund surplus (OMB 2008).

If only a bookkeeping exercise, why 'fully fund' Federal pension plans?

Though fully funding Federal pension plans is recognized as bookkeeping exercise, the move to accrual budgeting has been embraced by policy-makers, budget experts, and accounting organizations because it makes the cost of personnel transparent. With accrual budgeting, decisions on whether to increase hiring, enhance benefits, or use contractor support must be made with a full recognition of the total cost. For example, if a decision were made to double the size of the military force in FY 2009, the DoD budget would need an additional $17 billion to cover the new retirement accrual obligations in that year alone. If the accrual budgeting of the Military Retirement System were dismantled and replaced with a cash 'pay-as-you go' system, then the DoD would not have had to consider the cost of retirement benefits for the new personnel in its decision or its budget, as they would not show up for another 20 years (DoD 2006).

Several branches of the Federal government have supported the move to transparency. The President's FY 2003 Budget proposed to move all of the remaining Federal pension and retiree health benefits not yet fully funded to an accrual budgeting basis. This would have ensured that the employer's share of the annual cost of all Federal pensions and retiree health benefits would be reflected in the human resource budgets of those agencies where employees worked. The Office of Management and Budget (OMB) Controller stated that it was the right time for such an improvement, given the increased sensitivity to the need for accuracy and transparency in accounting. The Comptroller General of the US and Chair of the Joint Financial Management Improvement Program (JFMIP) also issued a supportive statement on behalf of the JFMIP Principals stating that including these accrual costs in data used for budgetary decision-making would enhance the planning and the evaluation of the cost of operations, and improve consistency, transparency, and accountability for results. Similar statements were issued by the Association of Government Accountants and the American Institute of Certified Public Accountants.

These efforts to improve budgetary reporting were not favored by all. Congress did not pass legislation to enact the Administration's proposal in FY 2003 or in later years. In fact, there were several attempts by the Armed Services Committees to reverse DoD accrual budgeting and to reduce the transparency of the true cost of military manpower, by transferring certain defense accrual costs to the Department of Treasury and spending the resulting excess DoD appropriation on other projects. Such a move would have directly increased the budget deficit by the total accrual amount since it would have increased Federal outlays to the public.

The first Congressional attempt to alter accrual budgeting was successful. In 2003, Congress increased military retirement benefits for certain members receiving monthly Veterans Affairs (VA) disability benefits, and it required the Department of the Treasury to pay the annual marginal accrual increase associated with the new benefits instead of DoD. In FY 2007, for example, this gimmick understated DoD's annual manpower costs by $2.5 billion (4.7% of basic payroll) and increased the deficit by a like amount (DoD 2006). The second Congressional attempt to alter accrual budgeting was enacted in the National Defense Authorization Act for FY 2005. Section 725 of this law eliminated the requirement for DoD to use annual appropriations to pay the accruing cost of post-retirement health care for retirees over age 65, and it also transferred the requirement to the Department of Treasury. However, both the Office of Management and Budget and the Congressional Budget Committees have continued to charge the cost of this legislation against the DoD appropriation, essentially nullifying the intent of the enacted budget change. Without such a united agreement on technical scoring, this law would have caused the deficit to increase by more than $60 billion over five years or required enactment of offsetting reductions of the same magnitude in Federal programs (US Senate 2006).

Two years later, the House Armed Services Committee again included similar language in its version of the Defense Authorization Act for FY 2007, and this time the proposed bill included language that would have made it difficult for OMB and the Congressional Budget Committees to charge the legislation against the DoD appropriation. The Senate version of the bill did not include the accrual change so, before the bill was conferenced, letters of strong opposition to the House version were written to the House and Senate Armed Services Committees by the Office of Management and Budget, the Secretary of Defense, the Department of Treasury, the Senate and House Budget Committees, and the Senate Appropriations Committee. The letters cited the $11 billion annual windfall that DoD would reap that would increase the deficit, as well as the importance of transparent costs in the budgets of Federal agencies. As a result of this strong opposition, the final enacted law dropped the language to remove DoD's accrual obligation (US Senate 2006).

Conclusion

Most US Federal retirement plans are now fully funded. Nevertheless, as the plan assets must legally be invested in Federal securities, fund surpluses are used to lower the overall Federal government budget deficit. As a result, unlike the private sector, current taxpayers are not charged with the cost of future Federal retirement obligations.

Since private-sector plans are not allowed to invest in company investments, full funding does result in charging current management with the cost of future retirement obligations. However, similar to the private sector, Federal funding does require the employing Federal agency to budget for the accruing liability of retirement for its current personnel. Policy decisions regarding the number of Federal civilian and military personnel and the design of their retirement benefits are then made with a better understanding of the cost. If decisions are made to increase personnel or benefits, then offsetting savings must be found in order to live within both agency and Federal budget totals. This allows for more fiscal security in the long-term.

References

US Department of Defense (DoD) (2006). *Valuation of the Military Retirement System as of September 30, 2006.* DoD Office of the Actuary. Washington, DC: US Department of Defense.

US Government Accountability Office (GAO) (1996). *Public Pensions, Summary of Federal Pension Plan Data.* Report to Congressional Requesters, (GAO/AIMD-96-6). Washington, DC: US Government Accountability Office, February.

US Office of Management and Budget (OMB) (2008). *FY 2009 President's Budget.* Washington, DC: US Office of Management and Budget, February.

US Office of Management and Budget (OMB) (various years). *News Release.* Washington, DC: US Office of Management and Budget.

US Senate (2006). *Budget Bulletin.* Senate Committee on the Budget. Washington, DC: US Senate, September 20.

Part II

Implementing Public Retirement System Reform

Chapter 9

Reforming the German Civil Servant Pension Plan

Raimond Maurer, Olivia S. Mitchell, and Ralph Rogalla

Throughout the developed world, public sector employees have traditionally been promised a pay-as-you-go (PAYGO) defined benefit (DB) pension plan. In such a system, current pensions are paid through taxes or contributions made by the working generation. These systems, however, face increasing financial difficulties, since a shrinking working-age group has to support more and more retirees. If these developments continue and the systems remain unaltered, civil servants pension benefits sooner or later will have to be reduced or contributions increased, in either case requiring unpopular political decisions. At the same time, it is often argued that moving public employee pension plans toward funded systems may offer a resort to the deteriorating financial situation of these plans. The rationale behind this argument is that accumulating assets and investing them in the capital markets will strengthen the rights of plan participants, increase transparency, and might generate enhanced returns, which in turn help to reduce civil servants' pension costs. This chapter explores the feasibility of implementing a funded pension system for German civil servants who have been promised an unfunded DB plan which faces future shortfalls.

In some countries, civil servant pension plans are well funded, as in the United States or the Netherlands (Mitchell et al. 2001; ABP 2006). But German civil servant DB plans are promised benefits related to final salary and service years, yet few of these promises are backed by assets. As political decisionmakers have grown more conscious of the economic costs of public pensions, some action has already been taken. The German state of Rhineland-Palatinate was the first to introduce a fully funded pension scheme for newly recruited civil servants in 1996, which is currently endowed with 20–30 percent of the salaries of those covered by the plan. The state of Saxony followed along these lines and introduced a comparable scheme in 2005, which fully covers all employees who joined civil service since 1997. Both states essentially restrict their funds' investment universe to government bonds, and thereby forego the opportunity to improve the funds' financial situation by earning higher returns in equity markets. This is in sharp contrast to empirical evidence on international public pension plans' investment strategies. For instance, Dutch-based ABP, the pension fund for those employed by the government and in education, only invests around 40 percent of plan assets into fixed-income securities, including a substantial fraction of corporate bonds (ABP 2007). Similar results are reported for the United States, where state pension plans on average only invest about one-third of their assets in bonds and other debt instruments (Wilshire 2007).

As German civil servants pensions are far from being fully funded, and since in those cases where plans have at least some assets, investment policies are particularly conservative, more efforts need to be made to provide political decisionmakers with reliable information on the opportunities and risks associated with moving toward a funded pension system for civil servants. To this end, this chapter studies the implications of partially prefunding the civil servants pension plan in the German state of Hesse. We introduce a hypothetical additional tax-sponsored pension fund for currently active civil servants, similar to those already introduced in Rhineland-Palatinate and Saxony. Contributions paid into the fund are invested in the capital markets and investment returns are used to alleviate the burden of increasing pension liabilities. Based on stochastic simulations of future pension plan asset development, we estimate the expectation as well as the Conditional Value at Risk (CVaR) of pension costs. These are then evaluated in an effort to determine the optimal asset allocation that controls worst-case risks while still offering relief with respect to expected economic costs of providing the promised pensions.

This study extends prior work by Maurer, Mitchell, and Rogalla (2008) in several ways. First, we give a more detailed overview on future structural changes in the civil service population, which will contribute to a further deterioration of the public pension plan's financial situation. Second, we introduce a more sophisticated stochastic asset model of the vector autoregression variety which includes stocks, bonds, and real estate as an alternative asset class available to the plan manager. Finally, we study the intertemporal risk and return patterns of the suggested investment policy for current and future taxpayers.

In what follows, we first offer a concise description of the characteristics of the German civil service pension plan. Next we evaluate future public plan obligations for taxpayers in a non-stochastic context and derive the payroll-related deterministic contribution rate that is able to finance accruing pension benefits in the long run. Drawing on these results, we take a plan manager's perspective to determine reasonable investment strategies for accumulating plan assets within a stochastic asset/liability framework. The final section summarizes findings and their implications for managing funded public sector pension plans in Germany.

German civil service pension plan design

Public sector employees constitute about 14 percent of the German work-force, classified into two groups: public employees and civil servants. The legal status of the roughly 3 million public employees is based on private sector law, while that of the 1.4 million civil servants is codified in public law. Initially, the rights and duties of civil servants were codified in the 1792 Prussian General Code, and with some modifications, the basic characteristics of this system are still in force and manifested after World War II in the German constitution (Gillis 1968). Key components include the fact that civil servants commit to work for public sector tasks for life, they have no right to strike, and they are subject to special disciplinary rules. In exchange for this commitment, the government provides them with an appropriate salary depending on specific career paths, offers particular pre-entry training, and supplies lifelong health care, disability, and pension benefits. In contrast to the United States, the legal status, the salary packages, and the retirement benefits for German civil servants are quite homogenous at the federal, state, and local levels.

At retirement, German civil servants receive a noncontributory, tax-sponsored, and cost-of-living-adjusted defined benefit type lifetime annuity[1] which depends on final salary, the number of pensionable years of service in the public sector, and the retirement age. The noncontributory plan for civil servants comes at the price of significantly lower gross salaries compared to other public sector workers with equivalent qualifications. German civil servants are neither offered complementary occupational pension plans nor covered by the national social security system.[2] Hence, their retirement benefits are higher than those of private sector workers who may be eligible for social security as well as supplementary occupational pension benefits (Heubeck and Rürup 2000).

Some argue that the generosity of civil servant pensions serves as partial compensation for their lack of portability, since accrued pension benefits are substantially reduced if the worker were to leave public employ.[3] Naturally, this substantially reduces turnover, particularly among older civil servants with long tenure. On the other hand, if a civil servant were to change jobs within the public sector, he would be permitted to remain in the same pension plan (even when moving from one state to another). From the plan sponsor's perspective, the relatively generous but non-portable DB pension scheme serves as a useful instrument for attracting, recruiting, and retaining a highly skilled and stable workforce.

Of late, however, German public pension plan generosity has been substantially reduced. In 2003, a new pension benefit formula was introduced that reduced the retirement benefit formula from 1.875 percent of final salary per year of service down to 1.79375 percent.[4] After a maximum of 40 pensionable service years, a retiring civil servant is promised a maximum replacement rate of 71.75 percent. A surviving spouse receives survivorship benefits of 55 percent (formerly 60%) of the deceased civil servant's pension. Orphans receive 20 percent and half-orphans 12 percent.

Current pensioners, who retired under the old formula with pension benefits worth 75 percent of their final salaries, will also be affected by the benefit cut. For several years, their post-retirement benefit increases will be marginally reduced, until their replacement rate will be cut to the same 71.75 percent. The nominal pension paid to a retired civil servant will nonetheless increase over time.

In the past, civil servants' standard retirement age has been 65, though they may retire as young as age 63 with a reduction of 0.3 percentage points per month. Special provisions for public safety workers with physically demanding jobs like police officers or fire fighters allow for retirement at earlier ages without a benefit cut. In mid 2007, however, several states as well as the federal government have followed Germany's social security system in moving gradually to 67 as the normal retirement age.

Deterministic valuation of future public pension obligations

Next we analyze the actuarial status of the civil servants' pension plan in the state of Hesse.[5] Our prior research has found that already-accrued public pension liabilities for the state are on the order of 150 percent of current explicit state debt (Maurer, Mitchell, and Rogalla 2008); this analysis assumes that these claims already accumulated will be financed from other sources. In this section, we conduct a deterministic actuarial valuation of pension liabilities that will accrue in the future to existing employees and new hires over the next 50 years.[6] We draw on a datafile provided by the Hessian Statistical Office which contains demographic and economic information on more than 100,000 active and retired civil servants in Hesse as of the beginning of 2004, including their age, sex, marital status, line of service (for active civil servants), and salary/pension payments. On average, 45 percent of the active workers are female, the average salary (in 2004) is €39,000, and it is a relatively old group, averaging age 45.

Figure 9-1 depicts the age distribution of the sample of active employees. This distribution peaks for employees in their late 40s and early 50s. Thus, in 15 to 20 years' time, a significant group of civil servants will retire in a concentrated fashion, and it will result in a jump in required pension payments. At the same time, there are relatively few active civil servants in

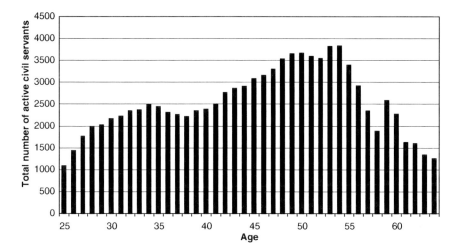

Figure 9-1 Age distribution of active civil servants in 2004. *Note*: Age distribution for all active civil servants ($N = 104,919$). *Source*: Authors' calculations using 2004 data provided by the German State of Hesse.

their late 50s or early 60s, a pattern attributable to generous early benefits in the past.

Demographic Assumptions. In what follows, we project pension accruals of future generations of employees. Our approach is to project the time path of age and salary for all civil servants through time (we assume that the marital status remains constant). When a position becomes vacant, a new civil servant is assumed to be recruited (with equal probability of being male or female); the new worker's age is assumed to be the average age of entering civil service, accounting for average time spent on position-related education or other types of public service that will be credited as pensionable years in civil service. The salary of the newly hired civil servant is assumed to be in line with the age-related remuneration for the position; the marital status is assumed to be that of the previous position holder. Since turnover other than retirement is virtually nil we assume no employee turnover prior to retirement; hence we do not account for early retirement, disability benefits, or dependents' benefits due to death in service. In terms of mortality projections, we use those derived by Maurer, Mitchell, and Rogalla (2008) who have prepared mortality tables specific to retired German civil servants based on a dataset for the state of Hesse covering the period 1994 to 2004. They show that retired civil servants tend to enjoy lower mortality than the overall population. Throughout this study we also employ these tables, accounting for decreasing future mortality rates according to the trend functions published by the *German Association of Actuaries* (see DAV [2004]). We also assume that the pension reforms are fully implemented, that is, maximum benefits only amount to 71.75 percent of final salary and the retirement age is 67.

Economic Assumptions. Three interrelated economic factors significantly influence the valuation of pension plan liabilities: anticipated inflation, expected salary growth rates, and investment returns on plan assets (see Hustead and Mitchell [2001]). While Germany has experienced only moderate inflation over the last decades, it remains an important factor for the valuation of future pension cash flows. For this reason, and because salaries as well as pensions tend to be maintained in real terms, this study therefore uses real financial values and investment returns throughout.

An issue that looms large in the public pension plan arena is what discount rate one should use in valuing future promised benefits (Waring 2008). Naturally, the discount rate selected directly influences both the reported pension liability and the contribution rate required to fund the promises. The current debate coalesces around whether public plans should use an actuarial versus an economic concept of liabilities.[7] Many actuaries select a discount rate which reflects projected (or historical) asset returns; accordingly, if a portion of the pension fund is held in equities, the selected discount rate will include an *ex ante* risk premium which may not, in fact, be realized *ex post*. This approach also tends to downweight future liabilities and upweight the benefits of investing in stock. By contrast, if returns are lower than expected, future generations of taxpayers may end up bearing the investment risk, if actual returns fall below the expected rates. This strategy is intended to smooth contribution rates required over time.

By contrast, many economists contend that a public plan should use a (nearly) risk-free rate on government bonds to compute liabilities, as this reflects the state's financing costs. We argue that the risk-less interest rate must be used for reporting the actuarial present value of pension promises for accounting purposes and for solvency planning, as well as for setting the contribution rates. Our simulation assumes that this real risk-free interest rate is 3 percent for the base case;[8] we also evaluate an alternative set of results with a real interest rate of 1.5 percent. Using a risk-free government bond rate is consistent with the often-recommended practice of nearly fully matching public plan assets and liabilities. Nevertheless, this does not mean that the public entity must, of necessity, automatically invest entirely in government bonds. Instead, it might be appropriate to invest at least part of the pension portfolio in more risky equities, depending on the plan sponsor's risk preferences.

Projected future benefits for current and future civil servants

In order to move the public DB pension plan toward funding, assets need to be built up and invested in the capital markets to back the accruing liabilities. Consequently, the plan sponsor's foremost task is to assess what contributions are required to finance the benefits based on pension liability patterns specific to the plan. As pension benefits for Hessian civil servants are calculated as a percentage of final salary times years of service, the normal cost of the plan (i.e., the cost accrued in each year supposing actuarial assumptions are realized) is determined according to the aggregate level percentage of payroll method. Total projected pension plan costs are stated as a percentage of active members' overall payroll (McGill et al. 2005); we derive the actuarial present value of future pension benefit obligations (PBO) based on future salaries and service years over the next 50 years (2004–53), evolving our initial population through time in line with the dynamics discussed earlier. We determine the value of future pension benefits for active and future civil servants based on the projected benefit obligation (PBO) formula:

$$\text{PBO} = \sum_i \frac{1.79375 \cdot \tau_i \cdot S_{67,i} \cdot \bar{a}_{67,i}}{(1+r)^{67-\text{Age}_i}} \tag{9.1}$$

where (for each civil servant i of Age_i) τ_i is the number of service years as of retirement, $S_{67,i}$ is the (expected) salary at retirement age 67, $\bar{a}_{67,i}$ is the immediate pension annuity factor, and r is the discount rate. After 50 years, we assume that the plan is terminated and conduct a discontinuance valuation.

The relative amount of the present values of pension liabilities to salary payments represents the deterministic annual contribution rate as a percentage of the payroll required to fund future pension promises.[9] In our non-stochastic analysis, we presume that these contributions are paid into the pension plan at the beginning of each year. Plan assets are invested in the capital markets and earn a fixed (i.e., non-stochastic) return equal to the rate at which plan liabilities are discounted for valuation purposes. Table 9-1 summarizes the results for our base case with a real discount rate of 3 percent (Column 1) as well as for our alternative setup, that is, a discount rate of 1.5 percent (Column 2). The present values of current workers' projected pension liabilities and salaries are reported along with the ratio of the present value of pension costs to salaries and, therefore, the notional contribution rate required to finance the pension promises.

In our benchmark case with the 3 percent discount rate, the present value of future pension liabilities comes to €20.8 billion (Row 1, Column 1), whereas salary payments have a present value of €111.5 billion

TABLE 9-1   Projected benefit liabilities and contribution rates: deterministic model

	Discount Rate	
	3%	*1.5%*
	(1)	*(2)*
(1) PV Pension Liabilities (in bn)	20.8	44.8
(2) PV Future Salaries (in bn)	111.5	149.3
(3) Contribution Rate: (1)/(2) (in %)	18.7	30.0

Notes: Authors' calculations using 2004 data provided by the State of Hesse. Base case defined with a 3% discount rate, alternative case uses 1.5%.

Source: Derived from Maurer, Mitchell, and Rogalla (2008).

(Row 2, Column 1). The ratio of present values representing the average required contribution rate is 18.7 percent of salaries for each future year (Row 3, Column 1). This comes close to the contribution rates for the civil servants' pension plan of Rhineland-Palatinate, which range from 20 to 30 percent depending on service level. It comes at no surprise that these results are highly sensitive to the discount rate applied. A lower discount rate increases both the present value of pension liabilities as well as the present value of salary payments. However, as pension liabilities have a longer duration than salary payments, contribution rates increase with falling discount rates. In our alternative setting with a real discount rate of 1.5 percent, the present value of pension liabilities more than doubles to €44.8 billion while discounted salary payments only increase by less than 50 percent to €149.3 billion (Rows 1 and 2, Column 2). Hence, the contribution rate rises to 30 percent (Row 3, Column 2).

Pension plan management in a stochastic environment

Uncertain capital market returns on pension plan assets are of major concern to DB pension plan sponsors. While market gains may reduce required contributions and therefore overall plan costs, excessive investment losses can also require a plan sponsor to make supplementary contributions in an effort to recover from funding deficits. Selecting an adequate asset allocation for plan funds is therefore of utmost importance to the plan manager.

Therefore in this section we evaluate the public plan sponsor's decision-making process, to identify a reasonable plan asset allocation in a world with uncertain investment returns. This requires formulating an intertemporal objective function guiding trade-offs between capital market risk and returns, as well as between supplementary contributions and cost savings.

Plan Design, Pension Manager Objectives, and Asset/Liability Modeling. We minimize the worst-case total cost of running plan over a future long-term time horizon. The funded pension scheme we model is designed as follows: at the beginning of every period t, regular contributions RC_t are paid into the pension plan by the plan sponsor. These contributions are determined by a fixed contribution rate CR of 18.7 percent of the current payroll for all civil servants participating in the plan, as derived in the previous section. Plan funds are used to pay for pension payments due at time t, while the remaining assets are invested in the capital markets.

At the end of every period, the plan manager has to analyze the plan's funding situation. Depending on the funding ratio, defined as the fraction of the current projected benefit obligation that is covered by current plan assets, solvency rules might require additional funds to be paid into the plan to recover funding deficits. By contrast, substantial overfunding might allow future contribution rates to be reduced. Specifically, in case the funding ratio in any period drops below 90 percent, immediate supplementary contributions SC_t are required to reestablish a funding ratio of 100 percent. If, on the other hand, fund assets exceed fund liabilities by more than 20 percent, CR will be cut by 50 percent. In case the funding ratio even rises above 150 percent, no further regular contributions will be required from the plan sponsor until the funding level decreases again. At the end of our projection horizon, we assume the plan is frozen and all liabilities are transferred to a private insurer together with assets to fund them.

The plan manager's investment policy aims at generating sufficient returns in order to reduce overall pension plan costs. At the same time, he tries to keep capital market fluctuations and thereby worst-case plan costs under control. Hence, the plan sponsor is interested in identifying the optimal allocation of pension funds across three broad asset classes: an equity index fund, a government bond index fund, and a real estate index fund.[10] Specifically, we assume that the plan sponsor seeks to minimize the worst-case cost of running the plan, specified by the Conditional Value at Risk at the 5 percent level of the stochastic present value of total pension costs (TPC).[11] The distribution of total discounted pension costs is derived from running a 10,000 iteration Monte Carlo simulation. Based on this, we identify the optimal asset allocation x fixed at the beginning of the projection horizon.[12]

Total pension costs are the sum of regular contributions (RC) and supplementary contributions (SC) made by the plan sponsor. All payments by the plan sponsor are discounted at the fixed real interest rate r, which reflects the government's financing cost. Thus, the optimization problem with respect to the vector of investment weights x (i.e., the fraction of assets invested in bonds, stocks, and real estate) is specified by:

$$\min_{x} CVaR_{5\%} \left(TPC = \sum_{t=0}^{T} \frac{RC_t + SC_t\,(1 + \xi)}{(1 + r)^t} \right) \tag{9.2}$$

The 5%-Conditional Value at Risk (CVaR) is defined as the expected present value of total pension cost under the condition that its realization is greater than the Value at Risk (VaR) for that level, that is:

$$CVaR_{5\%}\,(TPC) = E\,(TPC|TPC > VaR_{5\%}\,(TPC)) \tag{9.3}$$

The CVaR framework as a measure of risk is in many ways superior to the commonly-used VaR measure, defined as $P\,(TPC > VaR_a) = a$, that is, the costs that will not be exceeded with a given probability of $(1 - a)$ percent. In particular, the CVaR focuses not only on a given percentile of a loss distribution, but also accounts for the magnitude of losses in the distributional tails beyond this percentile.[13]

We argue that pension benefits as a rule should be covered by regular plan contributions. Hence, supplementary contributions ought to be required only as a last resort. In case a plan sponsor is often asked to make supplementary contributions, regular contribution rates are likely to be insufficient. To discourage making too few regular contributions, we include a penalty factor ξ for supplementary contributions. Thus, if one unit of supplementary contributions is required to recover a funding deficit, then $(1 + \xi)$ units are accounted for as plan costs. This penalty can also be interpreted as the additional costs in excess of the risk free rate of financing the required supplementary contributions, countering the notion that public monies paid into public pension plans are 'free' money.

At the same time, measures need to be taken to discourage overfunding the plan significantly. The sponsor might find it appealing to excessively short government bonds and invest the proceeds into the pension plan in an effort to 'cash in' on the equity premium. To this end, we disallow funds being physically transferred out of the plan; the minimum contribution rate in any single period is zero. In case plan assets exceed plan liabilities after plan termination, these funds are lost from the perspective of the plan manager as they are not accounted for as revenues in his objective function. Later we relax this assumption.

Stochastic Asset Model. We model the long run stochastic dynamics of future returns on assets accumulated in the pension plan using a first-order vector autoregressive (VAR) model, which is widely used by practitioners as well as in the academic literature (Campbell and Viceira 2002; Hoevenaars, Molenaar, and Steenkamp 2003). The pension plan's investment universe comprises broadly diversified portfolios of equities, bonds, and real estate investments. Our asset model draws on the specification employed by Hoevenaars et al. (2008), who extend the models in Campbell, Chan, and Viceira (2003) as well as in Campbell and Viceira (2005) by including additional asset classes, in particular alternative investments like real estate, commodities, and hedge funds. Following the notation of Hoevenaars et al. (2008), let z_t be the vector

$$z_t = \begin{pmatrix} r_{m,t} \\ s_t \\ x_{1,t} \\ x_{2,t} \end{pmatrix} \tag{9.4}$$

that contains the real money market log return at time t ($r_{m,t}$), the vector $x_{1,t}$, which includes the excess returns of equities and bonds relative to $r_{m,t}$ (i.e., $x_{i,t} = r_{i,t} - r_{m,t}$), the vector $x_{2,t}$, which includes the excess return of real estate relative to $r_{m,t}$, and a vector s_t describing state variables that predict $r_{m,t}$, $x_{1,t}$, and $x_{2,t}$. We include the nominal 3-months interest rate (r_{nom}), the dividend-price ratio (dp), and the term spread (spr) as predicting variables.[14]

While historical return data are easily available for traditional asset classes, this does not hold for alternative investments, like real estate in our case. Typically, return time series for these asset classes are comparably short. This imposes difficulties when trying to calibrate the model. The large number of parameters to be estimated can lead to these estimates being unreliable as data availability is insufficient. To resolve this problem, restrictions are being imposed on the VAR with respect to $x_{2,t}$. In particular, we assume that $x_{2,t}$ has no dynamic feedback on the other variables. In other words, real estate returns are influenced by the returns on traditional asset classes and the predictor variables, while these in turn do not depend on the development of real estate returns. To this end, let y_t be the vector

$$y_t = \begin{pmatrix} r_{m,t} \\ s_t \\ x_{1,t} \end{pmatrix} \tag{9.5}$$

The dynamics of y_t are assumed to follow an unrestricted VAR(1) according to

$$y_{t+1} = a + By_t + \varepsilon_{t+1} \tag{9.6}$$

with $\varepsilon_{t+1} \sim N(0, \Sigma_{\varepsilon\varepsilon})$. The return on real estate investments are modeled according to

$$x_{2,t+1} = c + D_0 \cdot y_{t+1} + D_1 \cdot y_t + H \cdot x_{2,t} + \eta_{t+1} \tag{9.7}$$

with $\eta_{t+1} \sim N(0, \; \sigma_{re})$. The innovations ε_{t+1} and η_{t+1} are assumed to be uncorrelated, as contemporaneous interrelations are captured by D_0. Based on this setup and following Stambaugh (1997), we can then optimally exploit available data by estimating the unrestricted VAR Equation 9.6 over the complete data sample and by using the smaller sample only for estimating the parameters in Equation 9.7.

The unrestricted VAR model is calibrated to quarterly logarithmic return series starting in 1973:I and ending in 2007:I. The real money market return is the difference between the nominal log 3-months Euribor and inflation (Fibor is used for the time before Euribor was available). Log returns on equities and log dividend-price ratios draw on time series data for the DAX 30 – an index portfolio of German blue chips – provided by DataStream. We use the approach in Campbell and Viceira (2002) to derive return series for diversified bond portfolios. The bond return series $r_{n,t+1}$ is constructed according to

$$r_{n,t+1} = \frac{1}{4} y_{n-1,t+1} - D_{n,t}(y_{n-1,t+1} - y_{n,t}) \tag{9.8}$$

employing 10 year constant maturity yields on German bonds, where $y_{n,t} = \ln(1 + Y_{n,t})$ is the n-period maturity bond yield at time t. $D_{n,t}$ is the duration, which can be approximated by

$$D_{n,t} = \frac{1 - (1 + Y_{n,t})^{-n}}{1 - (1 + Y_{n,t})^{-1}} \tag{9.9}$$

We approximate $y_{n-1,t+1}$ by $y_{n,t+1}$ assuming that the term structure is flat between maturities $n - 1$ and n,. As for equities, excess returns are calculated by subtracting the log money market return, $x_{b,t} = r_{n,t} - r_{m,t}$. The yield spread is computed as the difference between the log 10-year zeros yield on German government bonds and the log 3-months Euribor, both provided by Deutsche Bundesbank.

Deriving reliable return time series for real estate as an asset class is difficult due to the peculiarities of property investments.[15] In contrast to equity and bond indices, inhomogeneity, illiquidity, and infrequent trading in individual properties result in transaction-based real estate indices not being able to adequately describe the returns generated in these markets. Moreover, such price indices do not account for rental income, which constitutes a significant source of return on real estate investments. By contrast, it is comparably easy to construct indices that try to approximate the income on direct real estate investments by using the return on investing indirectly through traded property companies like real estate investment trusts (REITs). However, empirical evidence on these forms of indirect real estate investments suggests that they exhibit a more equity-like behavior.[16]

These indices are therefore a much less than perfect proxy for direct real estate investments (see Hoesli and MacGregor [2000]).

Appraisal-based indices, like the one this study draws on, are the most widely used representatives for real estate investments in the academic literature as well as among practitioners. These indices account for easy to sample continuous rental income as well as for returns from changes in property values, which are estimated through periodic appraisals by real estate experts. As individual properties' values are usually estimated only once a year and due to the fact that there is no single valuation date for all properties, not every return observation in the index can be substantiated with a new and observation date consistent appraisal of the overall property portfolio underlying the index. Moreover, annual appraisals often draw significantly on prior valuations. Consequently, returns derived from appraisal-based indices exhibit substantial serial correlation and low short-term volatilities that understate the true volatility of real estate returns. Different methodologies have been suggested to reduce undue smoothing in real estate return time series, which subsequently will exhibit more realistic levels of volatility.[17] In this study we employ the approach developed by Blundell and Ward (1987) that suggests transforming the original (smoothed) return series according to:

$$r_t^* = \frac{r_t}{1-a} - \frac{a}{1-a} r_{t-1} \tag{9.10}$$

where r_t^* represents the unsmoothed return in t and a the coefficient of first-order autocorrelation in the return time series. Under this transformation, expected returns remain constant, $E(r_t^*) = E(r_t)$, but the return standard deviation increases according to:

$$STD\left(r_t^*\right) = STD\left(r_t\right) \sqrt{\frac{1-a^2}{(1-a)^2}} \tag{9.11}$$

We rely on an appraisal-based index for a diversified property portfolio as elaborated in Maurer, Reiner, and Sebastian (2003), which provides quarterly returns on German real estate back to January 1980. The index is a value weighted index constructed from the returns on German open-end real estate funds' units. These fund units represent portfolios of direct real estate investments and liquid assets like money market deposits or short- to medium-term government bonds.[18] The return on direct property investments is then approximated by subtracting from the funds' returns their earnings resulting from investing in liquid assets.

While our asset/liability model is run on a yearly basis, the VAR is calibrated to quarterly data, resulting in higher reliability of parameter estimates due to a higher number of available observations. Quarterly returns

TABLE 9-2 Simulated parameters for stochastic asset case

	Expected Returns (%)			Correlations		
	Base case scenario	Low return scenario	Standard deviations	Equities	Bonds	Real Estate
Equities	6.57	5.07	23.4	1		
Bonds	4.08	2.58	7.02	0.17	1	
Real Estate	3.13	1.63	3.80*	0.09	−0.52	1

Notes: *: Unsmoothed volatility following Blundell and Ward (1987). Base case scenario relates to a discount rate of 3%, low return scenario relates to a discount rate of 1.5%. See the Appendix for estimated quarterly VAR parameters which generate these moments based on 10,000 simulations.

Source: Authors' calculations; see text.

generated by the asset model are aggregated and parameters a, c, σ_{re}, and $\Sigma_{\epsilon\epsilon}$ are adapted so that the model's simulated empirical return moments (see Table 9-2 and the Appendix) reflect those of annual historic returns.[19]

Optimal Asset Allocation under Stochastic Investment Returns. Next we derive the optimal investment strategy for plan assets assuming that the rate of regular contributions, *CR*, is fixed at a given ratio of projected benefit obligation to the present value of projected future salaries. From Table 9-1 we know that for a real discount rate of 3 percent, a fixed contribution rate of 18.7 percent of current salaries is sufficient to finance the PBO that comes to €20.8 billion in the deterministic case. Against this deterministic PBO and contribution rate, we benchmark our results for an environment in which investment returns are stochastic. In our base case, we will assume the same real discount rate of 3 percent and a penalty factor ξ for supplementary contributions of 20 percent. A following section will investigate into the impact of varying these assumptions.

Table 9-3 summarizes key findings for four distinct asset allocations, the three polar cases of 100 percent equities, 100 percent bonds, and 100 percent real estate investments as well as the optimal investment strategy, which is determined endogenously by minimizing the 5%-CVaR of total pension costs. Panel 1 of Table 9-3 contains the portfolio weights of equities, bonds, and real estate investments assuming a static asset allocation (Rows 1 to 3), the expected present value of total pension costs (Row 4), and the 5%-Conditional Value at Risk (Row 5). Expectation and 5%-Conditional Value at Risk of discounted supplementary contributions are shown in Panel 2 of Table 9-3 (Rows 6 and 7). Figure 9-2 provides closer insight into the dispersion of possible total pension cost outcomes for the four asset allocations under investigation, showing box plots of various percentiles of the overall cost distributions.

TABLE 9-3 Risk of alternative asset allocation patterns assuming fixed
contribution rate

Fixed contribution rate: 18.7% Deterministic PBO: €20.8 bn Real Discount Rate: 3%	100% Equities (1)	100% Bonds (2)	100% Real Estate (3)	Cost min. Asset Mix (4)
Panel 1				
(1) Equity weight (%)	100	0	0	22.3
(2) Bond weight (%)	0	100	0	47.2
(3) Real estate weight (%)	0	0	100	30.5
(4) Expected pension costs (€bn)	21.71	18.62	21.99	16.09
(5) 5%-CVaR pension costs (€bn)	36.27	26.48	25.88	21.02
Panel 2				
(6) Exp. suppl. contributions (€bn)	8.69	1.56	1.43	0.50
(7) 5%-CVaR suppl. contrib. (€bn)	21.51	6.74	5.05	2.85

Notes: Contribution rate in % of salaries. Supplementary contributions required in
case of funding ratio (i.e., fund assets/PBO) below 90% to restore funding ratio of
100%. Contribution rate reduced by 50% (100%) in case of funding ratio above 120%
(150%). Opportunity costs of supplementary contributions addressed by accounting
for a penalty of $\xi = 20\%$.

Source: Authors' calculations using 2004 data provided by the German State of Hesse.

When the fund is fully invested in equities, total expected pension costs
for active employees come to €21.71 billion (Row 4, Column 1) while
the 5%-CVaR amounts to €36.27 billion or about 75 percent higher than
the deterministic PBO benchmark of €20.8 billion (Row 5, Column 1).
In addition to the regular pension contributions of 18.7 percent of the
payroll, taxpayers face another expected €8.69 billion in supplementary
contributions, which rise to €21.51 billion in CVaR (Rows 6 and 7, Column
1). As one would expect, high volatility of investment returns result in high
dispersion of possible cost outcomes. From Figure 9-2 it can be seen that
overall pension costs may vary widely from €12.6 billion (5th percentile)
to €33 billion (95th percentile). Although high return volatility comes
with high expected returns, expected pension costs are substantial due to
the capped upside potential inherent in the plan design. While the plan
manager is fully liable for funding deficits resulting from capital market
losses, he is not able to recover excess funds in an effort to reduce overall
pension costs. Thus, there is a strong disincentive for the plan manager to
overinvest plan funds into equities.

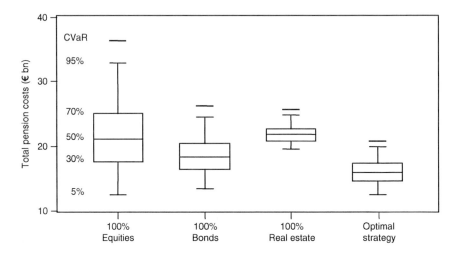

Figure 9-2 Range of pension costs under alternative asset allocations. *Note*: Total pension costs defined as net of regular and supplementary contributions using 3% discount rate. Annotations refer to the respective percentiles of total pension cost distributions for various asset allocations. *Source*: Authors' calculations; see text.

If, on the other hand, plan funds were fully invested in bonds, worst-case pension costs would only come to €26.48 billion, while expected costs would even drop to €18.62 billion (Rows 4 and 5, Column 2). Expected returns are moderate and therefore the cap on excess fund withdrawal is only of minor relevance. However, returns are still sufficient to earn some excess income over the discount rate, cutting expected costs down below their deterministic value. Lower volatility of investment returns results in lower dispersion of costs, ranging from €13.5 billion (5th percentile) to €24.6 billion (95th percentile). This keeps worst-case pension costs under control. On average, only €1.56 billion in supplementary contributions are required while their 5%-CVaR amounts to €6.74 billion, less than one-third compared to the all-equities allocation (Rows 6 and 7, Column 2).

Column 3 of Table 9-3 presents the results for an investment strategy that allocates all plan funds to real estate, the least risky single asset class under consideration in this study. Consequently, with an overall amount of €25.88 billion, worst-case pension costs are the lowest compared to the other polar cases (Row 5, Column 3). This also holds for expected and worst-case supplementary contributions, which come to €1.42 billion and €5.05 billion, respectively (Rows 6 and 7, Column 3). Low investment risk, however, comes at the cost of low expected returns. Real estate investments hardly outperform the fixed discount rate. Thus, there is not much of a risk premium to cash in and the upside potential is heavily limited. Expected pension costs amount to €21.99 billion, which exceeds those in the other polar cases as well as the deterministic PBO (Row 4, Column 3).

The optimal investment strategy given the fixed contribution rate of 18.7 percent of salaries is depicted in Column 4 of Table 9-3. It consists of 22.3 percent equities, 47.2 percent bonds, and 30.5 percent real estate investments (Rows 1–3). Equities acquire a significant share in the optimal portfolio, indicating that current investment policy for the few funded German pension schemes, that is, only investing in pure bond portfolios, might not be a favorable solution. Nonetheless, optimal equity weights are considerably lower than the almost 60 percent reported for US state pension plans (Wilshire 2007). Allocating a substantial fraction of assets to real estate is in line with the results of Ziobrowski and Ziobrowski (1997) and Firstenberg, Ross, and Zisler (1988), among others. In a more recent study however, Craft (2001) argues that in an asset/liability framework allocations to private real estate investments should only range from 12 to 16 percent. This is more in line with empirical observations of real estate allocations varying between 5 and 10 percent (see Wilshire [2007]; ABP [2007]). To a certain extent, the relatively high allocation to real estate in this study may be attributed to the underlying pension plan design. Due to the pension plan's up-side potential being restricted for political reasons, the plan manager will favor more stable real estate investments compared to riskier assets like equities.

Given the optimal investment strategy, expected pension costs for active employees are reduced to only €16.09 billion (Row 4, Column 4), more than 20 percent below the €20.8 billion required in the deterministic case. This cost reduction can directly be attributed to the considerable benefits, which can be expected from investing in diversified portfolios. From the outset, the fund is endowed with 18.7 percent of payroll, while actual pension payments are initially negligible. Expected returns well above the discount rate at which the benchmark contribution rate was derived and moderate return volatilities enable the fund to quickly accumulate considerable assets. The possibility of being able to reduce the actual contribution rate increases through time, while the risk of having to make supplementary contributions to reduce funding deficits diminishes.

This optimal funding and investment strategy also keeps worst-case risk under control. The 5%-Conditional Value at Risk of total pension costs, or the expected cost in the 5 percent worst cases, only amounts to €21.02 billion (Row 5, Column 4), almost equal to the deterministic benchmark. Supplementary contributions are also low. Their present value only comes to €500 million in expectation and even in the worst case—again defined as the 5%-CVaR—they only amount to €2.85 billion, slightly more than half the cost that was reported for the least risky pure real estate investment (Rows 6 and 7, Column 4).

The benefit of diversification can also be seen in Figure 9-2 with pension costs for the optimal asset allocation ranging from €12.5 billion (5th percentile) to €20 billion (95th percentile). This range is smaller than for pure equity or bond investments, while investing only in real estate will result in an even smaller range. However, the overall level of costs resulting from following the optimal strategy is substantially lower compared to the pure real estate investment case. Only investing in real estate will result in the 5th percentile of overall costs being only marginally lower than the 95th percentile of costs in the optimal case.

As a result, introducing an at least partially funded public pension plan that follows an optimized investment policy could be expected to substantially reduce the economic cost of providing covered pensions, while simultaneously keeping the consequences of capital market volatility under control.

Figure 9-3 provides deeper insight into the temporal structure of risks and rewards of following the cost minimizing investment strategy (i.e., 22% stocks, 47% bonds, 31% real estate). Panel A depicts the time path of the probability of having to make supplementary contributions due to substantial underfunding resulting from unfavorable investment returns (solid line). It indicates that there is a relatively low risk of additional contributions in the first decade of operations (much less than 10% probability), and a negligible risk thereafter. The other two lines depict the probability of the regular contribution rate being reduced by 50 (dashed line) or even 100 percent (dotted line). It can be seen that the probability of enjoying partial or full contribution holidays because of overfunding rises with time. Ten years into the program, the probability of a contribution holiday is only 2 percent, but 35 percent after 20 years. In other words, the risk of additional contributions is front-loaded, but the potential benefits savings are back-loaded.

Panel B of Figure 9-3 indicates that the expected value of required supplementary contributions (solid line) is highest at 12 years, where it amounts to €40 million (the dotted line represents expected savings due to contribution holidays). Ten years after the program is launched, the expected savings amount to €8.3 million, and rise to €145 (578) million in year 20 (40). The dashed line shows our estimate of the 'worst case' value of supplementary contributions measured by the 5%-CVaR risk metric. This suggests that, with a low probability, the plan sponsor might have to contribute substantially more during the early period: €800 million at the 10 year mark, and €360 million after 20 years. Reinforcing the message of Panel A, the optimal investment strategy greatly reduces the burden on future generations while controlling the risk on current contributors.

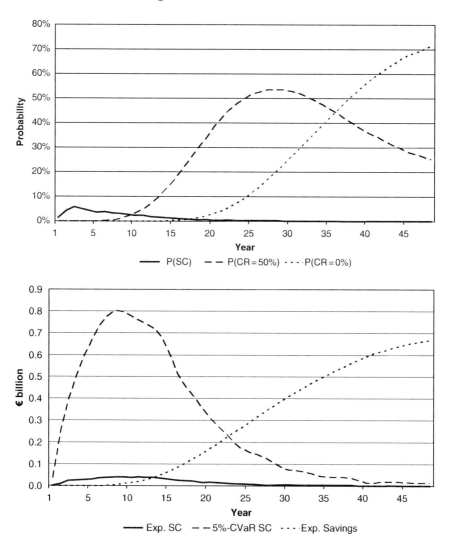

Figure 9-3 Time paths of supplementary public pension contributions and cost savings under optimal asset allocation strategy. Panel A. Probabilities of supplementary contributions and contribution holidays over time. Panel B. Magnitudes (in billions of 2004 euros) of expected supplementary contributions and cost saving due to contribution holidays. *Note.* P(SC): probability of supplementary contributions being required in any period. P(CR = 50%)/P(CR = 0%): probability of regular contribution rate being reduced to 50%/0%. Exp. SC: expected value of supplementary contributions in any given period. 5%-CVaR SC: 'worst case' value of supplementary contributions in any given period. Exp. Savings: expected value of cost savings due to cuts in contribution rates in any given period. *Source:* Authors' calculations; see text.

Further Results. Naturally, the results derived so far depend on model calibration. To check for robustness, we have analyzed optimal pension fund investment strategies for a selection of alternative parameterizations. While it is impossible to investigate all sensitivities, the findings presented in the following text provide a good understanding of the basic interrelations. Results are summarized in Table 9-4 for three alternative parameter sets. For ease of comparison, Column 1 repeats the result derived earlier for our base case. Alternative A investigates the impact of the penalty factor on supplementary contributions by redoing the analysis using a penalty factor for supplementary contributions of $\xi = 0$ (Column 2). We then study the influence of expected asset returns on the optimal asset allocation (Alternative B, Column 3). To this end, we analyze the plan assuming a real discount rate of 1.5 percent (instead of the 3% in our base case) together with the low return scenario from Table 9-2. Finally, we ease the restriction on withdrawing assets from the pension plan in an extremely overfunded situation by imposing a small cost on withdrawals (Alternative C, Column 4). Panel 1 of Table 9-4 presents optimal investment weights into equities, bonds, and real estate (Rows 1–3), as well as the expectation and the 5%-CVaR of the present value of total pension costs (Rows 4 and 5). Rows 6 and 7 in Panel 2 again present the expectation and worst-case realization of the present value of supplementary contributions. Finally, Rows 8 and 9 present the expected value as well as the 5%-CVaR of withdrawals from the pension plan.

In our base case, we levy a penalty of 20 percent on supplementary contributions, giving plan managers an incentive to follow a sustainable investment policy, which only relies on extra payments as a last resort. Moreover, this penalty was introduced to support the notion that such payments do not come for free but rather involve some form of financing costs. If supplementary contributions were free of extra costs, the plan manager would engage in a more risky investment strategy. Under these circumstances (Column 2, Rows 1–3), low risk real estate investments would be significantly reduced by more than 6 percentage points to an overall investment weight of 24.2 percent, while the weights of equities and bonds would both increase by about 3 percentage points to 25.6 percent and 50.2 percent, respectively. Equity exposure, however, continues to be comparably low, since the plan's upside potential is still limited. Having to account for such a penalty increases overall pension costs. Hence, it comes at no surprise that reducing the penalty factor will automatically reduce plan costs. For a penalty factor of 0 percent, expected plan costs come to €15.6 billion, while their worst-case value amounts to €20.5 billion (Column 2, Rows 4 and 5). Both figures are about €500 million below the ones reported for a penalty factor of 20 percent. Expected and worst-case supplementary contributions in Rows 6 and 7 of Column 2 are also lower

TABLE 9-4 Optimal asset allocation patterns for alternative parameterizations

	Base Case (1)	Alternative A (2)	Alternative B (3)	Alternative C (4)
Fixed contribution rate (in %)	18.7	18.7	30	18.7
Deterministic PBO (in €bn)	20.8	20.8	44.8	20.8
Real discount rate (in %)	3.0	3.0	1.5	3.0
Penalty factor on suppl. contributions	0.2	0.0	0.2	0.2
Penalty factor on withdrawals	–	–	–	0.2
	(1)	(2)	(3)	(4)
Panel 1				
(1) Equity weight (%)	22.3	25.6	22.5	53.1
(2) Bond weight (%)	47.2	50.2	47.5	46.9
(3) Real estate weight (%)	30.5	24.2	30.0	0.0
(4) Expected pension costs (€bn)	16.09	15.56	33.65	−2.46
(5) 5%-CVaR pension costs (€bn)	21.02	20.54	44.79	16.02
Panel 2				
(6) Exp. suppl. contributions (€bn)	0.50	0.49	0.59	1.68
(7) 5%-CVaR suppl. contrib. (€bn)	2.85	2.63	4.79	6.71
(8) Exp. withdrawals (€bn)	0.00	0.00	0.00	17.37
(9) 5%-CVaR Withdrawals (€bn)	0.00	0.00	0.00	3.42

Notes: Contribution rate % of salaries. Supplementary contributions required in case of funding ratio (i.e., fund assets/PBO) below 90% to restore funding ratio of 100%. Contribution rate reduced by 50% (100%) in case of funding ratio above 120% (150%). Withdrawal of funds exceeding 180% of pension liabilities (subject to respective penalty factor).

Source: Authors' calculations using 2004 data provided by the German State of Hesse.

than their counterparts in our base case (Column 1). Their decrease due to the reduced penalty factor, however, falls short of the 20 percent one might expect. This results from the slightly more aggressive optimal investment policy.

Discounting pension liabilities with a reduced real rate of 1.5 percent increases the deterministic PBO to €44.8 billion and the corresponding contribution rate to 30 percent of the payroll (Table 9-1, Column 2, Rows 2 and 3). Assuming that expected returns on assets drop by the same 1.5 percent, the optimal asset allocation will generate worst-case costs of €44.79 billion (Row 5 Column 3), virtually equal to the deterministic PBO. Expected pension costs come to €33.65 billion, down 25 percent compared to their non-stochastic counterpart (Row 4, Column 3). The optimal asset allocation consists of 22.5 percent equities, 47.5 percent bonds, and 30 percent real estate (Column 3, Rows 1–3). In essence, this equals the optimal allocation in our base case. The weight of real estate is marginally reduced by 0.5 percentage points, which are evenly distributed to equities and bonds. Thus, the interrelations between the asset classes as well as between plan assets and plan liabilities and the overall plan design determine optimal portfolio weights to a far greater extent than the absolute level of investment returns.

Finally we allow the plan manager to almost completely participate in the upside potential of investing plan assets more aggressively into equities. This alternative permits the plan manager to recover assets that exceed liabilities by more than 80 percent.[20] To prevent the manager from treating the pension as a hedge fund, we levy a 20 percent penalty on withdrawals. Now, investing in equities becomes much more appealing to the plan manager, as he is now rewarded for accepting higher return volatility with higher expected investment returns. Equity weights in the optimal portfolio rise by more than 30 percentage points to about 53 percent (Row 1, Column 4). While bond holdings remain virtually constant, assets are no longer invested into real estate due to their lack of expected return (Column 4, Rows 2 and 3). As expected investment returns significantly outperform the discount rate at which plan liabilities are valued, pension costs decrease substantially. In expectation, the plan exhibits negative pension costs of €2.46 billion (Row 4, Column 4). This means that after initially paying contributions into the plan for some years, investment returns on accumulated plan funds are sufficient to finance ongoing pension payments and even allow withdrawals that exceed earlier contributions in present value terms. Withdrawals come to €17.4 billion in expectation, and even in the worst case, almost €3.5 billion can be withdrawn from the plan (Rows 8 and 9, Column 4). Worst-case risks in this scenario are also well under control. While worst-case supplementary contributions come to €6.71 billion, more than double the amount of the base case (Row 7,

Columns 1 and 4), and the 5%-CVaR of total pension only amounts to €16 billion, 20 percent less than the deterministic pension cost (Row 5, Column 4).

Conclusion

As in many countries, civil servants in Germany are promised an unfunded DB pension. These benefits represent a significant liability to taxpayers, one which is currently not recognized as explicit state debt. We analyze the implications of moving Hesse's civil servants pension plan toward funding. We focus only on future benefit accruals, assuming that pensions paid to current retirees as well as claims already accumulated by active civil servants will be financed from other sources. With a non-stochastic framework based on a real discount rate of 3 percent, the annual contribution rate would be around 19 percent of salary which would be sufficient to cover future benefit accruals. Drawing on these results, we scrutinize alternative asset allocation strategies within a stochastic asset/liability framework. Here, we seek to minimize the worst-case costs of providing the promised pensions. In our base case, we find that, given the contribution rate of about 19 percent, the optimal investment policy for pension plan assets comprises 22 percent equities, 47 percent bonds, and about 31 percent real estate investments. Following this funding and investment policy will curtail worst-case pension costs to the deterministic PBO, while expected costs fall below these by almost 25 percent.

These results indicate that moving toward a funded pension system for German civil servants could be beneficial to both taxpayers as well as employees. Taxpayers can expect substantial cost reductions due to the favorable impact of earning investment returns in the capital markets, while their exposure to investment risks is limited for reasonable investment policies. Civil servants, in turn, benefit from being less exposed to discretionary pension cuts in times of tight government's budgets. Additionally, they might enjoy greater flexibility as pension claims backed by assets are much more portable than unfunded promises. Finally, we argue that public plans that hold 60 percent or more in equities, as is true in the US public case, is likely too aggressive. Nevertheless, investing in pure bond portfolios as in the few German pension schemes that hold some assets provides stability, but can be quite expensive.

Acknowledgments

This research was conducted with support from the TransCoop Program of the Alexander von Humboldt Foundation. Additional research support was provided by the Pension Research Council of the Wharton School of the University of Pennsylvania. We are grateful for useful comments from Peter Brady, Peter König, Steven Haberman, and for data support from the Hessian Statistical Office. Opinions and errors are solely those of the authors and not of the institutions with whom the authors are affiliated.

Appendix

TABLE 9-A1 Estimated quarterly VAR parameters

	$r_{m,t}$	$x_{e,t}$	$x_{b,t}$	dp_t	spr_t	$r_{nom,t}$
Parameter estimates						
$r_{m,t}+1$	−0.0338	0.0035	−0.0226	−0.2118	−0.0350	0.5455
$x_{e,t}+1$	0.1267	0.0116	0.0920	1.9727	0.5572	−2.8218
$x_{b,t}+1$	−0.1710	−0.0176	0.1106	−0.3946	0.9146	1.5958
dp_t+1	−0.0099	0.0012	−0.0094	0.9274	−0.0169	0.0464
spr_t+1	0.0467	0.0005	0.0458	−0.0196	0.9729	0.3110
$r_{nom,t}+1$	−0.0268	0.0010	−0.0173	0.0434	−0.0869	0.7718
D_0	−0.1218	−0.0068	−0.2699	−0.3993	−0.2348	−0.5134
D_1	−0.0915	−0.0073	−0.0033	0.1551	0.3570	0.3802
Error correlation matrix						
$r_{m,t}$	0.54					
$x_{e,t}$	−0.05	11.55				
$x_{b,t}$	0.19	−0.07	3.00			
dp_t	0.06	−0.87	0.12	0.30		
spr_t	0.01	0.05	−0.42	−0.10	0.62	
$r_{nom,t}$	0.21	−0.16	0.12	0.23	−0.35	0.15
H	−0.4897					
σ_{re}	0.0065					

Source: Authors' calculations; see text.

Notes

[1] To be precise, the benefits of retired civil servants are adjusted according to the general salary increase of active civil servants.

[2] Civil servants are exempt from unemployment insurance and the state covers a certain fraction of health care expenses for civil servants and their families. These fractions range from 50—85 percent, depending on family status, number of children, and state (Börsch-Supan and Wilke 2003).

[3] If, for example, a civil servant were to quit service and take a job in the private sector, he would sacrifice about 50 percent of his accrued pension claims. In this case, the state pays the employee's foregone employer contributions to the national social security system.

[4] To compensate for this cut in pension benefits, civil servants are allowed to (voluntarily) invest up to 4 percent of their salary (with a ceiling of €2,100 per year) into tax sponsored personal retirement account also known as 'Riester accounts'; see Maurer and Schlag (2003).

[5] Being part of former West Germany, Hesse's civil service population appears to be rather representative of the approximately 1.5 million active (which is about 4.5 percent of the German workforce) and 900,000 retired civil servants in Germany as a whole; this section draws on Maurer, Mitchell, and Rogalla (2008).

[6] This time horizon could be easily extended, but after 50 years, all active workers will be fully included in the new funded system.

[7] See Blake (2006), Gold (2003), and Waring (2008).

[8] The difference between the average nominal par yield of long term German government bonds and the average inflation rate for the post-World War II period is about 4 percent. Inflation protected bonds in the Eurozone currently yield about 2 percent. This market is currently not well developed for government bonds (especially those with long durations) which supports the assumption of a real interest rate of 3 percent.

[9] As noted above, we set aside pension benefits of current retirees as well as those already accumulated by currently active civil servants and assume that these will be covered by some other financing arrangement. Thus, only future benefit accruals by active civil servants will be covered by this scheme.

[10] We assume investments in index funds to prevent the state from systematically influencing asset prices.

[11] For a comparable objective function using the Value at Risk see Albrecht et al. (2006).

[12] We deliberately do not dynamically optimize investment weights and contribution rates over time. While this might by appealing from a theoretical perspective, political decision makers will most likely be unable to implement this in practice. Moreover, empirical evidence on pension plan asset allocation suggests that investment weights are rather constant in real-world pension schemes (see Haberman et al. [2003]).

[13] For a detailed discussion of the advantages of the CVaR over the more widely acknowledged VaR see, for example, Artzner et al. (1997, 1999) and Rockafellar and Uryasev (2002).

[14] The state variables included here are commonly used in the strategic asset allocation literature (see e.g., Campbell and Shiller [1988, 1991]; Fama and French [1989]; Campbell, Chan, and Viceira [2003]; Campbell and Viceira [2005]; Cochrane [2005]; Brandt and Santa-Clara [2006]).

[15] For an extensive discussion of design and characteristics of real estate indices we refer to—among others—Hoesli and MacGregor (2000) and Albrecht and Maurer (2005).

[16] In a survey by Eichholtz (1997), correlations between common equities and property company shares range from 0.12 to 0.96.

[17] Other methods to unsmooth real estate return time series have been suggested by—among others—Firstenberg, Ross, and Zisler (1988), Ross and Zisler (1991), Geltner (1993), Fisher, Geltner, and Webb (1994), and Barkham and Geltner (1994).

[18] A thorough analysis of the institutional design of German open-end real estate funds, as well as their risk and return profile can be found in Maurer, Reiner, and Rogalla (2004).

[19] Mean real log returns on bonds in our time series come to almost 5 percent per year while equities only yield an excess return of 1.5 percent. We reduce expected bond returns to 4 percent, considering this to be more appropriate in the long term.

[20] Formally, we expand the total pension cost in Formula 2 to $TPC = \Sigma(RC_t + (1 + \xi_1) \cdot SC_t - (1 - \xi_2) \cdot W_t)$, where W_t are the withdrawals in the case of a funding ratio higher than 180 percent and ξ_2 is the penalty factor.

References

ABP (2006). *ABP Annual Report 2006.* Heerlen, The Netherlands: ABP Investments.

ABP (2007). *Strategic investment plan ABP 2007–2009.* Heerlen, The Netherlands: ABP Investments.

Albrecht, Peter and Raimond Maurer (2005). *Investment- und Risikomanagement,* 2nd ed. Stuttgart, Germany: Schäffer-Poeschel.

—— Joachim Coche, Raimond Maurer, and Ralph Rogalla (2006). 'Understanding and Allocating Investment Risks in a Hybrid Pension Plan,' in D. Blitzstein, O. S. Mitchell, and S. P. Utkus, eds., *Restructuring Retirement Risks.* Oxford: Oxford University Press, pp. 204–25.

Artzner, Philippe, Freddy Delbaen, Jean-Marc Eber, and David Heath (1997). 'Thinking Coherently,' *Risk,* 10(11): 68–72.

—— —— —— —— (1999). 'Coherent Measures of Risk,' *Mathematical Finance,* 9(3): 203–28.

Barkham, Richard and David M. Geltner (1994). 'Unsmoothing British Valuation-based Returns without Assuming an Efficient Market,' *Journal of Property Research,* 11(2): 81–95.

Blake, David (2006). *Pension Finance.* Chichester: Wiley.

Blundell, Gerald F. and Charles W. Ward (1987). 'Property Portfolio Allocation: A Multi-factor Model,' *Land Development Studies,* 4: 145–56.

Börsch-Supan, Axel and Christina B. Wilke (2003). 'The German Public Pension System: How it Was, How it Will Be.' MRRC Working Paper 2003–41. Ann Arbor, MI: Michigan Retirement Research Center.

Brandt, Michael W. and Pedro Santa-Clara (2006). 'Dynamic Portfolio Selection by Augmenting the Asset Space,' *Journal of Finance,* 61(5): 2187–2217.

Campbell, John Y. and Robert J. Shiller (1988). 'Stock Prices, Earnings and Expected Dividends,' *Journal of Finance,* 43: 661–76.

—— —— (1991). 'Yield Spreads and Interest Rate Movements: A Bird's Eye View,' *Review of Economic Studies,* 58: 495–514.

—— and Luis M. Viceira (2002). *Strategic Asset Allocation: Portfolio Choice for Long-Term Investors.* Oxford: Oxford University Press.

—— —— (2005). 'The Term Structure of the Risk-Return-Trade-off,' *Financial Analysts Journal,* 61: 34–44.

—— Yeung L. Chan, and Luis M. Viceira (2003). 'A Multivariate Model for Strategic Asset Allocation,' *Journal of Financial Economics*, 67: 41–80.

Cochrane, John H. (2005). *Asset Pricing*. Princeton: Princeton University Press.

Craft, Timothy M. (2001). 'The Role of Private and Public Real Estate in Pension Plan Portfolio Allocation Choices,' *Journal of Real Estate Portfolio Management*, 7(1): 17–23.

DAV (2004). *Herleitung der DAV-Sterbetafel 2004, R für Rentenversicherungen*. Köln: Deutsche Aktuarvereinigung.

Eichholtz, Piet M. (1997). 'Real Estate Securities and Common Stocks: A First International Look,' *Real Estate Finance*, 14(1): 70–74.

Fama, Eugene F. and Kenneth R. French (1989). 'Business Conditions and the Expected Returns on Stocks and Bonds,' *Journal of Financial Economics*, 25: 23–49.

Firstenberg, Paul M., Stephen A. Ross, and Randall C. Zisler (1988). 'Real Estate: The Whole Story,' *Journal of Portfolio Management*, 14: 22–34.

Fisher, Jeffrey D., David M. Geltner, and R. Brian Webb (1994). 'Value Indices of Commercial Real Estate: A Comparison of Index Construction Methods,' *Journal of Real Estate Finance and Economics*, 9(2): 137–64.

Geltner, David M. (1993). 'Estimating Market Values from Appraised Values without Assuming an Efficient Market,' *Journal of Real Estate Research*, 8(3): 325–45.

Gillis, John R. (1968). 'Aristocracy and Bureaucracy in Nineteenth-Century Prussia,' *Past and Present*, 41(December): 105–29.

Gold, Jeremy (2003). 'Risk Transfer in Public Pension Plans,' in O.S. Mitchell and K. Smetters, eds., *The Pension Challenge: Risk Transfers and Retirement Income Security*. Oxford: Oxford University Press, pp. 102–15.

Haberman, Steven, Christopher Day, David Fogarty, M. Zaki Khorasanee, Martin McWhirter, Nichola Nash, Bernard Ngwira, I. Douglas Wright, and Yakoub Yakoubov (2003). 'A Stochastic Approach to Risk Management and Decision Making in Defined Benefit Pension Schemes,' *British Actuarial Journal*, 9(3): 493–618.

Heubeck, Klaus and Bert Rürup (2000). *Finanzierung der Altersversorgung des öffentlichen Dienstes*. Frankfurt: Peter Lang Verlag.

Hoesli, Martin and Bryan D. MacGregor (2000). *Property Investment: Principles and Practice of Portfolio Management*. Harlow, England: Pearson.

Hoevenaars, Roy P., Roderick D. Molenaar, and Tom B. Steenkamp (2003). 'Simulation for the Long Run,' in B. Scherer, ed., *Asset Liability Management Tools*. London: Risk Books.

—— —— Peter C. Schotman, and Tom B. Steenkamp (2008). 'Strategic Asset Allocation with Liabilities: Beyond Stocks and Bonds,' *Journal of Economic Dynamics and Control*, 32(9): 2939–70.

Hustead, Edwin C. and Olivia S. Mitchell (2001). 'Public Sector Pension Plans,' in O.S. Mitchell and E.C. Hustead, eds., *Pensions in the Public Sector*. Philadelphia, PA: University of Pennsylvania Press, pp. 3–10.

Maurer, Raimond and Christian Schlag (2003). 'Money-Back Guarantees in Individual Pension Accounts: Evidence from the German Pension Reform,' in O.S. Mitchell and K. Smetters, eds., *The Pension Challenge: Risk Transfers and Retirement Income Security*. Oxford: Oxford University Press, pp. 187–213.

Maurer, Raimond, Frank Reiner, and Steffen Sebastian (2003). 'Financial Characteristics of International Real Estate Returns: Evidence from the UK, US, and Germany,' *Journal of Real Estate Portfolio Management*, 10(1): 59–76.

—— —— and Ralph Rogalla (2004). 'Return and Risk of German Open-end Real Estate Funds,' *Journal of Property Research*, 21(3): 209–33.

—— Olivia S. Mitchell, and Ralph Rogalla (2008). 'The Victory of Hope over Angst? Funding, Asset Allocation, and Risk Taking in German Public Sector Pension Reform,' in D. Broeders, S. Eijffinger, A. Houben, eds., *Frontiers in Pension Finance*. Cheltenham, UK: Edward Elgar, pp. 51–79.

McGill, Daniel M., Kyle N. Brown, John J. Haley, and Sylvester J. Schieber (2005). *Fundamentals of Private Pensions*, 9th ed. Oxford: Oxford University Press.

Mitchell, Olivia S., David McCarthy, Stanley C. Wisniewski, and Paul Zorn (2001). 'Developments in State and Local Pension Plans,' in O.S. Mitchell and E.C. Hustead, eds., *Pensions in the Public Sector*. Philadelphia, PA: University of Pennsylvania Press, pp. 11–40.

Rockafellar, R. Tyrrell and Stanislav Uryasev (2002). 'Conditional Value-at-Risk for General Loss Distributions,' *Journal of Banking and Finance*, 26: 1443–71.

Ross, Stephen A. and Randall C. Zisler (1991). 'Risk and Return in Real Estate,' *Journal of Real Estate Finance and Economics* 4(2): 175–90.

Stambaugh, Robert F. (1997). 'Analyzing Investments whose Histories Differ in Length,' *Journal of Financial Economics*, 45: 285–331.

Waring, M. Barton (2008). 'Between Scylla and Charybdis: Improving the Cost Effectiveness of DB Retirement Plans,' in O.S. Mitchell and G.W. Anderson, eds., *The Future of Public Employee Retirement Systems*. Oxford: Oxford University Press, forthcoming.

Wilshire Consulting (2007). *Wilshire Report on State Retirement Systems: Funding Levels and Asset Allocation*. Wilshire, CA: Wilshire Associates Incorporated.

Ziobrowski, Brigitte J. and Alan J. Ziobrowski (1997). 'Higher Real Estate Risk and Mixed-Asset Portfolio Performance,' *Journal of Real Estate Portfolio Management*, 3(2): 107–15.

Chapter 10

The Outlook for Canada's Public Sector Employee Pensions

Silvana Pozzebon

Occupational pension plans are a key component of Canada's retirement income system. Assets held by occupational pensions or registered pension plans accounted for 60 percent of the total CAN$1.9 trillion of assets amassed in the country's retirement programs in 2006.[1] Occupational pension plans of public sector employees in turn play an important role in the Canadian retirement regime. With almost two-fifths of Canada's retirement assets held by public sector pension funds, the latter represented the largest share of the country's pension assets in 2006 (Statistics Canada 2008). The nine largest Canadian pension funds were also associated with the public sector, accounting for 46 percent of the total market value assets of CAN$693.1 billion accumulated in Canada's 100 top pension funds (in 2006).[2]

In terms of employment, the public sector corresponded to 21 percent of the Canadian paid labor force in 2006.[3] This sector includes civil servants and employees of government enterprises at various levels (federal, provincial, territorial, and local), as well as provincial and territorial employees of publicly-funded educational, health, and social service institutions.

The turbulent employment and market environments of recent years have spurred considerable interest in occupational pensions in Canada among practitioners, policymakers, and a few researchers. One area that remains largely unexplored concerns public sector employee pension plans, the subject of this chapter. In what follows, we first examine the relative importance of public and private sector employee pension plans in Canada and review their general characteristics drawing largely from administrative data collected by Statistics Canada (various years) through the *Pension Plans in Canada Survey.* We then turn to a discussion of funding issues and other challenges faced by public sector plans.

Relative importance of public and private sector plans

Registered pension plans (RPPs) are the most common type of occupational pension arrangement in Canada.[4] For reasons of simplicity, RRPs will be referred to as either occupational pension plans or employer-sponsored pension plans in what follows. Voluntarily-sponsored by employers or unions, RPPs must comply with federal income tax law to obtain favorable tax treatment for both employer and employee contributions within stipulated limits, as well as for investment earnings. RPPs are also subject to minimum standards prescribed by federal and provincial pension regulations. Some public sector employee groups (e.g., civil servants, teachers, and members of legislative assemblies) are covered by special pension statutes. These employee groups under special statutes differ among jurisdictions and in some instances, there is a degree of complementarity between special statutes and the general pension legislation applicable in the jurisdiction.

As Table 10-1 shows, a number of parallels can be drawn between the registered pension plan membership distribution of public and private sector employees. The 5.8 million Canadian RPP participants at the beginning of 2007 were almost evenly divided between the public and the private sectors. Moreover, the share of pension plan membership as a percentage of the country's paid workers was also similar in the two sectors (18% for the public sector versus 20% for the private sector). Differences in membership distribution between the sectors exceed similarities however. Public sector plan membership appears to be heavily concentrated (Table 10-1), with three-fifths of public sector RPP members employed by provincial government bodies or enterprises at the beginning of 2007. Analysis of additional data not reported in Table 10-1 indicates that the vast majority of public sector RPP members were found in two industrial classifications: 67 percent in public administration and 26 percent in educational services, health care, and social assistance.[5] By contrast, private sector plan members work in a wider range of industries with the largest proportions being in manufacturing (25%), followed by trades (18%), construction (13%), and finance (12%).

Membership gender patterns between the public and private sectors also diverge, as shown in Table 10-1. Sixty percent of public sector plan participants were female with proportions reversed in the private sector where 62 percent of members were male. These numbers do not reveal the fact that females represent a steadily growing share of plan members in both sectors over time. The proportion of females in the public sector increased from 37 percent in 1974 to 60 percent in 2007, while in the private sector, the proportion almost doubled from 20 to 38 percent during

TABLE 10-1 Overview of public and private sector Registered Pension Plans (RPPs), Canada, 2007 (at January 1)

	Public (%)	Private (%)
Active members in RPPs (total: 5.8 million)	47	53
Number of RPPs (total: 18,594)	7	93
Male members in RPPs (total: 3.0 million)	36	64
Plan assets as % of reserves held in all RPPs (total: 1.1 trillion CAN$, market value)	67	33
Members in sector:		
Members as % of Canadian paid labor force	18	20
Members as % of paid labor force in sector	86	25
Male	40	62
Sub-sector of employment		
Municipal	24	–
Provincial	59	–
Federal	16	–
Other	1	–
Plan size		
1–99 members	1	7
100–999	3	26
1,000–9,999	11	35
10,000–29,999	12	11
30,000+	73	21

Sources: Author's calculations based on Statistics Canada (n.d. Table 183-0002, n.d. Table 280-0009, n.d. Table 280-0010, n.d. Table 280-0012, n.d. *Proportion of Labour Force and Paid Workers Covered by a Registered Pension Plan [RPP]*).

the same period.[6] Among the explanations cited for this trend are the growth in female labor force participation, and employment shifts away from male-dominated areas such as heavy industry and manufacturing to female-dominated service industries (Schembari 2006).

The table also reveals that, compared to the private sector, most public sector plan members were concentrated in large plans. Almost three-quarters of the public sector members were in plans of 30,000 or more, whereas more than two-thirds of private sector members were in plans of 10,000 or fewer. These figures are consistent with the fact that plans in the public sector represented only 7 percent of the 18,594 RPPs in Canada at the beginning of 2007.[7]

Perhaps the most telling distinctions between the public and private sectors emerge from a study of RPP coverage rates. At the end of 2006, total RPP participants in Canada represented 38.1 percent of paid workers.[8] The RPP coverage rate fell from 44.7 percent in 1981 to 38.1 percent in 2006, with a consistent downward trend discernable since the early 1990s

(see Figure 10-1). The decrease in overall RPP coverage rates in Canada
has been driven by developments in the private sector. The proportion
of private sector paid workers who were members of employer-sponsored
pension plans has eroded slowly since 1991 from percentages in the mid- to
low-thirties during the 1980s to 25 percent at the end of 2006. By comparison, the share of public sector paid workers in RPPs experienced a one-time
jump from 76 percent in 1989 to 84 percent in 1991, rose slowly until 1999
and has been relatively stable since. As such, the 86 percent coverage rate
at the end of 2006 for the public sector stands in sharp opposition to the
situation in the private sector where only a quarter of the paid labor force
is covered by an occupational pension.

Several explanations have been offered for the decline of private
sector pension coverage in Canada. Among these are the structural
shifts in employment as mentioned earlier, complex legal requirements
which added to pension administrative costs, and an uncertain economic
environment increasing the financial burden of pensions for employers.
Differences in unionization rates between the private and public sectors
may also be telling since unions have traditionally sought to secure pensions

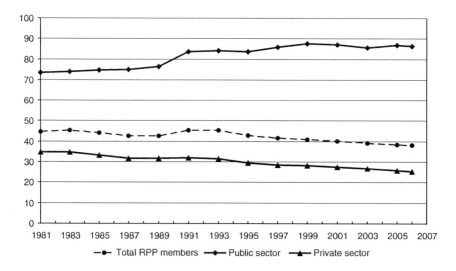

Figure 10-1 Percentage of paid workers covered by a Registered Pension Plan
(RPP), total and by sector, Canada: 1981–2006. *Sources*: Total percentages: 1981–
2003 data from Statistics Canada (2006*b*); 2005 data from Statistics Canada (2007*a*);
2006 data from Statistics Canada (n.d. Proportion of labour force and paid workers
covered by a registered pension plan). Sector percentages: Author's calculations
using: sources cited for total percentages; Statistics Canada (n.d. Table 183-0002,
n.d. Table 280-0009); Statistics Canada (2006*a*).

for their members. In fact, union density is fairly high in the public sector and has remained relatively stable at a little more than 70 percent (71% in 2006) since 1984. On the other hand, union density is considerably lower in the private sector and has decreased from 26 percent in 1984 to 17 percent in 2006 (Akyeampong 2004; Statistics Canada 2007*b*). Although a direct relationship cannot be established between RPP and union membership trends on the basis of these figures, it is interesting to note the parallels. Finally, the boost in public sector coverage in the early 1990s has been related both to the growth in female membership and changes to pension law extending RPP membership to part-timers (Schembari 2006).

Characteristics of public and private sector plans

General Plan Features. At the beginning of 2007, single-employer plans accounted for three-quarters of all the 5.8 million RPP members in Canada. Although slightly more than half of all single-employer plan participants worked in the public sector, the vast majority (89%) of this sector's members were in single-employer plans (Table 10-2). The normal retirement age of a small fraction of public sector plan members (15%) is set at the relatively early age of 60; it is 65 years of age for virtually all (96%) private sector plan members. Information on early retirement provisions is no longer made available. However, the author has not found evidence to dispute past evidence showing that unreduced early retirement benefits are prevalent in the public sector. Access to such benefits can be based on age and/or number of years of service combinations, such as the 55/30 rule for Canadian federal civil servants.

Table 10-2 also reveals that pension plans of the defined benefit (DB) type remain prevalent among Canadian RPP members, particularly among those who work in the public sector. Respectively, 81 percent of all RPP participants and 93 percent of public sector plan members were covered by such savings arrangements at the start of 2007.[9] DB plans have especially stood the test of time in the public sector. As Figure 10-2 shows, they have represented over 90 percent of the sector's members for over three decades even if a slight downward trend is perceptible. The percentage of private sector plan members in DB plans also remains important (67% at the beginning of 2007), but the decline is more pronounced than in the public sector. During the period from 1974–2007, coverage in the private sector fell by 21 percentage points versus 6 percentage points for the public sector.

By contrast, the share of plan members from both sectors in defined contribution (DC) plans has increased, rising considerably more rapidly in the private sector than in the public sector. Rising to a peak of 25 percent in

TABLE 10-2 General characteristics of public and private sector registered
pension plans, Canada 2007, at January 1 (percent of members)

	Public (2,730,676 members)	Private (3,037,604 members)
RPP members in single employer plans (total:4.3 million)	56	44
Single employer plan members in sector	89	62
RPP members in DB plans (total: 4.6 million)	56	44
DB plan members in sector	93	67
RPP members in DC plans (total: 0.9 million)	15	85
DB plan members in sector	5	25
Normal retirement		
Age 60	15	2
Age 65	80	96

Sources: Author's calculations based on Statistics Canada (n.d. Table 280-0012, n.d. Table 280-0013, n.d. Table 280-0016, n.d. Table 280-0024).

2007, the proportion of private sector plan members in DC plans was almost three times as high as it was in 1974 (9%). The public sector's share of members in DC plans was only 5 percent at the beginning of 2007 and this represented a decline of 1 percent from the previous peak. Additionally, data not presented here indicate that a small but rising percentage (from

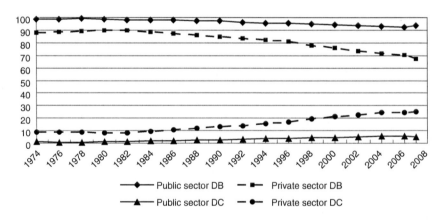

Figure 10-2 Percentage of registered pension plan members in defined benefit and defined contribution plans by sector, Canada: 1974–2007 (at January 1). *Source*: Statistics Canada (n.d. Table 280-0016).

1% in 2000 to 4% in 2007) of overall RPP members are covered by some sort of defined benefit/defined combination arrangement, and much of this change appears to be concentrated in the private sector.[10]

The trends noted in the earlier paragraphs are consistent with the movement discerned internationally regarding the shift from DB to DC plans, even if the latter is less marked in Canada than elsewhere (Schembari 2006). However, the growing importance of plans of the DC type in Canada is not entirely captured by statistics on RPPs as these do not include one increasingly popular retirement savings arrangement offered by private sector employers, *group registered retirement savings plans* (see Pozzebon [2005]).

Defined Benefit Plan Features. The overall generosity of RPPs of the DB type is higher for the public sector than the private sector, as is indicated in Table 10-3. Two factors likely explain this outcome. First, unlike the private sector, essentially all public sector plan participants must make contributions; and second, these are relatively more substantial in the public sector (contributions are discussed in more detail in the following text).

At the beginning of 2007, the pension formula of a representative public sector worker was based on a calculation using 2 percent of the average of the best four to five years of earnings.[11] By comparison, the benefit formula of only 58 percent of private sector plan members was earnings-based, with the remaining plans providing a flat benefit (and the latter are generally expected to result in lower pension benefits). The benefit calculation for private sector participants covered by earnings-based plans was also more varied: 66 percent were in plans using the average of best earnings which are likely to provide the most generous benefits in the earnings-based group; 14 percent were in plans using average of final earnings;[12] and 21 percent were in plans using average of career earnings, typically the least generous of the earnings-based group. Finally, the method for determining the pension benefit of slightly less than half of the private sector's members was based on a percent of annual earnings with 47 percent of this group covered by plans that used a multiplier of less than 2 percent.

Public sector employee pension plans were also relatively more generous than those of their private sector counterparts in providing automatic pension benefit adjustments that fully or partially compensate for increases to the consumer price index (CPI). The contrast between the two sectors is notable: the plans of more than three-quarters of public sector members included such an adjustment at the beginning of 2007, while those of approximately a sixth of private sector plan members did so. The share of members in both sectors belonging to plans offering benefit integration with the Canadian social security program—either the Canada Pension Plan (CPP) or the Quebec Pension Plan (QPP)—was important in both sectors, accounting for almost all public sector plan members and 74 percent of their private sector counterparts.

TABLE 10-3 Design features of public and private sector Defined Benefit Registered Pension Plans, Canada 2007, at January 1 (percent of members)

*Benefit integrated with CPP/QPP***	*Public (2,550,813 DB members)*	*Private (2,039,992 DB members)*
Benefit formula		
Flat benefit	0[+]	42
Earnings-based	100	58
Final average earnings	4	14
< 4 years	24	14
4 to 5 years	x	x
> 5 years	x	x
Average best earnings	93	66
< 4 years	7	22
4 to 5 years	92	76
> 5 years	1[E]	2[E]
Career average earnings	3	21
% Earnings per year of service	99*	48*
< 1.50	1[E]	16[E]
1.50–1.99	1	31
2.00	97	53
> 2.00	0	1
Automatic adjustment of pension to CPI	77	16
Full increase	39	13
Partial increase	54	79

Notes: Totals may not add to 100 due to rounding.

x Data not reported by Statistics Canada to meet the Statistics Act confidentiality criteria.

[+] Data rounded to 0. Only 165 RPP members in the public sector are covered by a flat benefit plan.

[E] Though data are not reported by Statistics Canada to meet the Statistics Act confidentiality criteria, percentage is estimated using data from remaining categories.

* Percentage calculated as follows: numerator is members in plans reported in the 'Total benefit rate based on percentage of earnings' category from Statistics Canada (n.d. Table 280-0022). This does not correspond to the numerator used for the 'earnings-based' entry in this table which is from Statistics Canada (n.d. Table 280-0017). Differences appear to be related to how hybrid and other combination plans are classified. Denominator is members in plans not classified as defined contribution in Statistics Canada (n.d. Table 280-0022) which includes hybrid and other combination plans.

** Percentage of members with benefit integration among plans classified under the category 'Total benefit rate based on percentage of earnings' from Statistics Canada (n.d. Table 280-0022). CPP is the government sponsored retirement income program for Canadians other than those living in Quebec. The latter are covered by the QPP.

Source: Author's calculations based on Statistics Canada (n.d. Table 280-0016, n.d. Table 280-0017, n.d. Table 280-0022, n.d. Table 280-0023, n.d. Table 280-0025).

TABLE 10-4 Contributions to public and private sector Registered Pension
Plans, Canada 2007, at January 1

	Public	Private
Employee contributions required (% of members)	99.7	64
Contributory plans based on % of earnings	89	59
Contributory plans based on variable rate	11	22
Employee contribution rate: % of earnings (% of members)		
< 5.0	1	48
5.0–5.9	6	33
6.0–6.9	12	16
≥ 7.0	81	3
% of contributions made by employer (total ER contributions 2007: CAN\$31.7 B)	64	84
Current service (net)	78	53
Actuarial deficiencies and unfunded liabilities	22	47

Source: Author's calculations based on Statistics Canada (n.d. Table 280-0018, n.d. Table 280-0026).

Contributions. Practically all public sector plan participants are in con-tributory plans (see Table 10-4). By comparison, slightly less than two-thirds of their private sector counterparts are required to make contributions. As to contribution levels, only 1 percent of the public sector membership made annual contributions of less than 5 percent of earnings to their pension funds at the start of 2007; 81 percent of members contributed at least 7 percent of earnings. The share of private sector plan members in these same two categories was quite different: 48 percent fell into the first group but only 3 percent into the second. Interestingly, the distribu-tion of members in the 'employee contribution rate' categories presented in Table 10-4 is fairly representative of the longer term situation in the private sector but not so in the public sector. The 2007 figures resemble those of the 1990s more closely than the distribution of subsequent years which showed higher percentages of members contributing between 5–6.9 percent of earnings and a lower share contributing at least 7 percent of earnings. As will be discussed further in the following text, funding issues offer a likely explanation for these patterns.

Overall, Canadian employers and employees contributed CAN\$31.7 billion to pension funds in 2007. The relative percentage of contribu-tions attributed to employers (versus employees) was lower in the public sector (64%) than in the private sector (84%). This difference may be partly attributed to the larger proportion of private sector members in non-contributory plans, which is consistent with employers assuming a larger share of overall costs. In fact, the proportion of contributions made by the sector's employers has been at least 70 percent in the period from 1974 to 2007 and remained consistently lower during the same time span in the public sector, ranging from 56 to 64 percent.

Consideration of the latter trends alone may be misleading, for example, if differences in contribution proportions between the sectors are merely reflecting dissimilar shares being allocated to funding liabilities. At first glance, Table 10-4 appears to support this premise. Yet additional analyses reveal that in both sectors, not only did the percentage of overall employer contributions reach a historic high in 2007, but more monies were being allocated to the reduction of pension deficits. With respect to the latter, the 47 percent figure reported on the last line of Table 10-4 represents a peak for the private sector. Similarly, the admittedly lower share of overall employer contributions in the public sector allotted to improve funding (22%) was also the highest it has been since 1993.[13]

Funding issues and other challenges

As the earlier discussion suggests, considerable effort has been expended in improving the funding situation of Canadian occupational pension plans in recent years. Much of the attention has been focused on the private sector, however. This is not unrelated to the stricter funding requirements imposed on the sector's employers and the implementation of special legislative measures to improve the solvency ratio of the plans they sponsor. Less is known about funding issues and developments in the public sector, so to these topics we turn next.

Trends in Public Sector Funding. Funding issues do not appear to have been much of a concern for most public sector pension plan sponsors in Canada as recently as 10–15 years ago. In the past, for instance, it was not unknown for governments to pay their share of retirees' benefits on a pay-as-you-go basis out of general revenue funds, where employee contributions were also deposited if they were not held in designated revenue funds invested in non-marketable government bonds. Such approaches to funding began to raise anxieties about the ability of public sector employers to secure the pension promise as demographic and economic conditions changed in the last two decades. Among the factors that appear to have played a major role were increased pressures for governments to balance budgets, the aging of the public sector workforce (many of whose members are part of the large baby boomer cohort), and increased life expectancies. Lobbying efforts by unions strongly established in the sector was another likely contributing factor.

Several approaches, many of them interrelated, have been used in an attempt to improve the funding status of Canadian public sector pensions in recent years. The widespread move to market-based investment of public sector pension assets is the most visible. In many cases this has also involved the establishment of autonomous funded schemes (as opposed to non-autonomous consolidate revenue funds, for example) to which both employers and employees direct contributions.[14]

The well-known Ontario Teachers' Pension Plan Board, set up in 1990, was probably a precursor of these trends that grew slowly during the 1990s, developed momentum toward the end of the decade, and continue today. A brief look at the situation of some of Canada's most important public sector pensions is suggestive. For example, the decade of the 1990s saw the creation of other autonomous funds in Ontario such as the Ontario Public Service Employees Union Pension Trust (OPTrust) which invests and manages the Ontario Public Sector Employees Union pension plan monies. In 1999, the British Columbia Investment Management Corporation (bcIMC), an independent body which provides investment services for several of the province's major public sector unions, came into being. A few months later, in April 2000, the Public Sector Pension Investment Board was established for federal civil servants.

The creation of independent funded entities in Canada has further been associated with the establishment of joint trusteeship of pension funds, although the two movements are not entirely concurrent. The little information available on joint trusteeship suggests that the phenomenon has grown beyond the early stages. Penetration of joint pension plan governance is most prevalent among the large public sector plans of two of Canada's foremost provinces, Ontario and British Columbia. Information available from the National Union of Public and General Employees (2007), a federation of unions in Canada, provides a good overview of existing joint governance arrangements among its affiliates scattered throughout the country.[15] The National Union of Public and General Employees (2007) also indicates that active lobbying has garnered commitments from the governments of at least two Atlantic Provinces to move toward joint trusteeship of public sector plans in these jurisdictions.

It is upheld that the joint trusteeship of pension plans implies a shared responsibility between the employer and employees that will result in the greater financial stability of the plan. From the employer's perspective, it can be argued that as an active participant with an obligation to assume half of the plan's liabilities, a union may interpret the notion of defending the interests of the employees differently than when it assumes solely a bargaining stance. For example, since pension costs cannot be as easily passed on to the employer in a joint trusteeship context, unions may pursue benefit improvements less aggressively at the expense of other considerations. Similarly, it may be that unions worried about securing the pension promise for their members will be in a better position to pressure reluctant employers to tackle funding questions.

Theory, of course, does not necessarily translate into practice. In the absence of any systematic data on the success of joint governance arrangements, the experience of several high-profile Canadian public sector plans that embrace joint trusteeship provides insights that inspire confidence in the approach (e.g., the Ontario Teachers' Pension Plan, the Ontario Public Sector Employees Union, and British Columbia's Public Service Pension Plan). Public documents testify to the efforts that are continuously being made to assure the financial health of these pension funds, some of which have been rather successful. There is also a noticeable transparency in the information provided, a factor probably not unrelated to the existence of joint trusteeship arrangements. In fact, several large public sector pensions under such agreements or the investment management entities with which they are associated, actively promote good governance practices among institutional investors. A glance at the membership list of the Canadian Coalition for Good Governance supports this.[16]

Investment Strategies. While little documentation exists to attest to the trends described earlier, Statistics Canada does collect data on trusteed pension funds, that is, those that operate according to the terms of a trust agreement. These funds accounted for 75 percent of total RPP plans assets in 2006.[17] As such, data on trusteed pension funds provide valuable information on the investment strategies of occupation pension plans. This is especially true for public sector funds which held 65 percent of total trusteed plans assets (CAN$873.6 billion) in 2006.

Policy changes implemented during the early 1990s permitted many large public sector funds to invest in equities (Anderson 2006).[18] As Figure 10-3 shows, this resulted in an increase in the proportion of assets held in stocks and a decline in that held in bonds at least until 1996. That year marked a shift in investment strategy, as fund managers attempted to reduce risk by diversifying plan portfolios. Consequently, exposure to stocks was lowered and that to pooled investment funds raised. The overall investment patterns for private sector trusteed funds are generally similar to those of the public sector from 1996 onward (see Figure 10-4) except with respect to exposure to stocks and pooled investments after 2004. According to their decreasing importance in the portfolio mix, the public–private sector asset distribution in 2006 was: 33 percent versus 42 percent in pooled investments, 32 percent versus 30 percent in stocks, 23 percent versus 19 percent in bonds, and 11 percent versus 8 percent in other investments.

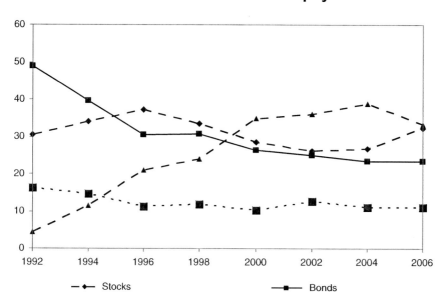

Figure 10-3 Asset allocation of trusteed public sector pension funds, Canada: 1992–2006 (percentage of total assets at market value). *Note*: Other investments include mortgages, real estate, cash, deposits, short-term funds, and miscellaneous assets. *Source*: Author's calculations based on Statistics Canada (n.d. Table 280-0005).

It is also interesting to note that a few of Canada's large public sector pensions have recently also become major players in the private equity market, by virtue of the investment sophistication they have developed and the size of their asset holdings.[19] They are attracted to the potentially high returns private equity markets can offer and have participated in innovative private equity partnerships with foreign partners both in Canada and abroad. Alternative investments, particularly infrastructure assets are a draw for public sector pensions in search of long-term stable returns.

Challenges. Lacking systematic data available on funding ratios for Canadian public sector plans, attempts to qualify their overall financial health would be misplaced. Nevertheless, this author ventures to say that experience in this regard is likely quite varied, as is true of the private sector. Moreover, as the previous section suggests, there is a degree of convergence between the sectors with respect to investment strategy. On the basis of the widely documented vulnerability of private sector pensions to market volatility, it is clear that, as public pension funds assume investment

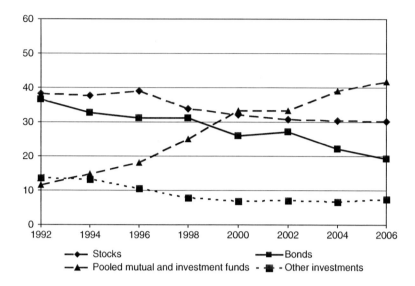

Figure 10-4 Asset allocation of trusteed private sector pension funds, Canada: 1992–2006 (percentage of total assets at market value). *Note:* Other investments include mortgages, real estate, cash, deposits, short-term funds, and miscellaneous assets. *Source:* Author's calculations based on Statistics Canada (n.d. Table 280-0005).

behaviors comparable to those of the private sector, they will face similar market risks and challenges.

Unlike private sector plans, it is improbable that those in the public sector will be confronted with a sponsoring employer's bankruptcy, but other employer-related funding threats exist. More specifically, governments at all levels still hold large pension liabilities. These amounted to CAN\$205.1 billion in 2006, with the federal government responsible for 64 percent of this total.[20] Note that liabilities at the federal level entail obligations that predate the move in 2000 to an autonomous funded pension arrangement.

There is reason for limited optimism in this area however. As the budgetary position of provincial governments has improved, several provinces have taken steps to reduce their pension liabilities (Lovely 2006).[21] For example, the government of Newfoundland and Labrador directed a CAN\$2 billion transfer payment from the federal government to the elimination of the unfunded liability of the province's teachers' pension in 2005 and it has since moved to reduce its pension liabilities toward other public service employees using debt-financed payments. Canada's three other Atlantic provinces, as well as the governments of Manitoba and Quebec, have also taken steps to decrease public employee pension liabilities by making special payments.

The situation of Quebec is noteworthy. This province accounted for 77 percent of the CAN$74 billion of pension liabilities accumulated by all governments other than at the federal level in 2006.[22] To better assess the relative size of this liability, consider that at 36 percent, Ontario employed the highest proportion of Canada's public sector workers in 2006 relative to Quebec which took second place at 24 percent, and British Columbia which came in third at 11 percent. Yet, the Ontario government's pension liabilities represented only 3 percent of total non-federal pension liabilities and British Columbia held less than 1 percent.

In an effort to improve the funding situation of its public sector employee pensions, the Quebec government established a designated fund in 1993, the Retirement Plans Sinking Fund, to which it has since regularly made optional annual payments (Finances Quebec 2008). These special contributions have been financed by issued government bonds and, in turn, monies accumulated in the designated fund have been invested in a mixed portfolio by the Caisse de Depot et Placement. The Caisse has also managed assets originating from employee contributions since the early 1970s. As of March 2008, the Quebec government reported that it had met approximately half of its pension actuarial obligations and projects to reach its goal of 70 percent earlier than anticipated. Notwithstanding these promising results, it should be recalled that debt-financed schemes such as this one, which are based on the expectation that investment returns will exceed the cost of borrowing, carry their own risks.

Demographic issues also pose considerable challenges for public sector pensions. As is generally true of Canada's workforce, public sector workers are aging. Many of these are baby boomers, so they are moving toward retirement *en masse*. Consider further that the Canadian public sector experienced an important expansion during the late 1960s and into the 1970s. Add to this the prevalence of unreduced early retirement benefits and the provision of some measure of inflation protection in public sector pension plans, and longevity has also increased in the overall Canadian population during the last decades. Taken together, this particular confluence of factors appears to be putting important pressure on public sector plans.

Moreover, the large group of baby boomers that joined the ranks of the public sector at approximately the same time is nearing retirement age. Many of the sector's workers have accumulated sufficient credits to be eligible for unreduced early retirement benefits and it appears they are opting for this choice.[23] As such, not only will this large group receive pension benefits (generally with some measure of inflation protection whose costs are difficult to predict) during an extensive retirement period, but pensioners are expected to live longer than actuaries had predicted. Coupled with the demographically driven decrease in the workforce, a decline in the ratio of active members to retirees can be expected. Overall, this scenario suggests that there will be insufficient funds in many public sector plans to meet retirement benefit requirements in the future, particularly if the large unfunded liabilities accumulated by governments at various levels remain on the books.

No systematic study of Canada's public sector pension plans confirms these outcomes, but anecdotal evidence is suggestive. In a recent submission to the Ontario Expert Commission on Pensions reviewing the province's pension legislation, the OPTrust expresses the belief that the ratio of active members to retirees is falling for many public sector pension plans (OPTrust 2007). The OPTrust further provides evidence of its own declining membership ratio attributed in part to high early retirement take-up rates. In the same vein, the case of the Ontario Teachers' Pension Plan is particularly revealing.[24] This pension plan recently ranked as the top pension service provider in North America and internationally, has a reputation for being a successful institutional investor. It has made an annual average return of 11.4 percent since 1990, consistently outperformed market benchmarks and generated surpluses from 1993 to 2005. But Teachers' has been at odds with funding shortfalls more recently. These are attributed to the declining ratio of active members to retirees resulting from early retirements and the longer life expectancy of pensioners. Because of the low ratio of contributors to pensioners, taking on additional investment risk is perceived as a less than optimal solution. Teachers' also judges that contribution increases alone (these have already been raised for 2006–09) will make it difficult to assure the plan's future viability. It is currently studying the situation in search of more creative solutions.

As suggested earlier, turning to market-based investment of pension funds is a popular option for those seeking to improve or maintain the financial health of public sector pension plans. While a well-crafted investment strategy can prove beneficial, it may not be sufficient going forward. Moreover, the search for higher returns carries corresponding risks. Other solutions will have to be considered. Increasing contributions is one of the more obvious and some public plans have already taken this route, but this option can place a disproportionate burden on active members. Benefit decreases or restructuring as well as less favorable early retirement conditions are other alternatives. These longer-term measures will require membership and retiree education and careful consideration to assure the equitable treatment of all. Clearly, there is scope for creativity in the search for solutions that will not impose undue costs on active members, retirees,[25] or both.

Conclusion

This chapter has shown that Canadian public sector RRPs have retained their traditional characteristics until recently, offering generous defined benefits to the vast majority of the sector's employees. This outcome is associated with the fact that essentially all public sector pension plan participants are required to make substantial contributions to their plans.

Public pensions appear less static when funding issues are considered. Coverage rates for private sector workers have fallen over time and a rising proportion of this sector's employees are members of DC plans. Efforts to increase the financial health of these plans have seen many public sector funds mimicking the market-based investment behavior and structure of the private sector, with the inherent risks and successes this entails. Positive models of joint pension fund sponsorship have also emerged in the public sector. But, even for those who have been successful forerunners on all these fronts, the Ontario Teachers' Pension Plan being a case in point, demographics will continue to represent a formidable challenge. In this context, the large unfunded pension liabilities held by governments are an additional cause for concern.

Notes

[1] Author's calculations based on Statistics Canada (2008). In addition to occupational pensions, Canada has a two-tier social security component providing basic income for the elderly (a quasi-universal flat benefit and low-income supplements through the Old Age Security programs) and an earnings-based benefit through the Canada Pension Plan/Quebec Pension Plan schemes; and individual registered savings plans.

[2] Sector affiliation of pension plans and calculations by author based on Kranc (2007).

[3] Author's calculations based on sources given in Figure 10-1.

[4] An increasingly prevalent occupational pension arrangement in Canada's private sector is the form known as group 'registered retirement savings plans' (group RRSPs). These are not subject to pension regulation, offer tax exemptions only for employee contributions and are essentially pools of individual registered retirement savings plans (RRSPs) to which employers facilitate access. The overlap between individual and group RRSPs as well as the lack of category specific data on these two types of savings vehicles can justify classifying group RRSPs as individual savings plans rather than occupational pension arrangements. This approach is often adopted in Statistics Canada publications and we follow their example here.

[5] Figures for manufacturing and construction are estimated by the author since Statistics Canada did not report data for these sectors due to confidentiality constraints. See Statistics Canada (n.d. Table 280-0011).

[6] Author's calculations based on Statistics Canada (n.d. Table 280-0008).

[7] Interestingly, a third of the more than 17,000 private sector RPPs had only one member. Statistics Canada (n.d. Table 280-0010).

[8] The unemployed, unpaid family members, and the self-employed with an unincorporated business are not considered paid workers.

[9] Aggregate data on RPP membership from Statistics Canada (n.d. Table 280-0008).

[10] Author's calculations based on data from Statistics Canada (n.d. Table 280-0016).

[11] To determine the benefit payable, this percentage is multiplied by the number of years of service.

[12] For two otherwise equivalent plans, if earnings in the final years before retirement are the highest, then final average earnings and best average earnings will yield the same pension benefit.

[13] Author's calculations based on Statistics Canada (n.d. Table 280-0026).

[14] The assets of the pension plan that regroups various categories of the province of Quebec's public sector employees, RREGOP, have been managed by the Caisse de Depot et Placement du Quebec since 1973. Since these assets represent monies originating only from employee contributions, RREGOP falls into a category distinct from those discussed in the paper.

[15] See especially Appendix 3 of National Union of Public and General Employees (2007).

[16] Interestingly, one of Canada's largest institutional investors of pension funds, the Caisse de Depot et Placement du Quebec, is absent from thiss list.

[17] Author's calculations based on Statistics Canada (2008).

[18] Much of this paragraph draws from Anderson's analysis (2006) of investment trends for total assets held in trusteed RPPs funds.

[19] This paragraph draws largely from Koumanakos (2007). The group of major players discussed here also includes the Canada Pension Plan Investment Board and the Caisse de Depot et Placement du Quebec which hold the assets of government administered social security programs.

[20] Author's calculations based on Statistics Canada (n.d. Table 385-0014).

[21] This paragraph draws from Lovely (2006).

[22] Data in this paragraph based on author's calculations using Statistics Canada (n.d. Table 183-0002, n.d. Table 385-0018).

[23] In 2007, the median age of retirement was 58.8 in the public sector and 62.4 in the private sector. Both sectors experienced a fall in the median retirement age during the 1980s (from the mid-1980s on in the public sector and a few years later in the private sector) to 1999, but the decline was more accentuated in the public sector. Since then the median retirement age has increased slightly in both sectors. Statistics Canada (n.d. Table 282-0051).

[24] This paragraph draws from Ontario Teachers' Pension Plan (2008a, 2008b).

[25] To avoid repetition, the URL for the E-STAT distributor is included in this reference only. The same URL applies for all subsequent references that mention the E-STAT distributor.

References

Akyeampong, Ernest B. (2004). 'The Union Movement in Transition,' *Perspectives on Labour and Income*, 5(8): Statistics Canada, Catalogue no. 75-001-XIE. http://www.statcan.ca/english/freepub/75-001-XIE/10804/art-1.htm.

Anderson, Robert (2006). 'Trusteed Pension Plans and Funds, 1990 to 2004,' *Canada's Retirement Income Programs 2006 Edition*, Statistics Canada, Catalogue 74-507XCD, CD-ROM.

Finances Quebec (2008). *2008–2009 Budget: Budget Plan (March)*. Quebec, Canada: Government of Quebec.

Koumanakos, Jamie (2007). 'Canadian LPs Take Outsized Role in PE,' *Buyouts*, 20(17): 32–33.

Kranc, Joel (2007). 'Restricted Access,' *Benefits Canada*, May: 19–37.

Lovely, Warren (2006). 'Funding the Pension Gap,' *Canadian Financing Quarterly*, CIBC World Markets, July: 1–6.

National Union of Public and General Employees (2007). *The Pensions Manual, Fourth Edition, October*. Ontario, Canada: National Union.

Ontario Teachers' Pension Plan (2008*a*). '2007 Report to Members,' (April). Toronto, Ontario. http://www.otpp.com/rm07/pdf/ReportToMembers2007.pdf.

—— (2008*b*). '1.6:1 Plan Maturity,' Toronto, Ontario. http://www.otpp.com/ar07/ar07_stateoftheplan.htm.

Ontario Public Service Employees Union Pension Trust (OPTrust) (2007). *Planning for the Future: Strengthening Ontario's Defined Benefit Pension System*. Submission to the Ontario Expert Commission on Pension, October 11. http://www.optrust.com/publications/OECPSubmission.pdf.

Pozzebon, Silvana (2005). 'The Future of Pensions in Canada,' in R. Clark and O.S. Mitchell, eds., *Reinventing the Retirement Paradigm*. Oxford: Oxford University Press, pp. 223–39.

Schembari, Patricia (2006). 'Employer-sponsored Pension Plans Over the Last 30 Years,' *Canada's Retirement Income Programs 2006 Edition*. Statistics Canada, Catalogue no. 74-507XCD, CD-ROM.

Statistics Canada (2006*a*). 'Table 1 Registered Pension Plan (RPP) members, by area of employment, sector, type of plan and contributory status, annual,' (table). *Canada's Retirement Income Programs 2006 Edition*. Statistics Canada, Catalogue no. 74-507XCD. CD-ROM.

—— (2006*b*). 'Table 21 Percentage of paid workers covered by a registered pension plan (RPP),' (table). *Canada's Retirement Income Programs 2006 Edition*. Statistics Canada, Catalogue no. 74-507XCD. CD-ROM.

—— (2007*a*). 'Pension Plans in Canada,' *The Daily*, June 21. http://www.statcan.ca/Daily/English/070621/d070621b.htm.

—— (2007*b*). 'Unionization,' *Perspectives on Labour and Income*, August. http://www.statcan.ca/english/freepub/75-001-XIE/comm/fact-2.pdf.

—— (2008). 'Pension Assets by Type of Plan, at Market Value,' (table) 'Preliminary Results of the Pension Satellite Account, 1990 to 2007,' *Latest Developments in the Canadian Economic Accounts*. Statistics Canada, Catalogue no. 13-605-X. http://www.statcan.ca/english/freepub/13-605-XIE/2008002/pdf/psa_e.pdf.

Statistics Canada (n.d.). *Proportion of Labour Force and Paid Workers Covered By a Registered Pension Plan (RPP)* (table). Summary Tables. Version updated July 8, 2008. http://www40.statcan.ca/l01/cst01/labor26a.htm?sdi=paid%20workers%20 covered%20registered.

—— (n.d.). *Table 183-0002 Public Sector Employment, Wages and Salaries, Monthly* (table). CANSIM (database). Using E-STAT (distributor). Version updated June 2, 2008. http://estat.statcan.ca/cgi-win/cnsmcgi.exe? Lang=E&ESTAT File=EStat\English\CII_1_E.htm&RootDir =ESTAT/.[25]

—— (n.d.). *Table 280-0005 Trusteed Pension Funds, Assets By Sector, Type of Plan and Contributory Status, Occasional* (table). CANSIM (database). Using E-STAT (distributor). Version updated April 7, 2008.

—— (n.d.). *Table 280-0008 Registered Pension Plan (RPP) Members, By Area of Employment, Sector, Type of Plan and Contributory Status, Annual* (table). CANSIM (database). Using E-STAT (distributor). Version updated July 3, 2008.

—— (n.d.). *Table 280-0009 Registered Pension Plans (RPPs), Members and Market Value Of Assets, By Jurisdiction of Plan Registration, Sector, Type of Plan and Contributory Status, Annual* (table). CANSIM (database). Using E-STAT (distributor). Version updated July 3, 2008.

—— (n.d.). *Table 280-0010 Registered Pension Plans (RPPs), Members and Market Value of Assets, By Size of Plan, Sector, Type of Plan and Contributory Status, Annual* (table). CANSIM (database). Using E-STAT (distributor). Version updated July 3, 2008.

—— (n.d.). *Table 280-0011 Registered Pension Plans (RPPs), Members and Market Value of Assets, By North American Industry Classification System (NAICS), Sector, Type of Plan and Contributory Status, Annual* (table). CANSIM (database). Using E-STAT (distributor). Version updated July 3, 2008.

—— (n.d.). *Table 280-0012 Registered Pension Plans (RPPs), Members and Market Value of Assets, By Type Of Organization, Type of Plan and Contributory Status, Annual* (table). CANSIM (database). Using E-STAT (distributor). Version updated July 3, 2008.

—— (n.d.). *Table 280-0013 Registered Pension Plans (RPPs), Members and Market Value of Assets, By Number of Employers Sponsoring the Plan, Sector, Type of Plan and Contributory Status, Annual* (table). CANSIM (database). Using E-STAT (distributor). Version updated July 3, 2008.

—— (n.d.). *Table 280-0016 Registered Pension Plans (RPPs), Members and Market Value of Assets, By Type of Plan, Sector and Contributory Status, Annual* (table). CANSIM (database). Using E-STAT (distributor). Version updated July 3, 2008.

—— (n.d.). *Table 280-0017 Registered Pension Plans (RPPs), Members and Market Value of Assets, By Earnings Base for Defined Benefit Plans, Sector and Contributory Status, Annual* (table). CANSIM (database). Using E-STAT (distributor). Version updated July 3, 2008.

—— (n.d.). *Table 280-0018 Registered Pension Plans (RPPs), Members and Market Value of Assets, By Employee Contribution Rate, Sector and Type of Plan, Annual* (table). CANSIM (database). Using E-STAT (distributor). Version updated July 3, 2008.

—— (n.d.). *Table 280-0022 Registered Pension Plans (RPPs), Members and Market Value of Assets, By Current Service Benefit Rate, Sector, Type of Plan and Contributory Status, Annual* (table). CANSIM (database). Using E-STAT (distributor). Version updated July 3, 2008.

—— (n.d.). *Table 280-0023 Registered Pension Plans (RPPs), Members and Market Value of Assets, By Type of Benefit Rate Based On Percentage of Earnings, Sector, Type of Plan and Contributory Status, Annual* (table). CANSIM (database). Using E-STAT (distributor). Version updated July 3, 2008.

—— (n.d.). *Table 280-0024 Registered Pension Plans (RPPs), Members and Market Value of Assets, By Normal Retirement Age, Sector, Type of Plan and Contributory Status, Annual* (table). CANSIM (database). Using E-STAT (distributor). Version updated July 3, 2008.

—— (n.d.). *Table 280-0025 Registered Pension Plans (RPPs), Members and Market Value of Assets, By Method of Automatic Adjustment of Pension for Defined Pension Plans, Sector, and Contributory Status, Annual* (table). CANSIM (database). Using E-STAT (distributor). Version updated July 3, 2008.

—— (n.d.). *Table 280-0026 Registered Pension Plans (RPPs), Contributions to Registered Pension Plans, By Sector, Type of Plan and Contributory Status, Annual* (table). CAN-SIM (database). Using E-STAT (distributor). Version updated July 3, 2008.

—— (n.d.). *Table 282-0051 Labour force survey estimates (LFS), retirement age by class of worker and sex, annual (years).* CANSIM (database). Using E-STAT (distributor). Version updated January 9, 2008.

—— (n.d.). *Table 385-0014 Balance Sheet of Federal, Provincial and Territorial General and Local Governments, Annual* (table). CANSIM (database). Using E-STAT (distributor). Version updated July 4, 2008.

—— (n.d.). *Table 385-0018 Federal, Provincial and Territorial Government Non-Autonomous Pension Plans Balance Sheet, as at March 31* (table). CANSIM (database). Using E-STAT (distributor). Version updated January 29, 2008.

—— (various years). *Pension Plans in Canada Survey.* http://www.statcan.gc.ca/.

Chapter 11

Unifying Pension Schemes in Japan: Toward a Single Scheme for Both Civil Servants and Private Employees

Junichi Sakamoto

Countries may be classified into two groups according to whether civil servants are covered by the same social security pension scheme as the one covering private employees, or whether special schemes apply to government workers, in which case they are generally not covered by the social security pension scheme that applies to private employees. The United Kingdom and Sweden represent the former case, where all employees are included in a single social security pension. There, civil servants are also provided with occupational plans. In the latter group, we have Germany (Maurer, Mitchell, and Rogalla 2009) and France; here civil servants are not covered by the social security pension schemes as are private employees. US federal government employees are in a transitional phase, where initially they had their own plan but new entrants after 1983 are covered by the national Social Security system; for this new group, the civil service pension represents their occupational pension on the national Social Security base.

Until the middle of the 1980s, Japan used to belong to the latter group. There were special schemes for national government and local government employees, and they were not in the national system covering private employees called the Employees' Pension Insurance (EPI) system. Benefit design, benefit levels, and contribution rates were totally different from each other. This structure began to change in 1984 when the government published a Cabinet Decision to unify all the occupation-specific compulsory programs and to finish the unification by 1995. While this plan was not realized by 1995, some of the schemes were merged with the EPI scheme rendering the coverage structure somewhat simpler. Benefit design and benefit levels also converged to a considerable extent.

Nevertheless, at present there still remain three occupation-specific schemes for employees other than the EPI scheme (see Figure 11-1).[1] Contribution levels still differ from one another, though benefit provisions are considerably equalized.[2] In 2007, the government once again submitted a bill to unify the remaining schemes by extending coverage of the EPI

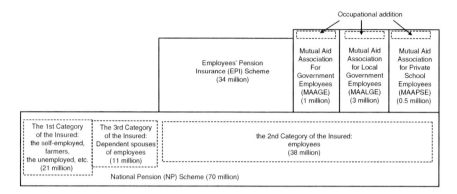

Figure 11-1 Japan's current social security pension schemes. *Note*: The figures in parentheses are the number of the insured by each scheme as of the end of March 2007. *Source*: Summary of the social security pension schemes in Japan by the Actuarial Subcommittee of the Social Security Council published on March 19, 2008 (Government of Japan 2008).

scheme to all workers including national and local government employees. At present, the ultimate shape of the fully merged system can only be outlined, as we shall show in the following text.

In what follows, we first describe how the different Japanese social security pension schemes cover the nation.[3] We then analyze reasons why the move to unify social security pension schemes began in 1984, with particular reference to the Mutual Aid Association (MAA) for Japan Railway Company Employees. Next we highlight aspects of the bill submitted to the Diet in 2007, along with the forces compelling the government to submit the bill and how issues of merger are addressed. We mention the complementary retirement benefit provisions for national and local government employees after the unification. Finally we summarize the process of unification and draw some lessons from the process, as well as offer thoughts about the future path of unification.

Evolution of the Japanese government employee pension scheme

After the Meiji restoration in 1868, the government that took over the Tokugawa Shogunate regime tried to construct an industrial country. It sought to consolidate the government by establishing a personnel system that would recruit competent persons for various administrative organs and by organizing the armed forces. It was in this context that the superannuation systems for civil servants and members of the armed forces were introduced. The government introduced a superannuation system for the Navy in 1875 and then for the Army in 1876. It also introduced a superannuation system for civil servants in 1884. It should be noted here that government employees at that time were classified into two groups: civil servants and public employees.[4] The superannuation system covered only the civil servants and members of the armed forces, but not for public employees more generally.

These superannuation systems were based on the concept that civil servants were people whose lives were 'bought' by the nation.[5] In other words, they were required to work for the government for life, reflecting the German concept of lifetime commitment (Kuhlman and Röber 2004). At the same time, however, this was a concept that the general public at that time could easily accept because of the tradition under the Tokugawa Shogunate regime whereby lords required lifetime loyalty of their servants and gave them a lifetime salary in return. In this sense, the superannuation was more like a salary than a retirement plan. It was financed in principle by the general revenue with civil servants contributing 2 percent of their salary as a token of appreciation. The various superannuation systems were unified into a single system in 1923.

By contrast, public employees were covered by mutual aid associations introduced organization by organization. Once a government organization introduced its mutual aid association, its public employees were compulsorily covered and they paid contributions. The first mutual aid association was introduced in 1905 for public employees of the Yawata Iron Manufacturing Public Corporation. It began by providing compensation for workplace injuries but later added medical insurance and pension benefits for old-age, disability, and survivorship. Subsequently, the mutual aid associations for employees of other organizations like the Imperial Railway Agency were introduced.[6] These mutual aid associations were introduced by the government organizations in charge of day-to-day operations. By contrast, public employees of government planning offices (not in charge of day-to-day operations) were without pensions until 1949.

After World War II, the Japanese civil service system was reformed, and in 1947 the distinction between civil servants and public employees was abolished. Nevertheless the superannuation system for the people deemed to be civil servants in the old system was maintained, though the mutual aid association system was reformed and codified in 1949 as the Government Employees' Mutual Aid Association Act. This was done to extend the coverage to the people deemed to be public employees of the government branches for planning who were not in charge of day-to-day operations. The new mutual aid association system also equalized benefit provisions and qualifying conditions irrespective of which government organization or branch one belonged to.[7] It did not, however, cover the people deemed to be civil servants in the old system.[8]

Extending coverage of the mutual aid association system to those deemed to be civil servants under the old system was spurred in 1949, when the Imperial Railway Agency was separated from the Ministry of Transportation and became a public enterprise called Japan National Railway Company (JNR). New entrants to the JNR were covered by the mutual aid association system for government employees even if they were posted in positions that civil servants used to occupy. Existing employees, who had joined the JNR before it was made a public enterprise and were deemed to be civil servants, were still covered by the old superannuation system. This provoked feelings of inequality among JNR employees and gave rise to a movement to introduce a new mutual aid association for the JNR employees. In 1956, the Public Enterprise Employees' Mutual Aid Association Act was enacted which separated this group from the mutual aid association for government employees. Their benefit provisions were more generous than that of the mutual aid association for government employees.

Two other government organizations were also made into public enterprises around the same time: the Salt and Tobacco Monopoly Enterprise (in 1949), and the Nippon Telegraph and Telecommunications Enterprise (in 1952); their employees then were covered by the Public Enterprise Employees' Mutual Aid Association Act from 1956. It should be noted, however, that contribution rates were set for each enterprise. In what follows, we denote these mutual aid associations of the JNR, the Salt and Tobacco Monopoly Enterprise, and the Nippon Telegraph and Telecommunications Enterprise by the acronyms MAA for JR Employees, the MAA for JT Employees and the MAA for NTT Employees.[9]

Stimulated by the movement in the public enterprises, demand for equal pension treatment of government employees grew until in 1959, mutual aid association coverage was extended to those deemed to be civil servants under the old system. At this point, the traditional superannuation system was abolished and Japan departed from the concept that the civil servants were those whose lives were 'bought' by the government. The government decided to unify the system in the form of mutual aid associations believing that the concept of lifetime employment was no longer acceptable to the nation. Further, mutual aid associations had been satisfactorily managed up to then so it was easy to obtain political support for these entities. It was also judged that the reserve fund to be formed under the mutual aid association system might be more conducive to government employee welfare than when the government directly managed and controlled the money. Last, the Ministry of Finance feared that rising pension costs would have to be paid from the general budget, so establishing a dedicated scheme for these employees seemed sensible at the time.

Several insurers or financial units developed under the new system. Each of the government departments in charge of day-to-day operations (e.g., the Ministry of Post and Telecommunications, the Forestry Agency, etc.) formed its own financial unit and decided contribution rates independently. The rest of the government employees were in the financial unit administered by the Federation of National Public Service Personnel Mutual Aid Associations (FMAA). Subsequently these financial units were unified under a single unit administered by the FMAA in 1984.

The new mutual aid association system provided for retirement, disability, and survivor benefits.[10] The retirement benefit formula was based on the three-year average of the basic salary prior to retirement, and 40 percent of this amount was provided for 20 years of service. One additional year of service increased the percentage by 1.5 percentage points. So after 40 years the benefit was 70 percent of the three-year average basic salary prior to retirement. The contribution rate of the financial unit administered by the FMAA was set at 8.8 percent for the part financed by contributions, with a government subsidy financing the remaining part. The contribution rate was decided based on the static level contribution method.[11] It should be noted that the costs of paying benefits accrued prior to October 1959, called past service costs, were to be borne solely by the government.[12] The contributions shared by the government employees and the government as employer were, therefore, for the benefits corresponding to the service period after October 1959.[13]

Although the government employee pension scheme departed from the superannuation system, the mutual aid association system itself had the nature of an occupational pension. These schemes were not only for securing income after retirement, but also for compensating the loss of opportunity to increase savings caused by the restrictions imposed on government employees.[14] One consequence of this occupational nature was that benefits were indexed in line with the rise in government employees' salaries.[15]

Arrangements similar to the past service cost of the mutual aid association for government employees were introduced in the case of the public enterprises. The cost of paying prior service benefits (prior to 1956) is borne by the public enterprises, and contributions paid by the public enterprise employees were for benefits corresponding to service after July 1956.

The evolution of local government employee pensions

Pension schemes for local government employees followed a rather complicated process of evolution. Before the Local Government Employee Act was enacted in 1950, these workers also used to be classified into civil servants and public employees. At the prefectural level, civil servants were further subclassified into two groups: one was the group of civil servants deemed to be 'equal' to central government civil servants and it also included teachers of schools established by local governments and policemen. This group was covered by the superannuation system. The other group included locally recruited civil servants, and these were usually covered by schemes similar to but distinct from the superannuation system. Since such schemes were gradually introduced, their dates of inception varied from prefecture to prefecture.

Employees at the prefectural level were initially not covered by any pension scheme, until 1949 when the mutual aid association system for government employees was extended to cover them. At the same time policemen and teachers came to be covered by the mutual aid association system for government employees. This policy was based on the idea that the employees of prefectural governments were deemed to belong to the Ministry of the Interior.

At the municipal level, civil servants were covered by superannuation systems stipulated in local bylaws and their inception dates varied from municipality to municipality. Although some of them were covered by the EPI scheme, municipal public employees were not, in principle, covered by any scheme until 1955 when the Municipal Employees' Mutual Aid Association Act was enacted.

Finally in 1962, following the establishment of the new Government Employees' Mutual Aid Association Act of 1959, the Local Government Employees' Mutual Aid Association Act was enacted. This covered all the prefectural and municipal government employees by the mutual aid association for local government employees; benefits were the same as those of the mutual aid association for government employees. As was true for the mutual aid association for government employees, prior service cost for benefits prior to 1962 had to be borne by local governments.[16]

Evolution of the modern Japanese social security pension scheme

Private sector employees had no national pension system until 1940; while some firms provided occupational pensions, the number was very small. During the 1930s, as war loomed, the importance of maritime transportation rapidly increased. Nevertheless, seamen's jobs were strenuous and they had to retire quite young, and few wanted to be seamen. Furthermore, if a vessel carrying soldiers and arms was sunk in an attack, seamen's survivors were not compensated, while those of the members of the armed forces were compensated. In the face of seamen's complaints, the government in 1940 introduced Seamen's Insurance to make the occupation more attractive and retain the necessary number of seamen. At this time, the Seamen's Insurance provided not only pension benefits but also medical insurance, and the pensionable age for an old-age benefit was age 50.

While seamen received this special treatment, there was no general pension yet available for private employees in general. In 1922, responding to labor disputes, the government studied Bismark's German social insurance system and introduced a health insurance system. In 1942, the government then introduced the EPI scheme. At first it covered only male blue-collar workers employed by enterprises with 10 or more employees; subsequently, it extended the coverage to male and female employees including white-collar employees (in 1944). Also industrial enterprises were at first limited to those in the manufacturing and mining sectors, but in 1954 the plan was extended to all industries except for the service sector. The lower size limit of covered enterprises was also cut to 5 from 10 (in 1954) and then to one for legal entities in 1985.

After World War II ended in 1945, Japan suffered from economic turmoil: prices skyrocketed and many aspects of government were forced to change drastically. One of these changes included a reform in the civil service system, erasing the distinction between civil servants and public employees. As a natural consequence, the superannuation system and the mutual aid association system were unified into the single new mutual aid association system.

In the private sector, too, reform discussions broke out inasmuch as hyperinflation had seriously eroded benefit levels. In 1954, coverage of the EPI scheme was extended to employees of most enterprises.[17] The benefit formula was also changed from the one comprising of only an earnings-related part to one that includes both a flat-rate portion and an earnings-related portion. Nevertheless, efforts to boost benefit levels were rejected by employers, whereupon three occupational groups decided to withdraw from (or not participate in) extended coverage of the EPI scheme. The first group involved private schools which established their own mutual aid association, ignoring the effort to extend EPI coverage to private educational organizations.[18] The second group included public employees of municipalities, some of whom had been covered by EPI; however they decided to withdraw from it and to establish their own mutual aid association in 1955. Later, in 1962, when the new mutual aid association system for local government employees was established, this one was absorbed by the new system. The third group comprised employees of agricultural cooperatives and fishery cooperatives; they too had been covered by EPI previously. Arguing that their jobs were like those of the local government employees, they claimed independence of the EPI scheme and established their own system. Thus, the Mutual Aid Association for Agricultural, Fishery and Forestry Cooperative Employees was established in 1959.[19]

In the late 1950s, as the economy recovered, there was much discussion about how to extend the health insurance program to the whole nation, so all could receive medical services. This discussion, spurred by demands from farmers and the self-employed to be included in social security pension schemes, led the government to begin thinking about covering the whole nation with a social security pension. While there was debate over including everyone in the EPI if they were not already in a mutual aid association or EPI, it was believed impossible because of the difficulty of measuring income for the self-employed and farmers.

Eventually a new scheme called the National Pension (NP) scheme was introduced in 1961, which covered self-employed, farmers, non-employed people, and employees of small enterprises with fewer than five employees. Both the benefits and the contributions under this system were flat rate; those with little or no income were exempted from paying contributions. Though initially it covered only the self-employed, farmers, etc, it was nevertheless the largest scheme at that time, including 20 million people in 1965, while the EPI scheme covered 18.7 million people.

Pension jealousy and long-term financial problems

Altogether then, in the 1960s there were 10 separate social security pension schemes including mutual aid associations. In the 1960s, Japan experienced economic growth and the benefit level of the EPI scheme and the NP scheme were greatly improved after 1965. But in the 1970s, problems in this complex structure gradually became conspicuous.

One reason had to do with the great difference of benefit provisions between the EPI scheme and the MAA schemes. Introduction of an automatic indexation provision of the EPI scheme in 1973 caused great public expectation for the EPI scheme and interest in comparing the benefit provisions with those provided by the MAA schemes.[20] It eventually led to people's awareness of the fact that there were disparities between the EPI and the MAA schemes. For example, the pensionable age for the EPI system was raised to 60 after the 1954 reform, while it remained age 55 for the MAA schemes. In addition, the EPI benefit was proportionate to the worker's career indexed average salary plus a flat-rate portion, while the MAA benefit was, generally speaking, proportional to final salary. In addition, the MAA benefit was much higher than under the EPI scheme, partly due to the fact that the average length of the covered period was also much longer in the case of the MAA schemes than for the EPI scheme.

In any case, demands grew to rectify the disparities, and pension jealousy or pension tension peaked in the mid-1970s. One reaction was to raise the MAA pensionable age to 60 with a transitional provision. It also began to be known that the financial prospects of some MAA schemes were gloomy and appeared not to be sustainable due to changes in industrial structure or employment structure. The particular ones mentioned were the NP scheme, the Seamen's Insurance, and the MAA for JR Employees.[21]

These problems were partly the result of urbanization as industrialization advanced, a process that began in Japan long before World War II but exacerbated in the 1960s and 1970s. This demographic shift resulted in a dire actuarial projection for the NP system in 1980 that indicated a decline in active participants in the near future and unsustainable contribution rates. The Seamen's Insurance system actually experienced declines in the numbers of active participants after 1970, reflecting the fact that advances in shipbuilding technology greatly reduced the number of sailors necessary to operate a ship. Further, Japan's maritime transportation industry had lost its international competitiveness because of its high cost, producing considerable redundancies. And restrictions imposed on economic activities outside the 200 sea mile zone further contributed to the pension scheme's downward spiral, requiring higher contribution rates almost every year after 1973.

Similarly the MAA for JR employees also began to experience changes in industrial structure during the 1970s. During this time, motorways came to connect many key Japanese cities, and roads were also improved for trucking; all of this produced redundancies in the JR Company. Their pension system fell into grave financial problems and after receiving help from other schemes in the 1980s, they were finally absorbed into the EPI scheme in 1997.

Pension reform in the 1980s

To cope with pension system financial problems caused by changes in industrial and employment structure, and to respond to the pension jealousy discussion, a massive reform in pensions was carried out in 1985. A first element of the reform involved the extension of NP system coverage to the whole nation; further, the NP scheme was restructured to provide flat-rate basic pensions, while schemes for employees including the EPI scheme and the MAA schemes were rearranged to provide only an earnings-related benefit. In the process, the government devised a 'Basic Pension Sub-account' in the National Pension Special Account, and the financing framework for basic pension benefits was established (see Figure 11-2).[22] As a result, the current NP scheme was born in the 1985 reform. This framework

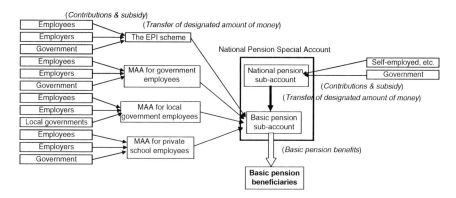

Figure 11-2 Financing basic pension benefits in Japan. *Source*: 2004 Actuarial Report of the EPI scheme and the NP scheme by the Ministry of Health, Labour and Welfare (Government of Japan 2005).

is no longer affected by changes in industrial structure because even if farmers do become employees, they will continue to support basic pension beneficiaries as contributors to the Basic Pension Sub-account of the NP Special Account.

The second major element of the 1985 reform was a change in MAA benefit formulas, where the approach moved away from a final salary formula toward a career average salary formula. It should be noted, however, that an amount equal to 20 percent[23] of the amount calculated by the new formula was added to the basic part of the MAA benefit; this was called the 'occupational addition.' This was added to MAA benefits because national government and local government employees were, from time to time, prohibited from saving on their own due to the code of conduct imposed upon them as public servants. The occupational addition was to compensate for such loss of opportunities. In any event, the occupational addition has been one of the main sources of pension jealousy, and proposed legislation has stipulated that the occupational addition be abolished.

A third element of the 1985 reform required the merger of the Seamen's Insurance and the EPI scheme.[24] As we have seen, the Seamen's Insurance scheme had suffered from a decline in active participants and faced worsening conditions. Fortunately, benefit provisions under the Seamen's Insurance plan were the same as those for mineworkers in the EPI scheme, so it was rather easy to merge it with the EPI scheme. A reserve fund corresponding to an amount that would have been accumulated to the same degree as the mine workers would have accumulated in the EPI scheme was transferred to the EPI scheme.

As a result, the 1985 reform partially solved many problems facing the NP and Seamen's Insurance schemes. The financial problems faced by the MAA for JR Employees were, however, left unsolved though the financial conditions were relieved to a certain extent by the introduction of the basic pension benefits. The problems with the MAA for JR Employees were grave because of the steep decrease of active participants. The 1985 reform also addressed the pension jealousy discussion, so by and large, the disparities were minimized. Nevertheless, differences including the occupational addition and other benefit provisions or contribution rates remain; these are the subject of current reform bills.

In the mid-1980s, with the Cabinet Decision of 1984, the Japanese government declared that the unification of social security pension schemes should be completed by 1995. Although full unification has not yet been completed, the process has been pursued and legislation was submitted to the Diet in 2007 to unify all social security pension schemes for employees. In the meantime, several schemes have been absorbed by the EPI. Several driving forces have been in play. One is pension jealousy, but another is the fact that some schemes actually faced insolvency. After this Cabinet Decision of 1984, all benefit reforms made in the EPI scheme were also reflected in the MAAs: for example, in 1994, the benefit indexation basis was changed from gross salary to disposable income, and this change was reflected in both the EPI and the MAAs. In 2000, the EPI old-age pensionable age was raised to 65 from 60, and so too in the MAAs. In 2004, the EPI introduced a modified indexation, and the MAAs also adopted the same index. This situation thus seems similar to that in Germany after 1992, where civil servant pensions have followed the reforms of the social security pension scheme (Börsch-Supan and Wilke 2003).

The MAA for JR Employees. As we have seen earlier, the MAA for JR Employees faced a steep decrease in active participants in the 1980s due to the shift of transportation on land from railway to lorry. This had a great impact on the financial basis of the MAA scheme and forced it to raise its contribution rates every year, from 10.24 percent in 1980 to 16.99 percent in 1984. Yet further contribution rates increases were in the offing, leading the government to require financial help from the MAA schemes for Government Employees, JT Employees, and NTT Employees beginning in 1984. Nevertheless this financial help did not solve the problems, so in 1990 the government required all employee schemes including the EPI scheme to help out the MAA for JR Employees. As this measure would stabilize the financial problem for the time being, the government set up in 1994[25] a group consisting of scholars and representatives from the social security pension schemes to work out measures to merge the MAA for JR Employees with the EPI scheme with the ultimate goal being the unification of the social security pension schemes for employees.

As of 1990, when the financial transfers began from all the schemes to the MAA for JR Employees, it turned out that the MAA for JT Employees was also in financial difficulties. Here the number of active participants fell from 38,000 in 1980 to 25,000 in 1990, mainly due to the invention of automatic tobacco-rolling machines which led to labor redundancies. As a consequence, the MAA for JT Employees was also provided with financial help by the 1990 framework.

In its 1995 report the working group suggested that the three MAA schemes for JR, JT, and NTT Employees should be merged with the EPI scheme as of 1997, and the remaining schemes for employees should also be gradually unified as they matured in the early years of the twenty-first century. One might ask why the MAA for NTT Employees was asked to merge with the EPI scheme, as this system was not in financial difficulty at that time. Nevertheless, the NTT Company had been privatized in 1985 and so the working group suggested that it should also be merged with the EPI scheme. (Incidentally, the JR Company was privatized in 1987 and the JT Company in 1985.) Following this report, a bill was passed in 1996 to merge the three MAA schemes with the EPI scheme and the merger took place in 1997. Thus the financial problems faced by the MAA for JR Employees were solved,[26] lagging behind the NP scheme and the Seamen's Insurance for more than a decade.

The Financial Framework for the Merger. When the working group decided to merge the three MAA schemes for JR, JT, and NTT Employees with the EPI scheme, they proposed a financial framework that would avoid imposing a new burden solely on the EPI scheme and distribute it among the remaining schemes for employees. Without such a framework, all of the financial imbalance would have gone for compensation solely by the EPI scheme. The working group suggested that it should be compensated for by all the remaining schemes for employees. Three principles formed the basis of the proposal:

(i) Benefits corresponding to the period after the merger would be supported by all active participants of the EPI scheme.

(ii) The three MAA schemes would transfer the bulk of the reserve fund to the EPI scheme. The amount is so calculated as to secure benefits promised when contributions were paid. In other words, it is roughly the reserve based on the unit credit method without revaluing pensionable remunerations.

(iii) Benefits corresponding to the period before the merger would be financed by the reserve fund transferred from each of the three MAA schemes, the national subsidy, and contributions paid by the active participants of JR, JT, and NTT Companies.[27] If these financial resources prove insufficient to finance the benefits, then the difference would be spread to all the schemes for employees.

A conceptual chart for the financial framework mentioned earlier appears in Figure 11-3. In the case of the MAA for JR Employees, the transferred reserve fund, the national subsidy, and the contributions were not enough

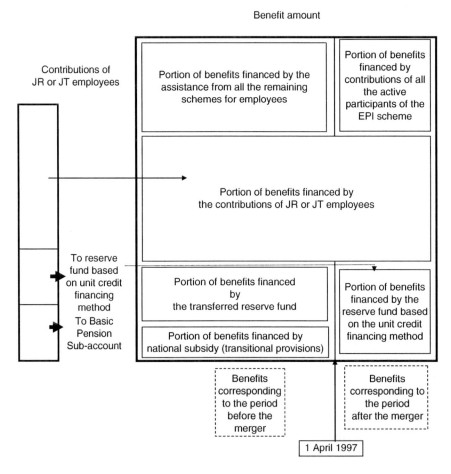

Figure 11-3 Merging the Mutual Aid Associations (MAAs) for Japan Railway Company (JR), Salt and Tobacco Monopoly Enterprise (JT), and Nippon Telegraph and Telecommunications Enterprise (NTT) employees with the Employees' Pension Insurance (EPI) scheme. *Source*: 2004 Actuarial Report of the EPI scheme and the NP scheme by the Ministry of Health, Labour and Welfare (Government of Japan 2005).

to pay the benefits, so the difference has been supported by the remaining schemes for employees. In the case of the MAA for JT Employees, the situation was the same and the shortfall of the benefit expenditure was covered by the other schemes. In the case of the MAA for NTT Employees, these financial resources were enough to pay the benefits so there have been no further transfers from the remaining schemes for employees.

Substantial reserves were transferred to the EPI scheme from each of the three MAA schemes on the merger. The actual reserve fund that the MAA for JR Employees held at the time of the merger was only JPY 0.3 trillion while the amount to be transferred was JPY 1.2 trillion; the clearing house corporation set up by the government to handle long-term debts when the JR Company was privatized is paying the difference over a 20-year installment period. The shortfall created by the merger of MAA schemes for JR and JT Employees has been compensated for by the remaining schemes for employees. The amount is based on financial projections, with the leveled annual shortfall totalling about JPY 0.13 trillion (in terms of the FY 2005 value); this is indexed to the rate of increase of yearly pensionable remunerations including pensionable bonuses for active participants of the schemes for employees. It is shared by the remaining schemes for employees.[28]

The Scheme for Agricultural, Fishery, and Forestry Cooperative Employees. In late 1990s, the Agricultural Cooperatives were forced to restructure their businesses due to globalization and deregulation. The number of active participants in the MAA for Agricultural, Fishery, and Forestry Cooperative Employees decreased from 511,000 in FY 1994 to 475,000 in FY 1999. Ultimately the MAA was merged with the EPI scheme in 2002, with a financial framework for the merger similar to that stipulated for the JR, JT, and NTT Employees schemes. The MAA for Agricultural, Fishery and Forestry Cooperative Employees transferred the reserve fund of JPY 1.6 trillion to the EPI scheme. The transferred reserve fund, the national subsidy, and contributions from active employees of the cooperatives were enough to finance the benefits corresponding to the period before the merger, so there was no need for support from the remaining schemes for employees.

In all, then, the 10 schemes that existed in the 1960s have been merged down to five with the NP scheme extending its coverage to the whole nation.

Ongoing merger efforts

In early 2001, the Cabinet published a decision stating that measures should be adopted to enhance the financial basis of employees' schemes and urged unification discussions should continue after the MAA for Agricultural, Fishery and Forestry Cooperative Employees was merged with the EPI scheme.[29] This Cabinet Decision also urged the MAA for Government Employees and the MAA for Local Government Employees to unify their financial bases which actually occurred in 2004; contribution rates are equalized as of 2009.[30] National pension reform occurred in 2004 with the introduction of an automatic balancing mechanism through modified indexation (Sakamoto 2005). The indexation is to be applied to all the schemes.

The political debate over pension mergers continued throughout 2004, in which the largest opposition party, the Democratic Party, campaigned on the pledge of a single social security pension scheme.[31] Shortly after the landslide victory of the ruling Liberal Democratic Party in the Lower House election in September 2005,[32] the government set up a formal meeting of the ministries[33] charged with the schemes to resolve problems of unification. The group's 2005 report referred to differences in contribution rates and benefit provisions, as well as questions about how to manage the pooled MAA reserve funds. They also noted the question of what to do with the occupational addition, how to treat benefits of national or local government employees corresponding to the period before the merger of the superannuation system with the mutual aid associations, etc. Around the same time, the government parties' Pension Reform Council issued a report recommending the equalization of contribution rate, abolishing different benefit provisions, abolishing the occupational addition, etc. Following this, a Cabinet Decision of 2006 was issued and a bill submitted to the Diet in April 2007, with these ideas. The bill went further to stipulate that the EPI scheme should be extended to national and local government employees as well as private school employees, and it also proposed all MAA schemes be restructured as branches of the EPI scheme.

Twenty-first century unification efforts

In early 2007, the government submitted to the Diet a new reform bill to unify the schemes for employees into a single scheme. It had several elements, first and foremost among them the extension of EPI coverage to national and local government employees and private school employees. Benefit provisions for future accruals are to be made uniform, including no further accrual of occupational additions after 2010.[34] Past benefits corresponding to the period before October 1959 must be cut by 27 percent to reduce the tax burden by reducing past service cost.[35] (There are alleviating provisions that the total benefit cut should not exceed 10 percent and that the annual benefit amount after the reduction should not

TABLE 11-1 Contribution programs for each scheme for employees

FY	MAA for Government Employees	MAA for Local Government Employees	MAA for Private School Employees	(%) EPI Scheme
Just before the 2004 actuarial valuation	14.38	13.03	10.46	13.58
2004	14.509	13.384	10.46(*)	13.934
2005	14.638	13.738	10.814	14.288
2006	14.767	14.092	11.168	14.642
2007	14.896	14.446	11.522	14.996
2008	15.025	14.800	11.876	15.350
2009	15.154		12.230	15.704
2010	15.508		12.584	16.058
↓	↓		↓	↓
2017				18.3
2018	18.3			
↓				
2027			18.3	

Note: *The initial date of the latest actuarial valuation of the MAA for Private School Employees was April 1, 2005.

Source: Ministry of Health, Labour and Welfare (Government of Japan 2005).

go below JPY 2.5 million.) Contribution rates are also to be made equal to those of the EPI scheme (with a transitional period) and future MAA contribution rates will be raised in step with EPI (namely by 0.354% every year); see Table 11-1.

Under the new structure, the MAAs are to become administrative branches of the EPI scheme, keeping records, collecting contributions, awarding benefits, paying benefits with partial financial interchange among the EPI sub-account and the MAA branches, managing and investing the reserve funds, etc. Active participants in the new scheme will be classified into four groups: active participants whose contributions will be collected by the Pension Sub-account of the Social Insurance Special Account; active participants whose contributions are to be collected by the MAA for Government Employees; active participants whose contributions are to be collected by the MAA for Local Government Employees; and active participants whose contributions are to be collected by the MAA for Private School Employees.

The MAA schemes will manage and invest the portion of their reserve funds; it is unclear whether the segregation will be notional or actual.[36] Given the current size of the reserve funds of the MAA schemes, there will certainly remain some reserve funds though the bill does not clarify how these remaining reserve funds will be utilized.[37] Investment principles for these funds will be determined by the Minister of Health, Labour and Welfare in consultation with other ministries, and every year the funds' investment performance will be published.

Assuming that the bill is adopted, what can be forecast for future government employee benefits? They will have the old-age basic pension benefit and the old-age EPI benefit, as well as new retirement benefits from newly-established occupational pension schemes that have yet to be established. They may also have retirement lump-sum benefits and personal savings including personal annuities. As yet, all the provisions of the to-be-established occupational pension scheme are not known, but it appears that its payment combined with employer-provided lump-sum benefits must not exceed the average retirement benefits of private companies with at least 50 employees. A 2006 survey found that the private benefit amount expressed as a lump-sum was JPY 29.8 million, while that which had been paid to government employees was JPY 29.6 million including the occupational addition of the MAA for Government Employees. If the portion paid by employees themselves was included, the private sector average was JPY 30.4 million while that of government employees was JPY 31.8 million. Overall the new occupational pension scheme will likely pay lower benefits than before.[38] It should also be noted that the new occupational pension scheme will be defined benefit; the fact that some government employees access to insider information precludes a defined contribution plan.

In 2007, political turmoil stymied the prospects for pension unification since the government party lost its majority in the Upper House. In addition, the Democratic Party has said it will not agree to the bill's passage[39] unless the whole nation is covered, including the self-employed. Adding to the debate was the recent revelation of the existence of 50 million unidentified records of the NP and the EPI schemes kept by the Social Insurance Agency, giving rise to massive public anxiety. Hence the reform agenda will continue to be debated for some time.

Conclusion

Looking back on efforts to unify the Japanese social security pension schemes, several factors enabled the process to proceed as far as it has. First, some schemes encountered financial difficulties due to changes in industrial structure. Second, the 1985 reform made benefit formulas the same which facilitated the later mergers. Third, strong political leadership helped drive the bill to unify the schemes.[40] Fourth, pension jealousy justified the claim that social security pension benefits should be equalized without exceptions.

There remain some outstanding matters to clarify in future years. For instance in some cases, the former insurers remain as administrative branches of the EPI scheme. Also the financial interchange is only partial. Nevertheless, progress has been made to strengthen the financial basis of the social security pension benefits and make the benefits and contributions equitable.

Notes

[1] The current Japanese social security pension provisions include two layers. The first layer is the National Pension (NP) scheme which covers the whole nation with a flat-rate basic pension benefit. Active participants in the NP scheme are classified into three categories: (*a*) the self-employed, farmers, the unemployed, etc; (*b*) the active employees below age 70; and (*c*) non-working dependent spouses. The second layer is for employees, and there are four schemes in this second layer: (*a*) the Employees' Pension Insurance (EPI) scheme for private employees, (*b*) the Mutual Aid Association (MAA) for government employees, (*c*) the MAA for local government employees, and (*d*) the MAA for private school employees. Both the EPI and the MAA schemes provide earnings-related benefits.

[2] Contribution rates as of April 2008 are 14.996 percent for the EPI scheme, 14.896 percent for the MAA for government employees, 14.446 percent for the MAA for local government employees, and 11.876 percent for the MAA for private school employees.

[3] For an outline of the current framework of Japanese social security pensions see Sakamoto (2007). Additional information is available from Government of Japan (1957, 1984, 1994, 1996, 2001, 2003, 2006*a*, 2006*b*, 2006*c*) and Yoshiwara (1987, 2004).

[4] Government employees were ranked. Their ranks were raised when they got promotions. Civil servants were those whose ranks were above or equal to a certain rank.

[5] A man named Toshinaga Kawaji studied the French police system in Paris and contributed to constructing the modern police system in Japan in 1870s. He concluded that civil servants can be thought of as commodities bought by taxes paid for by the general public.

[6] In 1907, the mutual aid association for employees of the Imperial Railway Agency was introduced.

[7] Some people deemed to be public employees were promoted to be civil servants. However, if both of their periods of service as public employees and as civil servants did not satisfy the qualifying period for the mutual aid association and for the superannuation system, they could receive only lump-sum payments and not pensions from either of them. There was no portability permitted between the superannuation and the mutual aid association system.

[8] Around this time, in 1950, Robert Myers, former Deputy-Commissioner of the Social Security Administration of the US government, came to Japan at the invitation of the General Headquarters and gave advice to the Japanese government about the reconstruction of the civil service pension schemes.

[9] The Japanese national railway was privatized in 1987 and became the Japan Railway Company. The Salt and Tobacco Monopoly Enterprise was privatized in 1985 and became the Japan Tobacco Company. The Nippon Telegraph and Telecommunications Enterprise was privatized in 1985 and became the Nippon Telegraph and Telecommunication Company. The names of the three public enterprise employees' mutual aid associations are derived from those companies' names after privatization.

[10] The mutual aid associations provided health insurance as well.

[11] The level contribution method is the financing method in which the contribution rates are set to be level throughout the period of equilibrium. By static we mean that we do not take account of the salary increase nor price increase in the future when we calculate the level contribution rate.

[12] Government employees from the period prior to October 1959 are very old and form a closed group, so the past service cost is decreasing. It was JPY 0.47 trillion out of the total expenditure of JPY 2.2 trillion in FY 2005.

[13] Ten percent of the contribution amount was subsidized by the government and the rest was shared equally by the employees and the employer (the government). This was changed later; currently the national subsidy is given by a fixed percentage of particular expenditure and the contributions themselves are shared equally by employees and the employer (the government).

[14] In Japan, government employees are forbidden to strike and are prohibited to hold stock.

[15] In 1973, benefit indexation was introduced in the EPI scheme.

[16] Past service costs of the local government employee plan amounted to JPY 1.2 trillion out of the total expenditure of 5.6 trillion in FY 2005.

[17] The exception was the service sector in the secondary classification of industry.

[18] Some universities decided not to participate in the MAA for Private School Employees but were covered by the EPI scheme, because they judged that their health insurance contributions would be larger if they had joined the MAA for Private School Employees. Most of the MAA schemes provided health insurance benefits for the participants as well.

[19] Unlike other MAA schemes, the MAA for Agricultural, Fishery, and Forestry Cooperative Employees did not provide participants with health insurance benefits. Instead, these employees were covered by a health insurance society that was a contracted-out insurer of the Health Insurance scheme provided by the government.

[20] The 1973 oil crisis caused daily goods prices to soar by 11.7 percent in 1973, 23.2 percent in 1974, and 11.7 percent in 1975. These inflation rates were reflected in the benefit amount according to the automatic indexation provision.

[21] In the 1970s, the company was still the Japan National Railway Company so it would be more accurate to denote it by the MAA for JNR Employees. However we denote it here by the MAA for JR Employees since later in 1987 the

JNR Company was privatized and became the Japan Railway Company as noted previously.

22 In order to finance the cost of paying the basic pension benefits, the Basic Pension Sub-account of the National Pension Special Account collects the designated amount of money from all the schemes, namely the EPI scheme, the MAA for Government Employees, the MAA for Local Government Employees, the MAA for Private School Employees, and the National Pension Sub-account of the National Pension Special Account. The self-employed, farmers, and such pay contributions to the National Pension Sub-account of the National Pension Scheme. The cost of paying the basic pension benefits is shared by these schemes in proportion to the number of active participants age 20–59 plus the number of dependent spouses age 20–59.

23 If the number of covered years was fewer than 20, then it was 10 percent, and if it was less than 1, then there was no occupational addition.

24 Strictly speaking, the pension provisions of the Seamen's Insurance were merged with the EPI scheme, and the rest of the provisions like health insurance and work injury provisions were left in the Seamen's Insurance.

25 The establishment of the 1994 working group was also based on the Cabinet Decision of February 1984.

26 It goes without saying that, every time they obtained financial help from other schemes, the MAA schemes for JR and JT Employees sought to reduce benefit costs including abolishing the occupational addition of the newly awarded and paying higher contributions than other active participants even after the merger.

27 Strictly speaking, they are the contributions left after the amount to be transferred to the Basic Pension Sub-account and the amount corresponding to the increased accrued liabilities during the year measured in the unit credit cost method are deducted. The contributions left are split into two parts to finance the benefits corresponding to the period before and after the merger in proportion to the benefit amount of each part.

28 Setting each scheme's share is rather complicated. To briefly outline the process, half of the level amount is shared in proportion to the total amount of the yearly pensionable remunerations including pensionable bonuses of each scheme. The remaining half is shared taking account of the cost rate of each scheme. The share is only on the schemes whose cost rates are not more than the cost rate of the EPI scheme. It of course includes the EPI scheme. The share is then decided in proportion both to the total amount of yearly pensionable remunerations including pensionable bonuses and to the difference of the cost rate of the scheme and that of the EPI scheme with some relief for the EPI scheme.

29 This was a continuation of the Cabinet Decision of February 1984. In fact, in March 1996, just before the bill to merge the three MAAs for former Public Enterprise (JR, JT, and NTT) Employees was submitted to the Diet, the Cabinet had also announced a decision to continue the effort to unify the framework of social security pension schemes for employees before system maturity in the twenty-first century. Both Cabinet Decisions, in this way, confirmed the direction of the Cabinet Decision of February 1984 and urged future governments to complete the policy implementation.

[30] Each of the two MAAs still remains as an independent insurer while the unification of the financial bases is carried out through financial interchange. The basic idea of this financial interchange is that the insurer with the lower cost rate (excluding the expenditure for basic pensions) gives cash to the insurer with the higher cost rate. Since this neglects the investment return, if one of the insurer becomes short of cash to pay benefits (including the expenditure for basic pensions), the other gives cash to the one from its surplus.

[31] During the 2004 Diet deliberations, the Democratic Party, which is the largest opposition party, tried to prevent the bill from passing the Diet by disclosing bribes by high-ranking officials of the Social Insurance Agency and by attacking several ministers who they said had not paid NP contributions for certain periods. The information was apparently provided by those supportive of the Democratic Party within the Social Insurance Agency. In the 2004 Upper House Election, the government parties lost only one seat which was sufficient to arouse anger against Social Insurance Agency staff. Ultimately the government decided to abolish the Social Insurance Agency and split it into two parts, the National Health Insurance Federation in charge of health insurance (mainly for small companies), and the Japan Pension Organization which is slated to take over the EPI and NP schemes. Interestingly, the new staffs will not be government employees. During this restructuring process, in 2007 it was revealed there were as many as 50 million unidentified records from both the EPI and NP schemes stored in the Social Insurance Agency, a revelation that apparently contributed to eventual fall of Prime Minister Shinzo Abe.

[32] This time the Prime Minister dissolved the Lower House when the bill to privatize Japan Post was rejected in the Upper House.

[33] They are the Cabinet Secretariat; the Ministry of Internal Affairs and Communications; the Ministry of Finance; the Ministry of Education, Culture, Sports, Science and Technology; and the Ministry of Health, Labour and Welfare.

[34] There are other small differences. For example, under the MAA schemes, survivors' benefits can be taken over by the parents of the deceased if they are alive when the children of the deceased reach the age of 18. Under the EPI scheme, it cannot be taken over. This case is to be treated in the same way as the EPI provisions. Another example is the income testing for the old-age beneficiaries actively covered by other schemes. If an old-age EPI beneficiary is actively covered by an MAA scheme, his/her old-age EPI benefit is not subject to income-testing while, if a retirement MAA beneficiary is actively covered by the EPI or another MAA scheme, his/her retirement MAA benefit is subject to income-testing. This case is, roughly speaking, to be treated in the same way as the MAA provisions. This sort of equalization is to be introduced.

[35] When the new MAA for Government Employees was introduced in October 1959, the contribution rate was 8.8 shared equally between employer and employees, so the government employees' share was 4.4 percent. For the superannuation system, on the other hand, the civil servants had paid 2 percent of their salary as a token of gratitude to the country. This was interpreted as having been short of the full contribution rate by 2.4 percent during the time of the superannuation system. Consequently it was decided to cut the benefits by 2.4/8.8 or roughly 27 percent.

[36] The reform bill only states the segregation and leaves the details to regulations that will be published when the bill passes the Diet.

[37] There are several options as to how to share the reserve fund. One approach would be to follow the path selected when the MAA for JR Employees was merged with the EPI scheme, but this was not adopted in this case since the JR scheme was on the verge of financial collapse while the MAAs for Government Employees, Local Government Employees, and Private School Employees are not.

[38] Government employees are not to be allowed to register in the DC scheme, probably because the new occupational pension scheme is to be introduced.

[39] The government parties control over two-thirds of the Lower House, so they can utilize the provision that the bill passes the Diet as long as it gains approval of more than two thirds of the whole seats in the Lower House even after the Upper House denies the bill. This provision was utilized to force passage of a bill providing fuel by the Self Defence Forces in the Indian Ocean to war vessels of allied nations engaged in the Afghanistan war. It is believed that too-frequent utilization of this provision will give the government parties a bad image causing them to lose elections, so they are understandably cautious when implementing the provision.

[40] It is not clear why the then-Prime Minister Junichiro Koizumi ordered the Chief Cabinet Secretary to come up with the bill to unify the social security pension schemes for employees. One apparent motivation might have been that in 2004, the Democratic Party refused to deliberate the bill, insisting that the true reform was the unification of all schemes and the coverage of both employees and the self-employed under a single scheme. Yet the Party's insistence seemed unrealistic relating especially to the treatment of the self-employed. Mr. Koizumi might have thought that he could win the next election by unifying employee schemes and curtailing government employee prestige.

References

Börsch-Supan, Axel H. and Christina B. Wilke (2003). 'The German Public Pension System: How it was, How it will be.' MRRC Working Paper 2003–41. Ann Arbor, MI: Michigan Retirement Research Center.

Government of Japan (1957). 'Kouseinenkin 15 Nenshi. (15-year History of the Employees' Pension Insurance Scheme),' Ministry of Health and Welfare.

—— (1984). 'Kouteki Nenkinseido no Kaikaku ni tsuite (On the Social Security Pension Reform),' Cabinet Decision, February.

—— (1994). 'Kouseinenkin 50 Nenshi (50-year History of the Employees' Pension Insurance Scheme),' Ministry of Health and Welfare.

—— (1996). 'Kouteki Nenkinseido no Saihensei no Suishin ni tsuite (Promoting the Unification of Social Security Pension Schemes),' Cabinet Decision, March.

—— (2001). 'Kouteki Nenkinseido no Ichigenka no Suishin ni tsuite (Promoting the Unification of Social Security Pension Schemes),' Cabinet Decision, March.

—— (2003). 'Kyousai Binran (Guidebook of the Mutual Aid Association for Government Employees),' Ministry of Finance.

Government of Japan (2005). 'Kouseinenkin Kokuminnenkin Heisei 16 Nen Zaisei-saikeisan Kekka (2004 Actuarial Report of the EPI Scheme and the NP Scheme),' Ministry of Health, Labour and Welfare, March.

—— (2006a). 'Hiyousha Nenkinseido no Ichigenkatou ni kansuru Kihonhoushin nitsuite (Principal Directions of the Unification of Social Security Pension Schemes for Employees),' Cabinet Decision, April.

—— (2006b). 'Hiyousha Nenkin Ichigenka no Kihonteki na Houshin to Susumekata ni tsuite (Principal Directions and Schedules of Unifying the Social Security Pension Schemes for Employees),' Memorandum of the Government and the Government Parties, December.

—— (2006c). 'Heisei 18 Nen Minkankigyou Taishokukyuuhu Chosa no Kekka (2006 Survey on the Retirement Benefits of Private Companies),' National Personnel Authority.

—— (2008). 'Heisei 18 Nendo Matsu Koutekinenkin Seido Ichiran (Fact Sheet of the Social Security Pension Schemes in Japan as at the end of FY 2006),' Actuarial Subcommittee of the Social Security Council, March 19.

Kuhlmann, Sabine and Manfred Röber (2004). 'Civil Service in Germany: Characteristics of Public Employment and Modernization of Public Personnel Management.' Working paper, Goethe-Institut. Konstanz, Germany: University of Konstanz.

Maurer, Raimond, Olivia S. Mitchell, and Ralph Rogalla (2009). 'Reforming German Civil Servant Pensions: Funding Policy, Investment Strategy, and Intertemporal Risk Budgeting,' in *The Future of Public Employee Retirement Systems.* Oxford: Oxford University Press.

Sakamoto, Junichi (2005). 'Japan's Pension Reform,' *World Bank Pension Reform Primer.* Washington, D.C.: World Bank.

—— (2007). 'Role of the Actuary in the Process of Unifying the Social Security Pension Schemes in Japan,' Paper presented at the International Actuarial Association/Pensions, Benefits and Social Security Section Colloquium in Helsinki, May 23.

Yoshiwara, Kenji (1987). 'Shin Nenkinhou (New Pension Act: 1986 Pension Reform),' *Zenkoku Shakaihoken Rengoukai* (National Social Insurance Federation).

—— (2004). *Wagakuni no Koutekinenkin Seido* (Social Security Pension Schemes in Japan: Its Evolution and Reforms). Tokyo: Chuo Hoki Press.

Chapter 12

Redefining Traditional Plans: Variations and Developments in Public Employee Retirement Plan Design

Keith Brainard

One reason an employer may provide his or her workers with retiree benefits is to attract and retain qualified employees who seek to maximize compensation and establish a reliable source of retirement income. In the case of state and local government employment, other stakeholders may also have retirement benefit objectives. For example, taxpayers seek to ensure that cost-effective and affordable public sector retirement benefits. Likewise, recipients of public services seek public employee compensation packages that facilitate the efficient and effective delivery of the public services on which they rely.

These and other objectives can be achieved through the use of various elements of retirement plan design, including features of both defined benefit (DB) and defined contribution (DC) plans. Ninety percent of employees of state and local government in the United States have a DB plan as their primary retirement benefit (US Bureau of Labor Statistics 2000). This fact, however, obscures an array of DC features that exist within or alongside traditional DB plans, incorporated to fulfill one or more objectives of one or more retirement plan stakeholders.

This chapter presents examples of DC plan elements functioning in concert with traditional DB plans sponsored by state governments. Specifically, it details a range of plan features adopted including the cash balance plan for state and county workers in Nebraska; the earnings limitation savings account at the Minnesota Teachers' Retirement Association; the investment earnings-based Permanent Benefit Increase provision at the Arizona State Retirement System (ASRS); the deferred annuity benefit at the Minnesota Teachers' Retirement Association; and the hybrid retirement plan at the Oregon Public Employees' Retirement System. These are a few instances of DC plan elements that exist in plans sponsored by state and local governments.[1]

In each instance, these DC elements were established to meet one or more particular stakeholder objectives. They illustrate that DB plans are flexible enough to meet key objectives for stakeholders, including employers, employees, taxpayers, and recipients of public services, while preserving core elements of retirement plan design.

Implementing a cash balance plan in the Nebraska Public Employee Retirement System

State and county workers in the Nebraska Public Employee Retirement System (NPERS) were among the 10 percent of US state and local government employees whose primary retirement benefit had been a DC plan. Throughout the 1980s and 1990s, NPERS conducted seminars for these employees, often accompanied by a professional financial planner, in an effort to educate participants on the importance of making good choices regarding their retirement accounts: diversifying retirement assets, rolling assets upon termination to another retirement plan, etc. Despite these efforts, a large percentage of participants remained heavily invested in low-risk stable value funds, and many took a distribution when terminating or changing jobs.

In 2000, the Nebraska Legislature launched a retirement benefits adequacy study of Nebraska state and county workers. The study's results affirmed what NPERS staff had believed all along: that on both an absolute basis and relative to comparable workers in neighboring states, Nebraska state and county workers were not accumulating assets sufficient to provide adequate retirement income (Buck Consultants 2000). In response, the Nebraska Legislature in 2002 established a new cash balance (CB) plan for all newly-hired county and state workers. Existing DC plan participants were given a one-time opportunity to switch, and approximately 30 percent of them elected to do so. (In late 2007, remaining DC plan participants were given a second opportunity to switch, and an additional 4% so elected.) Pursuant to the legislation that established the new plan, employee and employer contribution rates for the CB plan were established at the same level as under the legacy DC plan: employees contribute 4.8 percent of pay and employers contribute 156 percent of the employee rate (7.49%; the employer match for counties is 150%). Public employees in Nebraska also participate in Social Security.

Rather than going into individual accounts, CB contributions are pooled and invested in a diversified portfolio of stocks, bonds, and real estate, similar to those of other public pension funds. Participants' nominal accounts are credited annually based on the greater of 5 percent or the federal mid-term rate plus 1.5 percent.[2] In addition, the NPERS Board may authorize a dividend credit to CB plan accounts. This credit is based on investment performance and is determined in concert with the plan's actuary. Actual

TABLE 12-1 Earnings and dividend credit rates
applied to accounts in the Nebraska
Public Employee Retirement System
cash balance plan, 2003–2007

Year	Earnings Credit (%)	Dividend Credit (%)	Total Credit Applied (%)
2003	5.04	NA	5.04
2004	5.19	3.08	8.27
2005	5.45	2.80	8.25
2006	6.27	13.05	19.32
2007	6.12	2.73	8.85

Source: Buck Consultants (2007).

credits to member accounts since the program's inception are shown in
Table 12-1.

Retirement Benefits. The CB plan vesting period in Nebraska is three
years; members may retire at age 55 with three years of service. Generally,
the longer a participant waits to retire, the higher will be the benefit
since an older participant has a shorter actuarial payout period. An active
(working) participant who postpones retirement will increase his or her
retirement benefit not only due to the shorter payout period, but also
through a higher account balance resulting from additional contributions
and (most years) investment earnings. Retiring participants may elect to
annuitize any portion of their account balances, from 0 to 100 percent.
Annuities are based on the participant's age and are adjusted based on
the member's selection of optional factors, including a 2.5 percent cost-
of-living adjustment (COLA), period certain options, etc. The Nebraska
CB plan's assumed investment return is 7.75 percent; this assumption also
applies to annuities.

DB and DC Plan Features. The CB plan works like a traditional DB plan
in that: (*a*) assets are pooled and professionally invested in a diversified
portfolio; and (*b*) participants are assured a minimum benefit by virtue of
the 5 percent minimum guaranteed earnings credit. The plan functions
like a DC plan in that: (*a*) benefits are affected by market returns; and (*b*)
participants may take their entire balance, including employer contributions and investment earnings, as a lump sum at retirement.

As with a DC plan, the CB plan shifts some investment risk from the
employer to the participant, since the employer guarantees a minimum
return of 5 percent. As with a DB plan, the employer assumes investment
risk of 5 percent for non-retired participants, and the employer retains
longevity risk by providing an annuity based on the plan's assumed investment return of 7.75 percent.

In the case of the Nebraska CB plan, the legislature applied the same contribution rates that were used for the DC plan, while lowering investment risk and eliminating longevity risk for plan participants who elect to take an annuity at retirement. One possible concern about the CB plan design is that by permitting retired participants to access up to 100 percent of their cash balance, the plan leaves assets vulnerable to use for purposes other than for retirement income.

Death and Disability Benefits. The Nebraska plan's death benefit is payable to beneficiaries based on the value of the deceased member's account, and like the retirement benefit, it may be taken either as a lump sum or an annuity. This is consistent with death benefits offered by other state and local government retirement systems, although employers often will provide a supplemental life insurance policy for their workers. Members who meet criteria for disability can qualify for an annuity calculated in the same manner as a retirement benefit: on the basis of the account value and the member's age. The only difference between the manner in which the disability and retirement benefit are calculated is that disability applicants vest immediately. The disability benefit under the new CB plan provides access for participants to a benefit with assets that are professionally invested and that reflect the participant's salary and length of service, characteristics a DC plan often does not exhibit.

Preserving Cost Consistency. The NPERS Board may pay a dividend only if the actuarial required contribution rate is 90 percent or less of the statutory contribution rate. This creates a contribution rate cushion that prohibits the distribution of dividends unless the plan's funding condition is sound. Since inception of the plan in 2003, the combined employer and employee contribution rate has exceeded the plan's normal cost. Combined with excess investment returns that have permitted payment of a dividend credit each year from 2004 to 2007, the plan has had an actuarial surplus since inception. As of end 2007, the plan's funding level was 103.4 percent.

Earnings Limitation Savings Accounts (ELSAs) for the Minnesota Teachers Retirement Association

In recent years, many states have established or expanded opportunities for retired public employees to return to employment with the same employer who sponsors their retirement benefit, without forcing them to sacrifice the benefit due to IRS limits on in-service distributions. These often are referred to as 'return-to-work' provisions. Multiple factors create demand to enable retirees to return to work, including a rising retirement rate as growing numbers of Baby Boomers move closer to retirement age;

expanding difficulties among employers in replacing retiring workers creat-ing employee shortages in certain fields (e.g., teachers and engineers) and geographic areas (e.g., rural areas and inner cities); increasing employee interest in phasing out of the workforce, rather than experiencing a sudden cessation of employment followed by an equally abrupt onset of retirement; and a recognition among many retirees that either their retirement income is insufficient or not what they thought or hoped it would be. An additional factor prompting demand for retirees to return to work is health care costs which continue to grow faster than the rate of general inflation and which many retirees fail to fully consider prior to retiring.

Return-to-work provisions in several states illustrate public employers' efforts to strike a balance between allowing retirees to return to work while remaining compliant with tax rules. For instance, participants in the ASRS who reach normal retirement eligibility may return to work for an ASRS employer one year after retirement, as long as there was no agreement with their employer to hire the participant at the time the participant left. Alternatively, ASRS participants who meet normal retirement eligibility criteria may return to work for an ASRS employer without waiting, as long as two criteria are met: (*a*) there was no agreement between the participant and the employer for the participant to return to employment; and (*b*) the participant may work no more than 19 hours per week for any length of time, or 20 or more hours per week for no more than 20 weeks per year. These provisions are intended to either force the employee into retirement for at least one year, or to preclude participants from returning to work in a permanent, full-time capacity. Each of these consequences creates limitations for both the employer and the employee.

Connecticut permits retired public school teachers to receive retirement benefits and to be reemployed by a local board of education, or by any constituent unit of the state system of higher education, in a position designated by the State Commissioner of Education as a 'subject shortage area' for the school year in which the former teacher is reemployed. Such employment may be for up to one full school year and may, with prior approval by the board, be extended for an additional school year. Thus, this provision also is limiting for both employers and employees.

In fact, most return-to-work provisions including those in both Arizona and Connecticut are designed to limit the amount of time annuitants may work for their employer/retirement plan sponsor. These limits prove to be a hindrance to public employers' ability to fill certain positions and ensure the consistent delivery of certain public services. Another challenge with return-to-work provisions is one of public perception, since the idea of a public employee simultaneously receiving a paycheck and an employer-sponsored retirement benefit may provoke controversy and ill will toward public employees and their retirement benefits.

The Minnesota Teachers' Retirement Association (TRA) administers a program designed to remove barriers to return to teaching after retirement. Prior to 2000, in accordance with the rules then in place, any pension benefits withheld from retirees due to 'excess' earnings, reverted to the TRA Fund.[3] Because returning retirees did not wish to forfeit pension benefits, this policy created a disincentive to return to work and limited the ability of school districts to attract retired teachers to return. Motivated by statewide teacher shortages, Minnesota established a method in 2000 that would accommodate the needs of both public school employers and retired public school teachers who sought to return to work, while not limiting the returning employee's earnings or the length of time worked. This was accomplished by incorporating certain DC plan elements into the return-to-work provision, known as earnings limitation savings accounts (ELSAs).

Under Minnesota state law, teachers under age 65 who resume teaching for a TRA-covered employer after retirement are subject to an annual earnings limitation based on the Social Security rules. If a member earns more than the Social Security earnings limitation ($13,560 in calendar 2008), the annuity payable during the following calendar year is offset by $1 for each $2 earned in excess of the limitation.[4] Under the ELSA program, rather than confiscating a portion of the member's pension benefit and returning it to the TRA fund, the offset amount is deferred into an individual account that earns 6 percent annually. Members in the ELSA program do not make a contribution to the TRA pension benefit or earn additional service credit, and TRA employers do not pay pension contributions for their rehired annuitants. On the later of reaching age 65 or one year after termination of the TRA-covered employment that gave rise to the limitation, participants may receive a lump-sum payment of the total offset amount plus 6 percent interest compounded annually. (As of this writing, the yield on a 10-year US treasury bill is below 4.0 percent, making a guaranteed rate of 6 percent appear generous.) The TRA does not annuitize ELSAs; all or any portion of the payment may be rolled over to a traditional IRA or an eligible employer plan. ELSAs are nominal accounts invested by the same entity—the State Board of Investments—that invests the Minnesota state pension fund assets. ELSA assets are invested in the same manner as other assets in the TRA Fund, so the ELSA accounts are not individually managed by their account holders.

According to the TRA, some ELSA participants have expressed interest in annuitizing these accounts. Also some have complained about the required delay in accessing accounts until age 65 at the earliest: a participant who retires at 58 and returns for two years must then wait at least five years prior to being able to access his ELSA. ELSA members are able to designate a beneficiary for their accounts in the event of their death before distribution of their ELSA account.

As of June 2007, TRA had 1,389 retirees (3% of all benefit recipients) who had exceeded the earnings limitation since the program's inception and established an ELSA account. The total dollar value of ELSA accounts totaled approximately $18 million. The TRA or its actuarial consultant have not studied the possible effects of the ELSA program and whether school districts have chosen to rehire annuitants in lieu of hiring new teachers who would otherwise contribute to TRA. As structured, no actuarial cost is linked to this program since ELSA account holders are eventually paid their promised monthly benefits, albeit delayed until after age 65. This structure enables the ELSA program to avert allegations of so-called 'double-dipping.'

Investment earnings-based permanent benefit increase at the Arizona State Retirement System

Approximately two-thirds of state and local government pension plans provide their annuitants with some form of automatic cost-of-living adjustment (NASRA/NCTR 2007). Known as COLAs, these serve as a hedge against inflation which will erode the value of a retirement benefit. For example, over a 20-year period, an annual inflation rate of 3 percent will erode the value of a retirement benefit by 44 percent. Thus, the purchasing power of a $2,500 monthly benefit for a public school teacher retiring at age 65 will decline to $1,359 by age 85 (which is the median life expectancy of a 65-year-old female.) If she lived to age 95, the real value of her fixed nominal benefit would fall to $1,033. Most public pension plans that do not provide an automatic COLA periodically will approve either a permanent benefit increase or a one-time increase, sometimes known as a '13th check.' Some public funds such as the Teacher Retirement System and Employee Retirement System of Texas limit the legislature's authority to approve an ad hoc COLA based on the plan's actuarial funding status.

According to the Public Fund Survey, some public pension automatic COLAs are linked to changes in the consumer price index (CPI). These COLAs usually are capped, such as not to exceed 2 percent or 3 percent in one year. Some are established as a specific rate, such as 2 percent or 3 percent of the benefit, regardless of the CPI. Most automatic COLAs are compounded, meaning they are applied to the previous year's COLA-adjusted amount; those that are not compounded are known as simple, meaning that the COLA is applied to the annuitant's original benefit (NASRA/NCTR 2007). An automatic COLA is a relatively expensive benefit provision. For example, the South Carolina Legislature approved an automatic 1 percent COLA for current and future retirees of the South Carolina Retirement System. The projected cost of this benefit enhancement over the plan's 30-year funding period added $2.2 billion to the plan's $26 billion liability, resulting in a required increase to the contribution rate of approximately 2 percent of worker pay.

Employers and employees participating in the ASRS pay matching contribution rates determined by actuarial valuation. Other factors held equal, actuarial investment returns in excess of the plan's 8 percent return assumption reduce required contribution rates for both employers and employees. Likewise, returns below the assumption increase required contribution rates. Until 1994, annuitants in the ASRS relied on the legislature to provide periodic ad hoc COLAs. In that year, the state legislature approved an earnings-based permanent benefit increase (PBI) which provides a permanent benefit increase for ASRS annuitants funded with investment earnings above the plan's 8 percent investment return assumption.[5] If the ASRS fund's actuarial investment return were 10 percent, for example, the portion of the 'excess' 2 percent return (the difference between 10% and 8%) attributable to annuitants (retirees, beneficiaries, and disabilitants) would be set aside to increase benefits.

To calculate the amount of the increase, the plan's actuary pro-rates the portion of investment earnings that apply to current annuitants. The PBI provision limits the amount of the increase in any one year to 4 percent of the plan's annual retirement benefit liability; any amount over the 4 percent is set aside to fund increases in future years. The amount divided among annuitants is not based on the value of each annuitant's benefit, but rather on the basis of the annuitant's years of service credit. Thus, annuitants are rewarded for longer service, not higher salary. Annuitants with different final average salaries (which are used to calculate retirement benefits) but the same number of years of service will receive the same benefit adjustment. For the plan's annuitants, the timing of creating the PBI could not have been better. The period from 1995–2000 was marked by strong investment returns, and the ASRS fund participated in these returns. The PBI provision produced a benefit enhancement every year from 1994 through 2005, despite the fact that the fund experienced poor returns (as did most investors) in fiscal years 2001–03. This is because investment earnings generated during 1995–2000 were in excess of the 4 percent limit. For an annuitant retired before 1994 with the plan average of 18.6 years of service and an average monthly benefit, the average annual benefit increase from 1994 through 2005 was 3.3 percent, increasing the monthly benefit of an average annuitant by 45 percent, from $852 to $1,238.[6] The average increase in the CPI during this period was 2.5 percent. Because the benefit increase is based not on the base value of the benefit, but on the participant's years of service, the percentage increase varies by annuitant. Annuitants with lower earnings during their working years but who retired with the same number of years of service credit as an average salaried earner, received benefit increases higher than the average. The year 2006 was the first since the program's inception that annuitants did not receive a benefit enhancement.

When the PBI was established in 1994, the ASRS used a five-year smoothing period to calculate its actuarial investment return. In 2003, the ASRS switched to a 10-year smoothing period to calculate the actuarial value of assets. The ASRS also established a new, 10-year timeframe for calculating the PBI, beginning with 2002. Because of the poor investment returns in FY 02 and FY 03, notwithstanding strong returns in FY 04– 07, the fund is unlikely to distribute a benefit increase in the foreseeable future.

In the absence of the PBI, an automatic COLA, or ad hoc COLAs, the value of ASRS annuitant benefits would have been diminished by inflation, and the benefits of strong investment earnings would have been limited to the plan's active members, employers (taxpayers), and future taxpayers. The PBI permits annuitants to participate in the 'excess' investment earnings generated by the ASRS fund and reduces their exposure to inflation risk. By creating a mechanism to provide a COLA that is not automatic, the Arizona Legislature avoided creating an unfunded liability, although the PBI does reduce funds that would otherwise have been available to offset investment returns below the assumed rate.

The ASRS actuary acknowledges that without the PBI, the ASRS contribution rate would be lower than it is currently, although he has not calculated precisely how much lower. The actuary also has estimated that an automatic COLA of 1 percent would require an increased contribution rate of 3.62 percent. In calculating the cost of ASRS liabilities, the actuary assumes an investment return of 8 percent, meaning that no assumption is made for payment of a PBI. Of course, by allocating a portion of 'excess' investment earnings, the PBI provision reduces assets that would be available to offset negative actuarial experiences, including periods of actuarial returns that are lower than expected. But if the alternative to the PBI were to be a typical automatic COLA, the PBI would result in an actuarial cost only with assets that already have been accrued, thereby reducing the risk to the plan sponsor (and active annuitants, whose contribution rate also is affected by the plan's actuarial experience) of unfunded liabilities that would accrue automatically.

The value of a DC plan is a function of contributions to the individual account plus investment earnings less expenses. Retirement income produced by a DC plan thus depends on the value of each individual's account and investment earnings. Once a participant stops contributing to his retirement plan (as typically occurs in retirement), the value of his DC account—and the income the account generates—becomes limited by its investment performance. As with a DC plan, the PBI allows individual account holders to benefit from strong investment returns and to suffer the effects of inflation when returns are poor.

By establishing an earnings-based COLA, the ASRS has created a mechanism to reduce annuitants' inflation risk, paid for with a combination of current and future active members and current and future employers (taxpayers). Also, by recognizing the basis on which the plan will pay a COLA, the plan increases the likelihood that the COLA will be pre-funded rather than imposing the full cost of the COLA on future taxpayers.

Deferred annuity benefit at the Minnesota Teachers Retirement Association

Employee turnover is a fact of life for employers in every economic sector, regardless of the type of retirement plan an employer offers. Actuarial assumptions used for public DB plans recognize that many participants will leave the plan before they begin to draw a retirement benefit, or they will withdraw their assets rather than taking a retirement benefit. From the standpoint of the retirement plan, a problem with turnover is that retirement assets may be diminished through forfeiture of employer contributions and, in the case of DB plans, through low interest rates (if any) paid on assets of withdrawing participants. Terminating employees who are vested in their DB plans and who elect to leave their assets with the plan are exposed to inflation risk. The farther away is the terminating participant from drawing his retirement benefit, the greater the inflation risk exposure. Thus, DB plan participants who leave before qualifying for retirement benefits usually face unpleasant choices: either withdraw their contributions with little or no interest, thereby abandoning their employer's contributions, or leave their contributions with the plan until they reach retirement, exposing their future retirement benefit to inflation.

To address the problem of DB plan asset loss, the Minnesota Teachers' Retirement Association maintains a so-called deferred retirement annuity benefit, available to vested members (after three years) who terminate prior to reaching the plan's minimum retirement age of 55. To qualify for the benefit, terminating participants must leave their contributions with the TRA. Upon reaching retirement eligibility which occurs as early as age 55 for a reduced retirement benefit and age 66 for a normal (unreduced) retirement benefit, a participant may begin to receive a retirement benefit

(TRA 2008). The deferred annuity benefit is calculated in the same manner as for other, non-terminating participants, by multiplying the participant's years of service by his or her final average salary, and by the TRA retirement multiplier of 1.7 percent. The calculation for deferred annuity participants then is increased by 2.5 percent for each year since the participant terminated. This 2.5 percent escalator (which is greater for workers hired prior mid-2006) can partially offset the effects of inflation between the time the participant terminates and when the participant begins taking his retirement benefit.

A comparison of the difference the TRA deferred annuity benefit can make to a terminating participant's retirement benefit is shown in Table 12-2. Here we compare two plans, A and B. Plan A does not offer a deferred annuity benefit while Plan B does. Normal retirement eligibility in both plans is age 66 with at least three years of service, and the retirement multiplier is 1.7 percent of salary. A participant terminating employment at age 46 with 20 years of service and a final average salary of $50,000 in Plan A will receive an annual pension benefit of $17,000 on reaching age 66, as long as he or she leaves his or her contributions with the plan. An inflation rate of 3 percent will reduce the real value of that benefit by nearly 46 percent, to $9,245. The same employee participating in Plan B with the deferred annuity benefit would also qualify for a pension beginning at 66. But because the deferred annuity benefit has increased the value of the benefit by 2.5 percent each year, at age 66, the Plan B participant will receive an annual benefit of $27,856, ($15,378 on an inflation-adjusted basis) a reduction in the real value of the benefit of just 9.5 percent, compared to the $17,000 that Plan A will provide.

A terminating participant who elects to refund his contributions plus the 6 percent interest may invest his withdrawn retirement assets and purchase an annuity comparable to that provided by the TRA. The TRA deferred annuity benefit provides a mechanism for terminating participants to secure a retirement annuity protected (largely) from inflation and one that enables the participant to avoid the task of rolling over his assets and making investment decisions for the remainder of his working and retired life.

The cost to the TRA of the deferred annuity benefit is estimated to be 0.45 percent of payroll. This cost represents the actuarial gain the plan would realize if terminating participants who take advantage of the deferred annuity benefit, instead withdrew their benefits, leaving the employer's contributions with the plan. The TRA deferred annuity benefit is like a DC plan in that it permits retirement assets to continue growing despite the plan participant's terminating employment, just as DC plan assets would; and by enabling the withdrawn participant to receive the employer's contributions.

TABLE 12-2 Comparison of inflation-adjusted
benefit with and without the
Minnesota Teachers' Retirement
Association deferred annuity benefit

Year	Plan A ($)	Plan B ($)
	17,000	17,000
1	16,490	16,915
2	15,995	16,830
3	15,515	16,746
4	15,050	16,663
5	14,598	16,579
6	14,161	16,496
7	13,736	16,414
8	13,324	16,332
9	12,924	16,250
10	12,536	16,169
11	12,160	16,088
12	11,795	16,008
13	11,441	15,928
14	11,098	15,848
15	10,765	15,769
16	10,442	15,690
17	10,129	15,611
18	9,825	15,533
19	9,530	15,456
20	9,245	15,378

Source: Author's calculation as described in text, drawing
on information from TRA (2008).

Individual account plan sponsored by the Oregon Public Employees' Retirement System

In the face of falling DB plan funding and sharply higher, and unsustainable, projected costs, the Oregon governor and legislature revised the plan design of the Oregon Public Employees' Retirement System (PERS) in 2003. It terminated an old DB plan design whose cost had become unsustainable and established mandatory participation in both a DC and a DB plan. Since 2004, all mandatory employee contributions to PERS have been directed to the DC component of the retirement benefit, known as the Individual Account Plan, or IAP. With these changes, the Oregon governor and legislature were able to contain what had become unsustainable liability growth while preserving desirable features of both DB and DC plans.

PERS is the predominant public retirement system in the state, providing retirement and other benefits for employees of the state, public schools, and most political subdivisions. It includes over 160,000 active members and more than 100,000 annuitants. Combined assets held in the Oregon DB fund exceed $60 billion. PERS has long featured a retirement plan design containing both a DB and a DC plan, an atypical combination among state and local governments. Until 2003, the DB plan retirement multiplier had been 1.67 percent (the median public fund multiplier is 1.85%; NASRA/NCTR 2007). The accompanying DC component permitted participants to benefit from market gains with no exposure to downside risk. For example, if the fund containing DC plan accounts earned 15 percent in a year, participants got nearly all of that credited to their accounts. If the fund return was negative, participants still received a guaranteed 8 percent earnings credit.

Consecutive years of negative returns in 2001 and 2002 eroded the plan's funding level, which then declined precipitously, and projected plan costs were rising to unsustainable levels requiring projected employer contribution rates well above 20 percent. The Oregon governor and legislature responded by devising a new plan that reduced the DB plan retirement factor to 1.5 percent and also eliminated the guaranteed earnings feature in individual accounts. The new IAP features individual accounts invested in the same portfolio as the $60+billion PERS DB plan, so DC plan assets are now managed by the same professional investors who manage the big DB fund, relieving participants of the responsibility for managing their retirement assets. Moreover, investing in the DB fund costs less than most DC plans, and gives participants exposure to asset classes such as real estate and private equity, that they are unlikely to otherwise have access to in other DC plan accounts. Participants contribute 6 percent of pay to the IAP, and employers may (and most do) make the contribution on participants' behalf. Employer contributions finance the DB portion of the benefit. Upon retirement, in addition to their DB plan benefit, participants may elect to take their IAP assets either as a lump sum, in equal installments over a 5, 10, 15, or 20-year period, or as an annuity based on the account balance and participant's age.

IAP management costs have declined each year since the plan was established in 2004: 39 basis points in FY 07, down from 53 basis points in FY 06 and 86 bp in FY 05. Plan costs may continue to decline if growth in asset values outpaces growth in expenses, many of which are fixed. Low costs are an important factor contributing to participants' ability to accumulate retirement assets. Due to robust investment returns and low costs, the combined value of its individual accounts has grown to $1.9 billion in 2007

TABLE 12-3 Earnings credit applied to individual accounts in the Oregon Public Employee Retirement System, 2004–2007

Year	Earnings Credit (%)
2004	12.77
2005	12.80
2006	14.98
2007	9.46

Source: PERS (2008).

since plan inception. The IAP's low costs are enabled by annual, rather than daily, updating of account values and by investing IAP assets solely in the PERS fund, in which investment costs are less than 50 basis points. Although this is higher than other public pension funds of similar size, the Oregon Investment Council which invests the PERS assets has a long and successful investment track record, consistently outperforming most of its peers. This outperformance is attributable partly to higher-than-average allocations to alternative assets, including private equities.

Retiring participants who elect to annuitize or to withdraw their assets over a certain period (rather than withdraw them as a lump sum) continue to benefit from pooling, professional asset management, and alternative asset classes. Table 12-3 shows earnings credited to individual accounts since their inception in 2004. The earnings credit reflects the amount available for distribution and takes into account the fund's investment return and all expenses.

Employer response to the new plan design has been positive since the reforms stabilized liability growth and reduced both costs and cost volatility. Controlling plan liabilities and costs was particularly important to Oregon public employers and taxpayers, considering how high those costs had been projected to rise. In concert with other plan design changes, the establishment of mandatory individual accounts and investing them with professionals in a common fund is a central feature of the new plan design that has restored the sustainability of retirement benefits for public employees while leveraging key features of both traditional DB and DC plans.

Other states, including Washington, Ohio, and Indiana maintain retirement plan designs similar to that in Oregon, in which a DC plan accompanies mandatory participation in a DB plan. Table 12-4 presents and compares key features of these retirement plan designs.

TABLE 12-4 Defined benefit plans with mandatory defined contribution components sponsored by state governments

	Indiana PERF	Indiana TRF	Washington DRS	Ohio PERS	Ohio STRS	Oregon PERS
Applicable group(s)	Mandatory for all participants	Mandatory for all participants	Optional	Optional for new hires and non-vested workers since 2002	Optional for new hires & non-vested workers from 2001	Mandatory for new hires since August 2003
Normal retirement age/yrs of service	65/10, 60/15, Rule of 85 at age 55	65/10, 60/15, Rule of 85 at age 55	65/5	60/5, 55/25, any/30; 48/25 law enforcement	60/5	65/any, 58/30; 60/any, 53/25 public safety
DB plan multiplier	1.1%	1.1%	1.0%	1%; 1.5% for years > 30	1.0%	1.5%; 1.8% for fire and police
Employer funds DB plan benefit?	Yes	No pre '96 hires; yes since	Yes	Yes	Yes	Yes
Social security?	Yes	Yes	Yes	No	No	Yes
Employer contribution to DC plan	Employers (ER) may make employee (EE) contributions which vest immediately. State makes contributions for its EEs.	ERs may elect to make EE contributions, which vest immediately	No	ER contributions divided among DB, DC, D&D & retiree health care. Five-year vesting period for ER contributions	ER contributions divided among DB portion, DB UAAL, and retiree health care. 5-year vesting period for ER contributions	ERs may elect to make EE contributions

(cont.)

TABLE 12-4 (*Continued*)

	Indiana PERF	Indiana TRF	Washington DRS	Ohio PERS	Ohio STRS	Oregon PERS
Employee DC plan contribution	3.0%	3.0%	5% to 15%, depending on EE election	9.5%, including 0.1% for admin fees	10.0%	6.0%
DC plan investment options	Six investment options administered by the fund, ranging from conservative to aggressive	Six investment options administered by the fund, ranging from conservative to aggressive	Either the Total Allocation Portfolio, which mirrors DB plan fund, or 10 self-directed funds ranging from conservative to aggressive plus balanced funds	Nine sponsored options ranging from conservative to aggressive.	Eight options ranging from conservative to aggressive and a guaranteed return option	All DC plan contributions are invested in the DB plan fund

Default DC plan investment option	Guaranteed Fund earns a rate established annually by the Board. Current rate is 6%.	Guaranteed Fund earns a rate established annually by Board. Current rate is 6%.	Total Allocation Portfolio, which mirrors the DB plan fund	Moderate pre-mixed portfolio	Money market fund	DB plan fund
DC plan withdrawal options	Annuity, rollover, partial lump sum (LS) and annuity; deferral until age 70½	Annuity, rollover, partial LS and annuity (limited to after-tax assets), deferral until age 70½	DB plan fund: LS, direct rollover, scheduled payments & personalized payment schedule. Self-Directed: same as DB plan fund, plus annuity purchase	Annuity; partial distributions; payments for guaranteed term; mo'ly payments of designated amount; deferral until age 70½	Annuity; LS and rollover	LS payment or equal installments over 5, 10, 15, or 20-year period.
Info online	www.in.gov/perf	www.in.gov/trf	www.drs.wa.gov (Go to 'my plan 3 account')	www.opers.org	www.strsoh.org	oregon.gov/ PERS (Click on OPSRP & IAP)

Source: Author's compilation based on data provided by plan sponsors; see 'Info Online.'

Conclusion

This chapter focuses on instances where DC plan elements have been incorporated into or alongside DB plan structures sponsored by US state and local governments. The cases described include the cash balance plan administered by the Nebraska Public Employees' Retirement System; the Earnings Limitation Savings Accounts and Deferred Annuity Benefit sponsored by the Minnesota Teachers' Retirement Association; the Permanent Benefit Increase sponsored by the Arizona State Retirement System; and the hybrid retirement plan sponsored by the Oregon Public Employees' Retirement System. Each of these and similar mixed plan designs were implemented to accomplish one or more particular stakeholder objectives. These plan designs may offer lessons to employers and others seeking opportunities to rebalance various and sometimes competing stakeholder objectives, such as redistributing risks or costs, enhancing benefits, and promoting longer employment.

Notes

[1] Other examples of DC elements incorporated into state-sponsored DB plans not discussed here include options to increase the portability of pension assets by permitting the purchase and transfer of retirement benefit service credits among public retirement systems and in some cases, from service earned in the private sector to public retirement systems; partial lump sum options, which permit retiring public employees to take a portion of their annuity as a lump sum with an actuarial reduction in their annuity; deferred retirement option plans, which permit retiring public workers to continue working and defer their retirement benefit into an individual account, where it is invested by the plan sponsor until the worker ceases employment; automatic enrollment in a supplementary DC plan for workers whose primary retirement benefit is a DB plan; and establishment of cash balance plans in lieu of participating in Social Security.

[2] The federal mid-term rate is based on the average market yield of outstanding market obligations of the United States with maturities of at least three but not longer than nine years.

[3] Prior to 2000, there was an annual earnings limit for retirees under age 65 and a higher earnings limit for retirees age 65–69. For ages under 65, the penalty was $1 for every $2 over the earnings limit. For retirees ages 65 to 69, the penalty was $1 for every $3 over the higher earnings limit. Retirees age 70 and older had no earnings limitation.

[4] Members who reach normal retirement age (65, 10 months for those born in 1942) can earn $36,120 between January 1, 2008 through the month prior to turning age 65 and 10 months. Members reaching the full retirement age by January 1, 2008 are not subject to the earnings limitation.

[5] This statute has been modified since its inception to pay a COLA up to the full increase in the CPI, rather than one-half; to lower the threshold of investment

return from 9 percent to 8 percent; and to increase the maximum annual adjustment from 3 percent to 4 percent. See Arizona State Legislature (2008).

⁶ Based on data provided to the author by the Arizona State Retirement System.

References

Arizona State Legislature (2008). *Revised Statutes Section 38–767*, Benefit Increases. Phoenix: State of Arizona.

Buck Consultants (2000). *Benefit Review Study of the Nebraska Retirement Systems*, August. New York, NY: Buck Consultants.

—— (2007). *Actuarial Valuation of the Nebraska State Employees' Retirement System*, December. New York, NY: Buck Consultants.

Minnesota Teachers' Retirement Association (TRA) (2008). *Handbook of Benefits and Services 2008*. Saint Paul, MN: Minnesota Teachers' Retirement Association.

National Association of State Retirement Administrators and National Council on Teacher Retirement (NASRA/NCTR) (2007). *Public Fund Survey*. Washington, DC: National Association of State Retirement Administrators and National Council on Teacher Retirement.

Oregon Public Employees Retirement System (PERS) (2008). *Comprehensive Annual Financial Report for the Fiscal Year Ended 6/30/07*. Tigard, OR: Oregon Public Employees Retirement System.

US Bureau of Labor Statistics (2000). *Employee Benefits in State and Local Governments, 1998*. Bulletin 2531. Washington, DC: US Bureau of Labor Statistics.

Chapter 13

Defined Contribution Pension Plans in the Public Sector: A Benchmark Analysis

Roderick B. Crane, Michael Heller, and Paul J. Yakoboski

In this chapter we provide a perspective on best practice benchmarks for the design of defined contribution (DC) plans in cases where such plans are the primary, or core, employment-based retirement benefit sponsored by a public sector employer, as opposed to a supplemental benefit. These benchmarks are based on the assumption that providing an adequate and secure retirement income for participants is the primary objective for the plan.

We first discuss plan design principles that support an effective core DC plan and from these principles, we derive design best practices. Our discussion of best practices for primary DC plans in the public sector is not intended to define an 'ideal' plan design. No single plan design is best for all situations. Rather, the purpose of highlighting best practices is to provide a basis for identifying strengths and weaknesses of design that may affect the ability of a plan to provide an adequate and secure level of retirement income. We conclude the chapter with an analysis of existing public sector core DC plans relative to these best practice standards.

The public sector pension environment

The primary vehicle for providing core retirement benefits in the public sector has long been the defined benefit (DB) pension plan. DB plans specify how much monthly benefit a participant will receive once he or she retires. In the private sector, a DB participant is generally not required to make contributions to the plan, but most public sector DB plans require employee contributions. DB plans do not require the participant to make investment decisions. Typically, the risks of funding the promised benefits lie with the plan sponsor who is responsible for adequate funding of the program and management of money invested to support the plan. Over 90 percent of full-time public sector employees participate in DB pension plans for the major source of employer-provided retirement benefits (McDonnell 2002).

By comparison, about 14 percent of full-time public employees participate in DC retirement plans for their primary employer-provided retirement benefit (McDonnell 2002). DC plans define how much the sponsor
and participant can or must contribute to an individual account created
for each participant. When the participant retires, retirement benefits
are based on the total amount contributed plus investment gains, minus
expenses and losses. Typically, the participant decides how the money is
invested and takes the risk of poor investment performance if his or her
choices do not perform well. Some examples of public sector DC plans
include 401(a) money purchase plans, 401(k) plans, 403(b) tax-deferred
annuity plans, and 457(b) deferred compensation plans. The 14 percent
figure cited earlier translates into over two-million public-sector employees
who rely in whole or in part on DC arrangements for their employer based
core retirement benefit.

The design and funding of core DC plans in the public sector is far too
important to be left unexamined even though far fewer public employees
participate in them compared to DB plans. In the same fashion as the DB
plans that cover most public employees, core DC plans are vital to the
economic security of thousands of existing retirees and beneficiaries and
are an important component of the compensation structure of state and
local governments that offer them.

Plan objectives in the public sector

Public employers are faced with a range of competing objectives in their
capacity as a retirement plan sponsor. They will certainly want their retirement plans to promote effective and efficient workforce management by
helping to attract and retain quality employees and to subsequently facilitate the orderly and timely movement of employees out of the workforce.

Public sector entities, however, do not necessarily view the retirement
plans they sponsor strictly through the lens of an employer. A principal
function of government is to ensure the general welfare of society. This
makes the public sector uniquely concerned with the adequacy and security
of public employee retirement benefits. If the core DC retirement plans
they sponsor fail in this regard, a consequence may be an increased burden on the social welfare programs that they also sponsor. As stewards of
taxpayer dollars, all considerations are to be carefully balanced.

We assume that the primary objective of the public employer as a DC plan
sponsor is to provide adequate and secure retirement income throughout
retirement for its employees. Other objectives, such as workforce management considerations or additional employee financial security considerations (e.g., providing death and disability benefits) are appropriate

components of a comprehensive retirement benefit policy, but we consider them secondary for purposes of this chapter. As such, they do not directly influence our best practice benchmarks, but certainly would impact the 'ideal' plan design in any specific instance.

Several implications for best practice core DC plan design in the public sector flow from this primary objective. First, plans should be designed with participation and vesting requirements that maximize accumulations. Plans should provide a total contribution level and investment structure that together are expected to accumulate sufficient assets to fund an adequate retirement income for each participant. Finally, plans should have a payout design that provides an adequate and secure level of income throughout retirement.

In a DC framework, retirement income adequacy and security is a shared responsibility between employer and employee. So plan design should also provide participant access to independent, expert, and personalized education, planning, and advice services during both the accumulation phase and through retirement. Active employer engagement and oversight helps ensure alignment between plan design and plan administration. It also helps ensure that investment, administrative, and other professional service providers are meeting performance and service standards and that their fees are reasonable and competitive.

Best practice implications

Our recommendations for best practice design of core DC plans in the public sector result from specifying plan feature benchmarks that operationalize the abstract implications discussed earlier. Again, these are the implications of an assumed primary plan objective to provide adequate and secure retirement income. Table 13-3 summarizes these benchmarks.

Eligibility and Participation. Certain eligibility and participation design features contribute to greater participant accumulations and are therefore considered best practices: mandatory enrollment, low or no age restrictions on participation, and waiting periods of no more than one year before participation begins.

We are not prepared to endorse mandatory enrollment of part-time employees as a best practice. While it can be argued that is desirable under an objective of providing adequate and secure retirement income for public sector employees, the workforce needs of and financial implications for public plan sponsors are still evolving around this proposition. Voluntary participation opportunities should be considered as an alternative for these employees, however.

TABLE 13-1 Retirement income targets

Pre-Retirement Salary ($)	Gross Retirement Income Target (as % of Pre-Retirement Salary)
20,000	89
30,000	84
40,000	80
50,000	77
60,000	75
70,000	76[a]
80,000	77[a]
90,000	78[a]

[a] Increasing target replacement rates at higher salaries are the result of higher marginal income tax rates for these salary levels.

Source: Georgia State University/Aon Consulting (2004).

Contribution Levels. Best practice contribution design must result in an adequate retirement income. This implies non-elective, that is mandatory, contributions by the employer and/or employee. However, assuming typical investment returns, what is the appropriate contribution level? This in turn depends upon the level of retirement income that should be considered 'adequate.'

Retirement income adequacy is typically considered in terms of the percentage of a participant's salary immediately prior to retirement that is replaced during retirement (Aon Consulting 2004). This 'replacement ratio' is measured at the time of retirement and then throughout retirement to determine if it has been affected by inflation.

Public policy makers need to set retirement income replacement objectives for employees at the designated normal retirement date. Wage replacement objectives can vary by class of employee (e.g., regular employee versus public safety) and may reflect differences in pay levels and Social Security benefits. Table 13-1 presents target replacement ratios designed to maintain pre-retirement standards of living into retirement from the Georgia State University/Aon Consulting RETIRE Project (2004).

These replacement targets are higher than the traditional 70 percent target often used as conventional wisdom. The 75 to 89 percent figures reflect, in part, the higher costs of retiree health care that current and future retirees are likely to experience.

What Contribution Rate is Needed? If a 75 to 89 percent wage replacement target is adopted, what contribution rate (assuming reasonable investment returns) is required to achieve that objective?

Table 13-2 provide illustrations of wage replacement outcomes assuming various contribution rates at various salary levels compared to the Georgia State University/Aon replacement targets for given salary levels. These calculations assume an individual is hired at age 30 and retires at 65, salary increases at 4.5 percent annually, the pre-retirement investment rate of return is 7 percent per year, the annual growth rate in average national wages for Social Security indexing purposes is 3.5 percent, a single life annuity is purchased at retirement, and the payout rate is based upon 5 percent interest and the Annuity 2000 mortality table (with ages set back 2.5 years). In Table 13-2, the DC plan benefits replace the same percentage of pre-retirement income at all salary levels. Social Security provides a decreasing level of replacement income for higher salary levels because of its progressive nature.

Based on this analysis, in order to maintain pre-retirement standards of living, best practice calls for a core DC total contribution rate of at least 12 percent of pay if covered by Social Security and 18 to 20 percent of pay if not. Public safety employees would need to have significantly higher contribution rates in order to support earlier retirement ages common to those job classifications. It should be noted that all projections of income replacement rates are very sensitive to changes in the underlying economic assumptions, including salary growth rate, pre-retirement investment return, and assumed annuity payout rate.

We make no best practice recommendation regarding employer versus employee share of this total contribution. The objective of adequacy does not imply an implication regarding who funds the benefit. However, if retirement income security is considered a shared employer and employee responsibility, it could be argued that the appropriate benchmark would be a 50/50 split. Any employee contributions should be mandated and paid pre-tax.

Vesting. We have adopted the view that best practice regarding vesting for retirement benefits should be independent of when participation begins under the plan. A participant should earn a non-forfeitable right to all employer contributions, that is, be 100 percent vested, with one-year of employment service. This provides a reasonable hurdle for participants to earn non-forfeitable retirement benefits, while plan sponsors are not funding benefits for very short-term employees.

Therefore, if immediate participation is adopted by a plan sponsor, best practice allows for the imposition of a vesting period of up to one year. If participation is delayed for one year, best practice calls for immediate vesting in employer contributions. Graded vesting schedules are often confusing and more difficult to administer and, while acceptable, are not considered a best practice.

TABLE 13-2 Retirement income replacement projections under a defined contribution plan

Initial Salary	Replacement from DC Plan (as % of final salary) [a]	Replacement from Social Security (as % of final salary)	Combined (as % of final salary)	Income Replacement Target[b]	(Gap)/Surplus
10% of Pay Total Contribution Rate					
$30,000	41.8%	33.8%	75.6%	84.0%	(8.4%)
$50,000	41.8%	28.6%	70.4%	77.0%	(6.6%)
$70,000	41.8%	23.5%	65.3%	76.0%	(10.7%)
12% of Pay Total Contribution Rate					
$30,000	50.2%	33.8%	84.0%	84.0%	(0.0%)
$50,000	50.2%	28.6%	78.8%	77.0%	1.8%
$70,000	50.2%	23.5%	73.7%	76.0%	(2.3%)
14% of Pay Total Contribution Rate					
$30,000	58.5%	33.8%	92.3%	84.0%	8.3%
$50,000	58.5%	28.6%	87.1%	77.0%	10.1%
$70,000	58.5%	23.5%	82.0%	76.0%	6.0%

[a] Income replacement shown as a percentage of final pay. Calculations assume an individual is hired at age 30 and retires at 65, salary increases at 4.5 percent annually, the pre-retirement investment rate of return is 7 percent per year, the annual growth rate in average national wages for Social Security indexing purposes is 3.5 percent, a single life annuity is purchased at retirement and the payout rate is based upon 5 percent interest and the Annuity 2000 mortality table (with ages set back 2.5 years).

[b] Derived from Georgia State University/Aon Consulting (2004).

Source: Authors' calculations.

TABLE 13-3 Best practice recommendations for core defined contribution plan design in the public sector

Plan Design Feature	Best Practice Benchmarks
Eligibility and participation	• Mandatory enrollment • Low or no age restrictions on participation • Waiting periods of no more than one year for participation
Vesting	• 100% vested after one year of employment
Contributions (Employer and Employee)	• Non-elective contributions by employer and/or employee • Total at least 12 % of pay if covered by Social Security and 18 to 20 % of pay if not covered by Social Security
Investments	• Mandatory or default investment into lifecycle target-date funds • When participants are given choice, a limited menu of 15 to 20 options covering the major asset classes
Distributions	Pre-retirement: • No lump sum distributions at job change, other than small balance cash-outs • No hardship withdrawals • No plan loans Retirement: • Require minimum level of mandatory annuitization in vehicle providing inflation-protected income • Limited lump sum distribution availability
Administrative structure and fees	• Single vendor recordkeeping structure • Single point of contact for participants • Larger plans standard: total administrative and investment costs not to exceed 100 basis points
Other participant services	• Broad-based employee investment education • Individual-specific investment advice • Services delivered through multiple modes: call center, Internet, and in-person

Source: Authors' compilations.

Investments. If investment allocations are made with the objective of generating adequate retirement income, as opposed to, say, maximizing wealth, then best practice calls for mandatory or default investment into a lifecycle target-date fund. Lifecycle target-date funds ensure appropriate investment diversification, rebalance automatically, and regularly adjust investment allocations to limit risk based on the number of years until planned retirement. Such funds have the advantage of eliminating the need for investment decision-making by plan participants. They have the additional potential advantage of enhancing investment diversification by including asset classes (e.g., alternative investments and real estate) not typically found in traditional participant directed fund menus.

Lifecycle funds custom designed for a plan should be considered by the sponsor in certain cases because they can develop investment allocation strategies and glide paths that account for specialized employment and retirement patterns unique to a class of workers, such as public safety officers, for situations where workers do not participate in Social Security and for specific plan designs such as when the core DC plan is part of a combination DB/DC arrangement.

When participants are given choice, best practice calls for a limited non-overlapping menu of investment options (about 15 to 20 in number) covering the major asset classes. This will allow participants the opportunity to manage their own risk and return needs without overwhelming them with numerous and in many cases redundant options.

Pre-Retirement Distributions. Ensuring an adequate retirement income implies minimizing leakage from participants' accounts prior to retirement. Such leakage can occur at job change if individuals receive a lump sum distribution of their vested account balance and fail to preserve it for retirement via a rollover. Leakage can also occur through hardship distributions and plan loans. With a hardship distribution, the funds leave the retirement system. Plan loans are paid back with interest by the participant, however, there is the possibility of default by the participant, plus the interest payments on the loan may be less than what the borrowed funds would have otherwise earned had they remained invested in the plan.

Best practice plan design would not allow lump sums at job change; a limited exception could be made for small benefit accruals that do not exceed a threshold (e.g., $5,000) established by the plan sponsor to control the cost of administering numerous small value accounts. Best practice design would also not allow hardship withdrawals and loans.

Retirement Distributions. Best practice plan design ensures a secure stream of income throughout retirement. Best practice therefore limits participant ability to withdraw funds as a lump sum at retirement and requires that a minimum amount of the account be annuitized through a vehicle providing inflation protection. Such vehicles include participating guaranteed annuities, a variable payout annuity, and specialized inflation-protection annuities.

Annuitization of an account balance is the only means for an individual to guarantee a steady stream of income in retirement for life (and the lifetime of a spouse.) In addition, the value of these annuitized payments should be protected (at least partially) against erosion by inflation overtime else payment levels that were adequate at the beginning of retirement may no longer be so after a number of years in retirement.

How much of a participant's account balance must be subject to mandatory annuitization? If the primary purpose of the plan is to provide adequate retirement income, then annuitization of a relatively high percentage of the account could be required. This would be consistent with the general practice among public sector DB plans which typically require accrued benefits to be taken as an annuity. Social Security benefits should be considered when determining the appropriate level of annuitization of core DC plan account balances.

Administrative Structure. High administration and investment fees reduce the ultimate level of retirement income for participants of DC plans. Multiple vendor structures and agent–broker delivery models are generally more expensive than single recordkeeper administrative platforms. While investment choices may be supplied by several fund companies, best practice calls for one point of contact for participants regarding all aspects of the plan.

Plan features, plan size (participants and assets), asset allocation levels, geographic service area, administrative, and participant service levels are just some of the variables affecting a plan's administration costs and fees making it difficult to establish a best practice standard. It is possible, however, to establish standards that would help public core DC plan sponsors evaluate whether their costs and fees bear further examination. Larger plans should be able to take advantage of available economies of scale to deliver plan services at lower cost; total costs (administrative and investment fees) for a quality, state-of-the-art core DC plan should be available for 100 basis points or less for larger plans.

Education and Advice. Best practice design provides broad-based retirement planning and investment education services to participants. A higher best practice hurdle is the provision of individual-specific investment advice where a participant is provided with specific recommendations regarding the investment allocation of their contributions and account balances across the options available in the plan. Such guidance will factor in participant age, planned retirement age, current retirement accumulations, saving rates, tolerance for risk, and other factors. The mode for delivering personalized retirement services will need to reflect the multiple ways that individuals access information, for example, by phone, through the Web, and in person. While technology can enable more effective communication, it will not replace the need for one-on-one consultation, particularly as individuals approach retirement.

Public sector plans today

This section examines the 'typical' features of public sector core DC plans relative to our best practice benchmarks. While many features of a 'best practice' DC plan are met by many public sector plans, there is variance in this regard.

Two sets of plans are examined; those covering general public sector employees under 'state' plans and those covering public higher education employees. Plans in the state plan group include the Alaska Defined Contribution Retirement Plan, the Colorado Public Employees' Retirement Association (PERA) Defined Contribution Plan, the District of Columbia Defined Contribution Plan, the Florida Retirement System Investment Plan, the Michigan 401(k) Plan, the Montana Public Employee Retirement System Defined Contribution Retirement Plan, the Nebraska Defined Contribution Plan (which closed to employees hired after 2002), the North Dakota Public Employee Retirement System (PERS) Defined Contribution Plan, the Ohio Public Employee Retirement System Member-Directed Plan, the South Carolina Optional Retirement Plan, and the West Virginia Teachers Defined Contribution Plan.

The public higher education plans examined are those of Indiana University, Michigan State University, Purdue University, the State University of New York, the University of Iowa, the University of Michigan, and the University of Washington.

This is not an exhaustive list of public DC plans. These plans were chosen to be illustrative of common practice in the public sector. Among our sample of public sector plans, there is a high degree of uniformity along certain dimensions, for example, the mandatory nature of participation and the presence of non-elective sponsor and participant contribution levels. On the other hand, there is notable variance in the levels of these contribution rates. A summary table of the plan comparisons is provided in the Appendix.

Participation. Mandatory participation is the best practice benchmark for a core DC plan and employee participation is mandatory in all state plans examined here. The only caveat is in the case of an optional retirement plan, as in Colorado, Florida, Montana, North Dakota, Ohio, and South Carolina. In these situations, participation in a retirement plan is mandatory, but the individual chooses whether to participate in the primary DB plan or the primary DC plan. In cases where the individual fails to make such an election, he or she is typically defaulted into the DB plan. In Montana and North Dakota, all new hires are automatically enrolled in the DB plan, but then have a limited period of time (one year in Montana and six months in North Dakota) to switch into the DC plan if they so choose.

Participation is also mandatory in all of the public higher education plans examined. In the State University of New York and University of Iowa programs, the individual must choose between participation in the DB plan or the DC plan.

Another issue regarding participation is presence of a service requirement that must be fulfilled before the individual is eligible to participate in the plan. Best practice plan design not only involves mandatory participation, but also calls for eligibility within one year, if not immediately. Among the public plans examined here, not only is plan participation mandatory, but it is also typically immediate. The District of Columbia plan where individuals must be employed for one year before becoming eligible is an exception. Purdue also has a waiting period of up to three years for certain positions. At Michigan State University, the University of Michigan and the University of Washington, retirement plan participation is mandatory, but only after a two-year period of service, plus in the Michigan schools the service requirement is combined with an age requirement of 35. Individuals may participate in the plans prior to it becoming mandatory.

Contribution Levels. Best practice calls for non-elective contributions by the employer and/or employee that will result in an adequate retirement income assuming typical investment returns. This implies mandated contribution levels totaling at least 12 percent of pay if covered by Social Security and 18 to 20 percent of pay if not covered by Social Security. All of the public sector DC plans in our sample satisfy this benchmark to the extent that employers contribute to workers' accounts a specified percentage of pay and the employee's contribution rate is also specified by the plan.

In the state plans examined where workers are covered by Social Security, total contribution rates range from 4 percent to 12.3 percent; two of eight such plans meet or exceed the 12 percent best practice benchmark we set. Among state plans where workers are not covered by Social Security, total contribution rates range from 13 percent to 18.15 percent and two of four plans meet or exceed the 18 percent best practice rate.

In the higher education plans examined, combined employer and employee non-elective contribution rates were a minimum of 10 percent, typically in the range of 15 percent, and as high as 20 percent (for older participants at the University of Washington.) In all plans workers participated in Social Security and six of seven plans meet or exceed the 12 percent best practice benchmark. Non-elective contribution rates vary within some state and higher education plans based on position, salary, years of participation, or age.

Depending on the plan, there may or may not be the opportunity for additional discretionary contributions by the participants, which may or may not be matched by the plan sponsor. Michigan's public sector plan is a 401(k) and has employee elective contributions with an employer match. Among the higher education plans examined here, five of the seven allowed additional elective employee contributions and two of those matched employee contributions to a limit.

Projected Income Replacement Percentages. Table 13-4 shows projected income replacement rates at retirement for the plans examined here; replacement rates are presented based both on the DC benefit only and the DC benefit combined with Social Security.

If the contribution rate is a level percentage of pay (or one varying by age or years of service), the projected income replacement percentage arising from the DC plan will be independent of the individual's starting salary. A contribution schedule that varies depending on the level of annual salary (e.g., if integrated with Social Security) will result in replacement percentages that vary by the level of initial salary. Social Security replacement percentages will vary considerably by salary, with higher replacement percentages associated with lower-paid individuals.

As discussed previously, one study projects that an individual needs to retire with a total salary replacement percentage (including Social Security) in the range of 75 percent to 89 percent of final pay. While a 10 percent contribution rate may come close to achieving this goal for lower-paid individuals (due to relatively higher Social Security replacement ratios), a higher contribution rate of at least 12 percent of salary is more likely to achieve this goal for the majority of employees.

Vesting. Participants are always immediately fully vested in their contributions as well as the earnings on those contributions. Best practice calls for them to be immediately vested in employer contributions or to earn full vesting with no more than one year of employment. In our sample of state plans, the vesting norm is fulfilling a service requirement as a plan participant. The exception among the state plans examined here is that of South Carolina where individuals are immediately vested in employer contributions. The vesting schedule may be graded or cliff. The norm is graded vesting over a period of five years, though there is variation in the period of service required; full vesting occurs after one year in Florida, but takes 12 years in the West Virginia Teachers Plan.

Immediate vesting is the near universal norm in the public higher education plans examined here. The exception is the SUNY plan which has 100 percent cliff vesting after one year of service.

Investment Options. In every plan examined here the employee has complete control of how the account funds are invested across the options offered by the plan. In the case of such participant choice, best practice calls for a limited non-overlapping menu of about 15 to 20 investment options covering the major asset classes.

The number of options offered in the state plans examined here ranges from nine in Ohio to 70 in South Carolina. South Carolina has four

TABLE 13-4 Projected income replacement rates at retirement for selected public core DC plans

Plan	Total Contribution Rate	DC Retirement Plan [a]			DC Retirement Plan Plus Social Security Benefits [a]		
		Initial Salary					
		$30,000	$50,000	$70,000	$30,000	$50,000	$70,000
Alaska DC Retirement Plan PERS[b]	13.00%	54.3%	54.3%	54.3%	54.3%	54.3%	54.3%
Alaska DC Retirement Plan TRS[b]	15.00	62.7	62.7	62.7	62.7	62.7	62.7
Colorado PERA DC Plan[b]	18.15	75.9	75.9	75.9	75.9	75.9	75.9
District of Columbia DC Plan	5.00	20.1	20.1	20.1	53.9	48.7	43.6
Florida (FRS) Investment Plan	9.00	37.6	37.6	37.6	71.4	66.2	61.1
Michigan 401(k) Plan	10.00	41.8	41.8	41.8	75.6	70.4	65.3
Montana DC Plan	11.09	46.4	46.4	46.4	80.2	75.0	69.9
Nebraska DC Plan	12.30	51.4	51.4	51.4	85.2	80.0	74.9
North Dakota PERS DC Plan	8.14	34.0	34.0	34.0	67.8	62.6	57.5
Ohio PERS Member-Directed Plan[b]	18.13	75.8	75.8	75.8	75.8	75.8	75.8
South Carolina Optional Ret. Plan	11.50	48.1	48.1	48.1	81.9	76.7	71.6
West Virginia Teachers DC Plan	12.00	50.2	50.2	50.2	84.0	78.8	73.7
Indiana University—New Hire (after 1999)	10.00	41.8	41.8	41.8	75.6	70.4	65.3
Indiana University—Old Hire	15.00	62.7	62.7	62.7	96.5	91.3	86.2
Michigan State University	15.00	62.7	62.7	62.7	96.5	91.3	86.2
University of Michigan	15.00	62.7	62.7	62.7	96.5	91.3	86.2
Purdue University	11/15 on $9k	59.9	61.0	61.5	93.7	89.6	85.0

State University of New York	11 then 13 after 7 years	50.2	50.2	50.2	84.0	78.8	73.7
University of Iowa	15, except 10 for first 5 years under $4800	62.2	62.4	62.5	96.0	91.0	86.0
University of Washington	10 then 15 & 20 at ages 35 and 50	65.5	65.5	65.5	99.3	94.1	89.0

[a] Income replacement shown as a percentage of final pay. Calculations assume individual is hired at age 30 and retires at 65, salary increases at 4.5 percent annually, the pre-retirement investment rate of return is 7 percent per year, the annual growth rate in average national wages for Social Security indexing purposes is 3.5 percent, a single life annuity is purchased at retirement and the payout rate is based upon 5 percent interest and the Annuity 2000 mortality table (with ages set back 2.5 years).

[b] Participants under this plan are generally not covered under Social Security.

Source: Authors' calculations; see text.

providers offering between 15 and 22 options and, while participants may only have one provider at a time receiving contributions, they can keep assets with more than one of the providers. The number of investment options offered in public higher education is typically greater than the number offered elsewhere in the public sector. With the exception of the University of Washington, which offers 10 options, all other higher education plans examined here offer anywhere from 31 options to over 150 at the University of Michigan. The larger number of funds offered by these public universities is usually related to the existence of multiple service providers offering stand alone bundled arrangements.

Investment options that take specific asset allocation decisions out of the hands of the participant are a common offering in the state plans. Examples include a managed account in Alaska, target retirement date options in Colorado, North Dakota, and South Carolina, and life-cycle funds for Purdue University. All plans specify a default option for when a participant does not specify investment elections. In some cases, the default is a managed account or a target-date fund; in other cases, it is a relatively conservative investment, like a short term bond fund or a balanced investment fund. Best practice calls for default into a lifecycle target-date fund.

Pre-Retirement Distributions. Best practice would not allow lump sum distributions at job change when a participant's account balance exceeded a specified level set by the plan sponsor (e.g., $5,000) to prevent account leakage. Controlling pension asset leakage in this way is not done in the state or public university segments. All public plans examined here provide full lump sum distributions at job change.

Leakage can also occur through hardship distributions and plan loans and best practice design would not allow such features. In the state plans examined here, hardship withdrawals and plan loans are generally not available (the Michigan 401(k) plan is an exception). Likewise in the public university plans, hardship withdrawals and loans are not available (the exception being the Michigan State University plan).

Retirement Distributions. As discussed initially, the purpose of a core DC plan is to generate adequate retirement income for the lifetime of an individual (and his or her spouse). Thus the best practice plan design regarding retirement distributions is to limit the ability to withdraw funds as a lump sum combined with a requirement that a minimum amount of the account be annuitized through a vehicle providing some degree of inflation protection.

In the state plans examined here, full lump sums are always a distribution option. On the other hand, most of the state plans have annuitization as a distribution option (Colorado, Michigan, and Montana do not), but none require any degree of annuitization by the participant. The Ohio PERS Plan offers a special form of distribution where individuals can select a partial life annuity and a partial lump sum payment. The Florida Retirement System Investment Plan, the Nebraska Defined Contribution Plan, and the South Carolina Optional Retirement Plan also provide an inflation-hedged annuitization option. Florida offers a life annuity with a 3 percent annual increase in benefit payments and Nebraska offers a life annuity with a 2.5 percent annual increase. South Carolina offers a variable life annuity as well as a fixed annuity with increasing benefits. While not a perfect hedge against inflation, such vehicles do provide a means to at least partially protect benefit payments that are guaranteed to last a lifetime. All other state plans examined here provide no inflation hedge other than the ability to invest in equities after retirement.

Among the DC plans in higher education examined here, all have an annuitization option providing features that at least partially address inflation risk, including the use of variable life annuities and fixed life annuities with a feature for annual benefit increases. These plans, however, also offer full lump sums as a distribution option and do not require any degree of annuitization at retirement.

Administrative Structure. Best practice is a single recordkeeper structure. This has the primary benefit of providing a single point of contact for participants and may also help to control plan costs by taking advantages of the resulting economies of scale. Among the state plans examined here, almost all use a single recordkeeper structure; the exception being the South Carolina Optional Retirement Plan. Among public university plans however, multiple recordkeeper structures are the norm; all plans examined here have multiple recordkeepers.

Education and Advice. All of the plans reviewed provide their participants with basic information regarding the plan, such as how it works, the benefits of participation, its features, and the options that participants have, as well as the decisions that they need to make. In addition, plans also provide basic education about saving for retirement, such as understanding the different types of investment vehicles in the plan and how to construct an appropriately diversified portfolio. Education services typically also cover such issues as the benefits of dollar cost averaging through regular contributions, the benefits of compounding, and the value of benefit preservation (i.e., rollovers) at job change.

A higher best practice hurdle is the provision of individual-specific investment advice. Among the state plans examined here, the Colorado PERA, the Ohio PERS, and the West Virginia Teachers Plan do not provide investment advice (we were not able to ascertain whether investment advice is provided in the North Dakota PERS Defined Contribution Plan). Participant investment advice is provided by all the public university plans examined here, with the exception of the University of Washington which will likely be offering it by year-end 2008.

Conclusion

A DC plan with the primary objective of being the core source of retirement benefits needs to be designed with a focus on providing adequate and secure retirement income. From a plan design perspective, therefore, a core DC plan must incorporate features that increase the likelihood that this primary objective is met. In this chapter, we have proposed specific parameters for key plan features as best practice benchmarks in the public sector.

Typical core DC plans in the public sector today satisfy our best practice benchmarks in many instances. However, while many features of a 'best practice' DC plan are met by many public sector plans, there is variance in this regard.

Public sector employers and employees need and will be seeking better results and flexibility from their core DC retirement plans. While it is not expected that public employers will move away from their core DB plans as a primary method of delivering retirement benefits, interest in DC solutions will continue as public policy makers engage in the continuing efforts to make sure retirement benefits designs remain a good fit in an ever-changing employment environment.

TABLE 13-A1 Comparison of best practice benchmarks to major public sector core DC plans

Best Practice Benchmark	Plan Name				
	Alaska Defined Contribution Plan	Colorado PERA Defined Contribution Plan	District of Columbia Defined Contribution Plan	Florida Retirement System Investment Plan

Eligibility and Participation

Best Practice Benchmark	Alaska Defined Contribution Plan	Colorado PERA Defined Contribution Plan	District of Columbia Defined Contribution Plan	Florida Retirement System Investment Plan
Mandatory participation; no age restriction; no more than one year wait	Mandatory participation; no age restriction or waiting period	Mandatory participation; no age restriction or waiting period; optional to DB plan	Mandatory participation; no age restriction; one year waiting period	Mandatory participation; no age restriction or waiting period; optional to DB plan

Vesting

Best Practice Benchmark	Alaska Defined Contribution Plan	Colorado PERA Defined Contribution Plan	District of Columbia Defined Contribution Plan	Florida Retirement System Investment Plan
100% no later than after one year of service	Graded: 25% after 2 years, 50% after 3 years, 75% after 4 years, 100% after 5 years	50% immediate, graded to 100% over 5 years	Cliff: 100% after 5 years	Cliff: 100% after 1 year

Total Employer and Employee Contributions

Best Practice Benchmark	Alaska Defined Contribution Plan	Colorado PERA Defined Contribution Plan	District of Columbia Defined Contribution Plan	Florida Retirement System Investment Plan
12%+ of pay if covered by Social Security; 18–20% of pay if not covered by Social Security	Non-Social Security Teachers ER: 7% EE: 8% PERS ER: 5% EE: 8%	Non-Social Security ER: 10.15% EE: 8% For state troopers ER: 12.85% EE: 10%	Social Security Covered ER: 5% EE: 0% For detention officers ER: 5.5% EE: 0%	Social Security Covered Regular employees: ER: 9% EE: 0%. For Other employees: ER contribution ranges from 10.95–20% and EE: 0%

(cont.)

TABLE 13-A1 (Continued)

Best Practice Benchmark	Plan Name				
	Alaska Defined Contribution Plan	Colorado PERA Defined Contribution Plan	District of Columbia Defined Contribution Plan	Florida Retirement System Investment Plan	
Investments					
Mandatory or default into target-date lifecycle funds.	Default to qualified managed account	Default to balanced fund	Default to target date fund	Default to moderate risk balanced fund	
Limited array of 15–20 funds covering major asset classes.	12	13	13	20	
Individual investment advice through one or more providers.	Yes	No	Yes	Yes	
Pre-Retirement Distributions					
Small benefit distributions only before retirement age	Full lump sum available on termination	Full lump sum available on termination	Full lump sum available on termination	Full lump sum available on termination	
No hardship or loan distributions	Not available	Not available	Not available	Not available	

Retirement Distributions				
Minimum level of annuitization required	Annuity available, but not required	No annuitization option	Annuity available, but not required	Annuity available, but not required
Limited lump sum distribution	Full lump sum available	Full lump sum available	Full lump sum available	Full lump sum available
Provide inflation protected features	Only ability to invest in equities after retirement	Only ability to invest in equities after retirement	Only ability to invest in equities after retirement	Life annuity with a 3% annual increase in benefit payments
Administrative Structure				
Avoid multiple vendor recordkeeping structures	Single recordkeeper	Single recordkeeper	Single recordkeeper	Single recordkeeper
Other Participant Services				
Investment education, retirement, and financial planning services	Yes	Yes	Yes	Yes

(cont.)

TABLE 13-A1 (Continued)

Best Practice Benchmark	Plan Name					
	Michigan 401(k) Plan	Montana PERS Defined Contribution Retirement Plan	Nebraska DC Plan (closed to employees hired on or after 1/1/2003)	North Dakota PERS Defined Contribution Plan	Ohio PERS Member-Directed Plan

Eligibility and Participation

Mandatory participation; no age restriction; no more than one year wait	Mandatory participation; no age restriction or waiting period	Mandatory participation; no age restriction or waiting period (automatically enrolled in DB plan, but have 1 year to switch to DC plan)	Mandatory participation; no age restriction or waiting period	Mandatory participation; no age restriction or waiting period (automatically enrolled in DB plan; have 6 months to switch to DC plan)	Mandatory participation; no age restriction or waiting period (worker must choose participation in the DB, DC plan or combined plan within 180 days of hire)

Vesting

100% after 1 year of service	Graded: 50% after 2 years, 75% after 3 years, 100% after 4 years	Cliff: 100% after 5 years	Cliff: 100% after 3 years	Graded: 50% after 2 years, 75% after 3 years, 100% after 4 years	Graded over 5 years at 20% per year

Total Employer and Employee Contributions

	Social Security Covered ER: 4.0% EE: 0.0% (plus 100% ER match on elective EE contributions up to 3% of pay)	Social Security Covered ER: 4.19% EE: 6.9%	Social Security Covered ER: 7.5% EE: 4.8%	Social Security Covered ER: 4.12% EE: 4.0%	Non-Social Security ER: 8.73% for state employees, 8.65% for local employees, EE: 9.4%
12%+ of pay if covered by Social Security; 18–20% of pay if not covered by Social Security					
Investments					
Mandatory or default into target-date lifecycle funds	Default to short term fund	Default to balanced fund	Default to moderate premixed fund for employer contributions and stable value fund for employee contributions	Default to target date fund	Default to moderate balanced fund (60% equity, 40% fixed-income)
Limited array of 15–20 funds covering major asset classes	21	15	13	28	9
Individual investment advice through 1+ providers	Yes	Yes	Yes	?	No

(*cont.*)

TABLE 13-A1 (Continued)

Best Practice Benchmark	Plan Name				
	Michigan 401(k) Plan	Montana PERS Defined Contribution Retirement Plan	Nebraska DC Plan (closed to employees hired on or after 1/1/2003)	North Dakota PERS Defined Contribution Plan	Ohio PERS Member-Directed Plan
Pre-Retirement Distributions					
Small benefit distributions only before normal retirement age	Full lump sum available on termination	Full lump sum available on termination	Full lump sum available on termination	Full lump sum available on termination	Full lump sum available on termination
No hardship or loan distributions	Both available	Not available	Not available	Not available	Not available
Retirement Distributions					
Minimum level of annuitization required	No annuitization option	No annuitization option	Annuitization option available; not required	Annuitization option available; not required	Annuitization option available; not required
Limited lump sum distribution	Full lump sum available	Full lump sum available	Full lump sum available	Full lump sum available	Full lump sum available
Provide inflation protected features	Only ability to invest in equities after retirement	Only ability to invest in equities after retirement	Life annuity with a 2.5% annual increase in benefit payments	Only ability to invest in equities after retirement	Only ability to invest in equities after retirement

	South Carolina Optional Retirement Plan	West Virginia Teachers DC Plan	Indiana University Plan	Michigan State University Plan	Purdue University Plan
Administrative Structure					
Avoid multiple vendor recordkeeping structures	Single recordkeeper	Single recordkeeper	Single recordkeeper	Single recordkeeper	Single recordkeeper
Other Participant Services					
Investment education, retirement and financial planning services	Yes	Yes	Yes	Yes	Yes
Eligibility and Participation					
Mandatory participation; no age restriction; no more than one year wait	Mandatory participation; no age restriction or waiting period (must choose participation in either the DB or DC plan within 30 days of hire; DB is the default)	Mandatory participation; no age restriction or waiting period	Mandatory participation; no age restriction or waiting period	Immediate eligibility; mandatory participation after age 35 and 2 years of service	Mandatory participation; eligibility varies from immediate to 3 years of service depending upon position

(cont.)

TABLE 13-A1 (Continued)

Best Practice Benchmark	Plan Name					
	South Carolina Optional Retirement Plan	West Virginia Teachers DC Plan	Indiana University Plan	Michigan State University Plan	Purdue University Plan	

Vesting

100% after 1 year service	Immediate	Graded: 1/3 after 6 years 2/3 after 9 years 100% after 12 years	Immediate	Immediate	Immediate

Total Employer and Employee Contributions

12%+ of pay if covered by Social Security; 18–20% of pay if not covered by Social Security	Social Security Covered ER: 5.0% EE: 6.5%	Social Security Covered ER: 7.5% EE: 4.5%	Social Security Covered ER: varies from 10–12% depending on position (varies from 11–15% for those hired before 1989) EE: 0%	Social Security Covered ER: 10% EE: 5%	Social Security Covered ER: 11% on first $9,000 of pay and 15% thereafter EE: 0%

Investments

Mandatory or default into target-date lifecycle funds	Default into DB if do not specify investment choices	Default to balanced fund	Default to age-based life-cycle funds	Default to money market fund	Default to age-based life-cycle funds

	70	13	38	31	34
Limited array of 15–20 funds covering major asset classes					
Individual investment advice through one or more providers	Yes	No	Yes	Yes	Yes
Pre-Retirement Distributions					
Small benefit distributions only before normal retirement age	Full lump sum available on termination	Full lump sum available on termination	Full lump sum available on termination	Full lump sum available on termination	Full lump sum available on termination
No hardship or loan distributions	Not available	Not available	Not available	Both available	Not available
Retirement Distributions					
Minimum level of annuitization required	Annuitization option available; not required	Annuitization option available; not required	Annuitization option available; not required	Annuitization option available; not required	Annuitization option available; not required
Limited lump sum distribution	Full lump sum available	Full lump sum available	Full lump sum available	Full lump sum available	Full lump sum available
Provide inflation protected features	Variable life annuity and fixed life annuity with increasing benefits both available	Nothing other than the ability to invest in equities after retirement	Variable life annuity and fixed life annuity with increasing benefits both available	Variable life annuity and fixed life annuity with increasing benefits both available	Variable life annuity and fixed life annuity with increasing benefits both available

(cont.)

TABLE 13-A1 (Continued)

Best Practice Benchmark	Plan Name				
	South Carolina Optional Retirement Plan	West Virginia Teachers DC Plan	Indiana University Plan	Michigan State University Plan	Purdue University Plan
Administrative Structure					
Avoid multiple vendor recordkeeping structures	Multiple recordkeepers	Single recordkeeper	Multiple recordkeepers	Multiple recordkeepers	Multiple recordkeepers
Other Participant Services					
Investment education, retirement and financial planning services	Yes	Yes	Yes	Yes	Yes

	State University of New York	University of Iowa	University of Michigan	University of Washington
Eligibility and Participation				
	Mandatory participation; no age restriction; no more than one year wait	Mandatory participation; optional to DB plan	Immediate eligibility; mandatory participation after age 35 and two years of service	Immediate eligibility; mandatory participation after two years of service
Vesting				
	Cliff: one year	Immediate	Immediate	Immediate
	100% after one year service			
Total Employer and Employee Contributions				
	Social Security Covered ER: 8% during first 7 years of participation, 10% thereafter (Note: higher rates apply to members who joined plan prior to July, 1992) EE: 3%	Social Security Covered ER: First 5 years: 6.67% on first $4,800 and 10% thereafter; 10% after 5 years EE: First 5 years: 3.33% on first $4,800 and 5% thereafter; 5% after 5 years	Social Security Covered ER: 5% EE: 0% (100% ER match of EE elective contributions up to an additional 5%)	Social Security Covered Both ER and EE: 5% if under age 35; 7.5% between ages 35 and 50; 10% if age 50 and older
	12%+ of pay if covered by Social Security; 18–20% of pay if not covered by Social Security			
Investments				
	Default to money market fund	Default to age-based life-cycle fund	Default to age-based life-cycle fund	Default to money market fund
	Mandatory or default into target-date lifecycle funds			
	Limited array of 15–20 funds covering major asset classes	39	150+	10
	32			

(cont.)

TABLE 13-A1 *(Continued)*

Best Practice Benchmark	Plan Name				
	State University of New York	University of Iowa	University of Michigan	University of Washington	
Individual investment advice through one or more providers	Yes	Yes	Yes	No (but likely in 2008)	
Pre-Retirement Distributions					
Small benefit distributions only before normal retirement age	Full lump sum available on termination	Full lump sum available on termination	Full lump sum available on termination	Full lump sum available on termination	
No hardship or loan distributions	Not available	Not available	Not available	Not available	
Retirement Distributions					
Minimum level of annuitization required	Annuitization option available; not required	Annuitization option available; not required	Annuitization option available; not required	Annuitization option available; not required	
Limited lump sum distribution	Full lump sum available	Full lump sum available	Full lump sum available	Full lump sum available	
Provide inflation protected features	Variable life annuity and fixed life annuity with increasing benefits both available	Variable life annuity and fixed life annuity with increasing benefits both available	Variable life annuity and fixed life annuity with increasing benefits both available	Variable life annuity and fixed life annuity with increasing benefits both available	

Administrative Structure

	Multiple recordkeepers	Multiple recordkeepers	Multiple recordkeepers	Multiple recordkeepers
Avoid multiple vendor recordkeeping structures	Multiple recordkeepers			
Other Participant Services				
Investment education, retirement and financial planning services	Yes	Yes	Yes	Yes

Source: Authors' compilations; see text.

References

Aon Consulting, Inc. (2004). *Replacement Ratio Study, A Measurement Tool for Retirement Planning.* New York, NY: Aon Consulting, Inc./Georgia State University.

Georgia State University/Aon Consulting (2004). *RETIRE Project Report, 2004.* Atlanta, GA: Georgia State University.

McDonnell, Ken (2002). 'Benefit Cost Comparisons between State and Local Governments and Private-Sector Employers.' *EBRI Notes,* 23(10): 6–9.

Part III

The Political Economy of Public Pensions

Chapter 14

The Evolution of Public Sector Pension Plans in the United States

Robert L. Clark, Lee A. Craig, and Neveen Ahmed

The first US states provided retirement plans for their civil service employees beginning over a century ago. The subsequent spread of retirement plans across the states continued for more than a half a century before all of the states had adopted such plans.[1] General old-age assistance plans predated employee retirement plans in many states,[2] and state and local governments typically developed pension plans for teachers, police officers, and firefighters before the states extended similar benefits to other civil service employees (Clark, Craig, and Wilson, 2003). The creation and management of public sector pension plans in the twentieth century was an evolutionary process, with many of the early plans for local employees and teachers eventually being merged into single, state-wide systems, and these were frequently merged with plans covering general state employees. Coverage has now been extended to virtually all public sector employees in the United States.

This chapter begins with a review of the evolution of retirement plans from the establishment of the first state-employee plan in 1911 through the coverage of practically all state employees. In addition, in the next section we explore the relationship between public sector pensions and Social Security. Following that, we report findings from a survey of state retirement plan administrators, which covers past and current characteristics of the state plans. These findings shed light on how the states adjusted their pension plans once their employees were allowed to be covered by Social Security. We then provide a detailed assessment of how plan characteristics have changed over the past 25 years and highlight the differences between plans in which workers are covered by Social Security and plans in which workers are not covered. Finally, we present regression analysis to explain how and why retirement plans differ across the states.

The evolution of state employee pension plans

The first state retirement plan for (non-teacher) civil service employees was established in Massachusetts in 1911; however, few states rushed to follow that example. By 1916, only Illinois, New Jersey, and Pennsylvania had adopted plans (USBLS 1916), and by 1934, only nine states had retirement systems for general state employees (Social Security Board 1937). Recognition of the need to move elderly state employees out of public service employment, along with sincere concerns for their retirement income, became more acute with the onset of the Great Depression. The passage of the Social Security Act in 1935 contributed to discussions about the need for retirement plans for public employees and how public sector pensions would be structured and financed. Specifically, the initial exclusion of public employees from the Social Security system seems to have stimulated some states to take action and establish their own retirement plans.

Over the next two decades or so, almost every state passed legislation creating a retirement plan for general state employees. The US House of Representatives Committee on Education and Labor Pension Task Force (1978) reported that 45 percent of all large state and local pension systems were established (or had a major restructuring) between 1931 and 1950, and another 15 percent did so in both the 1950s and 1960s. By 1961, 45 states had established pension plans with only Idaho, Nebraska, North Dakota, Oklahoma, and South Dakota failing to develop a retirement plan (Mueller 1961),[3] and these states subsequently developed plans for their employees. Thus, widespread pension coverage of public employees is a surprisingly recent development.[4]

As a result of a perceived anomaly of federal law, the history of state pension plans is inextricably linked to the history of the national Social Security system in the US. At the time the Social Security system was created, legal concerns led Congress to exclude state and local workers from the system. Specifically, the issue was whether the Constitution granted to Congress the power to tax the states (as well as local governments). Since the Social Security Act required employers (in this case, the states) to remit a share of the payroll tax, it was perceived as a tax on the states. The evolution of case law on the matter during and following the Great Depression subsequently rendered moot many such concerns about the exercise of federal power, and in the 1950s, federal legislation permitted state and municipal governments to voluntarily include their employees in the Social Security system. Because most states and many municipal governments already provided pension plans for their workers by that date, the decision by state and local governments to enter the Social Security system raised a series of questions for policymakers. One was: Did those public employees who were brought into the Social Security system on a voluntary basis pay for that privilege in the form of a reduction in the benefit formula associated with their employer provided pension? We address this question in the following text.

When Congress first passed legislation permitting states to enter into voluntary agreements with the Social Security Administration (SSA) in 1950, it allowed public employees *not* covered by an employer-provided retirement system to participate in Social Security (Mitchell et al. 2000).[5] Additional amendments enacted in 1954 allowed state and local employees who were covered by an employer-provided retirement plan to obtain Social Security coverage at the election of the public employer and employees. Since coverage was voluntary under both of these provisions, public employers who had entered the Social Security system could, if they chose, also terminate this relationship. Thus, participation in the system was in principle something of a two-way street for the state and local governments. However, as part of the 1983 Social Security reforms, Congress repealed this option; thus states could no longer rescind their decisions to participate in Social Security. Once in the system, public employers were now required to remain in the system.[6] Finally, in 1991, Social Security coverage was made mandatory for all state and local employees who are not covered by an employer-provided retirement plan (Social Security Administration 2007).

By 2007, all 50 states had signed agreements, the so-called Section 218 agreements, with SSA allowing some or all of the public employees in each state to be covered by Social Security. Even today, however, many state and local employees still remain outside of the Social Security system. Indeed, one estimate is that approximately 28 percent of all state and local public employees remain outside the system (Streckewald 2005). The majority of public employees who do not participate in Social Security are police officers, firefighters, and teachers. The members of these groups were typically among the first non-military public workers to receive pensions in the United States; thus, employees in these occupations typically were already covered by a retirement plan when Social Security was established (Clark, Craig, and Wilson, 2003).[7]

There currently are seven states whose general state employees are currently outside the Social Security system: Alaska, Colorado, Louisiana, Maine, Massachusetts, Nevada, and Ohio.[8] In addition to general state employees, teachers and some local public employees are not covered in these states. Furthermore, some teachers and local employees in California, Connecticut, Illinois, Kentucky, Missouri, and Texas do not participate in Social Security (Munnell 2005).

The status of state-provided retirement plans following the states' voluntary entry into the Social Security system offers an interesting economic and public policy experiment. Employers and employees are often interested in allocating a portion of total compensation to retirement benefits. If the initial, that is the pre-Social Security, employer-provided retirement plan supplied the optimal level of benefits given the state's human resources objectives, employee preferences, and the cost of providing these benefits, then the introduction of Social Security would tend to encourage the states to reduce the generosity of their retirement benefits and reduce the employer contributions to their pension plans. If promised a Social Security benefit, and required to pay the payroll tax, workers would also tend to accept a reduction in employer-provided retirement benefits and employee contributions.

Mueller (1961) reported that when the various states began providing Social Security coverage to their employees, eight states made no reductions in the generosity of their own state retirement plan; 15 states modified their systems slightly, but in all cases, total retirement benefits, social security plus employer pension benefits, were greater than the retirement benefits earned prior to Social Security coverage; another eight states integrated their systems with Social Security and markedly reduced benefits payable under their state systems.[9] Although Mueller's study provides a useful snapshot of the impact of Social Security on public sector plans circa 1960, because a number of states subsequently overhauled their public sector pension plans, we sought to learn more about how the plans responded to the introduction of Social Security by surveying state pension plan administrators. Specifically, we asked them what, if any, changes were made in their retirement plans when the state allowed participation in Social Security.

Survey of state plan administrators

Ideally, a history of the evolution of state retirement plans would include the date that each state first established a retirement plan for general state employees, teachers, and other public sector employees, along with the date these public employees were first covered by Social Security. In addition, we would like to know if the plans altered the generosity of the employer-provided benefits when participation in Social Security was first allowed. This information has proven very difficult to find, as plan documents (published or on-line) rarely give a detailed history of the development of these plans. Primary and secondary sources indicate that, initially, many state and local governments provided some type of income relief to the elderly persons, and often legislatures and other government bodies awarded lifetime pensions through legislative action targeted at specific retirees (Clark, Craig, and Wilson, 2003). We also know that, over time, there has been considerable consolidation of retirement plans in many states, as the plans for teachers and municipal employees have been merged into a single plan managed at the state level. Plan documents often refer to the dates that the most recent consolidation of plans occurred, rather than indicating the date that the first plan covering state employees was established.

To fill in some of the gaps concerning the development of public pensions, we partnered with the National Association of State Retirement Administrators (NASRA) to develop a survey sent to the administrator of each US state plan. Plan administrators were asked to report the following: the year their plan was established; whether state employees were covered by Social Security; and if they were covered by Social Security, then to list the first year the employees participated in the Social Security system. In addition, the administrators were asked to explain the nature of any adjustments in benefits or contributions when employees were first covered by Social Security.

Administrators representing 31 of 50 state retirement plans responded to the survey. The responses to several questions provided important information on the development of public employee pension plans. In response to the question: 'In what year was your retirement system established?' plan administrators illustrated the slow spread of state retirement plans across the country during the twentieth century. Comparing these responses with other primary and secondary sources, leads us to conclude that some of the responses (and/or other secondary sources) emphasize the date of the last merger or consolidation of retirement plans, rather than the date of establishment of the first pension plan for state employees. For example, in the survey the Florida state plan indicates that it began in 1970; however, other sources indicate that a retirement plan existed in that state as early as 1927. Nevertheless, the pattern of development of state retirement plans reported here is broadly consistent with the pattern of development of state plans described earlier, indicating a surge in plan establishment beginning in the 1930s, reaching a peak in the 1940s, and continuing through the 1950s and 1960s.

The state administrators were also asked: 'In what year did your state first enter into the Social Security system?' and whether benefits and contributions to the state plan were reduced when workers were included in Social Security. Combining the data on year of establishment with year of entry into Social Security and whether any adjustments were made, we divided the states into four groups:

1. Plans established prior to the state entering Social Security where no adjustments were made in benefits or contributions to the state retirement plan.
2. Plans established prior to the state entering Social Security where benefits and contributions were reduced after the entry into Social Security.

3. Plans established after state employees were already covered by Social Security.
4. Plans in which state employees still remain outside the Social Security system.

In this sample of 31 states, 20 states had pension plans for their civil service employees prior to 1950. Of these, 18 entered the Social Security system, and of those that entered the system, 11 did not reduce benefits or contributions associated with the state retirement plan, while seven states reported that the plan structure was modified in conjunction with joining the system. In addition, there were 11 states that started their pension plans after their employees were included in Social Security, and nine of these entered the system at the time they created their plans. It would be logical to conclude that these states (and their employees) considered the cost and benefits of Social Security in developing their own pension plans. Finally, four states that responded to our survey remain outside of Social Security and could be considered as having evaluated the costs and benefits of Social Security and then decided to retain their own system without allowing their employees to participate in Social Security. Thus, at a first glance, we conclude that state plan administrators, legislatures, and public employees have considered the implications of being participants in Social Security and adjusted their own plans accordingly, and that their responses were quite diverse.

Evolution of plan characteristics covering state employees

The development of state employee pension plans after 1911 includes the establishment of pension plans for state workers by every state, and the structural modification of many of these plans as retirement systems for teachers and local employees were often merged into plans for general state employees. The extension of Social Security to public employees on a voluntary basis beginning in 1951 resulted in a wave of states deciding to allow their employees to be covered by Social Security. As noted earlier, many states altered their pension plans by reducing benefits and contributions to their own retirement plan or by integrating the state plan with Social Security. By the mid-1970s, these structural changes in the retirement systems of the various states appeared to have run their course. Yet, over the next 25 years, important plan characteristics continued to evolve, as public pensions generally became more generous in terms of benefits and allowed earlier retirement. This section describes the current status of state retirement plans and how they have evolved over the last two decades.

Despite the 30-year trend among private sector employers away from DB plans and toward a greater emphasis on DC plans, DB plans remain the dominant type of retirement plan in the public sector. In 2007, the US General Accounting Office reported that with the exception of Alaska and Michigan, all states offered DB plans as their primary retirement plan for general state employees.[10] In addition, two states, Indiana and Oregon, had adopted primary plans that included components of both DB and DC plans, and Nebraska had established a cash balance plan for its employees. In addition to their primary retirement plan, every state offered its employees the opportunity to participate in voluntary DC plans such as 403(b) or 457(b) plans. In contrast to the private sector, public employers often do not match employee contributions. Only 12 states match employee contributions to DC plans up to a specified limit (GAO 2007).[11]

The contrast between public and private plans sheds light on the history of public plans in the past few decades. Clark and McDermed (1990) argue that much of the early movement away from DB plans in the private sector was caused by two factors: one was the cost of government regulations, and the other was the structural changes in the economy that resulted in shifts away from industries that had traditionally used DB plans as an important human resource policy. In particular, the decline in employment in integrated manufacturing processes that benefited from low turnover, and the rise of service industries that valued labor mobility, helped drive down the share of the private sector labor force covered by a DB plan. These trends simply did not have the same effect on public sector employers. Similarly, Munnell, Haverstick, and Soto (2007) attribute the staying power of DB plans in public sector to differences in the labor force and regulatory environment facing public employers. Furthermore, they argue that the workforce in the public sector is older, more risk averse, less mobile, and more unionized than the private sector labor force. In addition, state and local governments do not face the same pressures on administrative costs and other requirements associated with government regulation of pensions in the private sector.[12]

There exists no detailed history documenting the improvements in state retirement benefits since the mid-1970s; nevertheless, several secondary sources provide useful snapshots that reveal changes in those plans over the last three decades. One problem in comparing these and similar snap shots is that the data sources are different, and the number and type of plans also vary across the reports. For example, in 1978, the Pension Task Force *Report on Public Employee Retirement System* (US House of Representatives 1978) estimated that retirement plans within state-administered systems, in which workers were included in Social Security, yielded average replacement rates of 45 percent for workers with 30 years of service in plans that were not integrated with Social Security. Similar workers who were not covered by Social Security received replacement rates that were about 57 percent of final earnings. These estimates imply a generosity parameter (percent of average salary per year of service) of about 1.5 percent per year of service for workers covered by Social Security and 1.9 percent per year of service for those outside the Social Security system.

Between 1988 and 1998, the Bureau of Labor Statistics published four surveys of employee benefits provided by state and local governments. The BLS Bulletin No. 2309 (USBLS 1988) reports that in 1987 the replacement rate for retirees who had 30 years of service and average earnings of $35,000 was 48.6 percent for retirees who were covered by Social Security and 61.6 percent for retirees from public employers who were not included in the Social Security system. USBLS Bulletin 2477 (USBLS 1996) reports that in the average replacement rates had risen to 51.0 for Social Security covered retirees and 62.6 for retirees without Social Security coverage. These values imply that the mean generosity parameter for public employees included in Social Security increased from 1.6 to 1.7 percent of final salary per year of service between 1988 and 1996. In contrast, the generosity parameter for public employees not in Social Security also rose slightly from 2.05 to 2.1 percent of salary per year of service.

More recently, Brainard (2007, 2009) reports median retirement benefit multipliers of 1.85 percent per year of service for Social Security covered workers and 2.20 percent for employees who are not covered by Social Security. These values imply a further increase in replacement rates for the retiree with 30 years of service to 55.5 for those with Social Security coverage and 66 percent for those who were not covered by Social Security. These three data sources indicate that the generosity of public pension plans was increased between the mid-1970s and 2007. A worker with 30 years of service retiring in 2007 could expect a replacement rate approximately 10 percentage points higher than a similar worker retiring in 1977.

A more comprehensive assessment can be made by comparing the replacement rate provided to employees under the same state plan at different points in time. Since 1982, the Wisconsin Legislative Council has collected information on the benefit characteristics of 85 large public pension plans, including the plans that cover general state employees in all 50 states (Wisconsin Legislative Council various years). To examine the changes in benefit formulas and contributions over the past quarter century, we reviewed the information contained in the Comparative Study of Major Public Employee Pension Systems compiled by the Wisconsin Legislative Council (various years). These reports have been published biannually covering the years 1982 to 2006. We have also examined the latest information on the websites of the various state employee retirement plans to supplement the 2006 Wisconsin data.

Table 14-A1 presents information from state retirement plans in 1982 on the normal retirement age specified in the plan, the number of years used to determine the final salary average, and the retirement multipliers in the benefit formula. These values are then contrasted with the data for 2006 to show how state employee retirement plans have evolved over the past 25 years. In general, the states have substantially increased the generosity of their pension plans over the years. Thirty-three states modified the normal retirement ages specified in the plans that allowed workers to retire at earlier ages with fewer years of service; while six states increased their normal retirement ages (NRA) somewhat, including Minnesota, which linked the NRA for state retirement benefits to the NRA for Social Security. Fifteen states reduced the number of years in the averaging period, thus raising final pension benefits; while only Alaska increased the number of years in its averaging period. Finally, 30 states increased the multipliers and/or eliminated Social Security offsets, and four states reduced the multipliers used to calculate retirement benefits. As a result of these changes, holding other factors constant, the typical state employee will retire with a higher replacement ratio in 2006 than in 1982.

To evaluate the impact of these changes, we have calculated the replacement rates in each state for a hypothetical worker retiring at age 65 with 20 years of service. The mean replacement rate in 1982 for plans in the seven states outside the Social Security system was 44.4 percent. By 2006, the mean replacement rate for these same states had increased to 47.9 percent. The rates for 30-year employees were 65.5 percent in 1982 and 73.0 percent in 2006. In contrast, the median replacement rates for states whose employees with 20 years of service who were also covered by Social Security were lower: 32.1 percent in 1982 and 37.3 percent in 2006. The rates for 30-year employees were 48.2 percent in 1982 and 58.2 percent in 2006. Interestingly, the increase in the median replacement was greater during this period for states outside the Social Security system, even though the 1983 amendments to Social Security resulted in a reduction in Social Security benefits for future retirees.

Overall, 39 states increased the 30-year replacement rate for their workers; while in seven states, the 30-year replacement rates remained constant. Only one state, Florida, had a decline in its 30-year replacement rate. In these calculations, the increase in the median replacement rate for retirees from state governments results from two factors: one is an increase in the generosity factor in the benefit formulas, and the other is the reduction in the number of years used to determine final salary average. States also made their retirement plans more generous by allowing workers to retire at earlier ages. Figure 14-1 shows the distribution of income replacement

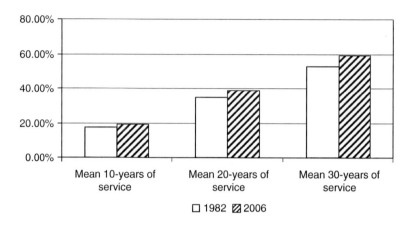

Figure 14-1 Mean income replacement rates, state pension plans, by years of service, 1982 and 2006. *Note*: Figures are the mean annual replacement rates of state employee pensions for workers retiring in 1982 or 2006, with 10, 20, and 30 years of service. *Source*: Authors' calculations from state retirement plan websites and Wisconsin Legislative Council (1982 and 2006).

rates by years of service and year. The chart illustrates the increase in mean replacement rates as year of service increase and the across the board increase in benefits between 1984 and 2006.

In addition we have divided the replacement rate figures by Social Security coverage. Figure 14-2 illustrates the difference in replacement rates for state workers covered by Social Security and those not covered, in 1982. Similarly, Figure 14-3 illustrates the same differences for 2006. Taken together the figures show the extent to which replacement rates increase with job tenure and the absence of Social Security coverage, as well as the overall increase between 1982 and 2006. Furthermore, they show the increase in replacement rates between 1982 and 2006 for workers not covered by Social Security relative to those who were covered.

Other important characteristics of DB pension plans that influence the cost of the plan to the employer and the value to the employee include the vesting requirements and the contribution rates. Table 14-A2 reports these values for the state retirement plans in 1984 and 2006.[13] In 1984, 25 states imposed a 10-year vesting standard; 19 states had 5-year vesting; five states imposed vesting standards of four or eight years; and Wisconsin had immediate vesting. Over the intervening two decades, vesting standards were reduced by 17 states. In 2006, only 10 states imposed 10-year vesting compared to 28 with 5-year vesting. Ten states had vesting requirements of fewer than five years, and two states still had 8-year

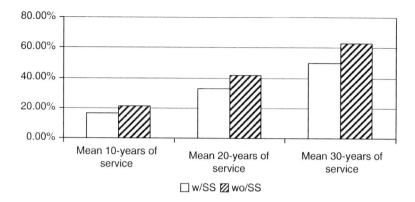

Figure 14-2 Mean income replacement rates of state pension plans, by social security coverage, 1982. *Note*: Figures are the mean annual replacement rates of state employee pensions for workers (with and without Social Security coverage) retiring in 1982 with 10, 20, and 30 years of service. *Source*: Authors' calculations from state retirement plan websites and Wisconsin Legislative Council (1982 and 2006).

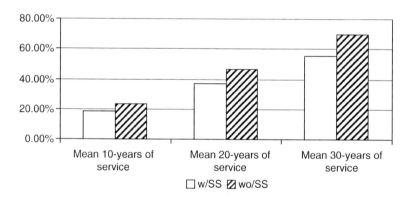

Figure 14-3 Mean income replacement rates of state pension plans, by social security coverage, 2006. *Note*: Figures are the mean annual replacement rates of state employee pensions for workers (with and without Social Security coverage) retiring in 2006 with 10, 20, and 30 years of service. *Source*: Authors' calculations from state retirement plan websites and Wisconsin Legislative Council (1982 and 2006).

vesting. The decline in the vesting period also represents an increase in the generosity of these plans.

Table 14-A2 also presents the employee and employer contribution rates for 1984 and 2006 for each state retirement plan. Over the past two decades 20 states increased employee contribution rates while eight reduced them. Using a survey of plan administrators, Brainard (2007) reports that the median employee contribution rates remained stable between 2002 and 2006. The employee contribution rate for states with Social Security coverage was 5.0 percent, and the contribution rates for employees that were not part of Social Security was 8.0 percent.

Explaining the variation of retirement benefits across state pension plans

Economists agree that the decision by an employer to offer a pension plan depends on employee preferences for current compensation relative to deferred compensation; the cost of providing a dollar of future income compared to receiving a dollar today; and how the pension might influence worker turnover and retirement rates. In the private sector, some companies offer pension plans but many do not; some employers provide DB plans, but most now use DC plans, and some firms have generous plans while others provide relatively low retirement benefits. Competitive pressures help sort workers and firms into the most desirable matches. In the public sector, all states offer retirement plans to their employees, and virtually all states have established and continue to maintain DB plans. Thus, there is much more homogeneity across the retirement plans offered by state governments; however, these plans still vary substantially in their generosity.

In this section, we attempt to explain differences in the replacement rates that career state employees will achieve, depending on their state of employment, and how these differences have evolved over time. Our efforts are limited by the limited number of states, only 50 in total (as well as the multi-collinearity in many of the factors that likely impact the level of benefits that state political leaders wish to provide the employees of the state). We estimate a rather simple model of the determinants of the generosity of state retirement plans. Research on employee compensation suggests that any such model should consider including: measures of a state's population growth; the financial condition of the state's pension fund; an indicator of collective bargaining strength of public employees; and the plan's connection or lack of connection to Social Security (see Clark, Craig, and Wilson [2003]; Craig [1995]; Fishback and Kantor [1995], [2000]; Gruber and

Krueger [1991]; Moore and Viscusi [1990]; and Munnell [2005]). Institutional factors also suggest that the overall level of coverage of a public sector plan might influence the generosity of benefits. Given the data limitations, the model we estimate is:

$$\text{Replacement Rate}_i = \alpha + \beta_1 \text{PopulationGrowth}_i + \beta_2 \text{FundingRatio}_i$$
$$+ \beta_3 \text{Union}_i + \beta_4 \text{SocialSecurity}_i$$
$$+ \Sigma \beta_j \text{Plan}_{ij} + \varepsilon_i, \tag{14.1}$$

where Replacement Rate$_i$ is the income replacement rate for a representative worker with 20 years of service in the *ith* state pension plan; PopulationGrowth$_i$ is the average annual compounded rate of population growth during the most recent 10-year period in the *ith* state; FundingRatio$_i$ is the ratio of pension plan assets to annual benefit expenditures in the *ith* state pension plan; the variable Union$_i$ is the share of the public sector employment covered by a collective bargaining agreement in the *ith* state; the term SocialSecurity$_i$ is a dummy variable that takes on the value one if the workers in the *ith* state plan are covered by Social Security, zero otherwise; and the Plan$_{ij}$ terms are dummy variables that take on the value one for, respectively, plans that cover only general state employees, plans that cover state employees and teachers, plans that cover state employees and local public employees, and plans that cover all three groups of employees; zero otherwise.[14]

We anticipate that the population growth and union variables will have positive coefficients in the estimated equation shown earlier. Population growth serves as a proxy for the overall economic climate of the state in question, and the union variable reflects the collective bargaining strength of the state's public sector workers. In addition, the signs on the pension funding ratio and the Social Security dummy variable should be negative. Pension plans with large liabilities relative to assets may have reached that level of funding due to relatively high replacement rates (Mitchell and Smith 1994). With respect to participation in Social Security, economic theory suggests that workers excluded from Social Security will tend to receive a compensating differential in the form of a higher replacement rate from their employer pension.

To estimate equation (14.1), we constructed a data set that includes the income replacement rate relative to the last year of earnings, which was calculated for a hypothetical worker in each state utilizing plan characteristics reported in the Wisconsin Legislative Council's *Comparative Study of Major Public Employee Retirement Systems*, published biannually from 1982 through 2006 (Wisconsin Legislative Council various years). In addition, to supplement the *Study*, we obtained information from the Web sites of each of the state plans. Key plan parameters used to calculate the replacement rates included the number of years used to calculate the final average salary, the generosity parameter, and the normal retirement age. The Social Security variable was also constructed from these sources.

In order to construct the replacement ratio for the hypothetical worker, we assumed that this worker had annual earnings of $50,000 in the fifth year before retirement, and this salary was increased by 3 percent per year until retirement, assumed to occur at age 65. The annual benefit for this worker is calculated under three different assumptions related to years of services; these are 10, 20, and 30 years of services. Finally, the replacement ratio is calculated under the previous assumptions using the benefit formulas for each state retirement plan for those states with DB plans. Other types of plans are excluded.[15]

As for the other variables, the population growth variables were created from data supplied by the *Statistical Abstract of the United States* (US Department of Commerce various years). Data for the construction of the funding ratio are from the Census Bureau's *Census of Governments: Employee Retirement Systems of State and Local Governments* (US Department of Commerce 2004),[16] and the unionization variable is from Hirsch an Macpherson (2007).[17] Table 14-1 contains means and standard deviations of the independent variables.

Estimation results for three versions of equation (14.1) are shown in Table 14-2. The first column contains the estimated coefficients for 1982 and the second column contains the results for 2006. The third column reports the findings from a pooled regression that includes observations from both years and interaction dummy variables indicating 2006.

TABLE 14-1 Descriptive statistics, means, and standard deviations of independent variables

Independent Variable	1982	2006
Population growth (%)	1.28 (1.08)	0.97 (0.82)
Pension funding ratio	18.52 (7.57)	19.99 (4.97)
Percent of government labor force unionized	40.90 (16.39)	38.53 (16.91)
Covered by Social Security	0.7763 (0.4195)	0.7763 (0.4195)
Plan includes state workers only (State dummy)	0.1447 (0.3542)	0.1447 (0.3542)
Plan includes state workers and teachers (State and teacher dummy)	0.0395 (0.1960)	0.0395 (0.1960)
Plan includes state and local employees (State and local dummy)	0.1842 (0.3902)	0.1842 (0.3902)

Source: Authors' compilations of state retirement system data; see text.

TABLE 14-2 Multivariate models of replacement ratios for state and local employees, with 20 years of service, 1982 and 2006

Independent Variable	1982	2006	Pooled with 2006 interactions
Intercept	39.28*** (4.41)	50.59*** (5.78)	44.14*** (3.60)
Population growth	2.48*** (0.85)	1.66 (1.18)	2.05** (0.88)
Pension funding ratio	−0.22** (0.11)	−0.15 (0.21)	−0.27** (0.12)
Percent of government labor force unionized	0.09* (0.05)	−0.11* (0.06)	0.05 (0.05)
Covered by Social Security	−8.33*** (2.42)	−10.40*** (2.68)	−9.65*** (0.02)
Plan includes state workers only (State dummy)	−1.69 (2.36)	4.53* (2.61)	−2.65 (2.48)
Plan includes state workers and teachers (State and teacher dummy)	−1.85 (3.62)	0.49 (3.94)	−2.38 (3.91)
Plan includes state and local employees (State and local dummy)	0.58 (2.11)	4.60* (2.38)	−0.25 (2.22)
Pop growth times 2006 dummy	–	—	−0.38 (1.41)
Funding ratio times 2006 dummy	–	–	0.32* (0.19)
% Govt LF union times 2006 dummy	–	–	−0.13** (0.06)
Social security coverage times 2006 dummy	–	–	0.49 (3.28)
State dummy times 2006 dummy	–	–	7.61** (3.40)
State and teacher dummy times 2006 dummy	–	–	2.93 (5.39)
State and local dummy times 2006 dummy	–	–	5.25* (3.06)
R^2 (adj)	0.4105	0.2951	0.378
F	5.48***	3.75***	4.95***
N	46	47	92

Notes: Standard errors are in parentheses. *–The probability of obtaining the resulting test statistic this large when the null hypothesis of $\beta = 0$ is true, is less than .10; ** less than .05; and *** less than .01.

Source: Authors' analysis of state retirement system data; see text.

In general, in the 1982 regressions, the signs of the coefficients are consistent with our expectations, as discussed earlier. A growing economy, as measured by population growth puts upward pressure on the replacement rate provided by the state retirement plan. The estimated coefficient indicates that a 1 percentage point increase in the population growth rate per year is associated with a 2.5 percentage point increase in the replacement rate. While this might seem like a large impact, the reader should note that the mean annual population growth rate among the states is only 1.4 percent per year so an increase of 1 percentage point represents a substantial increase in the rate of growth of a state's population.

As noted earlier, lower funding ratios reflect the higher costs associated with more generous retirement plans. The estimated coefficient on the fund ratio in the 1982 regression indicates that a reduction in the ratio of pension fund assets to annual expenditures of one year of pension costs is associated with a 0.22 percentage point increase in the replacement rate. The share of the government labor force that is unionized is expected to lead to higher compensation and more generous retirement benefits. The estimated union effect has the expected positive sign in 1982 as a 1 percentage point increase led to a 0.09 percentage point increase in the replacement rate. In general, participation in Social Security is expected to be associated with less generous employer provided retirement plans. The Social Security coefficient in the 1982 regression has the expected negative impact on the replacement rates from a public sector retirement plan. Controlling for the other variables in the equation, inclusion in Social Security reduced the replacement rate from a state plan by 8.3 percentage points.

With one notable exception, the results for the 2006 regressions are qualitatively similar to those for 1982. The key difference is in the sign of the coefficient on the share of the government labor force unionized; a 1 percentage point increase in the unionized share of the government labor force led to a 0.11 percentage point *decrease* in the replacement rate. Interestingly, a regression of this union variable on either the population growth or the funding ratio variables yields a negative and statistically coefficient. Thus it appears that by 2006, having a large share of the state's public sector work force in a union was a proxy for slow population (and economic) growth and pension finance problems. In short, the union variable may have switched from being an indicator of bargaining strength and larger pension benefits to an indicator of overall economic weakness. In addition, in the 2006 model, two of the variables indicating the coverage of public sector workers have positive and statistically significant impacts on replacement rates. The estimated coefficients on these variable suggest that when state employees are in a separate plan, that is, a plan that does not include teachers or teachers *and* local government employees, they receive replacement rates that are 4.5 percentage points higher than comparable workers in combined state, teacher, and local plans.

The results in Table 14-2 suggest some quantitative difference between the factors that explain the replacement rates in 1982 and 2006. To further test the possibility that the influence of these variables changed over time, we pool the observations from 1982 and 2006 and then created a dichotomous variable that takes the value one for 2006, zero otherwise. The 2006 indicator variable is multiplied times each of the explanatory variables in the basic equation. The results for the pooled sample are shown in the final column of Table 14-2. The estimated coefficients on the explanatory variables themselves are similar to those shown in columns 1 and 2 of the table. The interaction terms indicate whether the effect of the variables is significantly different in 2006 compared to 1982. As expected given the result in columns 1 and 2, the analysis finds significant differences in the 2006 impact of the funding ratio and the share of public sector work force that is unionized. In addition, the inclusion of the interaction terms yield positive impacts on a number of the plan-type variables, suggesting that these particular plans experienced an increase in their replacement rates over time compared to plans covering state and local employees plus teachers—that is, the omitted dummy variable.

Finally, we are interested in exploring the change in the replacement rates between 1982 and 2006, as reflected in Figures 14-1 through 14-3. In Table 14-3, we employ the same variables from equation (14.1) to explain the *change* in replacement rates between the two years. The coefficient on the union variable is the only statistically significant non-dummy variable, and it suggests that, as we noted earlier, a heavily unionized public sector labor force has had a negative impact on the generosity of state pension

TABLE 14-3 Explanation of the percentage change in replacement ratios for state employees with 20 years of service, between 1982 and 2006

Independent Variable	
Intercept	10.00** (4.68)
Population growth	−0.08 (0.97)
Pension funding ratio	−0.10 (0.17)
Percent of government labor force (Unionized)	−0.17*** (0.05)
Covered by social security	−0.17 (2.17)
Plan includes state workers only	6.26*** (2.12)
Plan includes state employees and teachers	0.23 (3.20)
Plan includes state and local government employees	3.31* (1.94)
R^2 (adj)	0.1850
F	2.46***
N	46

Notes. Standard errors are in parentheses. *–The probability of obtaining the resulting test statistic this large when the null hypothesis of $\beta = 0$ is true, is less than .10; ** less than .05; and *** less than .01.

Source: Authors' analysis of state retirement system data; see text.

funds over the past 25 years. A greater unionized share of the state's public sector labor force has reduced the rate of improvement in public sector pension benefits, holding other variables constant.

Conclusion

This discussion provides a brief history of the development of state retirement plans since the first plan was established early in the twentieth century and analyzes their subsequent changes, particularly during recent decades. The adoption of retirement plans for general state employees moved rather slowly during the first third of the century but with the passage of Social Security in 1935 which excluded public sector employees, many states began to establish their own retirement plans. However, the final states plans were not established until the 1960s. The relationship of these state retirement plans with Social Security is a story unto itself, and we have attempted to provide the basic outline of the response of states to the changing rules associated with the inclusion of public employees into the Social Security system.

Once established, public retirement plans have been merged with those for teachers and local employees in many states, and these consolidated plans are now the norm, although many states continue to offer retirement plans only for general state employees. The main story of the past three decades has been the increased generosity of state retirement plans. States have reduced the normal retirement age, increased the generosity parameters, and reduced the number of years in the averaging period. As a result, replacement rates have risen significantly. The history we provide may raise concerns for the sustainability of the current generosity of state retirement plans, especially in light of the emergence of very large unfunded liabilities associated with retiree health benefit plans that are provided by most states.

Finally, we have attempted to explain the variation in benefits across state retirement plans and how these differences have changed during the last 25 years. We draw the reader's attention to four key findings. First, our analysis indicates that a state's population and economic growth has led states to be more generous with their public sector pension plans. States that have seen their populations grow dramatically have tended to increase the replacement ratios that career workers can achieve. Second, we find that the funding status of state retirement plans has a negative impact on the generosity of the state's public sector pension plans. The logic of this finding is reasonably straightforward. Some states have well-funded plans in part because, relative to their less-well-funded peers, they pay smaller pensions. Third, the impact of public sector unionization on the generosity of the states' public sector pension plans has changed over time. In the early 1980s, unionization still had a positive impact on income replacement rates, presumably reflecting the greater bargaining power associated with a greater incidence of unionism in the public sector. Swings in unionization of only a few percentage points had relatively large implications for the differences in plan generosity. However, by 2006, the union effect had changed its sign. Today, the extent of unionization among public sector workers has a negative impact on the state's replacement rate.

Finally, we find that participation in Social Security reduced the typical worker's replacement rate from their state retirement plan by around 8 percentage points. Whether this is a large or small cost for participation in Social Security depends on any reduction in employee contributions to the state plan for those workers covered by Social Security and the overall benefits associated with Social Security coverage relative to the size of the payroll tax.

TABLE 14-A1 Benefit formulas and retirement ages for state employee pension plans, by state, 1982 and 2006

State	NRA[f]	Averaging Period[g]	Benefit Formula[h]
Alabama[b]			
1982	60(10); 30 yrs	3	2.0125
2006	60(10); 25 yrs	3	2.0125
Alaska[b, c]			
1982	55(5); 30 yrs	3	2.0
2006	60(5); 30 yrs	5	2.0 1st 10 yrs; 2.25 2nd 10 yrs; 2.5 20 plus
Arizona[c]			
1982	65; 62 (10); 60 (25)	5	2.0
2006	65; 62 (10); R80	3	2.1 1st 20 yrs; 2.15 next 5; 2.2 next 5; 2.3 over 30
Arkansas[b]			
1982	65 (10); 55 (35)	5	1.625 with SS offset; limit 100% of FAS including SS
2006	65 (5); 28 yrs	3	2.0
California[b]			
1982	60 (5)	5	2.418 with SS offset
2006	55(5)	1	2.0 at 55; 2.5 at 63

(*cont.*)

TABLE 14-A1   (*Continued*)

State	NRA[f]	Averaging Period[g]	Benefit Formula[h]
Colorado[c,e]			
1982	60 (20); 55 (30); 65 (5)	3	2.5 1st 20 yrs; then 1.0; limit 70% FAS
2006	65 (5); 55 (30); R80	3	2.5; limit 100% FAS
Connecticut[a]			
1982	55 (25); 65 (10); 70 (5)	3	2.0; limit 75% FAS
2006	62 (10); 60 (25)	3	1.83 with SS offset
Delaware[d]			
1982	62 (10); 60(15); 30 yrs	5	1.6; limit 75% FAS including SS
2006	62 (5); 60 (15); 30 yrs	3	1.85
Florida[c]			
1982	62 (10); 30 yrs	5	1.68, limit 100% FAS
2006	62 (6); 30 yrs	5	1.68
Georgia[a]			
1982	65; 30 yrs	2	1.5
2006	60 (10); 30 yrs	2	2.0; limit 90% earnings
Hawaii[c]			
1982	55 (5)	5	2.0
2006	62 (5); 55 (30)	3	2.0
Idaho[c]			
1982	65 (5); 60 (30)	5	1.67
2006	65 (5); R90	3.5	2.0; limit 100% FAS
Illinois[a]			
1982	60 (8); 35 yrs	4	1.0 1st 10 yrs increasing to 1.5 after 30 yrs; limit 75% FAS
2006	60 (8); R85	4	1.67; limit 75% FAS
Indiana[b]			
1982	65 (10)	5	1.1 plus money purchase
2006	65 (10); 60 (15); R85	5	1.1 plus money purchase
Iowa[c]			
1982	65	5	1.67
2006	65; 62 (20); R88	5	2.0 1st 30 yrs; 1.0 extra yrs
Kansas[c]			
1982	65	5	1.25
2006	65; 62 (10); R85	3	1.75

TABLE 14-A1 (*Continued*)

State	NRA[f]	Averaging Period[g]	Benefit Formula[h]
Kentucky[b]			
1982	65 (4); 30 yrs	5	1.6
2006	65 (4); 27 yrs	5	1.97
Louisiana[a, c]			
1982	60 (10); 55 (25); 30 yrs	3	2.5; limit 100% FAS
2006	60 (10); 55 (25); 30 yrs	3	3.3; limit 100% FAS
Maine[c, e]			
1982	60	3	2.0
2006	60 (5)	3	2.0
Maryland[c]			
1982	62 (5); 30 yrs	3	0.8 to SS cap; 1.5 over cap
2006	60 (5); 30 yrs	3	1.8; limit 100% FAS
Massachusetts[a, e]			
1982	65 (10)	3	2.5; limit 85% FAS
2006	55 (10); 20 yrs	3	0.5 to 2.5, age related limit 80% FAS
Michigan[a]			
1982	60 (10); 55 (30)	5	1.5
2006	60 (10); 55 (30)	3	1.5
Minnesota[a]			
1982	65 (10); 62 (30)	5	1.0 1st 10 yrs; 1.5 extra yrs
2006	SS NRA	3	1.7
Mississippi[c]			
1982	65; 30 yrs	5	1.63 1st 20 yrs; 2.0 over 30
2006	60 (4); 25 yrs	4	2.0 1st 25 yrs; 2.5 extra yrs; limit 100% FAS
Missouri[a]			
1982	65 (4); 60 (15)	5	1.2
2006	65 (5); 60 (15); R80	3	1.7
Montana[b]			
1982	60 (5); 65; 35 yrs	3	1.67
2006	60 (5); 65; 30 yrs	3	1.785 1st 25 yrs; then 2.0
Nebraska[a]			
1982	65	money purchase plan	
2006	55	money purchase plan	

(*cont.*)

TABLE 14-A1 (*Continued*)

State	NRA[f]	Averaging Period[g]	Benefit Formula[h]
Nevada[c,e]			
1982	60 (10); 55 (30)	3	2.5; limit 75% FAS
2006	65 (5); 60 (10); 30 yrs	3	2.6; limit 75% FAS
New Hampshire[c]			
1982	60	3	1.67 with SS offset
2006	60	3	1.67 to 65; 1.515 after 65
New Jersey[b]			
1982	60; 55 (25); 35 yrs	3	1.67
2006	60	3	1.82
New Mexico[b]			
1982	60 (20); 65 (5); 30 yrs	3	3.0; limit 80% FAS
2006	60 (20); 65 (5); 25 yrs	3	3.0; limit 80% FAS
New York[b]			
1982	62 (20)	3	2.0 SS offset; max 30 yrs
2006	62 (5); 55 (30)	3	1.67 1st 20 yrs; 2.0 20–29; 3.5 yrs over 30
North Carolina[d]			
1982	65; 30 yrs	4	1.57
2006	65 (5); 60 (25); 30 yrs	4	1.82
North Dakota[b]			
1982	65	5	1.04
2006	65; R85	3	2.0
Ohio[b, c]			
1982	65 (5); 30 yrs	3	2.0; limit 90% FAS
2006	60 (5); 30 yrs	3	2.2 1st 30 yrs; 2.5 extra yrs; limit 100% FAS
Oklahoma[b]			
1982	62; 58 (30)	5	2.0
2006	62 (6); R90	3	2.0
Oregon[c]			
1982	58; 55 (30)	3	1.67
2006	65; 58 (30)	3	1.5 plus money purchase
Pennsylvania[a]			
1982	60 (3); 35 yrs	3	2.0
2006	60 (3); 25 yrs	3	2.5; limit 100% high salary

TABLE 14-A1 (*Continued*)

State	NRA[f]	Averaging Period[g]	Benefit Formula[h]
Rhode Island[d]			
1982	55 (30); 60 (10); 25 yrs	3	1.7 1st 10 yrs; rising to 2.4; limit 80% FAS
2006	60 (10); 25 yrs	3	1.7 1st 10 yrs; 1.9 2nd 10 yrs 3.0 21–34; 2.0 over 35 yrs; limit 80% FAS
South Carolina[c]			
1982	65; 30 yrs	3	1.25 less than $4,800; 1.65
2006	65; 28 yrs	3	1.82
South Dakota[c]			
1982	65 (5)	3	2.0 with SS offset
2006	60 (3); R85	3	1.625 yrs prior to 7/1/02 1.55 yrs after 7/1/02
Tennessee[c]			
1982	60; 30 yrs	5	1.5 below SS cap; 1.75 over SS; limit 75% FAS
2006	60 (5); 30 yrs	5	1.5 below SS cap; 1.75 over SS; limit 94.5% FAS
Texas[a]			
1982	60 (10); 55 (30)	3	1.5 1st 10 yrs; then 2.0; limit 80% FAS
2006	60 (5); R80	3	2.3; limit 100% FAS
Utah[c]			
1982	65 (4); 30 yrs	5	2.0; limit 100% FAS
2006	65 (4); 30 yrs	3	2.0
Vermont[a]			
1982	65; 62 (20)	5	1.67; max 30 years
2006	62; 30 yrs	3	1.67; limit 50% FAS
Virginia[c]			
1982	65; 60 (30)	3	1.67 with SS offset
2006	65 (5); 50 (30)	3	1.7; limit 100% FAS
Washington[b]			
1982	65 (5)	5	2.0
2006	65 (5)	5	2.0

(*cont.*)

TABLE 14-A1 (*Continued*)

State	NRA[f]	Averaging Period[g]	Benefit Formula[h]
West Virginia[b]			
1982	60 (5)	3	2.0
2006	60 (5); R80	3	2.0
Wisconsin[c]			
1982	65	3	1.3; limit 85% FAS
2006	65; 57 (30)	3	1.6; limit 70% FAS
Wyoming[c]			
1982	60 (4)	3	2.0
2006	60; R85	3	2.125 1st 15 yrs; 2.5 after

[a] Retirement plan covers only state employees.

[b] Retirement plans covers state and local employees.

[c] Retirement plan covers state and local employees and teachers.

[d] State plan covers state employees and teachers.

[e] State employees are not covered by Social Security.

[f] NRA indicates the normal retirement age for the plan. States often have several criteria that employees can satisfy and thus qualify for unreduced pension benefits. The numbers presented in the table indicate the age and service needed to qualify for an unreduced pension benefit. For example, an entry of 60 (10) indicates that a worker reaching age 60 with 10 years of service has reached the normal retirement age. Some states allow workers to qualify for unreduced benefits with a minimum number of years of service. These requirements are shown by an entry like 30 years. Finally some states allow workers to reach the normal retirement age with a combination of age and years of service equal to some number such as 80. An entry of R80 indicates the NRA is reached when the worker's age plus years of service equal 80.

[g] Entries in this column indicate the number of years used to determine a worker's final average salary (FAS). In some states, the formula is based on the highest consecutive years of earnings while other states include the highest years of earnings but these years must be in the last 5 or 10 years of employment.

[h] The states with DB plans calculate retirement benefits by multiplying a generosity parameter times the FAS times the number of years of service. Values in this column indicate the generosity parameter in percent. Some states have formulas that are integrated with Social Security and other states place a limit or cap on benefits, typically specified as a percent of the final average salary.

Source: Authors' analysis of state retirement system data; see text.

TABLE 14-A2 Plan contributions and vesting requirements

State	Employee Contribution Rate	Employer Contribution Rate	Vesting Requirement
Alabama[b]			
1984	5.0	7.59	10
2006	5.0	7.78	10
Alaska[b, c]			
1984	4.25	13.62	5
2006	6.75	16.77	5
Arizona[c]			
1984	7.0	7.0	5
2006	9.1	9.1	Immediate
Arkansas[b]			
1984	Noncontributory	10–12	10
2006	5.0	12.54	5
California[b]			
1984	5.0–9.0	16.0–21.0	5
2006	6.0	10.356	5
Colorado[c,e]			
1984	8.0	10.2–12.5	5
2006	8.0	10.15	5
Connecticut[a]			
1984	Noncontributory	7.0	10
2006	2.0		5
Delaware[d]			
1984	3.0–5.0	14.4	10
2006	3.0 above $6,000	6.1	5
Florida[c]			
1984	Noncontributory	10.93	10
2006	Noncontributory	6.72	5
Georgia[a]			
1984	3.0–5.0	7.75	10
2006	1.25	10.41	10
Hawaii[c]			
1984	7.8	23.47	5
2006	6.0	13.75	5
Idaho[c]			
1984	5.3	8.82	5
2006	6.23	10.39	5
Illinois[a]			
1984	4.0	13.29	8
2006	4.0	$210.5 million	8
Indiana[b]			
1984	3.0	7.5	10
2006	3.0	4.7	10

(*cont.*)

Table 14-A2 (*Continued*)

State	Employee Contribution Rate	Employer Contribution Rate	Vesting Requirement
Iowa[c]			
1984	3.75	5.75	4
2006	3.7	5.75	4
Kansas[c]			
1984	4.0	4.8	10
2006	4.0	5.27	10
Kentucky[b]			
1984	4.0	6.25–7.25	5
2006	5.0	5.89	5
Louisiana[a, c]			
1984	7.0	9.2	10
2006	7.689	19.1	10
Maine[c, e]			
1984	6.5	15.47–15.9	10
2006	7.65	15.09	5
Maryland[c]			
1984	5.0 over SS	4.6–6.25	5
2006	2.0	9.18	5
Massachusetts[a, e]			
1984	7.0	Pay-as-you-go	10
2006	8.3	2.9	10
Michigan[a]			
1984	Noncontributory	8.85	10
2006	Noncontributory	13.6	10
Minnesota[a]			
1984	3.73	3.9	10
2006	4.0	4.0	3
Mississippi[c]			
1984	6.0	8.75	10
2006	7.25	10.75	4
Missouri[a]			
1984	Noncontributory	12	10
2006	Noncontributory	12.59	5
Montana[b]			
1984	6.0	6.417	5
2006	6.9	6.9	5
Nebraska[a]			
1984	3.6–4.8	156% of employee rate	5
2006	4.8	156% of employee rate	3
Nevada[c, e]			
1984	Noncontributory	15	10
2006	10.5	10.5	5

Table 14-A2 (*Continued*)

State	Employee Contribution Rate	Employer Contribution Rate	Vesting Requirement
New Hampshire[c]			
1984	4.6–9.2	n/a	10
2006	6.3	6.7	10
New Jersey[b]			
1984	4.96–8.73	n/a	10
2006	5.0	$7.97 million	10
New Mexico[b]			
1984	7.85	7.0–7.85	5
2006	7.42	16.59	5
New York[b]			
1984	3.0	9.2	10
2006	3.0	8.0	5
North Carolina[d]			
1984	6.0	10.03	5
2006	6.0	2.66	5
North Dakota[b]			
1984	4.0	5.12	10
2006	4.0	4.12	3
Ohio[b, e]			
1984	8.5	13.71–13.95	5
2006	9.0	13.54	5
Oklahoma[b]			
1984	4.0	14.0	10
2006	3.0–3.5	11.5	8
Oregon[c]			
1984	6.0	11.01–11.67	5
2006	8.0	8.04	5
Pennsylvania[a]			
1984	6.25	15.77	10
2006	6.25	3.52	5
Rhode Island[d]			
1984	6.0–7.0	10.4–6.6	10
2006	8.75	14.84	10
South Carolina[c]			
1984	4.0–6.0	7.0	5
2006	6.25	7.55	5
South Dakota[c]			
1984	5.0	5.0	5
2006	6.0	6.0	3

(*cont.*)

TABLE 14-A2 (*Continued*)

State	Employee Contribution Rate	Employer Contribution Rate	Vesting Requirement
Tennessee[c]			
1984	5.0	11.07–15.01	10
2006	Noncontributory	7.3	5
Texas[a]			
1984	6.0	8.0	10
2006	6.0	6.45	5
Utah[c]			
1984	8.95	8.95	n/a
2006	Noncontributory	11.59–14.52	4
Vermont[a]			
1984	5.0	10.26	10
2006	3.35	6.26	5
Virginia[c]			
1984	5.0	6.15–8.86	5
2006	5.0	6.62	5
Washington[b]			
1984	6.0	n/a	5
2006	6.0	2.25	5
West Virginia[b]			
1984	4.5	9.5–10.5	5
2006	4.5	10.5	5
Wisconsin[c]			
1984	5.0	6.5	Immediate
2006	5.0	4.5	Immediate
Wyoming[c]			
1984	5.57	5.68	4
2006	5.57	5.58	4

[a] Retirement plan covers only state employees.
[b] Retirement plans covers state and local employees.
[c] Retirement plan covers state and local employees and teachers.
[d] State plan covers state employees and teachers.
[e] State employees are not covered by Social Security.

Source: Authors' analysis of state retirement system data; see text.

Notes

[1] The member handbook for the New Mexico public employees' retirement association (PERA 2008: 5) states: 'New Mexico enacted legislation creating a public employees retirement system in 1947. New Mexico was the last state in the continental United States to establish a retirement system for its public employees.' However, this information conflicts with other secondary sources and with data

collected by the authors in their survey of current state plan administrators; see below.

[2] 'State welfare pensions for the elderly were practically nonexistent before 1930s' (Social Security Administration 2008). However, the Great Depression created a well-recognized crisis in old-age welfare, and by 1935, 30 states had adopted some form of old-age assistance program. Although these programs were authorized by the state legislatures, they were typically managed by the counties, and the establishment of a plan was often a county-level option (USBLS 1931, 1932).

[3] By 1961, the state employees in each of these states participated in Social Security (Mueller 1961).

[4] This statement must be qualified by the fact that as early as 1930, 21 states offered some type of pension benefit to their teachers, who made up the single largest group of state workers. Although teachers' salaries were typically paid by local school boards with some combination of state and local monies, the pensions were administered by the states (Clark, Craig, and Wilson, 2003).

[5] The authority allowing voluntary participation in Social Security by public employees is contained in section 218 of the Social Security Act. As a result, these state agreements are referred to as section 218 agreements. Each state's Social Security Administrator is responsible for managing these agreements.

[6] Interestingly, legislation enacted in 1986 requires that all state and local employees hired after March 31, 1986 must be covered by Medicare; to date, no such mandatory coverage is required for Social Security.

[7] Almost three quarters of the public employees who remain outside the Social Security system reside in just seven states: California, Ohio, Texas, Massachusetts, Illinois, Colorado, and Louisiana.

[8] State employees in Alaska were once included in Social Security; however, in 1980, Alaska withdrew its employees from the system.

[9] The Pension Task Force on public pension systems reported that some plans were terminated and restructured when public employees were first covered by Social Security (US House of Representatives 1978).

[10] In 1999, the GAO (1999) reported that 21 of the 48 states with DB plans had considered terminating their DB plan and replacing it with a DC plan. However, eight years later, the GAO (2007) still found only two states with DC plans.

[11] A 2006 survey by the National Association of Government Defined Contribution Administrators found that on average only 21.6 percent of eligible state employees made voluntary contributions into in these plans (GAO 2007). Likely causes of this low level of participation are the absence of matching employer contributions and the more generous benefits provided by primary pension plans in the public sector.

[12] Also see Munnell and Soto (2007).

[13] The data in Table 14-4 are for 1984 because the 1982 report did not include detailed information on contributions.

[14] Of the 46 state plans included in the 1982 regression, 11 plans cover only state employees, three plans cover state employees and teachers, 14 plans cover state and local employees, and 19 plans cover state and local employees and teachers.

In the regressions below, the dummy that represents plans for all three groups of workers is the omitted variable.

[15] For various reasons, not every state-run plan in the United States is included in either the Wisconsin study or our data set. For example, the Wisconsin study includes plans that cover workers other than state employees. Some states maintain separate plans for teachers or local government workers, and there are dozens of state-run plans that represent small, well-defined groups, such as state judges or legislators, that are excluded (see Mitchell et al. [2000]: Table 14-2 for a complete tabulation of systems.) In addition, in 1982 the following plans were omitted: Indiana Public Employees' Retirement Fund (PERF) and Teachers' Retirement Fund (TRF) had a hybrid, 1.1 percent contribution rate combined with a 'money purchase' annuity component; Nebraska School Employees Retirement System (SERS) had a money purchase plan; and Oregon Public Employees Retirement System (PERS) has 1.5 percent plus a money purchase plan. Also, Tennessee Consolidated Retirement System (TCRS) had an 'integrated table' plan, and Tennessee had some information missing; thus so we used the 1984 formula. For 2006, the deleted plans include: Indiana PERF and TRF has hybrid, 'money purchase' option; Nebraska SERS has a money purchase plan; and Oregon PERS has 1.5 percent plus a money purchase plan. For Arkansas, we used 2 percent; and for Massachusetts, we used 2.5 percent instead of 0.1–2.5 percent age-related state formula.

[16] This is not an indicator of the actuarial soundness of the state plans. However, as Hustead an Mitchell (2000: 6) note, when it comes to the financial state of these systems, 'the status of public plans is not always transparent or comparable across systems.'

[17] Data are available from the authors on request.

References

Brainard, Keith (2007). *Public Fund Survey Summary of Findings for FY 2006.* Georgetown, TX: National Association of State Retirement Administrators.

—— (2009). 'Redefining Traditional Plans: Variations and Developments in Public Employee Retirement Plan Design,' in O.S. Mitchell and G. Anderson, eds., *The Future of Public Employee Retirement Systems.* Oxford: Oxford University Press.

Clark, Robert and Ann McDermed (1990). *The Choice of Pension Plans in a Changing Regulatory Environment.* Washington, DC: American Enterprise Institute.

—— Lee Craig, and Jack Wilson (2003). *A History of Public Sector Pensions in the United States.* Philadelphia, PA: University of Pennsylvania Press.

Craig, Lee A. (1995). 'The Political Economy Public-Private Compensation Differential: The Case of Federal Pensions,' *Journal of Economic History*, 55 (2): 304–20.

Fishback, Price V. and Shawn Everett Kantor (1995). 'Did Workers Pay for the Passage of Workers' Compensation Laws?' *Quarterly Journal of Economics*, 110 (3): 713–42.

—— —— (2000). *A Prelude to the Welfare State: The Origins of Workers' Compensation.* Chicago, IL: University of Chicago Press.

Gruber, Johnathan, and Alan B. Krueger (1991). 'The Incidence of Mandated Employer-Provided Insurance: Lessons from Workers' Compensation Insurance,' in D. Bradford, ed., *Tax Policy and the Economy, Vol. 5*. Cambridge, MA: MIT Press, pp. 111–43.

Hirsch, Barry T. and David A. Macpherson (2007). *Union Membership, Coverage, Density, and Employment by State and Sector, 1983–2007*. Union Membership and Coverage Database from the CPS. Online at www.unionstats.com.

Hustead, Edwin C. and Olivia S. Mitchell (2000). 'Public Sector Pension Plans: Lessons and Challenges for the 21st Century,' in O.S. Mitchell and E.C. Hustead, eds., *Pensions in the Public Sector*. Philadelphia, PA: University of Pennsylvania Press, pp. 3–10.

Mitchell, Olivia S. and Robert Smith (1994). 'Public Sector Pension Funding,' *Review of Economics and Statistics*, 76(2): 278–90.

—— David McCarthy, Stanley C. Wisniewski, and Paul Zorn (2000). 'Developments in State and Local Pension Plans,' in O.S. Mitchell and E.C. Hustead, eds., *Pensions in the Public Sector*. Philadelphia, PA: University of Pennsylvania Press, pp. 11–40.

Moore, Michael J. and W. Kip Viscusi (1990). *Compensation Mechanisms for Job Risk: Wages, Workers' Compensation, and Product Liability*. Princeton, NJ: Princeton University Press.

Mueller, Marjorie (1961). 'Retirement Plans for State and Local Employees,' *Monthly Labor Review*, November: 1191–99.

Munnell, Alicia (2005). 'Mandatory Social Security Coverage of State and Local Workers: A Perennial Hot Button.' Issue Brief No. 32. Boston, MA: Center for Retirement Research at Boston College.

—— Kelly Haverstick, and Mauricio Soto (2007). 'Why Have Defined Benefit Plans Survived in the Public Sector.' State and Local Pension Plans Brief No. 2. Boston, MA: Center for Retirement Research at Boston College.

—— Mauricio Soto (2007). 'State and Local Pensions are Different From Private Plans.' State and Local Pension Plans Brief No. 1. Boston, MA: Center for Retirement Research at Boston College.

Public Employees Retirement Association of New Mexico (PERA) (2008). *Public Employees Retirement Association of New Mexico Member Handbook*. Santa Fe, NM: Public Employees Retirement Association of New Mexico.

Social Security Administration (2007). 'How State and Local Government Employees Are Covered by Social Security and Medicare.' SSA Publication No. 05–10051. Washington, DC: Social Security Administration.

—— (2008). *Historical Background and Development of Social Security*. Washington, DC: Social Security Administration.

Social Security Board (1937). *Social Security in America: Part II Old Age Security*. Washington, DC: Social Security Administration.

Streckewald, Frederick (2005). 'Social Security Testimony Before Congress.' Hearing before the House Ways and Means Subcommittee on Social Security, June 9. Washington, DC: Social Security Administration.

US Bureau of Labor Statistics (USBLS) (1916). 'Civil-Service Retirement and Old-Age Pensions,' *Monthly Labor Review*, June: 635–51.

US Bureau of Labor Statistics (USBLS) (1931). 'Operation of Public Old-Age Pension Systems in the United States, 1930,' *Monthly Labor Review*, June: 1267–80.

—— (1932). 'Operation of Public Old-Age Pension Systems in the United States in 1931,' *Monthly Labor Review*, June: 1259–69.

—— (1988). *Employee Benefits in State and Local Governments*. Bulletin No. 2309. Washington, DC: US Government Printing Office.

—— (1996). *Employee Benefits in State and Local Governments*. Bulletin No. 2477. Washington, DC: US Government Printing Office.

—— (1998.) *Employee Benefits in State and Local Governments*. Bulletin No. 2531. Washington, DC: US Government Printing Office.

US Department of Commerce, Bureau of the Census (various years). *Statistical Abstract of the United States*. Washington, DC: US Government Printing Office. http://www.census.gov/compendia/statab/.

—— (various years). *Census of Governments: Employee-Retirement Systems of State and Local Governments*. Washington, DC: US Government Printing Office.

—— (2004). *Census of Governments: Employee Retirement Systems of State and Local Government*. Washington, DC: US Government Printing Office. http://www.census.gov/prod/2004pubs/gc024x6.pdf.

US General Accounting Office (GAO) (1999). *State Pension Plans: Similarities and Differences Between Federal and State Designs*. GAO/GGD-99–45. Washington, DC: US Government Accountability Office.

—— (2007). *State and Local Government Retiree Benefits: Current Status of Benefit Structures, Protections, and Fiscal Outlook for Funding Future Costs*. GAO-07-572. Washington, DC: US Government Accountability Office.

US House of Representatives, Committee on Education and Labor (1978). *Pension Task Force Report on Public Employee Retirement Systems*. Washington, DC: US Government Printing Office.

Wisconsin Legislative Council (various years.) *Comparative Study of Major Public Employee Retirement Systems*. Madison, Wisconsin: Wisconsin Legislative Council.

Chapter 15

Pension Fund Activism:
The Double-Edged Sword

Brad M. Barber

Does institutional activism create value for shareholders? Proponents of activism argue that institutions are merely providing necessary monitoring of corporations with poor performance. Critics view activism as the actions of meddlesome portfolio managers spending investors' money to interfere in corporate policy. Who is right?

To answer this question, I begin from basic economic principles and analyze a simple framework where a portfolio manager has the unfettered objective of maximizing the value of an investment portfolio.[1] I argue that the benefits of institutional activism—narrowly for the investors at the institution and broadly for society—hinge critically on the prevalence of two agency costs. The first agency cost is the well-known conflicts of interest between shareholders and corporate managers; corporate managers may pursue projects that benefit themselves, but not shareholders. Effective monitoring by institutions can reduce these agency costs—benefiting not only their investors, but raising the value of stocks for all investors. I refer to this type of institutional activism as 'shareholder activism.'

The second agency cost, less widely discussed than the first, is the conflicts of interest between portfolio managers and investors. Portfolio managers may pursue investment policies that benefit their own objectives, but not those of investors. The large block of voting rights under the control of institutional portfolio managers presents the most obvious potential source of agency costs. Just as this voting power can be used to benefit shareholders through effective monitoring of corporations, the voting power can be abused by advancing the interests of portfolio managers[2] that are different from those of their investors and reduce the value of the portfolio they manage. Generally, institutional activism in this arena centers on social issues, such as disclosure of greenhouse gas emissions, divestment in Sudan, or tobacco firms. Thus, I refer to this type of institutional activism as 'social activism.'

Social activism may lead to desirable or important social benefits. For example, institutional pressure may cause corporations to reduce pollution or be more vigilant in monitoring child labor practices. But pollution abatement technologies and the monitoring of labor practices is costly. Consequently, the social gains will often hurt the bottom line and potential returns earned by shareholders. Thus, a portfolio manager who is attempting to maximize the value of an investment portfolio would not pursue social activism when it forces corporations to incur avoidable costs. Many investors choose socially responsible mutual funds precisely because these funds invest in firms that are consistent with their personal values. However, most institutions (e.g., public pension funds) are not provided with such a clear moral mandate from their investors.

The two agency costs create a tension that renders the ultimate gains of institutional activism an empirical question. While admittedly imprecise, I argue that simple empirical methods—short-run event studies and the long-run returns of portfolios of targeted stocks—are the best methods available to estimate the net benefits of institutional activism.

While institutional activism is widespread, my discussion and empirical analyses focus on the efficacy and prudence of California Public Employees' Retirement System (CalPERS) activism—a long-time leader in the institutional activism. For almost two decades, CalPERS has been active in pursuing corporate reforms. In recent years, this activism has come under increased scrutiny as CalPERS took public stands on a wide range of issues including corporate governance, greenhouse gas emissions, auto fuel efficiency, labor negotiations, investments in tobacco firms, Iran, Sudan, South Africa, and the independence of audit committees.

Using simple empirical methods, I estimate the gains to the high profile activism of CalPERS focus list firms over the period 1992 to 2007. My short-run analysis indicates that CalPERS activism yields positive, but small, market reactions of 21 basis points (bps) on the date focus list firms are publicly announced. These announcement effects are too small to conclude they are reliably positive. I and many others have previously concluded this evidence was more persuasive, but in the last two years—particularly 2006—the so-called 'CalPERS effect' has been negative. However, it is worth noting that these small effects, if truly caused by CalPERS activism, yield wealth creation of $1.9 billion dollars over the 16 year period that I analyze.

My long-run analysis yields intriguing, but inconclusive results. Portfolios of focus list firms earn annualized abnormal returns ranging from 2.1 to 4.5 percentage points annually at holding periods ranging from 6 months to 5 years. If these abnormal returns are causally linked to the activism of CalPERS, the wealth creation is enormous—as much as 20 times greater than the short-run benefits and as large as $39.4 billion through December 2007. Unfortunately, while economically large and positive, the estimates of long-run abnormal returns are not reliably positive. Long-run returns are simply too volatile to conclude that the long-run performance of focus list firms is unusual. I argue that previous studies, which document reliably positive long-run abnormal returns for focus list firms, either fail to account for the characteristics of focus list firms and/or rely on faulty statistics.

Having established a reasonable estimate of the value of CalPERS activities surrounding focus list firms, I review the nature of reforms that CalPERS publicly pursues at these firms through shareholder proposals sponsored by CalPERS at focus list firms. Without exception, the CalPERS proposals increase shareholder rights. Empirical research establishes a strong link between shareholder rights and firm value and provides strong support for prudence of CalPERS' initiatives designed to improve shareholder rights. Thus, these governance-related reforms at focus list firms are uniformly shareholder (rather than social) activism.

However, CalPERS has also pursued social activism unrelated to their annual focus list firms. Often, this social activism is pursued at the behest of either of state legislative action (e.g., divestiture from Sudan or Iran) or the 13-member board (e.g., tobacco divestiture) that oversees CalPERS investments. I review some of the high profile decisions made by CalPERS. Many of these decisions lack clear evidence—empirical or theoretical— that CalPERS activism would improve shareholder value. CalPERS manages the assets of over a million public employees, retirees, and their families. When there is no clear link to improvements in shareholder value, whether CalPERS activism is in the best interests of those whose money they manage depends critically on the personal preferences of investors.

The remainder of this chapter is organized as follows. The first section provides an overview of the theory underlying institutional activism. In the second section, I provide empirical evidence regarding the short-run and long-run performance of CalPERS focus list firms. In the third section, I review the nature of reforms pursued at focus list firms and provide anecdotes regarding other activism pursued by CalPERS outside of their focus list initiative.

Institutional activism: theory

In this section, I formally lay out a simple framework to analyze the expected effects of institutional activism.

Shareholders versus Managers. It is well known that conflicts of interest may arise between shareholders, who seek to maximize firm value, and firm managers, who may have interests other than value maximization (e.g., empire building or maximizing compensation packages). These conflicts create a cost for shareholders that lead to lower firm valuations. Absent these agency costs, the market would reach some maximum agency-cost-free valuation, call it V^*.

Absent any monitoring by investors, agency costs (A) take a (relatively) large percentage of this maximum valuation. Investors can reduce the agency cost bite taken out of the valuation pie by monitoring corporations, but monitoring is costly, varies in effectiveness, and, no doubt, has diminishing marginal returns. In the top graph of Figure 15-1, I represent agency costs as a decreasing, convex function of monitoring resources (M).

Large institutional investors invest tens of billions of dollars in stocks— generally in an index fund or at least an equity portfolio that tracks the market reasonably well. Nonetheless, even the largest institutional investors own only a small percentage of the total market. For example, CalPERS, with US equity investments of $80 billion in January 2008, owns approximately 0.5 percent of the total market, which is valued at approximately $16.5 trillion in December 2007. For CalPERS to justify investment in the monitoring of corporate managers as a value enhancing proposition, a dollar spent on monitoring must increase the value of monitored firms by *at least* $200 ($1/0.5%), since CalPERS only owns a small slice of the monitored firms. If CalPERS prudently spends $1,000,000 on monitoring each year, the expenditure would lead to a minimum increase in firm value of $200,000,000.

This analysis presumes the benefits of activism are limited to the firms that are directly pursued by an institution. But widespread monitoring by institutions can also deter corporate malfeasance. If corporations know that institutions stand ready to publicly excoriate firms that engage in practices that reduce shareholder value, corporations will be less likely to engage in these practices in the first place. The deterrence benefits of activism are exceedingly difficult to measure, but nonetheless provide additional justification for institutional activism.

In general, a savvy portfolio manager will choose a monitoring cost (M*) that maximizes the value of his portfolio (P*). In panel B of Figure 15-1, I depict the manager's portfolio value as a function of the monitoring costs that he incurs. In principle, the optimal level of monitoring (M*) will be achieved when the marginal cost of monitoring equals the marginal benefit (i.e., reduction in agency costs realized in the manager's portfolio). Unfortunately, in practice, it is nearly impossible to estimate precisely the marginal benefit of monitoring. Thus, it is difficult to determine ex-ante whether institutions are investing in an optimal amount of monitoring. Even with the benefit of over a decade of hindsight, it is difficult to precisely estimate the total value of the gains resulting from CalPERS activism. I discuss this issue at length in the empirical section of this chapter.

Free Riders. As the earlier analysis makes clear, while large investors incur monitoring costs, all investors enjoy the benefits of monitoring. On one hand, this is a positive externality created by the monitoring of the large investor. On the other hand, that others benefit from the actions of

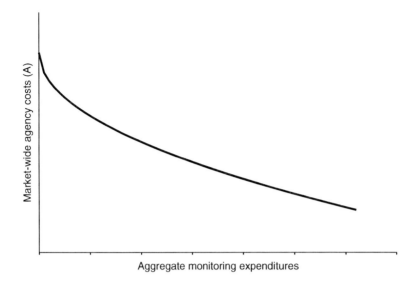

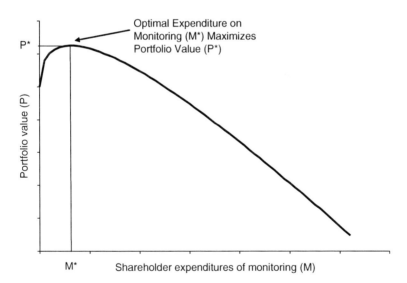

Figure 15-1 Relation between agency costs, monitoring expenditures, and portfolio value. Panel A. Agency costs and monitoring expenditures. Panel B. Shareholder expenditures on monitoring and portfolio value. *Source:* Author's depiction.

the large investor creates a free rider problem (Admati, Pfleiderer, and Zechner, 1994). To see this immediately, assume all investors choose a market index, but only the large investor incurs monitoring costs. It is obvious that small investors incur no monitoring costs but enjoy the benefits of monitoring by large investors ill outperform the large investor. An investor who delegates the management of his money to the large investor would flee the large investor and choose to manage his own money. And, of course, as the portfolio of the large investor shrinks, the incentive to monitor corporate actions is reduced.

To solve the free rider problem such that monitoring occurs in equilibrium, there must be either economies of scale to investment management or an institutional framework that encourages pooled investments.[3] Certainly both conditions hold in today's financial markets. With economies of scale to investment management (e.g., reduced transaction costs or improved diversification), the equilibrium size of a portfolio will be determined such that the transaction costs savings are exactly offset by the cost of monitoring (Admati, Pfleiderer, and Zechner, 1994). Furthermore, current investment practices encourage pooled investments. Corporations (or municipalities) provide employees with (generally) limited investment options for their retirement portfolios or manage a large investment portfolio that is intended to cover the beneficiaries of a corporate (or municipal) defined-benefit retirement plan.

Portfolio Manager versus Investor. Conflicts of interest can arise between investors and those who manage their money (e.g., portfolio managers). While investors seek to maximize the value of their invested wealth, portfolio managers may have incentives that are not fully aligned with this objective. In the context of shareholder activism, it is possible that a portfolio manager might have an interest in pursuing a political agenda (Romano 1993a, 1993b, 1995). Some argue that aspects of CalPERS activism are politically motivated. Perhaps the greatest controversy was raised when CalPERS voted to oust Safeway's CEO, Steven Burd, from Safeway's board of directors in May 2004 for his harsh dealing with employee unions. I discuss this and related issues in detail later when I examine the nature of CalPERS activism.

It is important to note that the conflicts of interest that arise between investors and portfolio managers hinge critically on the objectives of investors in the portfolio. Consider a simple example: A CEO pursues a policy of manufacturing the firm's products in the United States rather than overseas despite the fact that overseas manufacturing would be less costly. As a portfolio manager, you have a sizable stake in the company. You could attempt to rally support for ousting the CEO and replacing him with a CEO that would move the firm's manufacturing operations overseas; if successful, this would undoubtedly increase the value of the firm's stock. However, the investors in your portfolio uniformly oppose the wealth-maximizing initiative for moral reasons (e.g., perhaps the foreign manufacturers have lax labor or environmental standards and American jobs would be lost). If the portfolio manager were to pursue wealth maximization, he would not be serving the interests of his investors.

Heterogeneity in the moral or political views of investors in the institutional portfolio further complicates matters. Given the different objectives of investors within the portfolio, the portfolio manager cannot hope to satisfy everyone. These moral issues are invariably sensitive, but the point is simple: Once considerations other than wealth maximization are relevant for investors, aligning the interests of portfolio managers and investors becomes extremely difficult. Given the delicate nature of many of these ethical considerations, portfolio managers generally pursue policies that attempt to maximize shareholder value and avoid taking stands on sensitive moral issues. As the earlier example illustrates, whether this maximizes the utility, rather than wealth, of investors depends on their shared objectives.

Oversight of the Portfolio Manager. Strong oversight of the portfolio manager could prevent him from pursuing a political agenda that destroys the wealth of investors in his portfolio. In public pension funds, like those run by CalPERS and the California State Teachers' Retirement System (CalSTRS), legislature and a board provide oversight.

Boards are generally elected by the beneficiaries of the fund, appointed by an elected official, or designated based on their status as a government official. For example, the 13-member CalPERS board has six elected members, three governor-appointed members, and four statutory members (e.g., the state treasurer and the state controller).

Presumably, an effective board would remove a portfolio manager who pursues his own interests at the expense of investors. But boards are often political in nature. Indeed, CalPERS' board members started many of CalPERS' controversial initiatives. If the portfolio manager and board share political objectives, the board's oversight may be ineffective. Equally pernicious, a board may have a political interest in squelching prudent activism by a portfolio manager.

Consider the following example: A portfolio manager regularly pursues shareholder initiatives with strong and demonstrably positive effects on shareholder wealth. However, these initiatives tend to weaken the position and influence of top CEOs, who are strong supporters of members of the board that are assigned to oversee the portfolio manager. The corporate CEOs might use their influence with the board to put an end to the portfolio manager's shareholder activism.

Legislators also provide oversight of public pension funds. Divestiture is the most common example of legislative intervention. For example, the recent California state initiatives to require CalPERS and CalSTRS to divest of investments in Sudan and Iran resulted from extremely popular state legislation.

Not surprisingly, politics are a double-edged sword. Infusing politics into shareholder activism can lead to suboptimal outcomes in two ways. On one hand, politically-motivated boards could thwart valuable shareholder activism by a portfolio manager. On the other hand, lax oversight might enable a politically-motivated portfolio manager to pursue his social activism that reduces shareholder value and is not aligned with the values of his investors.

Evaluating the Portfolio Manager. Traditionally, portfolio managers are evaluated relative to an appropriate market benchmark (e.g., the S&P 500 or Russell 2000). Fancier evaluation tools might calculate alphas or abnormal returns relative to multiple benchmarks (or factors). Unfortunately, all of these methods miss the potential benefits of shareholder activism. Consider an index fund manager who invests in the S&P 500 and, by construction, is unable to earn a positive alpha. However, the fund manager pursues numerous shareholder initiatives that have demonstrably positive effects on share prices. This manager has improved the returns of his investors but since all investors in the marketplace benefit (the free rider issue discussed earlier), this performance boost does not show up in the form of a positive alpha.

A simple method for evaluating the activism of the portfolio manager is to measure the abnormal returns around the announcement of events related to shareholder activism. In an efficient market, the expected benefits of shareholder activism would be reflected in stock prices. Thus, the announcement of a shareholder initiative by an institutional investor should lead to share price changes if the announcement is unanticipated and leads to material changes in shareholder value. If prices do not react immediately to the announcement of a shareholder activism initiative, price effects may continue for some time after the announcement date. Given the controversy surrounding the degree of market efficiency in financial markets, it seems reasonable to analyze both the short- and long-run evidence.

The evidence from CalPERS

CalPERS formally began its corporate governance activities in 1987 under the leadership of then-CEO Dale Hanson. Between 1987 and 1992, CalPERS' staff would select companies to target. Many of the early reforms were targeted at the repeal of poison pills and staggered boards (Crutchley, Hudson, and Jensen 1998). Subject to CalPERS Board approval, letters were sent to the targeted company's CEO (Nesbitt 1994). In these early years, there was no formal announcement of the targeted companies. CalPERS activism would only become public when CalPERS formally sponsored a shareholder resolution. However, in 1992 CalPERS began publicly announcing its focus list in an effort to apply public pressure to targeted companies.

My empirical analyses concentrate on these focus list firms. It is important to note that CalPERS activism is not limited to these firms. As I discuss in detail at the close of this section, CalPERS has taken public stands on a wide range of issues.

Short-Run Returns. I begin with an analysis of the short-run returns around the public announcement of focus list for the 132 firms targeted by CalPERS over the period 1992 to 2007. Some firms appear on the focus list in multiple years.

Before summarizing the short-run evidence, it is useful to consider the conditions under which the short-run analysis would provide a reasonable approximation of the valuation impact of CalPERS activism. First, the market impact of the CalPERS announcement must be an unbiased predictor of the long-term valuation consequences. This would be true, for example, if financial markets were efficient, and the information contained in the CalPERS announcement were fully and immediately reflected in price.

Second, the announcement must be, to some extent, unanticipated. If market participants are fully aware that CalPERS plans to target the identified firms prior to the announcement, the press release would contain no new information. Similarly, if the announcement is partially anticipated, the short-run analysis around the press release date will underestimate the total valuation impact. Since CalPERS carefully guards the identity of focus list firms prior to the press release, this assumption seems reasonable.

Third, the information contained in the CalPERS announcement must be the revelation that CalPERS plans to work for change in the focus list firms. If CalPERS has information about target companies that is unavailable to market participants, the announcement might reveal this private information. For example, CalPERS might have attempted to effect change with target companies prior to the press release. If these attempts are successful, the firm might be removed from the focus list prior to the press release. Thus, to some extent, firms that remain on the focus list might have management that is unusually reticent to change corporate practices. Thus, the announcement of the focus list would have two bits of information: (*a*) CalPERS intentions to reform the focus list firms; and (*b*) management's reluctance to reform prior to the press release date. Assuming CalPERS pursues prudent corporate reforms, the former is likely positive news, while the latter is negative news. The mixture of positive and negative news in the public announcement would cause the researcher to underestimate the benefits of CalPERS activism.

Finally, the value of CalPERS activism must be limited to those firms that they publicly pursue. If CalPERS is able to successfully negotiate behind-the-scenes changes in corporate policy that redound to the benefit of shareholders, an analysis of only publicly announced intervention will underestimate the total value of activism. Similarly, monitoring may deter corporate malfeasance. It is impossible to precisely estimate the benefits of behind-the-scenes negotiations or deterrence, though both of these effects can contribute to the value of activism.[4]

In summary, the short-run analysis leans on the assumption of market efficiency and might underestimate the total benefit of CalPERS activism if the announcement is either partially anticipated or conveys some information about managerial entrenchment. In addition, the analysis misses auxiliary benefits of activism that might accrue from private negotiations or the potential deterrence of corporate malfeasance. For these reasons, short-run event time analysis yields a conservative estimate of the total benefits of CalPERS activism.

Several prior studies analyze the short-run returns around the public release of CalPERS focus list firms or CalPERS proxy initiatives. Wahal (1996), Smith (1996), and Del Guercio and Hawkins (1999) all analyze a small number of firms targeted by CalPERS in the 1987 to 1993 period and document short-run returns that are not reliably different from zero. Unfortunately, identifying a clean announcement date during this period is problematic, since CalPERS did not formally announce the focus list. Thus, the small sample size and the ambiguous announcement dates yield unreliable estimates of short-run abnormal returns.

English, Smythe, and McNeil (2004) and Anson, White, and Ho (2003) solve the announcement date problem by analyzing the period beginning in 1992, when CalPERS began announcing the constituents of their focus list firms in a formal press release. English, Smythe, and McNeil (2004) document reliably positive and economically large short-run returns of 0.98 percent for 63 focus list firms targeted from 1992 to 1997, while Anson, White, and Ho (2003) find positive but statistically insignificant returns of 0.26 percent for the 96 focus list firms targeted from 1992 to 2001.

I update the short-run results for the 132 firms targeted 1992–2007 and find positive but statistically insignificant market-adjusted returns of 0.12 percent (equally-weighted) or 0.21 percent (value-weighted). For the short-run analysis, I calculate market-adjusted returns for each firm on the announcement day using a CRSP value-weighted market index. For each year, I calculate an average market-adjusted return weighting each firm equally or by market cap. All data are from the Center for Research in Security Prices (CRSP) dataset. Table 15-1 presents the results of the short-run analysis by year. These results provide solid evidence that CalPERS shareholder activism, on average, improves shareholder value. In the

TABLE 15-1 Announcement day market-adjusted returns and valuation impact for CalPERS focus list firms by year, 1992 to 2007

Year	No. of Firms	Mean Market-Adjusted Return (%)		Valuation Impact ($ Mil)	Market Cap ($ Mil)
		Equally-Weight (%)	Value-Weighted (%)		
1992	12	0.32	0.01	14.0	93,763.2
1993	12	0.47	2.12	1,699.0	80,245.1
1994	10	−0.19	−1.14	−694.2	60,919.1
1995	9	0.20	0.13	20.2	15,341.6
1996	10	0.98	0.34	25.6	7,474.0
1997	10	0.15	−0.05	−6.9	12,950.0
1998	9	0.45	0.08	26.9	35,390.4
1999	9	0.53	0.12	18.7	16,040.4
2000	10	0.25	1.58	739.2	46,930.1
2001	5	0.36	−0.03	−1.0	3,707.6
2002	4	−0.10	1.35	480.5	35,640.6
2003	6	−0.66	−0.34	−45.6	13,323.6
2004	4	0.42	0.53	551.0	103,407.5
2005	5	−0.02	0.19	313.6	169,485.2
2006	6	−1.42	−1.75	−1,254.1	71,799.3
2007	11	−0.19	−0.24	−349.8	147,618.8
Mean		0.12	0.21	Sum 1,886.9	766,417.7
Std. Dev.		0.57	0.97		
t-statistic		0.76	0.81		

Notes: The CRSP value-weighted NYSE/ASE/Nasdaq market index is the benchmark. The announcement day is the date of the CalPERS press release for focus list firms.

Source: Author's computations; see text.

typical year, targeted firms experience a positive, but statistically insignificant, market reaction of 12 basis points (equally-weighted) or 21 basis points (value-weighted).[5]

A reasonable estimate of the total shareholder wealth created by the CalPERS activism can be calculated by multiplying the market-adjusted return for each firm by its market cap. In each year, the market cap of all firms targeted and the total shareholder wealth created by CalPERS activism are presented in the last two columns of Table 15-1. Over the last 16 years, CalPERS activism improved shareholder wealth by nearly $1.9 billion. Marketwide, this translates into an average annual wealth creation of $118 million. For CalPERS beneficiaries, the wealth is a much more modest $600,000 under reasonable assumptions.[6]

While the short-run analysis provides weak evidence that CalPERS activism creates shareholder value, does this activism benefit CalPERS investors? In other words, do the benefits that accrue to CalPERS investors justify CalPERS expenditures on activism? There are two relevant costs. First, shareholder activism requires fund resources to monitor and analyze firm governance and performance. Second, and more subtly, engaging in activism will preclude a firm from lending its securities in the targeted company. For many large investment funds, security lending is a reliable source of revenue. One might reasonably conclude that the staff costs and lost lending revenue are close to if not greater than the annual savings of $600,000.

This direct cost-benefit view is an overly simplistic view for two reasons. First, the CalPERS benefit is only the tip of the iceberg—all market participants benefit from CalPERS activism. Second, as discussed throughout the chapter, the short-run reaction to focus list announcements underestimates the total benefits to CalPERS activism.

Long-Run Returns. Of course, the analysis of short-term returns discussed earlier leans heavily on the assumption that markets respond immediately to the release of the CalPERS focus list. If markets are slow to respond to full implications of CalPERS activism, more information might be revealed in the analysis of long-run returns.

Several studies attempt to analyze long-run returns following the announcement of CalPERS focus list. Unfortunately, all of these studies focus on event-time returns, which are well-known to yield biased test statistics, and/or employ benchmarks that do not fully account for the characteristics of firms appearing on CalPERS focus list.[7] I elaborate on both of these issues in the following text.[8]

To get an initial sense for the long-run performance of the focus list firms, consider a simple event-time analysis, where day zero is defined as the date of the CalPERS announcement of the focus list firms. Figure 15-2 presents the mean cumulative market-adjusted returns (firm return less a value-weighted market index) for focus list firms for the three years leading up to the announcement date and for the five years following the announcement date. The focus list firms lag the market by a substantial margin in the years leading up to the announcement date. This is not surprising, since CalPERS explicitly uses poor stock performance to identify corporations that might require more careful monitoring.

What is more intriguing is the strong performance of these stocks following the announcement date. After five years, the average focus list firm has outperformed the market by over 20 percentage points. This is an impressive track record, but there are two problems with ascribing this strong performance to CalPERS activism. First, there is a benchmark problem. Clearly, the market index is not the appropriate benchmark for

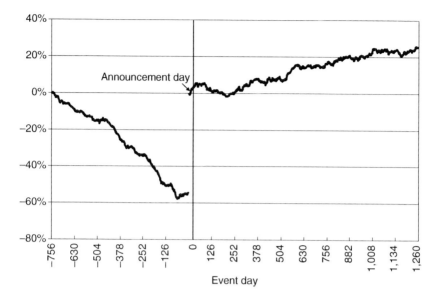

Figure 15-2 Cumulative market-adjusted returns for CalPERS focus list firms, 1992 to 2007. *Notes:* Event day 0 is the date of the CalPERS press release. Market-adjusted returns are calculated as a firm's return less the market return. On each event day, mean market-adjusted returns are calculated. The graph presents cumulative mean market-adjusted returns separately for (a) the period prior to the CalPERS announcement (left area) and (b) the period after the CalPERS announcement (right area). See text for a discussion of statistical significance. *Source:* Author's computations; see text.

focus list firms. CalPERS targets firms with poor performance, which—as we will see in subsequent analyses—tend to be value stocks rather than growth stocks. It is well known that value stocks tend to outperform growth stocks over long horizons, so clearly this firm characteristic must be carefully accounted for when assessing the long-run performance of the focus list firms.

Second, how do we assess whether the admittedly large long-run returns earned by focus list firms are a result of CalPERS activism or a mere chance outcome. To do so, we formally test the null hypothesis that the long-run returns are zero and lean heavily on statistical analyses. Unfortunately, statistics based on event-time returns such as those depicted in Figure 15-1 are notoriously unreliable (i.e., they tend to reject the null hypothesis more than they should). Though there are numerous issues, perhaps the most obvious is the explicit assumption that the returns earned by each focus list firm are independent. Security returns tend to be positively correlated. Thus, unless one can identify *all* factors that influence the cross-section of returns—a Herculean task—this assumption is almost certainly false.

Fortunately, there is a way to overcome the shortcomings of event-time analyses. The solution is simple: construct a calendar-time portfolio that invests in focus list firms. Firms are placed into the focus list portfolio at the close of trading on the date of the CalPERS press release. On any day, the return on the portfolio is merely a weighted average of returns on the focus list firms, where weights are proportional to each firm's market capitalization. This value-weighted portfolio can be thought of as a 'slice' of the market portfolio (or the CalPERS portfolio), which assumes varying investment holding periods in each focus list firm. In the analysis that follows, I vary the holding period from two weeks to five years.

The focus of the empirical analysis is the time series of daily returns on the focus list portfolio. Note that this analysis garners power from a longer time series (i.e., more daily returns) rather than more focus list firms. Thus, the analysis implicitly relies on the reasonable assumption that returns are independent over time. In contrast, the typical event time analysis, used in all prior analyses of the long-run returns of focus list firms, assumes each firm generates an independent observation and relies on the dubious assumption that returns are independent across firms.

The abnormal returns on this portfolio can be calculated using standard asset pricing techniques. It is now common practice in financial economics to estimate abnormal returns using the following four-factor model:

$$\left(R_{pt} - R_{ft}\right) = a + \beta \left(R_{mt} - R_{ft}\right) + s\,SMB_t + h\,HML_t + u\,UMD_t + \varepsilon_t$$

where R_{pt} is the return on the focus list portfolio, R_{ft} is the return on one-month T-Bills, R_{mt} is the return on a value-weighted market portfolio, SMB_t is the spread in returns between small and big firms, HML_t is the spread in returns between high and low book-to-market firms, and UMD_t is the spread in returns between stocks recently up and stocks recently down (a momentum factor).[9] The daily excess returns on the focus list portfolio are regressed on the daily realizations of the four factors. Positive coefficients on the size (SMB), book-to-market (HML), and momentum (UMD) factors represent tilts toward small firms, high book-to-market firms, and stocks recently up (respectively), while negative coefficients represent tilts toward big firms, low book-to-market firms, and stocks recently down. The parameter of interest in this regression is the intercept, which represents the daily portfolio 'alpha' or abnormal return after controlling for the style tilts of the portfolio.

The factor model regressions also address the second issue that plagues many of the prior studies of the long-run returns on focus list firms: the

TABLE 15-2 Daily abnormal returns (Alpha) to value-weighted portfolios of
CalPERS focus list firms at different holding periods, 1992 to 2007

Holding Period	Annualized Alpha (%)	Daily Alpha (%)	MRP	SMB	HML	UMD	Obs
Coefficient Estimate on:							
2 weeks	42.3	0.168	1.011	−0.139	0.713	−0.382	160
1 month	12.5	0.049	1.150	0.098	0.601	−0.474	336
6 months	4.5	0.018	1.221	0.282	0.473	−0.458	2,016
1 year	3.3	0.013	1.215	0.263	0.361	−0.377	3,821
2 years	2.9	0.011	1.177	0.208	0.284	−0.248	3,976
3 years	3.9	0.015	1.156	0.099	0.200	−0.132	3,976
4 years	2.1	0.008	1.111	0.030	0.074	−0.058	3,976
5 years	3.1	0.012	1.089	−0.010	0.117	−0.091	3,976
				t-Statistics			
2 weeks		1.48	6.35	−0.63	2.80	−2.93	
1 month		0.68	11.60	0.69	3.57	−5.74	
6 months		0.51	27.73	4.26	5.77	−9.91	
1 year		0.52	36.91	5.50	6.08	−11.07	
2 years		0.62	48.78	5.92	6.62	−10.00	
3 years		1.10	62.92	3.70	6.11	−6.98	
4 years		0.67	69.14	1.27	2.59	−3.51	
5 years		1.10	73.27	−0.48	4.44	−5.95	

Notes: Focus list portfolios are constructed assuming an investment in proportion to each
firm's market cap at the close of trading on the date of the CalPERS press release. The
holding period for each investment is varied. Abnormal returns (alphas) are calculated by
regressing the portfolio return less the risk free rate on market, size, value, and momentum
factors.

Source: Author's computations; see text.

use of benchmarks that do not adequately control for the characteristics of focus list firms. The independent variables provide explicit controls for the size, value, and momentum characteristics of the focus list portfolio.

Factor regression results for the period 1992 to 2007 are presented in Table 15-2. Focus list firms are added to the portfolio at the close of trading on the date of the CalPERS press release.[10] Coefficient estimates from the four-factor model are presented in the top half of Table 15-2 while *t*-statistics are presented in the bottom half. Each row of numbers represented the returns for a different holding period—ranging from two weeks to five years. The results of the daily regressions yield a daily alpha. To simplify the discussion, the daily alpha is annualized by multiplying the daily alpha by 252 (the number of trading days in a year).

The style tilts of the focus list portfolio are not surprising. Relative to the market portfolio, focus list firms have slightly greater than average market risk (i.e., betas greater than one), and are small $(s > 0)$,[11] value firms $(h > 0)$ with poor recent returns $(u < 0)$. The value and momentum tilts of the portfolio are consistent with CalPERS targeting poorly performing firms.

The abnormal returns (alphas) of the focus list portfolio are generally positive, but not reliably different from zero. At short horizons of two weeks and one month, the focus list portfolio earns impressive daily alphas of 16.8 and 4.9 bps per day (42.3 and 12.5 percentage points annually). At longer horizons of six months to five years, the daily alphas are consistently positive, though smaller—ranging from 2.1 percentage points annually to 4.5 percentage points annually. Note that these portfolio returns exclude the announcement return analyzed in Table 15-1 and thus would represent additional benefit to shareholder activism if we can conclude these returns are *caused* by the CalPERS intervention.

It is straightforward to estimate the cumulative abnormal gains on the focus list portfolio by summing the product of the size of the portfolio (V_t) and sum of the estimated intercept and residual from equation (1): $\sum_t V_t (a + \varepsilon_t)$. In Figure 15-3, we present the result of this estimation over holding periods ranging from two weeks to five years based on the returns of the focus list portfolio from 1992 through December 2007. For comparison purposes, the one-day valuation effects of $1.9 billion estimated in Table 15-1 are presented on the far left side of the graph. The estimates of long horizon gains on the focus list firms are generally positive, with the obvious exception of the four-year horizon.[12] In addition, the long horizon gains often are orders of magnitude larger than the one-day valuation effects. For example, the estimated gain at a two week holding period is $11.8 billion, but grows to $39.4 billion dollars assuming benefits accrue over five years following the CalPERS intervention.

While long-run returns on the focus list firms are economically large, they are not reliably positive. None of the t-statistics for the alphas presented in Table 15-2 are close to conventional levels of statistical significance. This underscores the Achilles heel of the analysis of long-run returns—volatility. While the alphas that we estimate are uniformly positive and economically large, we cannot conclude that they are unusual based on the available evidence.

The nature of CalPERS activism

Instead of leaning on return analyses to evaluate the activism of CalPERS, one can also analyze the nature of the reforms pursued by CalPERS. I

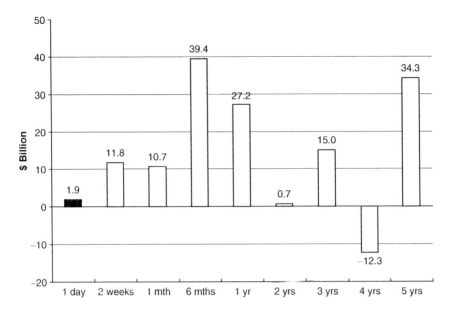

Figure 15-3 Cumulative gains from CalPERS shareholder activism for different horizons. *Notes*: Gains at one day are from Table 15-1 and include firms targeted from 1992 to 2007. Gains for horizons from 2 weeks to 5 years are based on four-factor abnormal returns in Table 15-2 and market capitalization of the focus list portfolio over the period 1992 to December 2007. See text for a complete description of the gain estimation. *Source*: Author's computations; see text.

identify 17 shareholder proposals sponsored by CalPERS that appear on the proxy statements of focus list firms in the five years after the year a firm is placed on the focus list. All shareholder proposals sponsored by CalPERS attempted to expand shareholder rights, most often by declassifying boards (seven proposals) or requiring independent board committees or directors (five proposals).

There is solid empirical evidence that firms with strong shareholder rights have higher valuations. Gompers, Ishii, and Metrick (2003) analyze the valuation of firms with varying levels of shareholder rights by constructing a shareholder rights score based on a number of firm practices including, for example, the presence of classified boards, unequal shareholder voting rights, and the presence of poison pills. They document that firms with strong shareholder rights (democratic firms) have mean valuations that are 33 percent greater than valuations of firms with few shareholder rights (dictatorial firms). La Porta et al. (2002) document higher valuations for firms in countries with better protection of investor rights. This evidence provides strong support that the nature of reforms pursued by CalPERS, which are clearly designed to expand shareholder rights, should improve shareholder value.

While CalPERS activism connected with focus list firms can be broadly justified from the scientific evidence cited earlier, CalPERS activism is not limited to focus list firms. Two examples are salient.[13] In 2000, CalPERS board voted 7 to 5 to divest all of its holdings in tobacco firms. CalPERS staff did not support the divestiture. Press accounts indicated that Philip Angelides, CalPERS board member and the California State Treasurer, was a strong advocate for this divestiture. Though this decision took place at a time when tobacco stocks were performing poorly, the decision was almost certainly motivated by moral, rather than investment, considerations. There is no evidence—theoretical or empirical—that tobacco firms should or do earn subpar rates of return. In addition, past performance is not a reliable indicator of future performance. In fact, recent evidence suggests sin stocks, like tobacco, earn superior returns precisely because they are spurned by large segments of the investment community (Hong and Kacperczyk 2005). According to press accounts of this decision, the CalPERS board did not consider the political or moral values of CalPERS investors when arriving at their decision.

The decision has proven costly for CalPERS investors. From October 2000 to December 2007, a dollar invested in tobacco stocks has grown to $3.90 while a dollar invested in the S&P 500 has increased to $1.16 cents. Given CalPERS divested of $365 million of tobacco stocks, it is reasonable to assume the CalPERS portfolio has taken a performance hit of about $1 billion.[14] CalSTRS also divested of tobacco stocks around the same time. Ironically, in late 2007 CalSTRS was reconsidering this decision (Chan 2007).

In 2004, Sean Harrigan, then-president of CalPERS board, was a key player in CalPERS involvement in a Safeway labor dispute. In 2003, United Food and Commercial Workers (UFCW) union organized a strike against Safeway over cuts in employees' health care benefits. In December 2003, acting at Harrigan's direction, CalPERS wrote Safeway CEO Steven Burd and urged Mr. Burd to wrap up union negotiations 'fairly and expeditiously' adding that 'fair treatment of employees is a critical element in creating long-term value for shareholders' (WSJ 2004a, 2004b). Besides being CalPERS president, Mr. Harrigan also served as the executive director of the UFCW's Southern California council.[15] If CalPERS intervened in the Safeway case to maximize shareholder value, there is little theory or empirical evidence to support this position. In stark contrast, there is a strong body of economic research supporting a link between shareholder rights and firm value—the main focus of many of CalPERS corporate reform efforts. To be sure, deft handling of labor relations clearly has implications for shareholder value. Unfortunately, there is no scientific evidence that provides an objective measure of good labor relations. This lack of scientific evidence and Harrigan's UFCW connections present obvious concerns about this particular intervention. Ultimately, only 17 percent of shareholders voted against appointing Burd to Safeway's board. The CalPERS board voted to remove Harrigan as a board member in December 2004.

When activism cannot be justified as a mechanism to improve shareholder value, the moral or political objectives of investors, not fund managers, should be considered paramount. It seems reasonable to ask whether the millions of people whose assets are managed by CalPERS would choose to hold tobacco stocks or intervene in labor negotiations.

Conclusion

Institutional activism is a double-edged sword. When prudently applied, shareholder activism can provide effective monitoring of publicly traded corporations. When abused, portfolio managers can pursue social activism to advance their personal agendas at the expense of those whose money they manage.

Social activism involves taking public stands on sensitive issues. Most institutions simply ignore these considerations when investing. Unfortunately, ignoring these considerations is not necessarily in the best interests of investors. It is possible that the vast majority of investors would approve of the divestment of tobacco firms. An institution that ignores these considerations would not be serving investors. It would seem reasonable to require a high level of investor support for an institution to engage in social activism. When institutions engage in social activism that cannot reasonably be expected to maximize shareholder value, the preferences of investors should be given top priority. Institutions must open lines of communication with investors; they must understand how investors stand on moral issues that might affect investment policy.

Moral issues are challenging and nettlesome. But do not throw the baby out with the bath water. Shareholder activism can provide important and effective monitoring of publicly traded firms *and* benefit shareholders. My analysis of announcement reaction of CalPERS focus list firms indicates these targeted and well-reasoned interventions have created $1.9 billion dollars of shareholder value. This is surely an underestimate of the total value of CalPERS activism for several reasons. For example, CalPERS' public announcements may be partially anticipated and convey negative information about managerial entrenchment. I am also unable to measure the value of CalPERS' private negotiations with firms or the extent to which CalPERS activism serves as a deterrent to corporate malfeasance.

Finally, though unreliably positive, the long-run returns of focus list firms are economically large and represent potential long-run gains as high as $39.4 billion.

With rare exceptions, CalPERS interventions in focus list firms are designed to improve shareholder rights. All shareholder proposals at focus list firms sponsored by CalPERS were designed to improve shareholder rights. There is strong empirical evidence that improving shareholder rights improves shareholder value. Institutional activism designed to improve shareholder value should be well grounded in scientific evidence—either theoretical or empirical (preferably both). When moral considerations affect investment policy, investor preferences should be paramount. Institutions should be carefully monitored to ensure they live up to these standards.

Acknowledgments

The author acknowledges Amanda Kimball for valuable research assistance. Ho Ho (CalPERS), Dan Kiefer (CalPERS), Craig Rhines (CalPERS), Ryoko Kita (UC Davis MBA student), and Paul Teng (Wilshire Associates) were very helpful gathering and understanding the data used in this study. David Blitzstein, Eugene Fama, Ken French, Bill Gebhardt, Michael Maher, Olivia Mitchell, Thomas Nyhan, Terrance Odean, Chris Solich, Dennis Trujillo, Robert Yetman, and Michelle Yetman provided valuable comments.

Notes

[1] This chapter is an update of Barber (2007).

[2] I use the phrase portfolio manager for expositional convenience. In practice, the portfolio manager may not be the source of these agency costs. For example, boards that oversee portfolio managers may encourage investment practices to advance board interests rather than investor interests.

[3] Thaler (1992) summarizes evidence that the strong free rider hypothesis is violated in many contexts (e.g., we contribute to public radio, we tip servers at places we will never visit again, we vote in elections when the chance that a single vote will sway an election is exceedingly small).

[4] For example, Qiu (2003) documents public pension fund ownership decreases the probability that a firm will become an acquirer. Several studies argue many acquisitions are motivated by managerial, rather than shareholder, interests. Thus, the decreased acquisitiveness of firms owned by public pension funds arguably redounds to shareholders' benefit.

[5] Each year is considered an independent observation since the event day is common for all firms within a year. Thus, the reader can calculate the t-statistics by

taking the ratio of the mean abnormal return across years and dividing by the standard deviation of the mean annual return.

[6] $600, 000 = 0.5 percent CalPERS ownership of the market times annual market wide wealth creation of $118 million.

[7] These studies include Nesbitt (1994), Del Guercio and Hawkins (1999), Crutchley, Hudson, and Jensen (1998), Prevost and Rao (2000), English, Smythe, and McNeil (2004), and Anson, White, and Ho (2004). All but Del Guercio et al. (1999) conclude the returns of focus list firms at long horizons are reliably positive. Of these studies, only Anson, White, and Ho (2004) explicitly control for the cross-sectional dependence. Del Guercio and Hawkins (1999) and English, Smythe, and McNeil (2004) control for size and value characteristics of focus list firms, which tend to be large value firms with poor recent returns. Crutchley, Hudson, and Jensen (1998) and Anson, White, and Ho (2003, 2004) rely on a market model, where parameters are estimated in the period *before* the focus list announcement. Using parameter estimates from the pre-announcement period will yield expected returns that are biased downward, since focus list firms perform poorly prior to the announcement. Downwardly biased expected returns will yield upwardly biased estimates of abnormal returns (see Nelson [2006]).

[8] See also Barber and Lyon (1997), Kothari and Warner (1997), Lyon, Barber, and Tsai (1999), Fama (1998), and Mitchell and Stafford (2000) for a discussion of these issues.

[9] The factor data and the details of their construction are available on Dr. Ken French's Web site: http://mba.tuck.dartmouth.edu/pages/faculty/ken.french/.

[10] Several firms are included on the CalPERS focus list in multiple years. Each firm is represented in the focus list portfolio only once. For example, in 1992 the focus list portfolio begins with a position in Chrysler. In 1993, Chrysler is again included on the CalPERS focus list. The focus list portfolio that assumes a holding period of two years would contain only one position in Chrysler, which would be divested two years after Chrysler's last inclusion on the CalPERS focus list.

[11] At the two week and five year horizon, the size factor is negative but not reliably different from zero.

[12] The long-run gain at four years is negative, while the mean alpha in Table 15-2 is positive at the same horizon. This is because the gains of Figure 15-3 depend on the alpha, size of the portfolio, and unexplained return (residual) on each day.

[13] There are other examples of activism unrelated to shareholder rights. CACI International has also been criticized by a CalPERS board member for having three civilian interrogators who are under Army investigation for their roles at Abu Graib prison. CalPERS was also widely criticized for voting against the appointment of Warren Buffett to Coca-Cola's board of directors. The vote against Buffett was a result of a policy of voting against audit committee members who approved significant non-audit contracts for the companies' auditors. This policy has been subsequently changed. CalPERS has also criticized auto companies for filing suit over California's clean car regulations.

[14] This estimate assumes: (1) CalPERS tobacco holdings earned returns similar to the industry returns, (2) divested tobacco stocks were invested in the S&P

500, and (3) divestment occurred month-end October, 2000. Tobacco industry returns are from Ken French's data library of industry returns using 30 industry portfolios.
[15] Public pension funds for Illinois, Connecticut, California, and the city and state of New York withheld support for Burd. Some published reports indicate the reason for their lack of support was Safeway's poor corporate performance, Burd's joint position as CEO and Board Chairman, and the lack of independence of Safeway's board.

References

Admati, Anat R., Paul Pfleiderer, and Josef Zechner (1994). 'Large Shareholder Activism, Risk Sharing, and Financial Market Equilibrium,' *Journal of Political Economy*, 102: 1097–130.

Anson, Mark, Ted White, and Ho Ho (2003). 'The Shareholder Wealth Effects of CalPERS Focus List,' *Journal of Applied Corporate Finance*, 15: 102–11.

—— (2004). 'Good Corporate Governance Works: More Evidence from CalPERS,' *Journal of Asset Management*, 5: 149–56.

Barber, Brad M. (2007). 'Monitoring the Monitor: Evaluating CalPERS Activism,' *The Journal of Investing*, Winter.

—— John D. Lyon (1997). 'Detecting Long-run Abnormal Stock Returns: The Empirical Power and Specification of Test Statistics,' *Journal of Financial Economics*, 43: 341–72.

Chan, Gilbert (2007). 'CalSTRS rethinks tobacco investment ban,' Sacramento Bee, September 6, p. D3.

Crutchley, Claire E., Carl D. Hudson, and Marlin R.H. Jensen (1998). 'Shareholder Wealth Effects of CalPERS' Activism,' *Financial Services Review*, 7: 1–10.

Del Guercio, Diane and Jennifer Hawkins (1999). 'The Motivation and Impact of Pension Fund Activism,' *Journal of Financial Economics*, 52: 293–340.

English, Philip C., Thomas I. Smythe, and Chris R. McNeil (2004). 'The "CalPERS effect" Revisited,' *Journal of Corporate Finance*, 10: 157–74.

Fama, Eugene F. (1998). 'Market Efficiency, Long-Term Returns, and Behavioral Finance,' *Journal of Financial Economics*, 49: 283–306.

Gompers, Paul, Joy Ishii, and Andrew Metrick (2003). 'Corporate Governance and Equity Prices,' *Quarterly Journal of Economics*, 118: 107–55.

Hong, Harrison G. and Marcin T. Kacperczyk (2005). '*The Price of Sin: The Effects of Social Norms on Markets*,' Sauder School of Business Working Paper. Vancouver, BC: Sauder School of Business, University of British Columbia.

Kothari, S.P. and Jerold B. Warner (1997). 'Measuring Long-horizon Security Price Performance,' *Journal of Financial Economics*, 43: 301–39.

La Porta, Rafael, Florencio Lopez-De-Silanes, Andrei Shleifer, and Robert Vishny (2002). 'Investor Protection and Corporate Valuation,' *Journal of Finance*, 57: 1147–70.

Lyon, John D., Brad M. Barber, and Chih-Ling Tsai (1999). 'Improved Methods for Detecting Long-Run Abnormal Stock Returns,' *Journal of Finance*, 54: 165–201.

Mitchell, Mark L. and Erik Stafford (2000). 'Managerial Decisions and Long-Term Stock Price Performance,' *The Journal of Business*, 73: 287–329.

Nelson, James M. (2006). 'The "CalPERS effect" Revisited Again,' *Journal of Corporate Finance*, 12: 187–213.

Nesbitt, Stephen L. (1994). 'Long-term Rewards from Shareholder Activism: A Study of the "CalPERS Effect," ' *Journal of Applied Corporate Finance*, 6: 75–80.

Prevost, Andrew K. and Ramesh P. Rao (2000). 'Of What Value are Shareholder Proposals Sponsored by Public Pension Funds?,' *Journal of Business*, 73: 177–204.

Qiu, Lily Xiaoli (2003). '*Public Pension Fund Activism And M&A Activity.*' Yale ICF Working Paper No. 03–24. New Haven, CT: The International Center for Finance at the Yale School of Management, Yale University.

Romano, Roberta (1993a). 'Public Pension Fund Activism in Corporate Governance Reconsidered,' *Columbia Law Review*, 93, 795–853.

—— (1993b). 'Getting Politics out of Public Pension Funds,' *American Enterprise*, 4: 42–9.

—— (1995). 'The Politics of Public Pension Funds,' *Public Interest*, 119: 42–53.

Smith, Michael (1996). 'Shareholder Activism by Institutional Investors: Evidence from CalPERS,' *Journal of Finance*, 51: 227–52.

Thaler, Richard H. (1992). *The Winner's Curse: Paradoxes and Anomalies of Economic Life*. Princeton, NJ: Princeton University Press.

Wahal, Sunil (1996). 'Public Pension Fund Activism and Firm Performance,' *Journal of Financial Quantitative Analysis*, 31: 1–23.

Wall Street Journal (WSJ) (2004a). 'Gadfly activism at CalPERS leads to possible ouster of president,' December 1, p. A1.

—— (2004b). 'Moving the Market,' December 2, p. C3.

Chapter 16

The New Intersection on the Road to Retirement: Public Pensions, Economics, Perceptions, Politics, and Interest Groups

Beth Almeida, Kelly Kenneally, and David Madland

US state and local pension plans have served as the cornerstone of retirement security for generations of teachers, police officers, firefighters, and other public servants for the last century. State and local governments continue to offer secure pension benefits to some 20 million workers and retirees, or 12 percent of the nation's workforce. As a group, these systems offer a cost-effective way to recruit, retain, and retire the workforce needed to deliver essential public services. But despite the strengths of the system, opposition to state and local pensions has emerged in recent years. Legislatures in several states including Alaska, California, Colorado, and Utah, have considered proposals that would drastically change how public employee retirement systems function. This chapter considers the question of how perceptions, politics, and interest groups—rather than sound economic and policy analyses—are shaping public pensions.

We begin with an overview of how state and local pension systems ensure retirement income adequacy for public employees and discuss how these systems are financed. We contrast the successful model of state and local pension systems with trends in the private sector toward increasing insecurity in retirement. We then turn to a discussion of how the public views pensions and the factors that drive public opinion on this issue. Finally, we examine the role that politics and ideological interest groups are playing in state policymaking and the overall public pension debate.

Public pensions and retirement living standards

Retirement security trends in the United States are troubling. Retirement plan coverage is declining in the private sector, personal savings are non-existent for most households, and six in 10 Americans are at risk of being unable to sustain their standard of living in retirement (Purcell 2007; Bureau of Economic Analysis 2008; Munnell et al. 2008*b*). But in the midst of this gloomy picture, there is a beacon of light: employees in the public sector are generally well positioned for a secure retirement, and state and local retirement systems stand out as a notable success story.

Traditionally, state and local employees are very likely to have access to at least one retirement plan at work and their primary plan is almost always a defined benefit (DB) pension plan. Three-quarters of state and local employees have a retirement plan, and of these, the majority, 86 percent, were covered by a DB plan in 2004 (Munnell, Haverstick, and Soto 2007). In a typical public sector DB plan, employees earn a benefit based on years of service and career-end salary (usually an average of the final three years' salary). The median benefit for Social Security-eligible public employees is 1.85 percent for each year of service. This means that after working 30 years, an employee would be eligible for a pension that would replace 55.5 percent of final earnings—an amount that, when added to Social Security and private saving, should meet generally-recognized standards of retirement income adequacy.[1] It is important to note that about one fourth of state and local employees do not participate in Social Security. For these groups, the median pension formula is higher—2.2 percent per year of service—which provides a benefit equal to 66 percent of final earnings after 30 years (Brainard 2007).

Almost all state and local employees also have the opportunity to participate in defined contribution (DC) plans, which in the public sector are known as 457(b) plans and/or 403(b) plans. Most states that offer a DB plan also offer a voluntary DC plan as a supplement, but participation rates tend to be low (GAO 2007a). For example, just 6 percent of state and local employees participated in both a DB plan and a supplemental DC plan in 2004 (Munnell, Haverstick, and Soto 2007). Low rates of voluntary participation could reflect the fact that public employees typically make substantial contributions to their DB plans, a fact which will be discussed further in the following text.

In a DC plan, benefits in retirement will depend on various factors including the amount contributed by employer and employee; the length of time funds remain in the account; whether funds are withdrawn; the amount of investment earnings; and the fees charged to the account. In a typical DC plan, there is a high degree of employee direction. The employee must decide how much to contribute (if at all), how to invest the funds, and how to make changes to these factors over time. Well-designed DC plans can be helpful supplements to DB plans, as they allow employees to save additional funds for retirement on a tax-advantaged basis that is in line with their own unique needs and circumstances. But DC plans can be problematic when they serve as the primary retirement vehicle, since workers generally fail to save enough, make poor asset allocation and investment decisions, cash out their accounts when they change jobs, and are reluctant to annuitize retirement wealth accumulated, even when doing so could enhance their well-being (Mitchell and Utkus 2004; GAO 2007*b*).

The state of Nebraska is a high-profile example of a public sector employer that for more than three decades offered a DC plan as the primary retirement plan to a large number of public employees, while it offered other state employees a DB plan. Yet that state found that the DC plan was not adequate to ensure that all workers would have sufficient retirement income, so in 2003 it established a new cash-balance DB plan for employees who otherwise would have had to rely only on the DC. This was done after concluding: 'We have had over 35 years to "test" this experiment and find generally that our defined contribution plan members retire with lower benefits than their defined benefit plan counterparts' (House Committee on Pensions and Investments 2000: 32). These and other research findings suggest that DB plans are a key component of a retirement system that seeks to ensure that employees will have sufficient assets to meet their needs in retirement (Engen, Gale, and Uccello 2005; Munnell, Webb, and Delorme 2006).

Because of their widespread access to DB plans (and in many cases, supplemental DC plans), most workers in state and local government have a good chance to earn retirement benefits that allow them to maintain a middle-class standard of living even after they stop working.[2] Retirement assets per worker in public sector retirement plans are more than two times greater than those in private sector plans (Munnell, Haverstick, and Soto 2007). The median public sector retiree receives a benefit of $22,000 per year. This amount, when combined with other reserves such as Social Security and/or private savings, provides middle-class teachers, public safety workers, and other public workers with the ability to maintain their living standards in retirement (McDonald 2008).

Public pension plans are a fiscally responsible way to finance retirement

The financing of state and local pensions is a shared responsibility between the employer (taxpayer) and employees. This is a key difference between DB plans in the public sector as compared to the private sector. In the private sector, the financing of promised benefits is typically the sole responsibility of the employer. Social Security-eligible public sector employees typically contribute 5 percent of pay to their pension plans, while non-Social Security eligible employees contribute 8.5 percent (Brainard 2009).

This model of cost-sharing is viewed positively by taxpayers, according to public opinion surveys to be discussed in the following text.

State and local pension DB plans tend to be funded rather than financed on a pay-as-you-go basis. Employer and employee contributions to these public pension plans are pooled in a trust and invested. The earnings on these investments help finance the benefits which eventually are paid out (Steffen 2001). In fact, investment earnings pay for the greatest share of benefits earned in public sector DB plans. Over the past decade, almost three-fourths of the funds that have flowed into state and local pension plans have been investment earnings. Only about one-fifth came from employer (taxpayer) contributions, and the remainder came from employee contributions (authors' calculation based on data from US Census Bureau 1996–2006).

Because of their group nature, public sector DB plans create significant economies for taxpayers and employees. Investment decisions in these plans are made by professionals, whose activities are overseen by trustees or other fiduciaries. This is in contrast to most DC plans where individuals often make poor investment decisions, where their inertia subjects their portfolios to acute imbalance, or at the other extreme, where engagement in excessive trading results in 'buying high and selling low' (Mitchell and Utkus 2004; Munnell and Sunden 2004). By contrast, public pension plan managers follow a long-term investment strategy (Weller and Wenger 2008). By pooling assets, DB plans can drive down administrative costs and reduce asset management and other fees (Hustead 2009). Asset management fees average just 25 basis points for public pension plans. By comparison, asset management fees for private 401(k) plans range from 60 to 170 basis points (Munnell, Haverstick, and Soto 2007). Because of these two effects, professional investment management and lower fees, it should not be surprising that professionally managed DB plans consistently outperform individually managed DC plans. One widely-cited estimate puts the difference in annual return at 0.8 percent (Munnell and Sunden 2004). Over a 30-year time period, this would compound to a 25 percent difference in total return.

DB plans create additional economies for participants and plan sponsors by pooling mortality and other risks. Mortality risk refers to the fact that an individual does not know his ultimate life span, which makes it extremely difficult to know exactly how much is needed to be certain that one will not outlive those savings. In a system of individual accounts, each person must accumulate enough saving to last for the maximum lifespan. By pooling the mortality risks of large numbers of people, DB plans need only accumulate assets sufficient to fund the *average* life expectancy. Thus, a DB plan will require fewer assets to be accumulated than a comparable DC plan, reducing costs by 15 percent to 35 percent (Fuerst 2004).[3] By combining the effects of professional management, lower fees, and risk pooling, actuaries have determined that DB plans are much more efficient than DC plans and that they provide pension benefits at a far lower cost (Fuerst 2004; Waring and Siegel 2007). Thus, to the extent that public retirement systems are supported (at least partially) by taxpayer funds, a DB plan design supports the goal of fiscal responsibility (Hustead 2009).

Despite their financial advantages, state and local DB plans have attracted attention from policymakers, researchers, the media, and others in recent years, because average funding levels had been on the decline, and in some cases, because of rising contribution requirements (GAO 2007*a*). As we will discuss in greater detail, DB plan funding levels have become a central focus of interest groups and others who seek to replace these plans with DC plans. Clearly, DB plans' funded status tends to ebb and flow over time with the ups and downs of asset markets, interest rates, and other macroeconomic factors. The funded status—the ratio of existing plan assets to the totality of current and future benefits—of state and local DB plans fell in the wake of the downturn in asset markets at the beginning of the 2000 decade, just as it did for DB plans in the private sector and other institutional investors. Prior to the downturn, public sector plans as a group had reported being fully funded (Brainard 2004). Of course there were exceptions to this general rule; a Government Accountability Office (GAO 2008) study reported that while most plans were soundly funded, 'a few have been persistently underfunded.' It concluded, 'Governments can gradually recover from these [stock market] losses. However, the failure of some to consistently make the annual required contributions undermines that progress and is cause for concern...' (GAO 2008: 26). In other words, regardless of the type of plan (DB or DC), if a plan sponsor postpones paying for it, the bill will grow and become more expensive to pay when it finally comes due.

For a solvent public plan sponsor, it may be neither critical nor particularly important for the DB pension to be constantly 'fully funded.' This is because a DB pension has a long time horizon, since benefits earned by participants in the plan do not have to be paid immediately. As a result, many DB plans take the long view, especially for public DB plans because they are backed by government entities that (unlike private corporations) have a very low risk of insolvency. In this instance, periodic swings in the plan's funded status can be viewed as a normal and expected feature. Cyclical downturns tend to be followed by improvements in asset markets, a phenomenon that economists describe as 'mean reversion' (Poterba and Summers 1988). Indeed, as asset returns have recovered and contributions increased in recent years, the average public plan's funded status has improved. In fiscal year 2006, for instance, the average plan was 85.8

percent funded (Brainard 2007). The GAO reports that 'a funded ratio of 80 percent or more is within the range that many public sector experts, union officials, and advocates view as a healthy pension system' (GAO 2007*a*: 35).

Proper funding may be harder to achieve in defined contribution plans

Some argue that the routine swings in funding that DB plans experience create untenable volatility in contributions for plan sponsors, but this is not necessarily the case. Disciplined funding practices and rules that reflect the going concern nature of DB pension plans can reduce the funding volatility of a pension plan, especially for public sector plans (Weller and Baker 2005; Weller, Price, and Margolis 2006; Giertz and Papke 2007). DC plan advocates also claim that because of the nature of the employer commitment in a DC plan (the employer simply commits to making a contribution rather than promising a certain benefit), such plans are always 'fully funded.' However, it is important to recognize that 'underfunding' *can and does* exist in a DC system, but it takes a different form. That is, when individuals compare the actual level of assets in their DC plan to what would be required to support an adequate retirement, they may find that their retirement needs are seriously underfunded.

From this perspective, the level of underfunding in DC plans is striking. According to the GAO, workers age 55–64 had a median account balance of $50,000 in 2004. If this were converted into an annuity at age 65, such an amount would provide an income of only $4,400 per year (GAO 2007*b*). Moreover, the GAO identified gaps in workers' ability to accumulate adequate retirement assets in DC plans, gaps that do not exist to the same degree with DB plans where participation typically is mandatory. That report concluded: 'DC plans can provide a meaningful contribution to retirement security for some workers but may not ensure the retirement security of lower-income workers' (GAO 2007*b*: 2).

This GAO 401(k) plan study stands in stark contrast to the agency's recent study of public sector DB plans, which concluded that the latter are generally on track to being fully funded. GAO found that the projected fiscal impact of fully funding pension obligations will be modest, so that state and local governments will be able to meet their future commitments with just a modicum of effort: 'Estimated future pension costs (currently about 9 percent of employee pay) would require an increase in annual government contribution rates of less than a half percent' (GAO 2007*a*: 2).

To fill the gap in retirement wealth for DC plans, most researchers estimate substantially larger increases in contribution rates would be required (VanDerhei 2006).

How the public perceives pension plans

Despite the health of public sector DB plans, legislatures in several states including Alaska, California, Colorado, and Utah, have recently considered whether to transition from a DB to a DC-only system. This may be because public policy debates can be driven by perceptions, politics, and interest groups rather than economic factors. We turn next to an evaluation of public opinion on the merits of DB plans compared to DC plans. As we shall show, the public's knowledge base is low; the public is divided about which one of the two systems is better; and judgments about the merits of one type of plan over the other are driven largely by ideological concerns and self-interest.

Low Knowledge Base. The US public does not know much about different types of pension plans. One survey showed that 40 percent of respondents said they have little knowledge of either 401(k) plans or DB plans (Hart Research Associates 2006). Workers also know relatively little about their own retirement plans (Mitchell 1988; Gustman and Steinmeier 1989; Reynolds, Ridley, and Van Horn 2005; Lusardi 2007). Further, a substantial minority of people will not even venture a guess as to the type of plan in place (Reynolds, Ridley, and Van Horn 2005). Perhaps the most striking evidence of the low level of knowledge is that only half of older workers could correctly identify whether they had a DB, DC, or combination plan (Gustman and Steinmeier 2004). As a result, expressed opinions about different types of pension plans should be seen against the very low level of information for most members of the public.

Public Opinion Divided on the Relative Merits of DB and DC. Little research exists about the public's preferences for DB or DC plans (Madland 2007). Available research indicates that, if forced to choose, people are evenly split about the merits of each type of plan. For example, in two nationally representative surveys, one found a slight preference for DBs but the other found a slight preference for DCs. (The question wording appears to explain the difference in the results.) A June 2005 Heldrich Center for Workforce Development at Rutgers University survey (Reynolds, Ridley, and Van Horn 2005) of 800 people currently in the workforce asked whether workers would prefer to receive their retirement benefits 'based on salary and years of service' or based on 'how much money is in the account.' A slight majority (51%) said they would prefer to receive retirement benefits based on salary and years of service, while 37 percent would prefer to do so based on how much is in the account, with 11 percent unable or unwilling to answer. A 2006 survey of 804 registered voters conducted by Hart Research Associates (2006) asked: 'Which is generally the better overall kind of retirement plan for workers—a pension plan or a 401(k)-type saving plan?' A slight majority (52%) answered that a 401(k) is better for workers, while 33 percent said a pension plan is better, with 15 percent unsure or unable to decide. This latter survey also asked what type of retirement plan public employees should have. Results are similarly divided. When asked about 'proposed change from pensions to 401(k)s for public employees,' 47 percent of voters strongly or somewhat opposed the plan, 44 percent of voters strongly or somewhat favored the proposal, and 9 percent said they were unsure.

Public Opinion Driven by Ideology and Self-Interest. Why people prefer one type of retirement plan over another is likely guided by the same forces that drive public opinion on a range of other economic policies: ideology and self-interest. Public opinion research commonly (although not always) finds that self-interest shapes how people think about economic policy questions (Cook and Barret 1992; Hasenfeld and Rafferty 1989; Ponza et al. 1989; Blekesaune and Quadagno 2003). If people believe that a policy will personally benefit them, they are more likely to support it. As a result, we should expect that, for example, government employees would be more likely to oppose switching public DB to DC plans. In fact, public employees should be especially likely to support DB plans because unions and other organizations communicate with them about the benefits of keeping such plans in the face of policy proposals to switch to DC plans. When organizations publicize issues, they prime people to think about the personal costs and benefits of an issue, making it more likely that people recognize their own self-interest and take action (Chong, Citrin, and Conley 2001).

Demographic factors such as age, income, and education, also help determine whether people believe that a given policy is in their self-interest and thus these factors also affect their policy preferences (Hasenfeld and Rafferty 1989; Ponza et al. 1989; Cook and Barret 1992; Blekesaune and Quadagno 2003). Ideology also is often theoretically and empirically linked to policy preferences (Hartz 1955; Schlozman and Verba 1979; McClosky and Zaller 1984; Feldman and Zaller 1992; Hasenfeld and Rafferty 1989; Cook and Barret 1992; Blekesaune and Quadagno 2003; Madland 2007). Americans tend not to have fully-fledged ideologies where every issue position matches a basic principle, and they tend to be rather ambivalent about their ideological leanings (Converse 1962; Free and Cantril 1968; Feldman and Zaller 1992; Hochschild 1981; Madland 2007). Nevertheless, Americans do have ideological leanings toward an individualistic, self-reliant ethic (Hartz 1955; Schlozman and Verba 1979), especially when compared to people in other countries. For example, surveys find that people of other nationalities are more likely to believe the government is responsible for providing a secure retirement, while Americans tend to believe they are personally responsible. A recent American Association of Retired People (AARP) poll found that half of all Americans believe individuals are responsible for themselves in retirement, compared to fewer than 40 percent of British and Germans, and fewer than 20 percent of French and Italians (AARP 2005).

While Americans may be more individualistic than other nationalities, they are not totally opposed to more collective solutions for retirement, supporting a division of responsibility between individuals, government, and employers for retirement savings. When asked in the 2005 Heldrich poll (Reynolds, Ridley, and Van Horn 2005): 'Who do you think should be primarily responsible for helping workers prepare for retirement? Workers, employers or the government?' some 39 percent of those surveyed said workers, 25 percent said employers, and 18 percent said government. Seventeen percent volunteered that all three should be responsible.

A related question in the 2006 Hart poll found similar results. The Hart survey asked: 'Do you personally think that being able to retire with financial security is a right that society should protect for all working people, or a personal goal that people are responsible for achieving on their own?' Forty seven percent of voters answered that retirement is 'a personal goal that people are responsible for achieving on their own,' while 39 percent answered that 'being able to retire with financial security' is a 'right for all working people.' Eleven percent of people surveyed answered 'both'—a choice that respondents had to volunteer on their own.

Ideological leanings would also seem likely to shape people's preferences for DB or DC plans. People who believe that the right way to live in retirement is to depend upon themselves rather than the government or the employer would be predicted to prefer DC over DB plans. A quick comparison of ideology and pension plan preference supports this expectation, and it shows that people who think individuals should be responsible for their own retirement are about 50 percent more likely to prefer DC plans than people whose ideology is not as individualistic.[4]

The expectation that ideology and self-interest influence how people think about DC and DB plans is tested more rigorously in the three regression models presented in Table 16.1 in the following text, using data from the Reynolds, Ridley, and Van Horn (2005) and Hart Research Associates (2006) public opinion surveys. Both surveys were nationally representative. The explanatory variables in each model include age, sex, education, income, union status, employment sector (public or private), the type of retirement plan a person has, and indicators of ideology and political party. Women appear to prefer interventions in the economy (Alvarez and McCaffery 2003) and thus are expected to be more supportive of DB

TABLE 16-1 Empirical determinants of the public's self-reported preferences for plan type and plan features

	Model Specification 1 Dependent Variable: Support for switching to 401(k) for public employees	Model Specification 2 Dependent Variable: Preference for a 401(k)-type savings plan	Model Specification 3 Dependent Variable: Preference for receiving benefits based on account balance.
	Coefficient	Coefficient	Coefficient
(Constant)	2.538	0.106	0.020
	(0.243)	(0.540)	(0.152)
Age	0.015	0.032	0.004
	(0.020)	(0.048)	(0.023)
Female	−0.259***	0.033	−0.026
	(0.106)	(0.245)	(0.052)
Education	−0.057	−0.042	0.015
	(0.039)	(0.088)	(0.026)
Income	−0.024	0.039	0.061***
	(0.030)	(0.069)	(0.019)
Union member	0.057	−0.136	−0.141**
	(0.150)	(0.324)	(0.072)
Public employee	−0.396***	−0.501**	−0.124**
	(0.125)	(0.275)	(0.068)
Have 401(k)	0.077	−0.048	0.131*
	(0.124)	(0.296)	(0.095)
Have DB pension	−0.018	−0.926***	−0.327***
	(0.154)	(0.347)	(0.103)
Individualistic ideology	0.201***	0.226**	0.079*
	(0.059)	(0.134)	(0.053)
Republican party support	−0.024	0.096	0.033
	(0.036)	(0.084)	(0.030)
	n=387	n=341	n=287

Notes: Reference category is not having a 401(k) or DB. Significance listed based on one-tailed tests.

* significant at greater than .1
** significant at greater than .05
*** significant at greater than .01

Sources: Authors' analysis of data from Hart Research Associates (2005 and 2006).

pensions. For partisan identification, a concept closely interrelated with ideology, people who identify with the Republican Party are less likely to support economic intervention and thus would be expected to be less supportive of DB pensions (Hasenfeld and Rafferty 1989; Cook and Barret 1992). Members of labor unions are more likely to support policies to ameliorate perceived flaws in the market, both because of their group interest as well as the greater likelihood that union leadership has framed the issue and communicated it to them (Nelson and Kinder 1996; Glasgow 2005). Finally, people's own experience with a DB or DC plan may shape their preferences, with people tending to support the kind of plan they have because they are more familiar with it. The dependent variables measure people's preferences for DB or DC plans for themselves and government employees, as described earlier.

The results indicate that ideology and self-interest are very strong predictors of people's opinions about DC and DB plans. People who believe in an individualistic ideology are much more likely to support DC plans, while people who work in the public sector are less likely to do so. In fact, these two variables—individualistic ideology and working in the public sector—are the only variables that are statistically significant in all three models. The result that ideology and self-interest drive public opinion about retirement plans is robust and holds up in alternative specifications. All other variables that are statistically significant in any of the models— such as women opposing changing public employee pensions to 401(k) plans—are in the predicted direction.

These results suggest that where voters and policymakers are predisposed to a particular ideological viewpoint, they may be swayed as much by political considerations as economic ones when it comes to making decisions about the ideal design of public pensions. Next, we turn to examine how political forces have played out in recent debates about the future of public pensions.

The role of politics and interest groups in the public sector DB debate

Given that there does not appear to be a groundswell of public concern about DB plans, and taking into account the public's lukewarm impressions on retirement plan design, an obvious question arises: Why have public sector DB plans become a political battleground in some states? One explanation is that partisan politics may play a role. Another explanation is that interest groups ideologically predisposed to more individualistic approaches to retirement may have been able to generate enough political momentum to raise the design of public sector pension plans as a public policy issue, despite the overall sound financial footing of public pensions. In this section, we first explore the issue of partisan views on retirement policy. We then provide an overview of some key interest groups that have focused on public pensions and highlight their role in recent state initiatives to convert public sector DB plans to DC plans.

Partisanship and Pensions. There is evidence that politics has been a key factor in recent debates on public sector DB plans. Munnell et al. (2008*a*) statistically examine the question of why some states have adopted DC plans as a primary plan, while others have not. They find that Republican control of the governorship and the state legislature is the greatest single predictor of whether a state made the switch to a DC plan. Other influential factors included union presence and sizeable employee pension contributions, both of which tended to reduce the likelihood of DC adoption. Surprisingly, other factors like lack of Social Security coverage and the plan's funded status did not have a statistically significant effect on whether a plan made a switch to DC. This finding is reinforced in the case studies presented in the following text. In Utah, California, and Alaska, the pension systems were all more than 80 percent funded, yet proposals were made (and in Alaska, adopted) to convert the system to a DC plan.

One explanation for these findings is that Republicans typically support DC plans because employees control the investments. DC plans are consistent with that party's political philosophy of individual responsibility for retirement savings. Thus, when Republicans are in control, changes or attempts at changing the nature of public pensions have been seen (Munnell et al. 2008*a*). However, the results from our analysis of opinion research indicate a paradox; individual Republicans are no more likely to support a switch to DC, after controlling for other factors (see Figure 16.1).

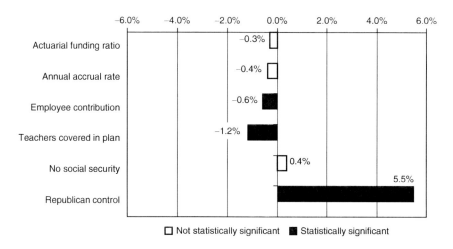

Figure 16-1 Effect of various factors on the probability of introducing a defined contribution plan. *Source*: Adapted from Munnell et al. (2008*a*).

Interest Groups and the Public Sector DB Debate. Another factor that has received less attention from researchers is the role of interest groups in advocating for changes to public pension systems. An interest group can be defined as an organized body of individuals sharing goals and who try to influence public policy (Berry 1989).

Throughout American history, interest groups have played a role in American politics. During the New Deal, the role of business interest groups was seen to influence policies that led to the formation of regulatory agencies. More recently it has been suggested that interest groups are growing too strong: one study showed the number of new interest groups grew 30 percent from 1960–80 (Berry 1989). Another study found a similar pattern, showing that 40 percent of interest groups were founded after 1960 and 25 percent after 1970 (Berry 1989). Both surveys showed that citizen groups were likely to have formed recently and confirmed that the increase is not a function of exaggerated rhetoric about the perils of modern interest groups.

Today's interest groups engage in a wide variety of activities. They may lobby branches of government at the local, state, or federal level. They also may seek to educate the American public or policymakers about issues, but they typically present only their side of an issue, offering facts and interpretations most favorable to their position. They are also active in agenda building: that is, interest groups frequently are responsible for bringing attention to their issue or position. These groups are consistent in pushing government to develop policies that, while advantageous to their own small constituency, do not benefit the broader public (Berry 1989).

In recent years, national and state-based interest groups have become key players in challenging the continuation of public sector DB plans and advocating a switch to DC plans. Tom Lussier, a former Massachusetts state legislator and pension system executive director, provided insight on the evolution of interest group involvement in public pensions. He indicated that, prior to the 1980s, state and local pensions were not on the radar screen of interest groups. But as public DB plans began investing in equities and the assets began to grow significantly, the plans became a target of interest groups active in pursuing anti-tax, free market, and individual responsibility/savings philosophies. These philosophies often did not take into consideration the economic benefits and efficiencies of public pensions (Lussier 2008).

The agenda pursued by these anti-tax, free market groups is perhaps best summed up by Grover Norquist, of the interest group Americans for Tax Reform (ATR). He said of public sector DB plans, 'just 115 people control $1 trillion in these funds. We want to take that power and destroy it' (Dreyfuss 2001: 16). Norquist and his group view public DB pensions as a battleground issue and they have actively planned state-by-state campaigns to dismantle public pension plans (Dreyfuss 2001). In recent years, like-minded groups including the American Legislative Exchange Council, Americans for Prosperity, the Club for Growth, the Manhattan Institute, and the Reason Foundation have sought to influence public opinion with reports, briefing papers, opinion pieces, and model legislation advocating DC over DB plans.

American Legislative Exchange Council. Founded in 1973, the American Legislative Exchange Council (ALEC) is a membership association for conservative state lawmakers who share 'a common belief in limited government, free markets, federalism, and individual liberty' (ALEC 2008a: 5). The organization generates research, policy papers and model legislation covering various issues before state governments.

In 2000, ALEC published an issue paper which argued that public employees should have access to 401(k) plans (Lathrop and Singer 2000). The paper did not acknowledge that access to DC plans was already widespread for state and local employees. Additionally, ALEC offered model legislation to state legislators promoting DC plans for public employees as a replacement for DB pensions (ALEC 2008b). This model legislation was introduced in Florida in 2000; though it was not adopted, the Florida legislature did enact a DC option for public employees (Lathrop and Singer 2000). The sponsor of the legislation, State Representative Ken Pruitt, was awarded ALEC's 'Hero of the Taxpayer' award winner. Pruitt was also nominated by ATR for ALEC's legislator of the year award. An ATR press release said that Pruitt was 'boldly paving the way for similar reforms across the country' (ATR 2000).

Americans for Prosperity. Americans for Prosperity is a Washington, DC non-profit organization that engages citizens to promote limited government and free markets on the local, state, and federal levels. The organization describes itself as working to educate citizens about economic policy and mobilizing citizens as advocates in the public policy process (Americans for Prosperity 2008). The organization has proposed closing down DB plans in favor of DC plans for public employees on the grounds that the latter are 'fairer to employees, employers, and taxpayers—and they do not incur unfunded liabilities' (Poulson 2006). The organization became involved with efforts in Colorado to change the public retirement system from DB to DC, to be discussed in the following text in greater detail.

Americans for Tax Reform. ATR is a national non-profit lobbying organization established to oppose tax increases, founded in 1985 by Grover Norquist. It serves as a national clearinghouse for a taxpayers' movement by working with approximately 800 state and county level groups. In recent years, ATR also has been active in efforts to privatize Social Security (ATR 2008). ATR's former chief economist Daniel Clifton has stated that the organization fully supports moving to a system of DC plans for state and local employees (Clifton 2004). A 2002 ATR policy brief on pension reform argues that states should move aggressively to transfer all state and local employees and schoolteachers from DB to DC plans to 'make full scale pension liberation a reality' (Ferrara 2002). The brief further argues that DC plans allow workers to earn higher benefits than traditional pension plans, save the employer administrative and funding costs, and help public employers recruit the best workers. In practice, DC plans have pitfalls when they are used as a primary retirement vehicle and often provide lower returns for workers, they are typically more expensive for employers for any given level of benefit, and they already are available as supplements to almost all public employees who desire to participate in them, facts not noted in ATR's writings on public pensions. Nevertheless, ATR endorsed DB to DC switch initiatives in California, and its reports were used to justify a successful proposal in Alaska to switch to a DC plan (Broder 2005; Persily 2005*a*).

Club for Growth. Established in 1999, this organization seeks to advance public policies that promote economic growth primarily through legislative involvement, issue advocacy, research, training, and educational activity. Its policy goals include cutting taxes, limiting government spending, and privatizing Social Security. The organization has a related political action committee that makes campaign contributions to candidates running for office, specifically in Republican primaries (Club for Growth 2008). Through its campaign-related activities, the Club for Growth actively supports Republican candidates looking to unseat moderate Republicans that the group deems at odds with its anti-tax, limited government agenda (Dewar 2004).

The Club was a particularly determined supporter of President Bush's 2005 campaign to overhaul Social Security by adding individual private accounts and spent millions to lobby on its behalf (Bailey 2005). The Club for Growth also was involved with the California pro-DC initiative, with a former director advocating for a DB to DC switch (Broder 2005). More recently, as part of its evaluation of candidates vying for the Republican presidential nomination, the group singled out former Massachusetts governor Mitt Romney, praising him for 'proposing to revolutionize the Massachusetts state pension system by moving it from a defined benefit system to a defined contribution system' (Club for Growth 2007: 5).

The Howard Jarvis Taxpayers Association. Founded in 1978, the Howard Jarvis Taxpayers Association is dedicated to the protection of Proposition 13, the California measure to cap property taxes, and the advancement of taxpayers' rights. This includes the 'right to limited taxation, the right to vote on tax increases and the right of economical, equitable and efficient use of taxpayer dollars' (Howard Jarvis Taxpayers Association 2008). This organization in 2005 indicated that it planned to put the DB to DC issue on the California ballot through the initiative process (Associated

Press 2005*b*). In 2007, the organization issued a study asserting that 'California's pensions are getting shakier' (Taub 2007), while the California Public Employees' Retirement System (CalPERS) and the California State Teachers' Retirement System (CalSTRS) disputed the findings. CalPERS called the report 'a highly contrived, biased study that fails to show the big picture' that 'hinged on a "snapshot" view of activity artificially constrained to a period of market downturn and the early stages of its recovery' (Taub 2007).

The Manhattan Institute. Established in 1978, the Manhattan Institute is a non-profit organization that aims to develop policy ideas that foster economic choice and individual responsibility (Manhattan Institute 2008). In a 2003 report entitled 'Defusing the Pension Bomb: How to Curb Public Retirement Costs in New York State,' Manhattan senior fellow E. J. McMahon contended that greater fairness for taxpayers and better retirement benefits for most government employees can be achieved by switching from the current DB pension system to a DC model. McMahon justified the DC approach in part by noting it is used by the vast majority of private companies (McMahon 2003). However, no discussion of the adequacy of these plans in the private sector was attempted.

A 2007 opinion piece by McMahon in the *Wall Street Journal* called into question DB pensions and voiced support for 401(k)-type plans for the public sector (McMahon 2007). A response letter to the editorial by the presidents of organizations representing state and local retirement administrators and trustees called the piece 'remarkably uninformed' about public pensions. In the letter, the signatories noted that the column failed to acknowledge that public pensions collectively are well funded, overseen by capable trustees, and subject to stringent laws, regulations, audits, and public oversight. The letter also noted that the column ignored that DB pension funds generate higher investment returns than 401(k) plans, portability has been built into public pensions, and that when offered a choice, the majority of public employees have eschewed DC plans and elected instead to participate in the DB benefit plan (Hanes and Williams 2007).

Reason Foundation. Founded in 1968, the Reason Foundation is a non-profit organization focused on advancing a free society by developing, applying, and promoting libertarian principles. Reason's Web site indicates that the *Wall Street Journal* says about the Reason Foundation, 'Of all the nation's conservative or free-market policy groups, it may be the most libertarian among them...and its ends up having the most direct impact on the actual functioning of government' (Reason Foundation 2008).

In June 2005, the Reason Foundation issued a report entitled, 'The Gathering Pension Storm: How Government Pension Plans are Breaking the Bank and Strategies for Reform' (Passatino and Summers 2005). The report characterizes pension benefits earned by public employees as 'extravagant' (Passatino and Summers 2005: 4), 'exorbitant' and 'unsustainable' (Passatino and Summers 2005: 5), but nowhere references data on actual levels of public pension benefits. It highlights the experience of a handful of examples of public plans that were experiencing significant funding challenges, then generalizes these exceptions to claim, 'Government employee pension systems across the nation are in crisis' (Passatino and Summers 2005: 3). In fact, at the time of the report's publication, public retirement systems were on average 85 percent funded (Brainard 2005). The national association representing state retirement administrators issued a response rebutting Reason's analysis point by point (Brainard 2006*b*). Reason's report urged all governments to shift new employees to 401(k)-style defined-contribution plans, remarking that in addition to purported economic benefits of this proposal, the '*moral* benefit is that it allows employees the freedom to manage their own retirement accounts and invest their own money as they see fit' (Passatino and Summers 2005: 5). More recently the Foundation continues to advocate a switch from DB to DC. In its March 2006 'Budget and Tax News,' the organization again indicated that the public pension 'crisis' has worsened, that taxpayers should worry, and that the problem is nationwide (Summers 2006).

Common Themes. Although each of the interest groups described earlier is a distinct entity, there is overlap in arguments made to support a switch to DC plans. Appeals to the supposed benefits of individual control over retirement decisions are frequent, as are claims that current DB plans are overly generous. Each of these groups also tends to suggest that failing to adopt DCs will result in dire consequences. For example, the term 'crisis' and the metaphor 'time bomb' are used frequently. Despite the fact that many of their claims are at odds with reality, we will illustrate in the next section that these interest groups have been surprisingly successful at creating an audience for their proposals, though it may be limited to those who share their free-market, individualistic ideology. This may be one reason why interest groups have had mixed success in actually achieving their legislative goals.

Recent attempts to convert public DB to DC plans

We now turn to an examination of recent attempts in four states to convert traditional DB to DC plans. We will see that in each case, partisan politics and/or interest groups have had a hand in triggering policy proposals and driving the political debate around public pensions.

Alaska In 2005, Alaska Republican Governor Frank Murkowski signed legislation switching the state's DB pension retirement systems to 401(k)-type DC accounts for teachers and state employees hired after July 1, 2006 (Inklebarger 2005). The DC individual account system is the only retirement plan for public workers, as Alaska's state and local employees do not participate in Social Security. At the time the legislation was enacted, the Alaska Public Employees Retirement System (PERS) provided retirement benefits to about 53,000 workers and retirees such as police officers and firefighters serving the state and 155 municipalities (Brainard 2006a). It also impacted the Alaska Teachers Employee Retirement System (TRS) which opened in 1955. In 2005, TRS included about 18,000 active and retired teachers and other education professionals in 57 school districts (Brainard 2006a).

The DC measure, introduced by Republican State Senator Bert Stedman, was 'one of the most contentious in the legislature' and one of the main issues during a two-week special legislative session (Inkelbarger 2005). The special session debate—at a time when Republicans controlled the legislature—was characterized as 'a nasty fight' over whether to end pensions for new public employees and teachers (Cockerham 2005a: A1). Consideration of the measure coincided with a push by the Bush administration to privatize Social Security. The White House reportedly became engaged in the Alaska pension battle when Alaska Senate President Ben Stevens contacted the White House to report problems securing votes to eliminate the DB system for public employees in Alaska. According to the *Anchorage Daily News*, a White House official phoned several Republican House members 'reminding them that President Bush's vision of Social Security reform is similar to the proposed overhaul of retirement benefits for Alaska's teachers and other public employees' (Persily 2005b: A1). The aide reportedly indicated that 'if legislators support the President, and support converting a portion of Social Security payroll contributions to private accounts, then it makes sense they would favor a similar system of individual investment accounts for Alaska public employees' (Persily 2005b: A1).

The measure also was reported to have roots back to Americans for Tax Reform. Democrats pointed out that the Senate Finance Committee's report on the pension legislation was 'lifted from a policy brief' by ATR; both the policy brief and the Senate Finance report 'tout the benefits of switching public employees from traditional pension plans to individual savings accounts, similar to the president's arguments for changing Social Security'(Persily 2005a: B1). Of the connection, Senate Minority Leader Johnny Ellis said he had the sense that the measure was 'part of a national conservative movement that is detrimental to public employees' (Persily 2005a: B1). Senate Finance Co-Chair Lyda Green reportedly denied 'a national political conspiracy,' but also indicated that there was nothing wrong if the committee report came from a conservative Web site saying, 'I'm not going to apologize for it' (Persily 2005*a*: B1).

The House and Senate had separate proposals to address the retirement system at a time when Alaska's public pension funds had prefunded some $13 billion in assets to pay for future costs. Similar to other public retirement systems, funding levels were lower in 2005 due to the market downturn in the early 2000s. The *Anchorage Daily News* reported that Alaska had one of the best-funded retirement systems in the country, and there was 'no good evidence that ending the pensions' would address current funding issues, and calls for more research on the issue (Cockerham 2005*b*: A1).

According to the former Alaska Division of Retirement and Benefits Director Melanie Millhorn, the pension shortfalls were due mainly to rising health care costs and a downturn in investments. The state Office of Management and Budget indicates that in 2001 and 2002, the fund's investments lost about 5 percent of their value. However, from 1999–2001, the medical costs, which were expected to rise between 5 and 6 percent, actually rose between 15 and 20 percent. As Milhorn said, 'If it weren't for rising health care costs, the pensions would be more than fully funded' (Volz 2005).

Meanwhile Sam Trivette, president of the Retired Public Employees of Alaska, also stated that the main cause of the shortfall was the cost of health care, not the pension. 'The pension component is well funded—over 100 percent,' he said. 'It is the health care component that has caused a drag on the systems' (Dillon 2005).

The Senate Finance Committee's bill did not address the funding gap in the retirement system, while the House State Affairs Committee proposal called for addressing the funding shortfall in 2005. With limited time left in the legislative session, some lawmakers indicated a preference to get another opinion and 'work over the summer and fall to see if there is a better answer than a total overhaul' (Persily 2005*a*: B1). Commenting on the failure of the Senate measure to address funding, House Minority Leader Ethan Berkowitz called the process 'an act of political bullying and arrogance' (Inkelbarger 2005).

The pension debate also became ensnarled with other issues. The Senate reportedly was refusing to approve almost a third of the proposed school state aid as a 'tactic to gain school districts' support for rewriting retirement benefits.' The House voted unanimously to reject the Senate's attempt to link school funding to rewriting retirement benefits (Persily 2005*a*: B1). And Governor Murkowski threatened to veto hundreds of millions of dollars in public works projects across the state 'unless the Legislature eliminates pensions for new public employees' (Cockerham and Persily 2005: A1).

As the regular session neared conclusion, Democrats in the House proposed a compromise plan to create an *optional* DC contribution plan for new hires (Volz 2005). The Governor vowed to veto any bill that did not include the Senate's proposal to place *all* new employees into a DC plan. In the final days of the legislative session, the Senate and the House became locked in a stalemate. The clock ran out and a special session was called (Cockerham and Persily 2005). Eventually, the Governor and Republican-controlled legislature secured passage of the DB to DC switch for new hires (Inklebarger 2005).

In an opinion piece published in the *Anchorage Daily News*, former Alaska attorney general John Havelock commented about legislation considered during the special session, including pension reform. He wondered why none of the legislative issues were discussed during the 2005 election campaign, nor included in the Governor's State of the State address, nor part of Murkowski's list of priorities. Havelock concluded that the special session 'illustrates a democratic process out of kilter' (Havelock 2005: B4). He said that 'none of the bills was adopted as a result of widespread urging by voters,' nor were voters urging candidates to reduce retirement benefits for new state employees (Havelock 2005: B4).

Despite enactment of the legislation, the final chapter on Alaska is yet to be written. Because the plan was adopted rapidly and in a single session, important technical questions remain open. More specifically, the law creating the individual account system may not be in compliance with Federal Internal Revenue Service regulations, which would mean new employee plans could lose their tax-deferred status. Additionally, the 2008 legislature is holding hearings on Senate Bill 183, which seeks to reverse the retirement plan legislation passed in 2005 (Burke 2008). The legislature moved toward a return to the DB plan when a Senate committee approved in March 2008 'a bill to reopen a DB plan to new teachers and government employees, and jettison a fledgling DC plan some say is harming the state's ability to attract and keep employees' (Kvasager 2008). Regarding passage of the measure State Senator Kim Elton said, 'We took a significant step backwards when we moved to a 401(k). It's coming home that we have a real problem with defined contribution. It's probably best synthesized in recruitment and retention. We're finding it far more difficult to recruit when almost every other public jurisdiction is offering a defined benefit plan' (Kvasager 2008).

California. In his State of the State address on January 5, 2005, California Governor Arnold Schwarzenegger called for an overhaul of the state pension system. The Republican Governor told the Democrat-controlled legislature that the pension system was 'out of control' and 'threatening our state.' He called for reform that would move new employees from a DB to a DC system that would be 'fair to employees and to taxpayers' (Associated Press 2005*a*), a proposal would affect both the CalPERS and the CalSTRS.

Later that month, *The New York Times* reported that the impetus for Mr. Schwarzenegger's plan was generated by the 'same anti-tax advocates, free-market enthusiasts and Wall Street interests pushing President Bush's Social Security initiative.' The proposal was 'supported by a number of Republican state lawmakers and is driven by the same ideology behind the effort to transform Social Security' (Broder 2005: 16). The *Times* predicted that outcome in California 'will not only have an impact on the state pension system, but will also provide an important marker of public opinion on proposed changes to Social Security' (Broder 2005: 16).

The initiative was endorsed by Americans for Tax Reform (ATR 2005; Broder 2005). Also supporting the Governor's proposal was Republican Assemblyman Keith Richman, who drafted legislation and filed the proposal as a ballot initiative. The Governor's staff indicated that he would campaign for the Richman ballot measure if the legislature failed to act (Wasserman 2005*a*). Also involved in the policy formulation was Stephen Moore, the former director of the conservative Club for Growth and who also was president of the Free Enterprise Fund, an organization dedicated to remaking Social Security. Moore said that the proposal 'aims toward giving people real ownership and a real stake in how the economy and the stock market perform' (Broder 2005: 16). Moore also reportedly saw the importance of California in impacting the national agenda, commenting that should the state move from a DB to a 401(k)-type DC system, 'the nation is likely to follow' (Broder 2005: 16). Several years later, Moore called for an effort to 'abolish these anachronistic guaranteed defined benefit pension systems and convert public employees to portable and cost-constrained 401(k)-type pensions' (Moore 2008).

At the time of the proposal, CalPERS was the largest pension system in the country with some $180 billion in assets for about 1.4 million workers and retirees. CalSTRS was the third largest system with about $125 billion in assets for some 750,000 members (Wasserman 2005*a*). Although the Governor described the plans as 'a looming train wreck,' *The New York Times* reported that 'even advocates of privatization in his own administration say the system is currently sound' (Broder 2005: 16). Together, the plans are 'nearly 90 percent funded, a level that most experts consider quite healthy' (Broder 2005: 16).

Opponents of the plan—which included almost all Democrats in the legislature, state employee unions, and plan trustees—said that the plans had been well-managed and provided critical retirement income for public workers. DB supporters also indicated that the state contribution to the system in 2005 was higher because of a downturn in the market. The state historically had benefited from a strong stock market and 'in some years has had to make no payments into the funds' (Broder 2005: 16).

The backdrop for the debate was quite complex. The Howard Jarvis Taxpayers Association was involved, proposing a ballot through the initiative process. Additionally, State Treasurer Phil Angelides—a Democrat and board member of both CalPERS and CalSTRS—formed a national coalition of state treasurers and pension fund officials to fight the governor's idea. He called the measure 'a major assault on the movement to reform corporate America following a wave of scandals.' Angelides said that the Governor's plan 'is part of a concerted effort to break apart the powerful voices of public pension funds that have stood up for ordinary investors in corporate boardrooms' (Wasserman 2005b). Interestingly, a loyalist of President Bush broke ranks and asked the Governor for an alternative to the DC switch. Gerald Parsky, chair of the University of California Board of Regents and chair of President Bush's 2000 and 2004 state election campaigns, said the measure would undercut recruiting and the economy. Parsky said, 'California's economic competitiveness will suffer if we cannot retain the nation's best and brightest faculty' and in today's global economy, 'California's intellectual capital is our state's chief competitive advantage' (LaMar 2005).

By April 2005, Governor Schwarzenegger abandoned his plan to convert the system primarily because public employees successfully leveraged the fact that the DC plan would not provide suitable death and disability coverage to workers, virtually killing the issue (Wasserman 2005c). In 2006, the Governor established a Public Employee Post-Employment Benefits Commission to propose ways to address growing pension and retiree health care obligations. The Commission was chaired by Republican DB supporter Gerald Parsky. The Commission issued a report in July 2007 that found that the total statewide pension system was 89 percent funded, and that since 2004, CalPERS and CalSTRS experienced annual returns in the double digits which are significantly higher than their assumed rates of return (LaMar 2005; Post-Employment Benefits Commission 2007).

Colorado. In 2006, the Colorado Public Employee Retirement Association (PERA) found itself facing proposals to convert its DB pension system to a DC system. The *Rocky Mountain News* called the 2006 legislative session 'the most challenging in PERA's 75-year history' (Milstead 2006b: 6B). At the time, the governorship was held by Republican Bill Owen, who supported drastic changes to the pension system and a switch to DC plans (Paulson 2006a). The legislature was controlled by Democrats.

As a matter of background, the retirement system was established in 1931 by the state legislature. PERA initially provided retirement benefits to state employees only, and then was called the State Employees' Retirement Association (SERA). By the end of its first 10 years, SERA had some 4,000 members, 112 retirees, and about $1 million in assets. For the first 20 years, investments were limited to US government bonds, or state, school, or municipal bonds. The rates of return averaged 2.75 percent (PERA 2008). Today, PERA is a substitute for Social Security for most public employees, and provides retirement and other benefits to nearly 280,000 active and retired employees of more than 400 government agencies and public entities in the state. The system has expanded its range of investments with assets in domestic and international stocks, corporate, government, and international bonds, real estate, and alternative investments (PERA 2008).

The editorial page of the *Denver Post* reported that while PERA was more than 100 percent funded in 2000, the stock market decline that same year left PERA funded at about 73 percent in 2006. This funding level, opined the paper, does not 'add up to a crisis' (Ewegen 2006a: E1). According to PERA, the funded status at the end of 2006 was 74 percent with a 15.7 percent return on investment and $38.8 billion assets. PERA's actuary indicated that this funding level is sufficient to pay benefits through the projected actuarial period of 30 years (PERA 2008).

In 2006, there were three major PERA legislative proposals. The first was proposed by House Republican Minority Leader Joe Stengel, which called for placing new public employees in a DC plan. The chief supporter of Stengel's bill was Fix PERA, an offshoot of the Americans for Prosperity Foundation. PERA's executive director testified that the measure was a 'gross overreaction.' A House Committee voted to postpone the bill indefinitely, which essentially defeated the measure (Milstead 2006a: 5B).

The failure of the Stengel bill left two major bills. Senate Bill 174 was sponsored by Democratic Senator Paula Sandoval and reflected PERA's proposal to maintain the DB system while taking steps to return the system to solid footing by restoring and accelerating the percentage contributed by employees to a previously higher level. Senate Bill 162 was led by Republican Senator David Owen and supported by Governor Owens. This legislation would have left current employees in the DB system and placed future employees in a DC plan (Paulson 2006b). With control of the state government split between a Republican governor and a Democratically-controlled legislature, a compromise solution was reached days before the legislative session concluded. The measure approved by the General Assembly maintained the DB pension system for all employees while restoring the funding level. The *Denver Post* reported that under the compromise legislation 'every new dollar the plan puts in PERA will come from employees, not taxpayers, mostly because employees agreed to contribute an additional 0.5 percent of their salaries into the fund for each of the next six years' (Ewegen 2006b: E1). This increase parallels a similar increase in employer contributions previously enacted in 2004. The proposal modified the structure of the PERA Board and also allowed newly-hired employees in higher education to choose either a DC or the DB plan (this provision later was modified to apply only to new employees of the community college system). Democratic Senator Sandoval sponsored the final compromise, which also raised the minimum retirement age for new employees from 50 to 55 (Ewegen 2006*b*).

Also of note was the fact that Fix PERA launched a related ballot initiative campaign. MSNBC reported that the 'libertarian leaning' proposal would have declared an 'actuarial emergency' and replaced the pension with a DC plan. Americans for Prosperity Foundation 'reluctantly withdrew the ballot measure' once compromise legislation was enacted and said in a press release that taxpayers are looking at 'an eventually bankrupt system' (Wolk 2006; Americans for Prosperity 2006).

Utah. In 2007, the Utah state legislature began consideration of a measure to convert the Utah Retirement Systems' (URS) DB plan to a DC system. Such a proposal would have affected 170,000 public employees and retirees, their families, and future workers (URS 2007). It was reported to be one of the 'thorniest issues of the Legislature' (Fahys 2007*a*). At the time, the data available showed the funding level to be at 96.5 percent (URS 2007). The measure was sponsored by Republican Representative John Dougall. He said that his bill would offer a choice 'to employees eager for incentives in a highly competitive job area' (Fahys 2007*b*). At a committee hearing on the bill, Dougall called the initiative 'an idea whose time has come' and an option that employees insist upon having. The lawmaker called it an employee benefit 'that when denied, would drive them to private-sector jobs where they can test their investment mettle' (Fahys 2007*a*).

In Utah, DB plans began for public employees in 1919 with the creation of the Fireman's Pension Fund. Until 1963, there were different plans for different classes of employees. That year, all public employee plans were consolidated under URS. The system began offering DC plans to employees in 1971, which were a precursor to what now are 457 plans that allow public employees to supplement their retirement security with individual savings accounts. In 1981, URS also began offering 401(k) plans for Utah public employees in 1981 (URS 2007).

While the 2000–02 bear market hurt the funding level of many public pension plans, the impacts were not quite so dramatic for URS. Its funded status did decline, but the system was more than 90 percent funded despite one of the most dramatic market fluctuations in history. This can be attributed to the fact that URS did not increase benefits and continued to make actuarially-required contributions during the 1990s bull market (URS 2007).

Utah's public employees' pension fund has grown to more than $17 billion, or nearly double the size of the state's annual budget, and it serves

163,000 people including schoolteachers, judges, police officers, county clerks, lawmakers, and ex-governors. According to the *Salt Lake Tribune*, it is considered 'an asset, the glossy polish on the state's sparkling financial rating' and 'rock solid, fully able to meet its obligations to retirees' (Fahys 2007*a*).

Nonetheless, the *Salt Lake Tribune* reported that a DB switch measure was triggered by 'a conservative Legislature' that was eager to 'join a nation-wide trend in business and government.' 'I feel quite comfortable with the choice option,' said Republican State Representative Merlynn Newbold (Fahys 2007*a*).

On February 24, 2007, the *Salt Lake Tribune* reported that new employees of the state Department of Information Technology (IT) Services would choose between a traditional state pension and a 401(k)-style DC retirement plan under a bill passed by the Republican-controlled House. The bill passed was a 'stripped-down version' of the original Dougall legislation intended to move all new hires to the DC system (Fahys 2007*b*). Dougall fended off several efforts to kill the legislation, including one that would have created a year-long study. The original measure eventually was defeated, as was Dougall's proposal to allow new transportation and IT hires to choose which system to join (Fahys 2007*b*).

A cost estimate for implementing the measure suggested that state agencies might have to come up with as much as \$18.4 million to deal with the drain on the retirement fund (Fahys 2007*b*). An article reporting on the failed measure drew attention to the fact that Republicans have tended to be more supportive of personal retirement accounts than Democrats, noting that the GOP controls the Utah legislature. The article reported that critics of the bill argued that switching state employees from a DB to a DC plan 'would create the unintended actuarial consequence of starving the DB plan of contributions' (Defined Contribution & Savings Plan Alert 2007).

To summarize recent activities in the states, interest groups have had a significant impact on the debate over state and local retirement plans in recent years. Because of the long-term nature of retirement plans, the ultimate effects of some of these efforts will not be fully felt for decades. It appears that interest groups' pursuit of their ideological goals are a major reason why proposals to dismantle DBs have risen to the forefront in some states, as evidenced in their broad statements and actions in states such as Alaska, California, and Colorado. It also appears that in recent years, these interest groups saw an opportunity to gain traction on the issue in light of rising contribution requirements to public plans that were the result of the 2000–2002 bear market. Interestingly, there did not appear to be active interest group involvement in the Utah debate where the funding and contribution levels did not spike during the bear market. Although interest groups managed to create an audience for their positions with politicians who were ideologically aligned, their rather mixed record in passing legislation to effect a switch from DB to DC suggests that these interest groups may be talking past the public voters and unaligned legislators of either party.

Conclusion

This chapter has explored how public perceptions, political dynamics, and interest groups are shaping the US public pension debate and policymaking. Public pensions have been a successful, shared enterprise between public employees and taxpayers. They have successfully met employees' needs for a secure source of retirement income that is adequate to maintain a middle-class standard of living. At the same time, they have collectively met the test of fiscal responsibility expected by the tax-paying public.

Challenges to public sector DBs do not appear to stem mainly from economic considerations, nor public dissatisfaction. Rather, the public has a low knowledge base and is undecided on the issue. But, where individuals do have a viewpoint, it is often driven by ideological or political beliefs. There does not appear to be a groundswell of discontent on the issue of public pension and no demand rising up from ordinary citizens for wholesale changes. Instead, efforts to dismantle public pensions have been tied to partisan politics and organized ideological interest groups. Specifically, while prior research suggests that Republican party control is a strong predictor of whether a state makes the switch from a DB to a DC plan, we find that individual Republican voters are no more likely than Democrat or Independent voters to support such a switch, after controlling for other factors, including an ideological predisposition to individualism.

These findings may help to explain the patterns we observe in the states examined. That is, the switch from DB to DC has not been a response to demands from the electorate, nor a response to economic factors. Rather, partisan politics and ideologically motivated interest groups have been a primary driver behind efforts to dismantle public sector DB pension plans.

Notes

[1] VanDerhei (2006) notes that a commonly-used rule of thumb dictates that retirees should seek to replace 75–90 percent of their pre-retirement income to maintain their living standards in retirement.

[2] Although most state and local employees have DB plans, it is important to note that 14 percent of state and local employees must rely on a DC plan alone (Munnell, Haverstick, and Soto 2007).

[3] DC plan sponsors could come close to approximating these economies by offering annuity distribution options. In practice, however, most DC plans do not offer annuities (Perun 2007).

[4] Based on cross-tabulations of the data from Hart Research Associates (2005, 2006).

References

AARP (2005). 'International Retirement Security Survey,' October. Washington, DC: AARP.

Alvarez, R. Michael and Edward J. McCaffery (2003). 'Are There Sex Differences in Fiscal Policy Preferences?,' *Political Research Quarterly*, 56(5): 5–17.

American Legislative Exchange Council (ALEC) (2008a). 'Inside ALEC: July 2008.' Washington, DC: American Legislative Exchange Council.

—— (2008b). 'Public Employees Portable Retirement Option (PRO).' Model Legislation & Talking Points. Washington, DC: American Legislative Exchange Council.

Americans for Prosperity (2006). 'Americans for Prosperity Withdraws PERA Ballot Initiative; Sees Some Gains And Continued Problems With Compromise Bill,' Washington, DC: Americans for Prosperity. http://www.americansforprosperity. org/index.php?id=1426&state=co.

—— (2008). 'About Americans for Prosperity: Our Missions,' Washington, DC: Americans for Prosperity. http://www.americansforprosperity.org/index. php?static=203.

Americans for Tax Reform (ATR) (2000). 'Taxpayers Salute State Rep. Ken Pruitt: Leadership Earns Him National Recognition.' ATR Press Release, May 5. Washington, DC: Americans for Tax Reform.

—— (2005). 'Schwarzenegger on Pension Reform: Let's Slow Down and Get it Right.' ATF Press Release, April 7. Washington, DC: Americans for Tax Reform.

—— (2008). 'ATR Opposes All Tax Increases as a Matter of Principle.' Mission Statement. Washington, DC: Americans for Tax Reform. http://www.atr.org/ home/about/index.html.

Associated Press (2005a). 'Text of Gov. Schwarzenegger's State of the State Address.' January 5. San Francisco, CA: reprinted on SFGate.com. http:// www.sfgate.com/cgi-bin/article.cgi?f=/g/a/2005/01/05/transcript05. DTL.

—— (2005b). 'California Teachers Pension Board Votes Against Governor's Pension Privatization Plan,' February 3. New York, NY: reprinted in the Associated Press Archives. http://nl.newsbank.com/nl-search/we/Archives.

Bailey, Holly (2005). 'Social Security: A New Campaign,' *Newsweek*, February 21: 8.

Berry, Jeffrey M. (1989). *The Interest Group Society*. Glenview, IL; Boston, MA; London: Scott, Foresman/Little Brown.

Blekesaune, Morten and Jill Quadagno (2003). 'Public Attitudes towards Welfare State Policies: A Comparative Analysis of 24 Nations,' *European Sociological Review*, December19: 415–27.

Brainard, Keith (2004). *Public Fund Survey Summary of Findings for FY 2003*. Georgetown, Texas: NASRA.

—— (2005). *Public Fund Survey Summary of Findings for FY 2004*. Georgetown, Texas: NASRA.

—— (2006a). *Public Fund Survey Summary of Findings for FY 2006*. Georgetown, Texas: NASRA.

—— (2006b). 'Response to Reason Foundation Study, "The Gathering Pension Storm,"' Georgetown, Texas: NASRA.

—— (2007). *Public Fund Survey Summary of Findings for FY 2006*. Georgetown, Texas: NASRA.

—— (2009). 'Redefining Traditional Plans: Variations and Developments in Public Employee Retirement Plan Design,' in O.S. Mitchell and G. Anderson, eds., *The Future of Public Employee Retirement Systems*. Oxford: Oxford University Press.

Broder, John (2005). 'Schwarzenegger Aims at State Pension System,' *The New York Times*. January 23: 16.

Bureau of Economic Analysis (2008). *News Release: Personal Income and Outlays*, January. Washington, DC: Bureau of Economic Analysis.

Burke, Jill (2008). 'Labor Unions Push for Better Benefits,' March 16. Anchorage, AK: KTUU-TV.

Chong, Dennis, Jack Citrin and Patricia Conley (2001). 'When Self-Interest Matters,' *Political Psychology*, 22(3): 541–70.

Clifton, Daniel (2004). *Remarks to the National Association of State Pension Administrators, Portable Public Pensions: The Inevitable Reform*. ATR Speech, August 10. Washington, DC: Americans for Tax Reform.

Club for Growth (2007). 'The Romney Record: Promise and Puzzlement,' August 21. Washington, DC: Club for Growth and Club for Growth PAC. http://www.clubforgrowth.org/2007/08/mitt_romneys_record_on_economi.php.

—— (2008). *About Club for Growth*. Washington, DC: Club for Growth and Club for Growth PAC. http://www.clubforgrowth.org/about.php.

Cockerham, Sean (2005a). 'Legislature Back in a Knot; No Deals: Stevens Says Senate Won't Release Bill until House Votes; Hawker Calls Process Embarrassing,' *Anchorage Daily News*, May 15: A1.

—— (2005b). 'House Rejects Top Bills; Vote: Governor and Senate Set on Passing Retirement, Workers' Comp,' *Anchorage Daily News*, May 18: A1.

—— and Larry Persily (2005). 'Legislators Refuse to Blink; Retirement: Special Session under Discussion to Help Senate, House Agree on Future of Pensions,' *Anchorage Daily News*, May 9: A1.

Colorado Public Employees' Retirement Association (PERA) (2008). 'Colorado PERA Mission and Vision Statements.' Denver, CO: Colorado Public Employees' Retirement Association. https://www.copera.org/pera/about/overview.stm.

Converse, Philip (1962). 'Information Flow and the Stability of Partisan Attitudes,' *Public Opinion Quarterly*, 26(4): 578–99.

Cook, Fay Lomax and Edith Barret (1992). *Support for the American Welfare State, The Views of Congress and the Public*. New York, NY: Columbia University Press.

Defined Contribution & Savings Plan Alert (2007). 'Utah Rejects DC Alternative to State DB Plan,' March 16. New York, NY: Institutional Investor.

Dewar, Helen (2004). 'GOP Club for Growth Shows Limited Clout,' *Washington Post*, May 23: A06.

Dillon, R.A. (2005). 'Kelly, Wilken Won't Rehash Benefit Plans,' *Fairbanks Daily News-Miner*, December 18. http://nl.newsbank.com/nl-search/we/Archives.

Dreyfuss, Robert (2001). 'Grover Norquist: "Field Marshal" of the Bush Plan,' *The Nation* 272(18): 11–16.

Engen, Eric M., William G. Gale, and Cori E. Uccello (2005). 'Lifetime Earnings, Social Security Benefits, and the Adequacy of Retirement Wealth Accumulation,' *Social Security Bulletin* 66(1): 38–56.

Ewegen, Bob (2006a). 'A 3 Percent Solution for PERA Rescue Plan for Retirement Group's Finances Might Be Simple,' *The Denver Post*, March 5: E1.

—— (2006b). 'Session Two-Tone Legislators Got Down to Work,' *The Denver Post*, May 14: E1.

Fahys, Judy (2007a). 'Pension Versus 401(k),' *The Salt Lake Tribune*, February 19.

—— (2007b). 'Employees May Have to Choose 401k or Pension,' *The Salt Lake Tribune*, February 24.

Feldman, Stanley and John Zaller (1992). 'The Political Culture of Ambivalence: Ideological Responses to the Welfare State,' *American Journal of Political Science*, 36(1): 268–307.

Ferrara, Peter (2002). 'Creating Portable Pensions for Government Employees,' ATR Policy Brief, April. Washington, DC: Americans for Tax Reform.

Free, Lloyd and Hadley Cantril (1968). *The Political Beliefs of Americans, A Study of Public Opinion*. New York: Simon and Schuster.

Fuerst, Donald (2004). 'Defined Benefit Plans: Still a Good Idea?' *AARP Global Report on Aging*. Washington DC: AARP International.

Giertz, J. Fred and Leslie Papke (2007). 'Public Pension Plans: Myths and Realities for State Budgets,' *National Tax Journal*, 60(2): 305–323.

Glasgow, Garret (2005). 'Evidence of Group Based Economic Voting: NAFTA and Union Households in the 1992 US Presidential Election,' *Political Research Quarterly*, 58(3): 427–434.

Government Accountability Office (GAO) (2007a). 'State and Local Government Retiree Benefits: Current Status of Benefit Structures, Protections, and Fiscal Outlook for Funding Future Costs,' GAO-07-1156. Washington DC: US Government Accountability Office.

—— (2007b). 'Private Pensions: Low Defined Contribution Plan Savings May Pose Challenges to Retirement Security, Especially for Low-Income Workers,' GAO-08-8. Washington DC: US Government Accountability Office.

—— (2008). 'State and Local Government Retiree Benefits: Current Funded Status of Pension and Health Benefits,' GAO-08-223. Washington DC: US Government Accountability Office.

Gustman, Alan and Thomas Steinmeier (1989). 'An Analysis of Pension Benefit Formulas, Pension Wealth and Incentives from Pensions,' in R. Ehrenberg, ed., *Research in Labor Economics*. Greenwich, CT: JAI Press, pp. 53–106.

—— —— (2004). 'What People Don't Know about Their Pensions and Social Security,' in W. Gale, J. Shoven and M. Warshawsky, eds., *Private Pensions and Public Policies*. Washington, DC: Brookings Institution, pp. 57–125.

Hanes, William and Meredith Williams (2007). National Association of State Retirement Administrators and National Council on Teacher Retirement Joint Letter (unpublished) to the Editor of the *Wall Street Journal*. October 4.

Hart Research Associates (2005). 'Retirement Security Survey,' July.

—— (2006). 'Retirement Security Survey,' July.

Hartz, Louis (1955). *The Liberal Tradition in America; An Interpretation of American Political Thought Since the Revolution*. New York: Harcourt, Brace.

Hasenfeld, Yeheskel and Jane Rafferty (1989). 'The Determinants of Public Attitudes Toward the Welfare State,' *Social Forces*, 67(4): 1027–48.

Havelock, John (2005). 'Special Session Evaded Accountability,' *Anchorage Daily News*, June 6: B4.

Hochschild, Jennifer L. (1981). *What's Fair: American Beliefs About Distributive Justice*. Cambridge, MA: Harvard University Press.

House Committee on Pensions and Investments, Texas House of Representatives (2000). Interim Report 2000: A Report to the House of Representatives 77th Texas Legislature.

Howard Jarvis Taxpayers Association (2008). 'Our Mission.' Sacramento, CA: Howard Jarvis Taxpayers Association. http://www.hjta.org/ourmission.

Hustead, Edwin C. (2009). 'Administrative Costs of State Defined Benefit and Defined Contribution System,' in O.S. Mitchell and G. Anderson, eds., *The Future of Public Employee Retirement Systems*. Oxford: Oxford University Press, forthcoming.

Inklebarger, Timothy (2005). 'Murkowski Signs Pension Changes into Law,' *The Associated Press State & Local Wire*, July 27.

Kvasager, Whitney (2008). 'Alaska Moves to Return to DB Plan,' *FundFire*, March 24.

LaMar, Andrew (2005). 'Bush Ally Attacks Schwarzenegger's Plans to Remake Public Pensions,' *San Jose Mercury News*, March 3.

Lathrop, Matt and Anne Singer (2000). 'Bringing Pensions into the 21st Century: How to Modernize Public Pensions,' Issue Brief. Washington, DC: American Legislative Exchange Council.

Lusardi, Annamaria (2007). '401(k) Pension Plans and Financial Advice: Should Companies Follow IBM's Initiative?,' *Employee Benefit Plan Review*, 62(1): 16–17.

Lussier, Tom (2008). Interview with author. Washington, DC, February 2008.

Madland, David (2007). 'A Wink and a Handshake: Why the Collapse of the US Pension System Has Provoked Little Protest,' Unpublished dissertation. Washington, DC: Graduate School of Arts and Science at Georgetown University.

Manhattan Institute (2008). 'Manhattan Institute: Celebrating 30 Years.' About Manhattan Institute. New York, NY: Manhattan Institute for Policy Research. http://www.manhattan-institute.org/html/about_mi_30.htm.

McClosky, Herbert and John Zaller (1984). *The American Ethos, Public Attitudes towards Capitalism and Democracy*. Cambridge, MA: Harvard University Press.

McDonald, Ken (2008). 'Retirement Annuity and Employment-Based Pension Income, Among Individuals Age 50 and Over: 2006,' *EBRI Notes*, 29(1): 2–7.

McMahon, E.J. (2003). 'Defusing the Pension Bomb: How to Curb Public Retirement Costs in New York State,' Civic Report 40. New York: Manhattan Institute.

—— (2007). 'Pensions and Palm-Greasing,' *The Wall Street Journal*, October 3: A18.

Milstead, David (2006a). 'Plan to Dump PERA Dies in House Panel; Two Measures to Alter State Pension Program Remain,' *Rocky Mountain News*, February 9: 5B.

—— (2006b). 'Teachers Union and Others Oppose PERA Reform Plan; Two-Tier Proposal Politically Motivated, Coalition Maintains,' *Rocky Mountain News*, April 11: 6B.

Mitchell, Olivia (1988). 'Worker Knowledge of Pensions Provisions,' *Journal of Labor Economics*, 6: 21–39.

—— Stephen Utkus (2004). *Pension Design and Structure: New Lessons from Behavioral Finance*. Oxford: Oxford University Press.

Moore, Stephen (2008). 'The Unions Go to Town... and Bankrupt America's Cities,' *The Weekly Standard*, 13(27): 11–12.

Munnell, Alicia H. and Annika Sunden (2004). *Coming Up Short: The Challenge of 401(k) Plans*. Washington, DC: Brookings Institution Press.

—— Anthony Webb, and Luke F. Delorme (2006). 'Retirements at Risk: A New National Retirement Risk Index,' Center for Retirement Research Special Project. Boston, MA: Boston College.

—— Kelly Haverstick, and Mauricio Soto (2007). 'Why Have Defined Benefit Plans Survived in the Public Sector?,' Center for Retirement Research State and Local Pension Plans, No. 2. Boston, MA: Boston College.

—— Alex Golub-Sass, Kelly Haverstick, Mauricio Soto, and Gregory Wiles. (2008a). 'Why Have Some States Introduced Defined Contribution Plans?,' Center for Retirement Research State and Local Pension Plans, No. 3. Boston, MA: Boston College.

—— Mauricio Soto, Anthony Webb, Francesca Golub-Sass, and Dan Muldoon. (2008b). 'Health Care Costs Drive Up the National Retirement Risk Index,' Center for Retirement Research Issue in Brief, No. 8–3. Boston, MA: Boston College.

Nelson, Thomas and Donald Kinder (1996). 'Issue Frames and Group-Centrism in American Public Opinion,' *Journal of Politics*, 58(4): 1055–78.

Passatano, George and Adam Summers (2005). 'The Gathering Pension Storm: How Government Pension Plans Are Breaking the Bank and Strategies for Reform,' Reason Foundation Policy Study 335, June. Los Angeles, CA: The Reason Foundation.

Paulson, Steven (2006a). 'Owens Says Fixing State Pension Plan a Top Priority,' *The Associated Press State & Local Wire*, January 4.

—— (2006b). 'Battle Looms over Changes to State Retirement Plan,' *The Associated Press State & Local Wire*, April 23.

Persily, Larry (2005a). 'Lawmakers Consider Retirement Overhaul; Shortfall: House, Senate Proposals Seek Solutions to Rising Pension Plan Costs,' *Anchorage Daily News*, April 3: B1.

—— (2005b). 'White House Enters Fray on Pensions,' *Anchorage Daily News*, May 9: A1.

Perun, Pamela (2007). 'Putting Annuities Back into Savings Plans,' in T. Ghilarducci and C.E. Weller, eds., *Employee Pensions: Policies, Problems, and Possibilities*. Champaign, IL: Labor and Employment Relations Association, pp. 143–62.

Ponza, Michael, Gred Duncan, Mary Concoran, and Fred Groskind (1989). 'The Guns of Autumn: Age Differences in Support for Income Transfers to the Young and Old,' *Public Opinion Quarterly*, 52(4): 441–46.

Post-Employment Benefits Commission (2007). 'Governor's Public Employee Post-Employment Benefits Commission Releases Report on Funding Status of Public Pension,' State of California Press Release, July 12. Burlingame, CA: State of California.

Poterba, James A. and Lawrence Summers (1988). 'Mean Reversion in Stock Prices: Evidence and Implications,' *Journal of Financial Economics*, 22: 27–59.

Poulson, Barry (2006). 'Colorado Voters Should Insist on a Defined Contribution Plan,' *Pueblo Chieftain*, March 14.

Purcell, Patrick. (2007). 'Pension Sponsorship and Participation: Summary of Recent Trends,' *CRS Report for Congress*. RL30122. Washington DC: Congressional Research Service.

Reason Foundation (2008). 'About Reason,' Los Angeles, CA: The Reason Foundation. http://www.reason.org/aboutreason.shtml.

Reynolds, Scott, Neil Ridley, and Carl E. Van Horn (2005). 'A Work-Filled Retirement: Workers' Changing Views on Employment and Leisure,' *WorktrendsSurvey*, Vol. 8.1. New Brunswick, NJ: John J. Heldrich Center for Workforce Development, Edward J. Bloustein School of Planning and Public Policy, Rutgers, The State University of New Jersey.

Schlozman, Kay Lehman and Sidney Verba (1979). *Injury to Insult: Unemployment, Class, and Political Response.* Cambridge, MA: Harvard University Press.

Steffen, Karen (2001). 'State Employee Pension Plans,' in O.S. Mitchell and E.C. Hustead, eds., *Pensions in the Public Sector.* New York: Oxford University Press, pp. 41–65.

Summers, Adam (2006). 'Public-Sector Pension Crisis Worsens Billions in Unfunded Liabilities Should Worry Taxpayers,' *Budget & Tax News*, Reason Commentary, March. Los Angeles, CA: The Reason Foundation.

Taub, Stephen (2007). 'Taxpayer Group, CalPERS in Pension Flap,' *CFO.com*, February 13. http://www.cfo.com/article.cfm/8695646.

Utah Retirement System (URS) (2007). 'Executive Summary of the Utah Retirement System Conversion from a Defined Benefit Plan to Defined Contribution Plan Issues Paper,' January 19. Salt Lake City, UT: Utah Retirement System.

US Census Bureau (various years). 'Table 2a. Revenues of State and Local Government Employee Retirement Systems,' *State and Local Government Employee-Retirement Systems: Revenues of State and Local Government Employee-Retirement Systems by State and Level of Government.* Washington, DC: US Census Bureau, Governments Division.

Van Derhei, Jack (2006). 'Measuring Retirement Income Adequacy: Calculating Realistic Income Replacement Rates,' *EBRI Issue Brief*, No. 297. Washington, DC: Employee Benefits Research Institute.

Volz, Matt (2005). 'State House Makes New Retirement Plan Optional,' *The Associated Press State & Local Wire*, May 4.

Waring, M. Barton and Laurence B. Siegel (2007). 'Don't Kill the Golden Goose,' *Financial Analysts Journal*, 63(1): 31–45.

Wasserman, Jim (2005*a*). 'Voters May Face Choice to Change State Pensions to 401(k) Plan,' *The Associated Press*, January 5.

—— (2005*b*). 'Schwarzenegger Pension Plan Faces Fight,' *Associated Press*, February 2.

—— (2005*c*). 'Schwarzenegger Abandons Pension Overhaul,' *Associated Press*, April 8.

Weller, Christian and Dean Baker (2005). 'Smoothing the Waves of Pension Funding: Could Changes in Funding Rules Help Avoid Cyclical Under-Funding,' *Journal of Policy Reform*, 8(2): 131–151.

—— Mark A. Price, and David M. Margolis (2006). 'Rewarding Hard Work: Give Pennsylvania Families a Shot at Middle Class Retirement Benefits,' Center for American Progress Report. Washington, DC: Center for American Progress.

—— Jeffrey Wenger (2008). 'Prudent Investors: The Asset Allocation of Public Pension Plans,' Unpublished manuscript. Boston, MA: University of Massachusetts Boston.

Wolk, Martin (2006). 'Colorado Unions Rally, Save Pension Plan. Ballot Initiative Would Have Forced Switch to Individual Accounts,' *MSNBC Interactive*, June 20.

Index